Copy-2005

www.brookscole.com

www.brookscole.com is the World Wide Web site for
Brooks/Cole and is your direct source to dozens of online
resources.

At *www.brookscole.com* you can find out about
supplements, demonstration software, and student
resources. You can also send email to many of our
authors and preview new publications and exciting
new technologies.

www.brookscole.com
Changing the way the world learns®

Ethical Decisions for Social Work Practice

Ethical Decisions for Social Work Practice

SEVENTH EDITION

Ralph Dolgoff
University of Maryland, Baltimore
Frank M. Loewenberg
Bar-Ilan University
Donna Harrington
University of Maryland, Baltimore

THOMSON
—————✳—————™
BROOKS/COLE

Australia • Canada • Mexico • Singapore • Spain • United Kingdom • United States

THOMSON

BROOKS/COLE

Executive Editor: *Lisa Gebo*
Assistant Editor: *Alma Dea Michelena*
Editorial Assistant: *Sheila Walsh*
Marketing Manager: *Caroline Concilla*
Marketing Assistant: *Mary Ho*
Advertising Project Manager: *Tami Strang*
Project Manager, Editorial Production:
Jennifer Klos

Print Buyer: *Rebecca Cross*
Permissions Editor: *Kiely Sexton*
Production Service: *Shepherd, Inc.*
Copy Editor: *Michelle Campbell*
Cover Designer: *Paula Goldstein*
Cover Printer: *Webcom*
Compositor: *Shepherd, Inc.*
Printer: *Webcom*

Printed in Canada
1 2 3 4 5 6 7 07 06 05 04 03

For more information about our products,
contact us at:
Thomson Learning Academic Resource Center
1-800-423-0563
For permission to use material from this text,
contact us by:
Phone: 1-800-730-2214
Fax: 1-800-730-2215
Web: http://www.thomsonrights.com

Library of Congress Control Number: 2003112632

ISBN 0-534-64142-3

Brooks/Cole—Thomson Learning
10 Davis Drive
Belmont, CA 94002
USA

Asia
Thomson Learning
5 Shenton Way #01-01
UIC Building
Singapore 068808

Australia/New Zealand
Thomson Learning
102 Dodds Street
Southbank, Victoria 3006
Australia

Canada
Nelson
1120 Birchmount Road
Toronto, Ontario M1K 5G4
Canada

Europe/Middle East/Africa
Thomson Learning
High Holborn House
50/51 Bedford Row
London WC1R 4LR
United Kingdom

Latin America
Thomson Learning
Seneca, 53
Colonia Polanco
11560 Mexico D.F.
Mexico

Spain/Portugal
Paraninfo
Calle/Magallanes, 25
28015 Madrid, Spain

Contents

CHAPTER 3

Guidelines for Ethical Decision Making: Concepts, Approaches, and Values   40

Feb. 2

CHAPTER 4

Guidelines for Ethical Decision Making: The Decision-Making Process and Tools   57

Feb. 23

PART 2 | ETHICAL DILEMMAS IN PROFESSIONAL PRACTICE   73

Mar. 2

CHAPTER 5

Confidentiality and Informed Consent   73

CHAPTER 6

Client Rights and Professional Expertise   100

Mar. 9.

CHAPTER 7

Value Neutrality and Imposing Values   114

Mar. 16

CHAPTER 8

Equality, Inequality, Limited Resources, and Advocacy   124

Mar. 16

Mar. 16 .

Mar. 23

Mar. 23.

Preface

Social workers and all citizens in the United States are living through perilous times. Wars and worldwide terrorism and other factors make for an age of anxiety, affecting people of all ages and groups, and reducing the resources available to human service organizations and social workers as they work to serve clients, patients, and others. Shortages of resources inevitably lead to difficult ethical choices that agencies and individual social workers are unable to avoid, including choosing between those who need services and those who equally need services.

Concurrently, every day, citizens of the United States (and elsewhere) learn of unethical acts in business and industry. Executives of major American corporations inflated their earnings' reports, thus driving up the price of their shares, from which they profited immensely. In many cases, these actions were both illegal and unethical. The list of businesses included many major enterprises such as Enron and Arthur Anderson. Unethical behavior was also reported in academia, scientific research, the legal profession, government, and in the media.

Ethical problems arise whenever and wherever people deal with human lives, human survival, and human welfare. These are activities in which social workers are involved daily. For this reason, we believe that concern for ethical conduct should be included in every curriculum for professional education. Those who teach in the area must keep in mind Thomas Aquinas's caution that when it comes to ethics "we cannot discuss what we ought to do unless we know what we can do" (*Commentary on De Anima*, I. 1.2). In other words, teaching the theory of ethical action is not worth much unless we also teach the skill of making ethical decisions. In this book, therefore, we will follow this dual focus. Some have said that virtue cannot be taught in a college classroom and that ethical dilemmas cannot be resolved by textbooks. However, we believe that the principles and techniques of ethical assessment and ethical decision making do have a place in a professional curriculum.

At the same time, we agree with those who have suggested that the concern of instructors should be less focused on presenting solutions to dilemmas than with efforts to encourage students to be alert in discovering and perceiving ethical issues, to become clearer about the values that affect their decision making, in considering competing arguments, in examining both the strengths and limitations of their own positions, and in reaching for thoughtfully reasoned conclusions. Our approach to ethical decision making is designed to assist social workers in reasoning carefully about ethical issues, to help them clarify their moral aspirations at the level demanded by the profession, and to achieve a more ethical stance in practice.

The exemplars presented and the exercises at the end of each chapter have been prepared to heighten students' sensitivity to the ethical aspects of social work practice, to aid them in developing a personal approach to such issues, and to help them consider the essential elements in ethical decision making in professional practice. Suggestions for additional readings also appear at the end of each chapter. In addition, we added graphics for some of the decision making tools and provided Internet sites so readers can look for the most up-to-date information.

In our continuing effort to make this book more useful, this edition has been completely updated and includes the latest research. We have added or augmented material on the following:

Technology and direct practice

Genetics

HIV and Family issues

Family violence and elder abuse

End-of-life issues

Accountability and evidence-based practice

Research and evaluation issues

A pluralism of identities (multiculturalism)

Family and marital therapy

Many new exemplars relevant to social work today

Information on Health Information Portability and Accountability Act (HIPAA); and NASW Professional Review

We have retained the two ethical decision screens. We have received numerous comments that the screens have proved helpful in the rank-ordering of ethical principles and ethical obligations, thus helping social work practitioners identify priorities among competing ethical obligations. Our intent has been to suggest some principles and guidelines that can substantially help social workers making ethical practice decisions, and we have been gratified by the wide use of the screens. Although ethical and moral perfection remains an unattainable goal, social workers, like all others, must continue to strive toward that goal.

The exemplars in this book are taken from the real world, but none of them occurred in exactly the way described or to the people identified in each situation. Neither names nor other identifying information came from social agency records nor from social workers who worked with these people. Many new exemplars have been added to reflect newer areas of practice. Needless to say, the exemplars do not always typify good or desirable practice. They were chosen simply to illustrate ethical problems occurring in the real world of practice.

We thank our colleagues and students for helping us think through many of the issues involved in social work ethics. We also want to thank the peer reviewers for their very helpful feedback on this edition. They are: Ellen Burkemper, Saint Louis University; Ellen Dunbar, California State University, Stanislaus; David Dupper, University of Tennessee; Barbara L. Torgusen, University of Alabama and Margaret Tynan, California State University, Stanislaus. Our thanks and appreciation to Bernetta Hux for her assistance, to the Health Sciences and Human Services Library of the University of Maryland Baltimore, and to the Milton S. Eisenhower Library of the Johns Hopkins University. Dr. Howard Altstein, Dr. Eva Sivan, Pat Hicks, Kathleen Walsh, and many students shared with us ethical dilemmas they encountered in practice situations.

We are pleased that our seventh edition is being published by Brooks-Cole, and we appreciate the helpfulness of Alma Dea Michelena and all those at Thomson who have worked on bringing this seventh edition to fruition.

Finally, we thank our friends and spouses who have continued their everlasting patience with our not-so-minor foibles.

Ethical Choices in the Helping Professions

Most social workers are confronted every day with the necessity of making ethical decisions. Some may have an opportunity to think about all possible options, perhaps to talk things over with a colleague or to consult with an expert. More often, social workers—even student social workers—are alone when they must make difficult ethical decisions. They cannot delay making a decision because of the immediacy of the problem that faces them. At best, they have a few hours or a few days to consider what should be done.

❖ 1.1 The Guevara Family Struggle: Report or Not?

The Guevara family is working very hard to get by economically. Mr. and Mrs. Guevara both work full time. Their four children—three of whom are in elementary school—return home in the early afternoon. The oldest child, Rosa, is 13 years old. She is expected to feed, supervise, and care for the other children. She has done a great job of taking care of her siblings. However, a neighbor reported the Guevaras to Child Protective Services, accusing them of neglect. Social worker Morgana Elam has been assigned to this case. Mrs. Guevara tells her that this is the way it is done in their culture. She and her husband want to make a better life for their children. They have explored every possible child care alternative but have found none that is better. If one of them has to cut back on employment, a paycheck will be lost with no assurance that other work will be found. After checking, Ms. Elam found she also could not suggest an alternative. The children all appear healthy and happy.

Is this a critical situation? The Guevaras are committed to making a better life for their family. By any objective standard the children do not appear neglected. Nevertheless, this situation poses a number of ethical dilemmas. Can you identify some of these? What ethical issues does this situation pose? Where will this social worker find help with the ethical aspects of this practice problem? How will this social worker decide what course of action to follow?

This situation poses a number of ethical dilemmas for Ms. Elam. One should note that, in addition to the parents, children, and social worker, there are others involved—such as neighbors and society. In this case, however, we will limit our focus to the family and social worker. In this book we consider only professional ethical dilemmas, and the social worker is confronted by a number of such dilemmas whose solutions should be congruent with ethical professional practice. We will briefly analyze three of these dilemmas.

The root ethical problem in this situation is that every social worker, including Ms. Elam, fills two professional social work roles: (1) a helper/enabler and (2) a societal control agent. The conflict between these two roles triggers a number of ethical dilemmas. What is good for one participant is not necessarily what is best for another. A decision that is best for now may not be so for the long run. We also need to consider the degree of damage that can be permitted to occur before the social worker must intervene.

Competing Values   Client self-determination, protection of human life, and enhancing the quality of life are three values to which all social workers are committed. As is so often the case, in this instance the social worker cannot honor all of them simultaneously. If the social worker substantiates the neglect report, she may undermine the family's self-determination and perhaps their long-term quality of life. On the basis of the family's experience so far, everyone is physically safe. If she does not substantiate and report the situation as neglectful, there is always the risk that something will occur that Rosa cannot handle. Weighed against that risk is the commitment of the parents to gain through hard work an improved quality of life for their family. There may be good reasons for giving priority to one, rather than the other, of these values. Nevertheless, this is a problem in professional ethics that the social worker must first recognize as a dilemma and then seek to resolve through the involvement of family members in problem solving and seeking professional advice from supervisors and colleagues.

Multiple-Client System   Ordinarily, a social worker gives priority to her[1] client's interests, just as ordinarily she would respect the client's self-determination. These principles are relevant to this situation. However, the social worker also has responsibilities toward others, including the parents,

---

[1]Some social workers are men, many more are women. In recent years, many writers have used such terminology *as his or her* and *she or he*. Or they have used the plural, such as "social workers believe." However, these usages are clumsy and often tend to interfere with the clarity of the message. Since most social workers are women, we will refer to the social worker as *she* (except in exemplars where the worker has been identified as a man, as in Exemplar 4.1) and to the recipient of the service as *he* (except where the recipient is a woman, as in Exemplar 1.2). We hope that male social workers and female recipients will bear with our usage.

their children, and Child Protective Services, as well as herself, the community, and society. This practitioner must decide to whom she owes first obligations and may encounter additional ethical dilemmas as the situation evolves.

Value Dilemma   This situation confronts the social worker with additional value dilemmas. While she is committed to providing service to her clients, she is not at all sure which professional values are relevant in this situation. She does not want to undermine the family's self-determination or the parents' motivation to advance economically and provide a better life for the family. She also does not want to impose her own values on the family, thus undermining their culture. Will the least harm to the children and the family as a unit be done by verifying the family neglect report, which means the family may lose an important source of income, or not reporting, in which case there is at least some risk of danger for the children? Furthermore, reporting or not reporting may result in putting the agency's reputation at risk and diminish the worker's own standing and evaluation in the agency. How can she choose between these conflicting but important values?

In summary, in this situation, the social worker's ethics indicate that in her role as a helper/enabler, she must make certain the family is enabled to make its own thoughtful decisions, she must assist the family to know and analyze alternatives, and she must facilitate access to helping systems that make these decisions possible. In terms of her role as social control agent, the social worker must *not* intervene unless there is sufficient evidence of imminent and irreversible danger of major proportions.

There are many ways to prepare for this practice reality. First, it is important to recognize that every decision in social work practice includes ethical aspects. Next, social workers need knowledge and skill to clarify these aspects of practice in order to engage in effective ethical decision making. Knowledge and skill in this area (as in all other aspects of social work practice) must be developed and refined throughout a social worker's professional career.

This book has been written to help social workers, students as well as practitioners, prepare for informed and skillful reasoning in ethical decision making. Part of this preparation consists of considering the following questions: Who is my client? What obligations do I owe to my clients? Do I have professional obligations to people other than my clients? What about my family? My agency? My profession? What are my own personal values? Are these values compatible with the profession's values? With societal values? What are my ethical priorities when these value sets are not identical and are in conflict? What is the ethical way to respond when I have conflicting professional responsibilities to different people?

In this chapter, we introduce this complex and important topic and define what we mean by **ethical decision making**. There are those who charge that some social workers have not yet developed a strong enough sense of morality and that, therefore, they find it hard to cope with the ethical implications of their practice. Others think that social workers are aware of ethical issues that occur in practice but that they make decisions on the basis of incomplete knowledge, value judgments and biases, and insufficient conscious use of self.

Social work students and practitioners have repeatedly asked for guides to help them grapple with ethical practice issues. In the past, these requests were answered only by the adoption of codes of ethics that were helpful in some ways, but left too many questions unanswered. The requests for help continue because most social workers know instinctively that ethics are supremely important. Even those who have never heard of Gewirth tend to agree with him that ethical requirements "take precedence over all other modes of guiding action" (1978, p. 1).

The very subject of professional ethics was once almost completely ignored in the social work curriculum. Lately, however, there has been a significant change, and ethical content is being taught in all phases of social work education.

In an age when scientists have cracked the genetic code, put men on the moon, transplanted hearts, transferred an embryo from the test tube to the womb, and cloned sheep, almost anything is possible from a technological point of view. The key question now is how to decide what ought to be done. More and more social workers have come to recognize that they, too, face questions that go beyond the "techniques" of social work. This recognition has made the subject of professional ethics more visible in the professional social work curriculum. Since 1982, the Council on Social Work Education (CSWE) has required the inclusion throughout the curriculum of content about professional practice values and ethics. In addition, a number of states now require continuing education credits in ethics for maintaining social work licenses.

What does the term *ethics* mean? The word comes from the Greek root *ethos,* which originally meant custom, usage, or habit. In contemporary use it deals with the question of what actions are morally right and with how things ought to be. General ethics clarify the obligations that are owed by one person to another person. Some obligations, however, are based on the specific relations between two people (such as a mother and her son), or they are based on a particular role voluntarily accepted by one of the parties. The latter are special obligations that apply only to those who have consented to accept that role position (Fishkin, 1982, pp. 25–27). Professional ethics are a codification of the special obligations that arise out of a person's voluntary choice to become a professional, such as a social worker. Professional ethics clarify the ethical aspects of professional practice. Professional social work ethics are intended to help social work practitioners to recognize morally correct practice and to learn how to decide and act ethically in any professional situation.

CONTEMPORARY INTEREST IN PROFESSIONAL ETHICS

Jane Addams talked many years ago about the importance of ethical practice, but until recently most professional social workers were less than clear about the ethical aspects of practice. Even though it is difficult to avoid ethical problems in everyday practice, there have been "scientific" efforts in the helping professions. Many scientists have attempted to de-emphasize questions of morals, values, and ethics within the practitioner's purview. Social workers accepted this "scientific" stance and preferred objective explanations over moralistic ones. This approach, however, has not helped them in making ethical decisions when difficult problems arise, especially in such controversial practice areas as abortion, genetic and other technologies, potential HIV transmission, assisted suicide, allocation of scarce resources, and similar situations.

One of the paradoxes of modern times is that the interest in professional ethics is high while the level of morality of our society seems low. In the 20th century, more people were killed by violence than ever before. Hitler's genocide was not a one-time aberration, but has been imitated (perhaps on a smaller scale in Cambodia, Rwanda, and the Balkans as well as in other nations). At the same time, the Nuremberg Trials after World War II, the Civil Rights movement in the late 1950s and 1960s, and the many rapid advances in medical and computer technology have resulted in a greater awareness of human rights, including the rights of clients. The renewed interest in social work ethics is, in part, related to this emphasis on human rights. It is also an expression of the maturation of the social work profession. The growing interest in social work ethics may be partially the result of the intensifying concern of practitioners with the increasing tendency of clients to resort to litigation to resolve claims of ethical malfeasance and malpractice. As a result, in the last three decades, complaints and lawsuits against social workers insured by the National Association of Social Workers (NASW) Insurance Trust have increased (Houston-Vega, Nuehring, & Daguio, 1997). This pattern has continued because of the growing number of professionals in the field and the litigious nature of our society (Imbert, 2002).

Unethical conduct, corruption, and scandals in government as well as in industry have become commonplace. Almost daily, newspapers report unethical practices by corporate executives, legislators, scientific researchers, physicians, lawyers, accountants, and other professionals. The daily media headlines almost always involve ethical matters. Since the appearance of the sixth edition of this book, Americans have been exposed to the impeachment of President Clinton, industrialists and accountants using ethically questionable, if not illegal, accounting methods, insider trading scandals, Olympic Games corruptions, new dilemmas in medical research, the use of drugs in sports, and questionable political fund-raising methods. Ethical questions almost always are at the top of the public agenda. No wonder that courses in ethics are spreading rapidly and are offered today not only by universities but also by businesses, professional groups, and the military.

Social work practitioners are searching for ethical guidelines for their work. For many, neither science nor religion has provided satisfactory answers to the ethical problems they face. The renewed emphasis on professional ethics is due to a "desire to retrieve human values and moral concerns from the high-tech influence of science, professionalization and rapid technical innovation" that is so characteristic of all areas of contemporary life, including professional social work (Walrond-Skinner & Watson, 1987, p. 5).

ETHICAL PROBLEMS IN SOCIAL WORK PRACTICE

Some suggest that ethics are a problem that occurs only on very special occasions. They argue that in most practice situations a social worker requires only a high level of professional skill and insight since no ethical questions are involved. This approach to professional practice, established by Sigmund Freud himself, has been accepted by generations of practitioners in all of the helping professions. The assumptions underlying this approach are supported by a number of philosophers who argue that most actions do not involve any moral question but are the result of a free choice among the various available alternatives. These alternatives are located in the area that Fishkin (1982) identified as the "zone of moral indifference." Other philosophers insist that there are ethical implications or ethical aspects to almost every professional decision. We follow the latter approach because we believe that professional social workers are not merely technicians who solve problems but they are also moral agents.

An examination of social work practice will reveal that almost all practice principles involve (or are based on) ethical principles. One of the sources for ethical problems in social work practice may be located in the multiplicity and contradiction of values that characterize contemporary society. While we often speak of ethical problems, it would be more correct to speak of the *ethical dimensions* or *ethical aspects of social work practice problems.* In the past, it was assumed that ethical issues arose out of, and were limited to, the dyadic relationship between social worker and client. Current ethical concerns also include those that arise out of the newer practice models, which include many participants in addition to client and worker. The breakdown of consensus concerning societal means and goals, the increasing scarcity of resources that are available for social welfare, and the use of new technologies not only have intensified traditional ethical dilemmas but also have given rise to what may well be a new generation of ethical issues in social work practice

In this book, we will examine **ethical problems** and **ethical dilemmas.** Ethical problems raise the question: What is the *right* thing to do in a given practice situation? How can a social worker avoid unethical behaviors in that situation? Ethical dilemmas occur in situations in which the social worker must choose between two or more relevant, but contradictory ethical directives, or when every alternative results in an undesirable outcome for one or more persons. The seedbed for ethical problems in social work practice is graphically portrayed in Figure 1.1.

Any disagreement that different participants of the action system (Group B) have with regard to alternate decision options (Group A) or alternative assumptions (Group C) will intensify the difficulties that social workers will encounter in ethical decision making. Examples of such difficulties occur in the following situations:

- A client wants a service that may affect another member of the family who does not want to receive that service: An adult daughter may want to place her aged father in a nursing home, but the aging father wants to remain in his own home.

Figure 1.1 | Ethical Problems in Social Work Practice

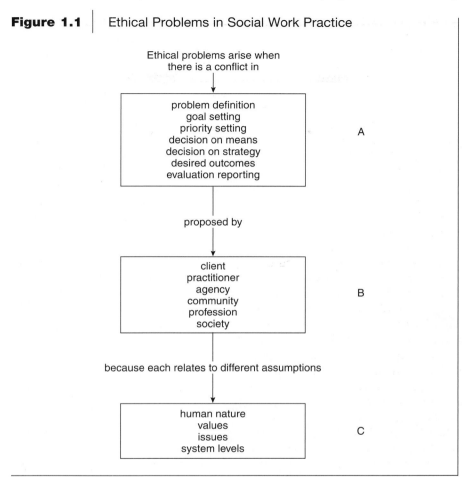

- Conflicting values impinge on the decision facing the social worker: A young woman asks whether her fiancé (who is your client) is HIV positive, while the client wants to keep this information secret.
- The community and the profession have different priorities: Everyone agrees that something must be done about domestic violence, but community leaders believe that better police protection is more important than building another shelter.
- The social agency prescribes a treatment modality based on one social work theory, although the practitioner knows that another approach is indicated for a particular client: The agency is committed to psychodynamic therapy, whereas research evidence indicates that in this situation cognitive-behavioral therapy is usually more effective.

Some social workers try to ignore the ethical problems and dilemmas that arise in these and similar situations, either because they are uncomfortable with making ethical decisions or because they think they already have the answer. Other social workers are aware of the ethical aspects of these problem situations but are uneasy because they think that they do not yet have the skill to deal with ethical problems of this nature.

Two causes of ethical problems are (1) competing values and (2) competing loyalties. Social workers may benefit from paying special attention to these causes.

Competing Values   An ethical dilemma may arise when a practitioner is faced with two or more competing values, such as justice and equality, or confidentiality and protecting life. Examples of conflicts regarding confidentiality are found in Chapter 5 (Exemplars 5.1 and 5.2), justice and equality in Chapter 8 (Exemplar 8.4), and protecting life in Chapter 12 (Exemplar 12.6). Similarly, in a period of rapidly shrinking budgets, no practitioner can ignore considerations of efficiency and effectiveness, even though these constraints may do violence to what is thought to be best for a particular client. A worker may feel equally committed to two values, even when both cannot be actualized in a specific situation.

Competing Loyalties   When competing or conflicting groups make claims for the social worker's loyalties, she may face an ethical dilemma. A classic example of this dilemma is the social worker who represents both the agency and the client, with each making conflicting demands. There is little need to point to the more obvious examples of this cause of ethical problems. Even less blatant incidents, such as a request for giving preferential treatment to relatives and friends, can be problematic from an ethical point of view. Multiple loyalties are also a source of ethical quandaries when a social worker serves a multiple-client system, as is so common today. In these circumstances, identifying the person or unit that should receive priority becomes a key ethical issue.

Several exemplars from social work practice will now be examined. Consider how ethical issues arise in each exemplar. The ethical problems faced by the social worker who has been assigned to work with Ms. Gabelli in Exemplar 1.2 are similar to, yet different from, those faced by worker Morgana Elam in Exemplar 1.1

❖ 1.2 Blanca Gabelli Costs Too Much

Blanca Gabelli, an 84-year-old retired physician, participates in a day treatment program and resides in an assisted living residence. Recently, she has become slightly more forgetful, falls more frequently, and has been somewhat less able to care for herself. She has also become increasingly irascible, and several staff members have complained about her demanding behavior. Your supervisor has asked you, as the social worker who serves the residents, to arrange a transfer to a nursing home because Ms. Gabelli is a "pain," requires too much effort, and is upsetting staff members who have many other duties in the residential program.

Although you believe that Ms. Gabelli is not yet in need of nursing home care, you contacted the one possible nursing home to arrange for a transfer. You just received a call from Ellen Brito, the nursing home administrator, who is asking about Ms. Gabelli's health, behavior, and attitudes. How should you respond?

Let us consider some of the ethical choices this social worker might make.

Goal Setting

Who should set the goals in this situation? If you comply with your supervisor's demand, you and your supervisor determine Ms. Gabelli's future while also undermining her sense of autonomy. Do you and your supervisor have an ethical right to do so? What part should Ms. Gabelli play in deciding her own living arrangements?

Role Conflict

A social worker is an agency employee. What are the implications if you do not comply with your supervisor's demand? Does the social worker's role require that you always comply with the suggestions of your supervisor or that you always serve as Ms. Gabelli's protector? Whose interests should receive priority consideration? Your supervisor's? the agency's? yours? Ms. Gabelli's? society's?

Value Dilemma

This social worker's supervisor is demanding that the worker comply with the agency's decision. In addition, her supervisor is asking her to lie and manipulate the situation so that the agency can transfer Ms. Gabelli. This social worker, however, personally and professionally places a high value on honesty. In what ways do her professional and personal values clash? Should the social worker tell Ms. Gabelli what her supervisor said? How honest should this social worker be and with whom?

Another set of ethical problems faces Sharon Gillette, the social worker in the following exemplar.

❖ 1.3 A Plane Crashes into the Pentagon

It was 10:15 A.M. in Arlington when the phone in the Gillette home rang. Sharon Gillette's husband had left for work over an hour ago. About half an hour after he left, the radio and TV reported a plane crashed into the Twin Towers in New York City. Moments ago another plane crashed into the Pentagon. Just a few minutes later many sirens sounded and smoke appeared in the sky to the east, indicating that a major catastrophe had occurred. People in Arlington and Washington and surrounding areas were anxious, not knowing what to expect. Mrs. Carlyle, who babysits for Sharon's children, called to say she was frightened and could not get there this morning. Now the phone rang again. The Civil Emergency Center asked Sharon, a professional social worker, to report immediately for duty at her assigned Emergency Center because many people were injured and in shock. Others were looking for loved ones. What was she to do?

Competing Values   Is it right for Sharon to leave her family? What mother can leave her children frightened and confused by a major disaster being reported on every TV channel? On the other hand, what are her obligations as a social worker to the families being served at the Emergency Center? This social worker cannot simultaneously be in her home with her children and at the Emergency Center.

Ambiguity   Sharon would have been far less troubled by her decision if she had known that no harm would come to her children or if she had known for certain that her presence at the Emergency Center would make a critical difference in the lives of the victims of the crash. In addition, this decision had to be made very fast, thus increasing the stressfulness of decision making.

What other ethical issues does this case pose? Where in the *Code of Ethics* will this social worker find help with the ethical aspects of this practice problem encountered in emergency situations such as floods, hurricanes, outbreaks of violence, and war? How will the social worker decide what course of action to follow? The ethical aspects of the situation are relatively straightforward. As a social worker, Sharon is charged with professional responsibilities, perhaps especially in an emergency situation, but she also has responsibilities to her family, which in this case includes very young, frightened, and potentially at-risk children. Which of these two obligations has priority? In Chapter 14, we will discuss the responsibilities of agencies.

CAN PROFESSIONAL ETHICS BE TAUGHT?

Teaching professional ethics is based on the assumption that knowledge about ethics will lead to the acquisition of attitudes and values, and that these, in turn, will produce the desired ethical behavior. Is there any reason to think that studying ethics will motivate ethical behavior any more than studying biochemistry will inspire a person to become a physician? In fact, some have suggested that learning about ethics may not be the best way to promote ethical behavior. Social work students and practitioners who spend too much time reflecting about professional ethics may find themselves in the same situation as the centipede who became incapable of moving when it tried to understand how its legs worked. Further empirical research is needed to discover whether and to what extent learning about ethics is helpful. Educators still do not know much more about value-and-ethics education than Socrates did twenty-five hundred years ago when he told Meno that he did not know how values were acquired nor whether they could be taught at all. These questions still require answers.

The widely accepted view is that attitudes determine behavior, but some leading attitude theorists have proposed that behavior determines attitudes. Generally, it is held that our behavior is a direct consequence of our attitudes about the world, but the revisionist theorists suggest that a person tends to select beliefs and attitudes that are in consonance with or support his or her behavior (Bern, 1970; Festinger, 1957). Following the traditional theory, it is widely believed that social workers' values influence their professional practice, such as the selection of treatment methods. The CSWE requirement for curriculum content related to values and ethics is also based on the assumption that a student who learns to value professional ethics will, as a practitioner, choose to behave in ethical ways.

It may be that both approaches are correct. Deutscher, Pestello, and Pestello (1993) indicated that both the attitude-behavior and the behavior-attitude models are far too simplistic and unrealistic. Under some conditions, the relationship is reciprocal or reversed so that, at the same time, attitudes influence behaviors and behaviors influence attitudes. However, attitude is just one determinant of behavior as intentions, expectations of others, and beliefs about outcomes all influence behaviors (Manstead, 1996).

In earlier times, professional ethics were transmitted by watching a master practitioner. This apprentice model was satisfactory for training professionals as long as the new practitioner faced the same type of problems as did the master teacher. Social work's traditional emphasis on concurrent field instruction and educational supervision suggests a partial continuation of the apprentice model. In today's world of rapid changes, however, this model may no longer be optimally effective. Alternate teaching methods must be developed to supplement this traditional curriculum approach.

The impact of college and university curricula on changes in values and ethics is not entirely clear. Feldman and Newcomb (1994), on the basis of an examination of more than 1,500 empirical studies conducted over four decades in many different parts of the United States, reported some positive findings, though these differed for various types of colleges and curricula. Most interesting was their conclusion that, with few exceptions, faculty members exerted an impact only "where the influence of student peers and of faculty complement and reinforce one another" (1994, p. 330). Feldman and Newcomb surveyed primarily undergraduate colleges and focused on general value systems. There are only a few empirical studies of value changes in professional social work education. These raise some questions about the efficacy of teaching values. A number of studies report either negative outcomes or no significant changes (Varley, 1963; Varley, 1968; Hayes & Varley, 1965; Brown, 1970; Cyrns, 1977; Judah, 1979). Five other studies (Sharwell, 1974; Moran, 1989; Wodarski, Pippin, & Daniels, 1988; Frans & Moran, 1993; Rice, 1994) report some positive findings. However, all of these studies attempted to measure value changes as reflected by answers to a questionnaire and did not assess ethical behaviors in practice settings.

More than 40 years ago, Pumphrey (1959) noted that social work students viewed the teaching of values as something quite apart from (or even irrelevant to) practice. Changes have occurred since Pumphrey undertook her study, but a recent observer noted that too many students still think that the major objective of ethics education is to pass an exam at the end of the semester. It is no wonder that social work students, like medical students, are often unable to recognize ethical problems in practice situations (Reiser, Burstajn, Applebaum, & Gutheil, 1987).

It is doubtful whether an academic course limited to thinking and talking about professional ethics will suffice to make students more ethical practitioners. Thinking and talking must be supplemented by doing. Skill in using the decision-making tools that we will present in this book, as well as the discussions and exercises, should help to improve the ability of students and practitioners to reason more effectively about ethical issues, improve the quality of ethical decision making, and result in more ethical professional behaviors in day-by-day practice. At the same time, we try to avoid giving pat answers. Instead, we hope to convey the need for tolerance of ambiguity when it comes to professional ethics. In professional practice there is rarely, if ever, only one correct ethical way. Our approach is to focus on ethical applications in practice situations rather than merely on the philosophical foundations of professional ethics. We agree with Hokenstad (1987) that instruction that is limited to ethics and values and does not at the same time concern itself with knowledge and practice will not facilitate the development of ethical social work practice. The purpose of teaching professional ethics is to develop not philosophers or ethicists, but more effective and more ethical practitioners.

Social work educational programs are expected to provide specific knowledge about social work values and their implications, to help students to develop an awareness of their personal values, and to clarify conflicting values and ethical dilemmas. One goal of social work education is to educate social workers who are responsible for their own ethical professional conduct.

The following are reasonable objectives for a course in professional ethics. Students will do the following:

1. Become more aware of and more sensitive to ethical issues in professional practice
2. Identify and grapple with competing arguments by examining their limitations and strengths
3. Learn to recognize the ethical principles involved in their practice situations
4. Develop a greater understanding of the complexities of ethical decision making
5. Be able to reach thoughtfully reasoned conclusions and apply ethical principles to their professional activities
6. Be able to clarify moral aspirations and standards and evaluate ethical decisions made within the context of the profession

ABOUT THIS BOOK

In this book, we try to help students acquire skill in analyzing ethical quandaries, become aware of the ethical aspects of practice, and learn techniques and tools useful for making better ethical decisions. We will not present detailed prescriptions for solving specific ethical problems, nor will we offer a cookbook approach that indicates what to do in every practice situation. Instead, we will offer various models to help social work students and practitioners gain skill in analyzing and assessing the ethical dimensions of practice problems so that they can develop ethically appropriate professional behavior. We will suggest several analytic schemes that may help social workers resolve the ethical dilemmas they face in practice.

It is important to recognize that ethical practice is an individual, an organizational, a professional, and a social phenomenon. Though ethical conduct is intentional behavior for which each individual bears responsibility, the professional peer group and the agency setting can and must encourage professional behavior that is ethical. Joseph (1983, p. 47) noted that "ethical concerns are generated by the structural and interactional arrangements of organizations, as well as from their goals and objectives." For too long, ethics have been the exclusive concern of the individual. Ethics must become the concern of the social group—in this instance, the concern of each social agency—as well as of the total profession.

In Chapter 2, we review the relation between values, general ethics, and professional ethics. Widespread concern about the relationship between law and ethics has led us to include a section on the relationship of ethical and legal behavior. We will also examine the manifest and latent functions of professional ethics, as well as present a brief history of the evolution of professional ethics in the field of social work.

In Chapters 3 and 4, we develop our decision-making framework. After briefly presenting several basic ethical theories and various approaches to ethical decision making in the helping professions, we will develop two decision-making screens, specifically designed to help in assessing the ethical alternatives that social workers face in their day-by-day practice.

The remaining chapters of this book are devoted to the presentation of a number of ethical problems and ethical dilemmas in professional practice. Nine of the chapters in this section cover a variety of practice problems. Each ethical problem and dilemma is important in its own right, but no claim is made that any one is more important than any other. For each dilemma, we have presented some relevant background information in order to help the reader examine the ethical dilemmas that arise out of the exemplars presented. The decision screens developed in Chapter 4 should be applied in analyzing each of these ethical dilemmas.

In Chapter 14, we again discuss the question of who is responsible for professional ethics. From what we have written in this chapter and from the development of our argument throughout the book, it will not come as a surprise that we place the responsibility for professional ethics not only on each social worker but also on the employing organization and on the organized professional group.

Exercises and suggestions for additional readings will appear at the end of every chapter. The Codes of Ethics for the following six organizations can be found at the following Web sites: The National Association of Social Workers (http://www.socialworkers.org/pubs/Code or http://www.naswdc.org); the National Association of Black Social Workers (http://ssw.unc.edu/professional/ NABSW.html); the Clinical Social Work Federation (http://www.cswf.org/); the Canadian Association of Social Workers (http://www.casw-acts.ca); the Feminist Therapy Institute (http://www.feministtherapyinstitute.org/), and the American Association of Marriage and Family Therapists (http://www.aamft. org/resources/LRMPlan/Ethics/ethicscode2001.htm). Additional exemplars, a glossary, and a list of selected Internet sites will be found in the appendixes.

Ethical issues will continue to cause discomfort even after this book has been completed. This is so because every decision that a social worker makes entails ethical risks. Perhaps the most agonizing of these risks is the danger of making a choice that may hurt or damage a client or someone else. Every effort must be made to avoid such dangers; yet these hazards are unavoidable and must not lead to inaction. We hope that the tools for ethical decision making that we will present, as well as the discussions and questions that will be raised, will alert social workers to their ethical responsibilities and help them become more skilled and more ethical practitioners.

EXERCISES

1. Read one exemplar related to your interests in Appendix A. Try to answer the following questions:
   a. What ethical issues are involved in this exemplar?
   b. What provisions of the NASW *Code of Ethics* address themselves to the ethical issues you have identified?
   c. What ethical problems and ethical dilemmas that occur in this exemplar *are not* covered by the NASW *Code of Ethics?*
   d. What do you think is the ethical thing to do? Do you think there is more than one solution?
2. Compare and contrast the ethical principles that relate to confidentiality in two of the codes of professional ethics identified previously by their Web sites.
   a. Which code do you consider most helpful when a practitioner must make ethical decisions involving this principle? Why?
   b. Put yourself in the Morgana Elam situation (Exemplar 1.1). What options are open to you? Analyze these in terms of the four questions raised in Exercise 1.
3. Study your local TV and newspapers for one week. Identify the ethical issues that have implications for social workers.
4. In Exemplar 1.3, does the Civil Emergency Center have an ethical responsibility to provide child care services for volunteers or employees

who are called in on an emergency basis to deal with a disaster such as the airplane crashing into the Pentagon?

SUGGESTIONS FOR ADDITIONAL READINGS

A short list of readings that we have found particularly helpful is found at the end of each chapter. Emphasis is given to the more recent literature rather than to the classics. The readings may amplify points that have been made, present other points of view, or raise additional questions. Reference to an article does not necessarily mean that we agree with it. In each instance, we have found that the author has made a thoughtful contribution to one or more of the subjects discussed in the chapter. The articles are mentioned only by author and year, the full citation can be found in the bibliography at the end of the book.

Goldstein (1998) presents a critical analysis of the moral aspects of social work practice. Dean and Rhodes (1992) suggest that good clinical practice is not necessarily good ethical practice and recommend that ethical deliberation be a more explicit focus of practice and of practitioners' self-examination. Manning (1997) argues for moral citizenship to guide ethical social work practice. Brill (2001) argues that a gap between social work ethics and social work practice is growing. Gambrill and Pruger (1997) present debates regarding 19 issues. These include a chapter on the effectiveness of the NASW *Code of Ethics*, on the question of whether ethical standards are higher than the law, and on the unethical behavior of colleagues. Sparse empirical evidence is introduced, but the issues focus on practice, coercion, professional self-regulation, professional education and training, and special client populations.

2 CHAPTER | Values and Professional Ethics

The Preamble to the N.A.S.W. Code (1999), states that "the mission of the social work profession is rooted in a set of core values." This statement reflects the importance of values for social work. It is possible that few professions—perhaps with the exception of philosophy—concern themselves with values to the extent that social work does. Goldstein (1973) described social workers as "value laden individuals." For Vigilante (1974) social work values are "the fulcrum of practice." Frankl also emphasized the centrality of values, not only for professional practitioners but for everyone. Life without values has no meaning, but only creates an "existential vacuum." For Frankl, the "will to meaning" is considerably more important than the "will to pleasure" (Guttmann, 1996).

VALUES

Social workers, like so many others, often fail to distinguish between such terms as *values, ethics,* and *morality* (or *virtues*). They use them rather loosely as if they all have the same meaning. Values, however, are not the same as virtues, though the two terms are often used interchangeably. Neither are values the same as ethics. One popular dictionary offers 17 definitions of *value.* Timms (1983) reviewed reports and publications from a number of social science fields and found no less than 180 different definitions for the term. A survey of the social work literature suggests that social work writers have used many of these definitions.

Maslow (1962) once observed that values are like a big container that holds all sorts of miscellaneous and vague things. Many philosophers have used the term *value* as if it meant the same as being interested and curious about something, but John Dewey used the term in a more precise way by noting that it must also include some element of appraisal or preference. Most social scientists have followed Dewey's definition, indicating that values are meant to serve as guides or criteria for selecting good and desirable behaviors. Kupperman (1999, p. 3) suggests that a value refers "to what is worth having or being" and that it "is preferable that it exist rather than not exist." Values enhance a life or the world and define "those conceptions of desirable states of affairs that are utilized in selective conduct as criteria for preference or choice or as justifications for proposed or actual behavior" (Williams, 1967, p. 23). Kluckhohn adds that "a value is not just a preference but it is a preference which is felt and/or considered to be justified . . ." (1951, p. 306). Most writers draw attention to the differences between societal values, group values, and individual values. Usually, values at these different levels are complementary or reciprocal, though at times they may be in conflict. Within any one society, most people, most of the time, agree about a core of societal values.

PROFESSIONAL VALUES

Social work practitioners take their basic professional values from societal values, that is, from the values held by the larger society in which they practice. These professional values are most often compatible with societal values, but there may be important differences in emphasis, priorities, or interpretation. It stands to reason, just as there is wide agreement about societal values, so there must be a wide consensus about basic professional values.

The central role that values play in social work has been recognized by many, as was noted in the beginning of this chapter. According to McGowan (1995), professional values are primary in practitioners' decision making and action. The *Code of Ethics* of the National Association of Social Workers (1999 Revised, pp. 5–6) summarized the core values of the social work profession as follows:

1. Social workers elevate service to others above self-interest. (Service)
2. Social workers pursue social change, particularly with and on behalf of vulnerable and oppressed individuals and groups of people. (Social Justice)
3. Social workers treat each person in a caring and respectful fashion, mindful of individual differences and cultural and ethnic diversity. (Dignity and Worth of the Person)
4. Social workers understand that relationships between and among people are an important vehicle for change. (Importance of Human Relationships)
5. Social workers are continually aware of the profession's mission, values, ethical principles, and ethical standards, and practice in a manner consistent with them. (Integrity)
6. Social workers continually strive to increase their professional knowledge and skills and to apply them in practice. (Competence)

There is a general consensus about social work values. For example, most professional social workers agree that client participation, self-determination, and confidentiality are among basic social work values. However, disagreements are likely to occur when it comes to implementing these generalized professional values. Social workers may disagree about priorities, specific objectives, and the means necessary to put these generalized values into practice. Furthermore, little is known about how social workers' personal and professional values are used for practice decision making and whether the adherence to particular values differs by practice setting or field (Pike, 1996; Csikai, 1999). Thus the value "enhancing the dignity of life" may be used by one social worker to support a client's request for an abortion or assisted suicide, while her social work colleague may call on the same generalized value to support her professional decision to try to persuade the client to go through a full-term pregnancy or continue with palliative care. In fact, these examples illustrate how "nonprofessional" or "higher" values can affect practice decisions.

Bloom suggests that philosophic definitions of values do not really assist practitioners in the helping professions; according to him, the focus should be on "what values look like as expressed in action" (1975, p. 138). Professional values that do not provide guidance and direction are only of limited use. Nevertheless, they are important because ethical principles and rules can be derived from these values. When framed as a professional code of ethics, such rules and principles may provide social workers with the ethical criteria necessary for making difficult practice decisions. Note should be taken that ethical principles are always derived from values. A rule or principle that is not derived from values but from another source is not an ethical rule. Such a rule may be a bureaucratic rule, a principle derived from practice wisdom, or something else, but it is not an ethical rule.

ETHICS

How to move from values to behavior is a problem that is not limited to professional practitioners. It is a more general problem that has become the focus of attention of ethicists. **Ethics** are generally defined as that branch of philosophy that concerns itself with human conduct and moral decision making. Ethics seek to discover the principles that guide people in deciding what is right and wrong. Another definition points to a key function of ethics. "Ethics is not primarily concerned with getting people to do what they believe to be right, but rather with helping them to decide what is right" (Jones, Sontag, Beckner, & Fogelin, 1977, p. 8).

Though the terms *values* and *ethics* are often used interchangeably, they are not identical. Ethics are deduced from values and must be in consonance with them. The difference between them is that values are concerned with what is *good* and *desirable*, while ethics deal with what is *right* and *correct*. A person's right to privacy, a good and desirable thing, for example, is an important value of American society. One of the social work ethical rules deduced from this value states, "Social workers should obtain clients' informed consent before audiotaping or videotaping clients or permitting observation of services to clients by a third party" (NASW, 1999 Revised, Section 1, 1.03f).[1] In the same manner, privacy is a desirable value, while informed consent and confidentiality are the ethical rules and the correct ways of practice that are derived from this value.

Even though values are meant to serve as guides for selecting desirable behavior, they do not always lead to these results since a person's behavior is not always consistent with his or her professed values. Social workers, like other professionals, at times practice in ways that are inconsistent with professional values or in ways that do not reflect societal values. For example, client participation in decision making is highly valued by social workers, yet some practitioners do not always make sufficient effort to involve their clients fully. One reason for the lack of congruence between values and behaviors may be that values are usually stated at a very high level of generality, while behaviors are very specific. Another reason for this incongruence may be the gap between professed (or public) and real (or personal) values of the person. What additional factors do you believe contribute to the incongruence between values and behaviors?

There is broad agreement about the most generalized values, such as cooperation and success, but these are not sufficiently specific to help identify appropriate behavior patterns. The more specific a value, the more useful will it be as a behavioral guide. On the other hand, the more specific a value, the smaller the probability that it will gain wide acceptance. For example, everyone agrees that, family life is a highly desired value—that is, everyone agrees as long as that value is not defined in more specific operational terms that reflect today's various types of families. This generalized value, however, does not help an adult son who has to make difficult decisions about how to care for his paralyzed, senile father without increasing the tensions that already exist between his present wife and his children from a previous marriage. Nor will the son's social worker find any specific ethical referents that may provide her with guidance in this situation.

MORALITY

George Bernard Shaw (1932) once wrote, "I don't believe in morality." His reference may have been to traditional values and rules of behavior promulgated by some external authority. Yet it is hard to conceive of life in a society that is essentially amoral.

Morality consists of principles or rules of conduct that define standards for right behavior. One might hope that morality consists of a set of general rules that apply to everyone in a society. These rules are neither enacted nor revoked by a legislature but are accepted and changed by general consensus.

---

[1]Note: This reference is to the NASW *Code of Ethics* (1999, Revised). All such citations encountered subsequently in this work refer to the same source.

They define the relationship between the members of a society. As Goldstein observed, "a moral sense . . . involves not only individual thoughts and actions but relationships with others" (1987, p. 181). Although in the United States there is a broad consensus about some issues, we are witnessing a growing diversity and multimoralities. There are deep divisions in American society about such issues as euthanasia and the right to commit suicide, human cloning, abortion, gay and lesbian marriage, and the responsibilities of individuals, families, and governments. On another level, values are clashing among immigrant, racial, generational, religious, sexual-orientation, and ethnic and cultural groups, among others. Social workers are increasingly confronted by a diversity of values and moralities; they practice in a society where there is less and less consensus about what is *the* proper moral stance.

The Educational Policy and Accreditation Standards (2001) of the Council on Social Work Education expects every social work education program to provide specific knowledge about social work values. This curriculum content is based on the previously cited core values identified in the *Code of Ethics* and their ethical implications. The educational goals of such content includes assisting students to develop an awareness of their own values; developing, demonstrating, and promoting the values of the profession; and analyzing ethical dilemmas and the ways they affect practice, services, and clients.

The purpose of education that focuses on the core values of the profession is to help students understand and appreciate human diversity. This knowledge and appreciation are first steps to correct professional activity. Thus, knowledge and appreciation of race, color, gender, age, creed, ethnic or national origin, disability, political orientation, and sexual orientation are important for professional purposes. Such groups represent a diversity of values and perspectives and, for many social workers, raise value dilemmas, both for themselves and for their clients.

PROFESSIONAL ETHICS

Professional ethics provide the guide that enables a social worker to transform professional values into professional practice activities. Ethical principles do not describe professional practice, but provide screens for assessing practice options for their rightness or wrongness. Codes of professional ethics identify and describe the ethical behavior expected of professional practitioners.

Professional ethics are closely related to, but not identical to, general societal ethics. Just as social work values are derived from the values held by society but are not necessarily identical to those values, so professional ethics come from the same sources as societal ethics but may differ from them in important details. There may be differences in priorities, emphases, intensities, or applications. Illustrative of these crucial differences are the ethical principles governing the relationships among people. Both societal and professional ethics stress the principle of equality, but professional ethics give priority to the client's interests, ahead of the interests of all others. Figure 2.1 summarizes these differences.

Figure 2.1 | The Ethics of Interpersonal Relations

General ethics: All persons shall be respected as equals.
Professional ethics: All persons shall be respected as equals, but priority shall
                           be given to the interests of the client.

Figure 2.2 | The Overlap between General and Professional Ethics

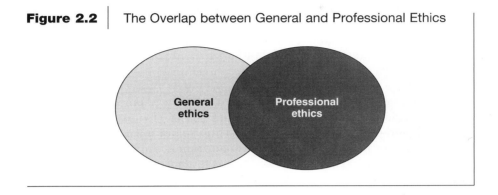

For social workers, this professional ethics principle is expressed in the standard of the NASW *Code of Ethics:* "Social workers' primary responsibility is to promote the well-being of clients" (NASW, 1999, 1, 1.01). The implications of this professional ethical principle for social workers and their practice are many because every social worker is almost continually forced to choose (knowingly or not) between general ethics and professional ethics (see Figure 2.2). It is, of course, often easier to deduce and formulate an ethical principle in theory than it is to apply it in practice. The framers of the CSWE *Educational Policy and Accreditation Standards* recognized the importance of professional ethics for social work practice. They therefore mandated that the values and ethics that guide professional social workers in their practice should be infused throughout the curriculum (Council on Social Work Education, 2002).

Some social workers can discuss professional ethics at length at staff meetings but fail to see how these principles affect their own practice, in the following exemplar the situation faced by one social worker will be analyzed; pay particular attention to the questions of professional ethics that this worker faces.

❖ 2.1 Diana Can't Go Out

Ms. Macedonia is a single parent, the mother of three children ranging in age from seven to sixteen. Her oldest daughter, Diana, is a 16-year-old high school student. Until the beginning of this school year, she received good grades, but at midterm she was failing all courses. She seems to have lost all interest in school. For the past three weeks, she has not been in school at all.

Ms. Macedonia is a clerical worker in the town's only industry. She goes to work early in the morning before her children leave for school and returns home late in the afternoon, hours after the children finish school. Ms. Macedonia is a good home manager. However, she has no friends and is always at home by herself.

Recently, Ms. Macedonia turned to the local family service agency to ask for help. She told the social worker that she felt depressed since she did not know what to do with Diana. By talking with both Ms. Macedonia and Diana, the social worker learned that Diana has to stay home every evening and every weekend because her mother does not want to be alone. Even though Diana wants to go out with her friends, her mother never allows her to do so.

Ms. Macedonia's social worker faced a number of practical and ethical questions, including the following: Who is "the client"? Whose interests should the social worker make a priority? Is it Diana or her mother who made the initial request for help? Or both? Is it ethical for the social worker to intervene with Diana even though she has not asked for help and who (on being contacted by the worker) claims to have no need for help? What other ethical considerations are evident in this case? For example, a social worker's primary responsibility to promote the well-being of a client does not mean that the welfare of other people should be ignored or harmed in order to satisfy the client's needs. Nor does the social worker's primary responsibility to the client relieve the social worker of her responsibility to the larger society and to the needs or problems of "nonclient" others.

No profession can establish for itself ethical rules that grossly violate the general ethical standards of the community. If a profession fails to take into consideration general societal ethics, it risks severe sanctions, including the possible revocation of part or all of its professional authority. Yet society recognizes that practice requirements make it impossible for professional practitioners to follow the identical ethical rules that people generally are expected to follow. Social workers, for example, may ask the kind of questions that in general conversation might be considered inappropriate or even an invasion of a person's privacy. However, before asking such questions, a social worker must be certain that this information is necessary and that she can keep it confidential.

Society often sets limits to what a social worker may do. These limits can add to the ethical problems that social workers face. In a number of foreign countries, particularly in some of the developing countries, social workers have been jailed because they chose to follow professional ethics and used a practice modality contrary to their government's expectations. Their fate highlights the fact that ethical problems in professional practice are real and at times can result in dire consequences. In a number of countries, including our own, some social workers have lost their jobs, have not received promotions, or have been shunned because they practiced in accord with professional ethical principles and in this way ran afoul of agency rules and expectations or certain societal values.

LAW AND ETHICS: THE PROBLEM OF UNETHICAL BUT LEGAL BEHAVIOR

Within the last two decades, Congress and all state legislatures have passed a large number of laws that affect social work practice. At the same time, the various state and federal courts, including the U.S. Supreme Court, have handed down a number of decisions that are of critical importance for social workers. "Good intentions" and "ignorance of the law" are no longer acceptable excuses for social workers who run afoul of the law. Lack of knowledge not only exposes practitioners to possible litigation for malpractice but may also contribute to unprofessional and unethical practices.

The purpose of this section is to help social work students and practitioners understand the interdependence of law and practice. We will also explore a number of key legal principles that are of vital importance for social workers. Less attention will be paid to specific legal questions because (1) in many instances the "law" differs in each of the 50 states, (2) law is constantly evolving, so if we were to discuss a specific law, there is a real possibility that it would be out of date even before this book is in the hands of the reader, and (3) we do not intend to make lawyers out of social workers.

Characteristics of Law

The word *law* has been variously defined by different authorities. According to Albert (1986), laws are concerned with protecting people against excessive or unfair power—government as well as private power. Black (1972) emphasizes the social control aspect of law; for him, law defines the normative relations between a state and its citizens. Selznick (1961) considers justice to be at the very center of any adequate definition of law. Others note that law tells people what they can and cannot do. The law informs them what is likely to happen if they are caught doing something that is prohibited (Van Hoose & Kottler, 1985). A crucial characteristic of law is that it is enacted by legislatures, interpreted by courts, and enforced by the threat of punishment. Its observance is held to be obligatory.

Law changes continually. At any given time it tries to reflect current knowledge and mores. The adaptation and change of law to reflect contemporary culture is exemplified by the evolution of the laws on abortion. When the California Supreme Court, in the *People v. Belous* case (1969), reversed the lower court conviction of an obstetrician who had been found guilty of procuring an abortion, it discussed at length the history of the statute that classified procuring an abortion as a crime. It noted that when the statute was enacted in 1850, almost every abortion resulted in the woman's death because of the complete lack of modern antiseptic surgical techniques. The legislature in the mid-19th century, therefore, limited abortions to those rare cases in which the danger to the woman's life from continuing the pregnancy was greater than the danger of her dying from the abortion. The Court noted that nowadays abortions during the first trimester are relatively safe—in fact, statistically safer than going through with the pregnancy. For this and other constitutional reasons, the Court reversed the conviction under what it considered the antiquated abortion statute and thus, in effect, revised the law in line with contemporary knowledge and technology.

In societies where the broad moral consensus has eroded, laws may be more effective than "moral persuaders" because they are enforced by the police power of the state. Following the enactment of the Personal Responsibility and Work Opportunity Act (1996), several states began to challenge former court rulings related to the provision of public assistance. These challenges placed restrictions on benefits for new state residents who were treated differently than those who resided in them for some time. In 1999, the U.S. Supreme Court held in *Saenz v. Roe* that states could not treat long-term and new residents differently in relation to public assistance benefits.

No matter how defined, law is of direct and immediate concern to social workers. There are many different ways in which law affects social work practice. Laws authorize payment for specified services; laws direct that certain social services be provided for all who need them; laws authorize professional social workers to engage in some activities that other people are not allowed to perform, but they also limit social workers from other activities that can be performed only by practitioners of another profession. Laws require social workers to report certain information to designated government agencies. Since laws differ from state to state, we avoid mentioning specific ones. Our purpose is merely to indicate the importance of laws for all social workers, no matter whether they are agency-employed or in private practice. Yet some social workers remain ignorant of the law. They practice as if the law is of little or no concern to them.

Most experts agree that child abuse reports have increased over the past 30 years, but many cases continue to go unreported. All states now require that cases of suspected child abuse and neglect be reported to a designated public child protective agency, no matter whether the social worker is employed by a public or voluntary agency or is in private practice. As is evident from the following research, some social workers may practice as if the law does not apply to them, using various rationalizations why they should not report. Two national studies of the incidence of child abuse and neglect and the reporting patterns of a broad representative sample of professionals who serve children found that many professionals failed to report substantial numbers of the children they saw who had observable signs of child abuse and neglect. Professionals failed to report to authorities 56% of apparently abused or neglected children, more than 85% of fatal or serious physical abuse cases (life-threatening or requiring professional treatment to prevent long-term impairment), as well as 72% of the sexual abuse cases. These data translate for the period studied into 2,000 children with observable physical injuries severe enough to require hospitalization that were not reported and more than 100,000 children with moderate physical injuries that went unreported. Over 30,000 apparently sexually abused children went unreported. Noteworthy is the fact that these nonreporting rates were discovered among relatively well-trained professionals, not among those less well-trained (Besharov & Laumann, 1996). In a study of child abuse and maltreatment reporting by 258 experienced mental health professionals, 51% of the social workers included failed to report at least one time during their careers (Weinstein, Levine, Kogan, et al., 2000), while another study found that 66% of social workers do not report all observed cases of suspected child maltreatment (Delaronde, King, Bendel, & Reece, 2000). A study by Ashton (1999) suggests that "beginning social workers do not fully understand their role as mandated reporters" (p. 546). Further, social workers who approve of corporal punishment are less likely to report cases of child abuse or neglect (Ashton, 2001).

At one time it was thought that professionals feared that reporting might result in a lawsuit, but nowadays all jurisdictions provide immunity from civil and criminal liability to professionals who report child abuse and neglect cases (Daro, 1988). Weinstein et al. (2000) found senior mental health professionals experienced stresses when a report is to be made. As a result, 90% of these clinicians consulted at least one source about reporting. One explanatory theory offered for the reluctance and inconsistent reporting of suspected child abuse by mental health professionals is that, although they know the legal requirements, they have concerns about the impact of reporting on their treatment of clients. However, Weinstein et al. (2000) found that the mental health professionals' relationships with their patients were positive in almost 30% of the cases; 11% improved or improved after initial resistance; and there was no change in 32%. Seven percent experienced reporting as negative and continued their resistance. Only one in five (21%) terminated treatment.

Differences between Law and Ethics

What are the similarities and differences between law and ethics? Law has an ethical dimension. Thus Albert insists that "it is altogether misleading to say. . . that legal duties have nothing to do with moral duties" (1986, p. 9), but there are differences. While observance of the law is obligatory and enforced by threat of punishment, compliance with ethical principles is voluntary and reinforced only by a moral respect for values. Professional ethics, however, may also be enforced by professional sanctions; such sanctions may range from a simple censure to cancellation of permission to practice. A professional who is guilty of unethical or unprofessional behavior may be punished by a court of law and also may be disciplined for the same offense by her professional association.

Whereas ethics are often characterized by a sense of ambiguity and indeterminacy, law is said to be definitive. Yet the outcome of legal disputes is far from certain or predictable. Legal rules are pliable; whether a particular legal rule will apply often depends on the arguments presented by one or the other side.

Law is enacted by legislatures and can be changed by a subsequent enactment or by legal interpretations. Ethical rules, though they do change over time, are generally resistant to deliberate changes. Yet there is a close relationship between law and ethics since laws are often based on ethical principles. Thus, the legal principle of *privileged communication* is based on the *privacy* value and the ethical principle of *confidentiality*. (See Chapter 5 for a discussion of these principles.)

Conflict between Law and Professional Ethics

Treating people wrongly does not become ethically right even when it is required or sanctioned by law. At times, a practitioner may follow the law and still be guilty of unethical professional behavior. In the past, a number of state legislatures enacted laws that mandated the involuntary sterilization of certain groups of felons and developmentally disabled persons. Can we say that a social worker who participated in these "lawful" programs practiced in an ethical manner? Many social workers claim that compliance with the law requiring the reporting and deportation of those who have entered this country illegally is contrary to professional ethics. Other social workers state that the application of the death penalty, even when authorized by law, is always unethical. Some suggest that there is a moral right, even a moral duty, to violate unjust laws (Pemberton, 1965). Social workers, for example, as advocates for civil rights or for humane treatment of persons with mental illness may engage in illegal behaviors, that is break the law for ethically principled reasons.

Yet there is a general assumption that human service professionals have an ethical duty to obey the law. However, "in some circumstances, competing ethical principles may be so fundamental that they justify disobedience of the law" (Melton, 1988, p. 944). This dilemma is highlighted by the *Tarasoff* decision (*Tarasoff v. Regents of the University of California*, 1976, 551 P2nd 334 at 340). The wider implications of this decision will be discussed in detail in Chapter 5. Here we will only note that in *Tarasoff* the California Supreme Court held that in some situations the welfare and safety of the community may be more important than the confidentiality principle. Some social workers view this legal requirement to break confidentiality as forcing them to choose in certain cases between the professional helping relationship, professional ethics, and law. Other social workers hold that a law cannot override professional ethical duties. Most, however, have accepted the principles of this decision. The *Code of Ethics* has been revised to reflect the *Tarasoff* decision (NASW Code, 1999 1, 1.07c); Most social workers no longer think that they have to choose between professional ethics and law in the duty to warn. In other situations, the dilemmas posed by the *Tarasoff* decision are still acute. For instance, consider a social worker whose clients include HIV-positive persons. What are the ethical and the legal requirements when such a client admits to his social worker that he continues to share needles or engage in unprotected sexual relations without notifying his partner of his condition? Must this social worker break confidentiality and warn the endangered partner? This ethical dilemma will be discussed in greater detail in Chapter 13.

When an ethical social worker discerns a wrong against an individual or a group, he or she is obligated to act. For example, the *Code* (6.04a) suggests social workers "should engage in social and political action that seeks to ensure all people have equal access to the resources, employment, services, and opportunities they require to meet their basic human needs and to develop fully." Thus, they are concerned not only with what ought to be but also with how to bring what *is* more in line with what *ought to be*. The feminist approach to ethics must include action to achieve equity for women within existing political, social, and economic structures. When such structures are not amenable to equity, they must be altered to be made more just (Brabeck & Ting, 2000, p. 29).

The NASW *Code of Ethics* in a discussion of the *Code's* purposes approaches this issue in a different manner:

> Instances may arise when social workers' ethical obligations conflict with . . . relevant laws or regulations. When such conflicts occur, social workers must make a responsible effort to resolve the conflict in a manner that is consistent with the values, principles, and standards expressed in this Code. If a reasonable resolution of the conflict does not appear possible, social workers should seek proper consultation before making a decision.

Malpractice and Unethical Behavior

A social worker's activities may be unprofessional, unethical, or both. An activity is unprofessional when it departs from the usual practice that a "prudent professional" would have rendered in the same situation. Such unprofessional conduct may be the result of professional negligence, lack of knowledge and skill, or misconduct. **Unethical behavior** violates the professional principles and standards promulgated by the profession's *Code of Ethics* in dealing with clients, colleagues, practice settings, the profession, and the broader society.

Failure to provide proper professional service (that is, rendering unprofessional service) can make a social worker guilty of malpractice liable to civil suits and/or criminal charges. Failure to provide ethical service can make a social worker liable to professional sanctions. In some situations, a social worker faces all three risks. For example, a social worker who has sexual relations with a client may face a civil damage suit, criminal charges, and professional sanctions for unethical behavior. (See Chapter 9 for a more extensive discussion of the ethical issues involved in client/social worker relations.) Having sexual relations with a former client may also be unethical and illegal, but after a lapse of a period of time, there may no longer be a case for civil liability. The length of the period of time differs in various states and also depends on the date of termination of therapy, when sexual contact occurred, and whether the failure to bring an action within the prescribed period was due to the effects of the sexual contact. The basic question, both legally and ethically, is not the elapsed time, but whether such relations still constitute an exploitation of the therapeutic relationship (Perry & Kuruk, 1993).

Legal remedies for malpractice can be classified into three categories: civil lawsuits (potential monetary damages), criminal complaints (potential criminal sanctions such as jail), and licensing board complaints (potential loss of license to practice for varying periods of times) (Sutherland, 2002). The type of proof necessary for conviction differs according to the charge and the law of a particular state. Among the legal considerations for action in sexual exploitation cases are the wording of the state's sexual exploitation and assault statutes; negligent breach of fiduciary duty; malpractice; negligent infliction of emotional distress; battery; intentional infliction of emotional distress; fraudulent misrepresentation; and breach of contract. Spouses may also assert separate and independent claims for the above and loss of consortium and alienation of affection (Advocate Web, 2002).

In a study of the incidence of unethical behavior and claims of malpractice by social workers from 1969 through 1990, Reamer (1995) reported that the two most common categories of claims involved incorrect treatment (18.6%) and sexual improprieties (18.5%), accounting for 37% of the cases. Not all claims have merit. However, for the period studied, over 41% of insurance payments were the result of claims concerning sexual propriety and just under 20% were for claims concerning incorrect treatment. In 1993, a study by the NASW Center for Policy and Practice found that of 226 alleged violations of prohibited sexual activity with clients 72 were substantiated. Strom-Gottfried (2000) analyzed almost 900 ethics cases filed with the NASW between July 1, 1986 and the end of 1997. Two hundred and sixty-seven cases were found to be substantiated violations after hearings (cases may include more than 1 violation; the total number of substantiated violations was 781). Of the boundary violations (dual or multiple relationships with clients), 40% were sexual relationship violations. The other categories of violations included issues of poor practice, incompetence, record keeping, honesty, confidentiality, informed consent, collegial violations, billing, and conflicts of interest. Civil suits to recover damages resulting from unprofessional actions or inaction are known as malpractice suits. The relatively low premium rates for malpractice insurance that social workers pay (in contrast to the premiums paid by physicians and other high-risk occupations) suggest that successful malpractice suits against social workers are still rare, but their number is increasing every year. In the early 1970s, there were almost no lawsuits against social workers, but since then the number of suits against social workers insured by the NASW Insurance Trust has increased dramatically (Houston-Vega, Nuehring, & Daguio, 1997). It must be remembered that all professions have experienced a growth in lawsuits in recent decades, which is characteristic of our increasingly litigious society. In the past, there might have been relatively few malpractice suits against social workers because most clients believed in their social workers' selfless dedication to client welfare. The relative scarcity also could have been due to a lack of common law to serve as a cause of legal action (Perry & Kuruk, 1993).

Social workers who want to protect themselves properly should know what is involved in malpractice. By learning how liability develops, they can take precautions that will reduce the hazards they may face. One need not be a lawyer to understand the principles involved. However, in specific situations, legal consultation is desirable. Nevertheless, it is important to keep one's perspective about malpractice and not panic. Social workers, however, should not

Table 2.1 | Necessary Conditions to Be Met to Win Malpractice Suits

A client must prove these four conditions in order to win a malpractice suit:

1. The defendant (that is, the social worker) must have a legal duty to provide a professional service to the plaintiff (client). Ordinarily, a social worker has such a legal duty once a person becomes a "client" (whether in an agency or in private practice).

2. The social worker's performance must have been negligent or below generally accepted professional standards of competence. What would other social workers have done under the same circumstances? "Good intentions" or "ignorance" are rarely an effective defense.

3. The plaintiff (client) must have suffered an injury or monetary loss.

4. The social worker's actions or inaction must have "caused" the alleged injury or loss.

underrate the potential risks they face. Table 2.1 summarizes the four conditions necessary for a client to win a malpractice suit.

There appear to be few limits to the reasons for which malpractice suits can be initiated. The list presented in Table 2.2, based on Besharov and Besharov (1987, pp. 519–20) and Corey, Corey, and Callanan (1998, pp. 141–46) shows the great range of malpractice actions.

Many social workers are familiar with several of the risks of malpractice listed in Table 2.2 and the general principles of malpractice litigation, but fewer are well informed about risk reduction methods (Houston-Vega, Nuehring, & Daguio, 1997). In the following section, risk reduction methods will be introduced. In one research study, 105 New Jersey social workers were asked whether a malpractice suit would be successful in the case of a therapist who asked the police to pick up an emotionally disturbed client. This client had threatened to assault his therapist because he imagined that the therapist had revealed confidential information about him. Only 29 respondents (27.6%) gave the correct answer to this vignette—that there was little or no basis for a successful malpractice litigation based on the therapist's actions. However, 61% gave the correct answer to another illustrative case example. The second such example involved a case where a depressed client threatened to commit suicide and also kill her two children. Social workers were asked whether there was a basis for a successful malpractice litigation against the worker if she failed to inform the client's husband of the threat. The correct answer was that her actions were very likely the basis for a successful litigation. The publicity given to the *Tarasoff* decision in professional journals may explain the higher percentage of correct responses in this instance. Nevertheless, even in this case, 40% of the social workers did not seem to know what is involved in malpractice litigation (Gerhart & Brooks, 1985).

The question remains: How can a social worker defend herself against the possibility of a malpractice suit? Knowledge and good practice are the best

Table 2.2 | Possible Bases for Malpractice Suits

1. Failure to obtain or document informed consent
2. Treatment without consent
3. Improper and incorrect diagnosis
4. Inappropriate treatment
5. Failure to consult with a specialist
6. Failure to refer to a specialist
7. Failure to prevent a client's suicide
8. Causing a client's suicide
9. Failure to protect a third party against damage
10. Inappropriate release of client from hospital
11. False imprisonment
12. Failure to provide adequate care for a client in residential care
13. Assault and battery
14. Sexual involvement with a client
15. Breach of confidentiality
16. Defamation
17. Violation of a client's civil rights
18. Failure to be available when needed
19. Abrupt or inappropriate termination
20. Inappropriate bill collection methods
21. Failure to report suspected child abuse
22. Failure to report suspected child neglect
23. Inadequately protecting a child
24. Violating parental rights
25. Inadequate foster care services
26. Failure to cure or failure to achieve satisfactory results
27. Client abandonment
28. Practicing beyond the scope of competency
29. Failure to control a dangerous client

defenses against liability. In addition, sound risk management can reduce the degree of risk by implementing a plan for practitioners and agencies that includes the following: (1) Risk management audit (licenses, registrations in order; protocols for emergency situations; insurance coverage paid; maintenance and safeguarding client records; and other factors all in order and up to date);

Table 2.3 | Protections from Malpractice Actions

1. Risk management audit, including
   - licenses, registrations in order;
   - protocols for emergency situations;
   - insurance coverage paid;
   - maintenance and safeguarding client records;
   - other factors all in order and up to date
2. Consultative relationship with legal counsel
3. Specialist consultants for
   - diagnosis and treatment;
   - second-opinion referrals;
   - ruling out organic pathology;
   - psychological testing;
   - evaluations regarding appropriateness of psychopharmalogical interventions
4. Continuing education

(2) Consultative relationship with legal counsel; (3) Specialist consultants (diagnosis and treatment; second-opinion referrals; ruling out organic pathology; psychological testing; evaluations regarding appropriateness of psychopharmalogical interventions); and (4) Continuing education (Kurzman, 1995).

There are additional means of protecting oneself from malpractice actions. One's practice can be limited to clients for whom the social worker is prepared by virtue of education, training, and experience. Other precautions are honesty and fidelity with clients, knowing one's limitations, and using consultation for difficult situations (Corey, Corey, & Callanan, 1998). Table 2.3 provides a list of how a social worker can protect herself from malpractice actions (Kurzman, 1995).

WHO NEEDS PROFESSIONAL ETHICS?

Do professional practitioners require special norms and ethical principles to guide their well-intentioned activities? Are not general ethical principles sufficient?

Whenever two ethical principles or two ethical rules provide contradictory directions, social workers need guidelines to help them decide which takes precedence. Professional ethics seek to provide such guidelines. There, however, are those who see no need for professional ethics. They argue that "common sense" or "practice wisdom" is all that a social worker needs in order to make the right decision. While no one should underrate the importance of sound judgment and practice wisdom, many recall the occasions when these simply were not sufficient to arrive at an ethically correct and effective practice decision.

Those who argue that professional ethics are not necessary for social workers cite one or more of the following arguments:

1. *Competence is enough.* Correct practice is based on competence and skill, not on the mastery of ethical principles. Many so-called ethical problems merely reflect poor practice. For example, good contracting will avoid many situations that are presented as ethical problems. Social workers will make more appropriate ethical decisions by becoming more competent.

2. *Each case is unique.* Every case is different and every client presents unique problems. No code of ethical principles can provide adequate guidance for every unique situation that a social worker faces.

3. *Scientific social work is value-free.* Scientific social work must pay more attention to knowledge and technology than to religion and morality. An exaggerated interest in ethics will deflect practitioners from developing further skill and knowledge, two areas that are most important for strengthening professional practice.

4. *There is no time.* Social work practitioners have no time for lengthy ethical reflections because practice demands that they act quickly. They do what they think is best for their clients. A code of abstract ethical principles will not help. If social workers were to analyze each ethical problem, they would never get anything done.

5. *Philosophers' ambiguity.* At least since Aristotle's days, philosophers have been unable to agree whether anyone can determine the truth of an ethical principle. Under these circumstances it is not possible to know the correctness of any ethical proposition. It is best not to fool ourselves into believing that professional ethics can help us know what is "right."

6. *Relativity.* What is thought to be "right" varies from country to country and even within a country at different times and for different population groups. In one society it is rude to come late for appointments, in another it is rude to come on time. Which is correct? In one culture a social worker is encouraged to recommend sexual abstinence when appropriate, while in another culture this option is taboo. Which is right? Within American society, different ethnic and cultural groups provide conflicting guidelines to what is "correct." In the social welfare field, the emphasis has shifted pendulum-like between individual well-being and societal welfare. Which emphasis best reflects professional social work ethics? Those citing this reason conclude that there are no fixed ethical principles that hold over time or space. Everything is relative, and there is no way of indicating which choice or option is correct.

7. *Instinct and "gut" feeling.* Practitioners usually know what is right in any given practice situation without having to turn to an authoritative ethical guide prescribed by some superior body. It is far better to trust a worker's intuition than to depend on the enforcement of bureaucratic rules.

8. *Coercion.* The adoption of a code of professional ethics will result in latent, if not overt, coercion to make practitioners act only in accordance with

that document. Such coercion contradicts the basic social work and societal value of self-determination. A code also tends to stifle professional creativity because it places every social worker in the same mold and expects the same routine standard behavior from every practitioner. Personal ethics and regard for client welfare are far more important for ethical behavior than any fear of sanctions imposed by a professional organization.

9. *Virtuous persons.* There is yet another argument, already made by Aristotle that all that is required for ethical decisions is that social workers be virtuous persons. When ethical decisions have to be made, people of good moral character will act ethically, based on their virtuous and morally schooled characters (Broadie, 1991).

10. *Wasted effort.* There are so few valid complaints about unethical behavior that a code of ethics and an enforcement machinery really are wasted efforts. Actually, there is much variability in the number of ethics complaints dealt with by the NASW. In 1987, there were 54 cases nationwide and 99 in 1993; but in 1996, the number was reduced to 70. The apparent decrease may be the result of an actual decrease in the incidence of unethical behavior or the result of the increased scope of state regulation of social work combined with diminished use of NASW processes (Strom-Gottfried, 2003). Is there an acceptable level of ethics complaints? Can any profession be satisfied that it has reduced unethical behavior by its practitioners to a bare minimum number?

These arguments against a code of professional ethics are not entirely persuasive. Some are fallacious, others distort reality. Here a brief response to some of the arguments must suffice. The philosophical and clinical bases for these arguments will be dealt with in greater detail in Chapter 3.

Anyone who practices social work knows that social workers seldom take time for drawn-out theoretical debates. Large caseloads and constant client demands for service do not leave time for calm contemplation and leisurely thinking. Ethical decisions, however, need not take a long time. Social workers need help in making correct choices, precisely because they have so little time, and in some cases, ethical choices that will need to be made can be anticipated.

Every social worker knows that each case is unique; yet there are commonalties. Ethical codes address these common elements. Principles and rules in a code of ethics are stated on a generalized level in order to permit adjustment to the unique features of each situation.

The voluntary acceptance of professional discipline, including a code of ethics, can hardly be viewed as a violation of the self-determination principle. A person becomes a professional social worker as a result of a voluntary decision.

Even though a code of professional ethics does not supply all of the answers that contemporary social workers need, there is a real demand for such a code. In time, improvements will make such a code even more useful. No code will ever provide "all" the answers—that is not and should not be a code's function.

CODES OF PROFESSIONAL ETHICS

Every occupation that strives to achieve professional status attempts to develop a code of professional ethics. Such a code usually contains a compilation of the ethical principles relevant to the practice of that profession, principles to which the members of that profession are expected to adhere. Many codes of professional ethics also describe the sanctions that will be invoked against those who are unable or unwilling to meet these expectations.

The code of almost every contemporary profession has been written with the following functions in mind:

1. Provide practitioners with guidance when faced by practice dilemmas that include ethical issues.
2. Protect the public from charlatans and incompetent practitioners.
3. Protect the profession from governmental control; self-regulation is preferable to state regulation.
4. Enable professional colleagues to live in harmony with each other by preventing the self-destruction that results from internal bickering.
5. Protect professionals from litigation; practitioners who follow the code are offered some protection if sued for malpractice.

Because a code of professional ethics tries to provide guidance for every conceivable situation, it is written in terms of general principles, not specific rules. Yet when we compare codes written two or three decades ago with those written in more recent years, we note that the contemporary ones tend to be more specific and try to cover a greater variety of specific situations. Thus, the NASW *Code of Ethics* of 1967 had many fewer paragraphs and was written in much more general terms than the later versions (adopted in 1979 and reconfirmed in 1984 and 1993). For example, the *Code* approved in 1996 and revised in 1999 more than doubled the number of standards found in the 1993 *Code*. On the other hand, the American Medical Association's (AMA) code of ethics (adopted in 1980) is much briefer than its previous code. Its most recent code (2001) includes only nine principles. One reason for the lack of detail in the current AMA code is the desire to prevent lengthy litigation that resulted from the detailed provisions of the previous code.

Internal inconsistencies between various paragraphs of the same code is one of the possible consequences of greater specificity. When there is greater specificity, various ethical principles often conflict with one another, even though each may be valid. One of the major problems of the 1999 *Code* is that it avoided the specification of a hierarchy of values, principles, and standards. This avoidance of any formulation of ethical principles in a hierarchical order provides the ingredients for many of the ethical dilemmas that we will examine in the following chapters. Another problem, suggested by Marcuse (1976) is that codes of professional ethics often fail to provide answers to ethical dilemmas because their orientation is more likely to be system-maintenance than system-challenging. At the same time, it must be remembered that codes of ethics "are not intended as a blueprint that would remove all need for the use of judgment or ethical reasoning" (Conte, Plutchik, Picard, & Karasu, 1989, p. 5).

Codes of ethics generally provide guidance only for good/bad decisions. They are far less effective in helping practitioners make decisions of the good/good and bad/bad variety. It is however, precisely these types of decisions that trouble many social workers. Good/bad decisions are those where one of the two options under consideration is thought to be correct or right, while the alternative is assumed to be incorrect or wrong. In most instances, social workers have no trouble making ethical decisions of the good/bad variety. Common sense and sound ethical judgment are usually sufficient to guide the practitioner's choice. Good/good decisions, on the other hand, are those where all of the options are beneficial, while bad/bad decisions are those for which all options result in some undesirable consequences (Keith-Lucas, 1977). In many of these latter situations, social workers need help to sort out the ethical aspects in order to make a correct decision.

Exemplar 2.2 illustrates a practice situation that includes an ethical dilemma that is not of the good/bad variety.

❖ 2.2 John Miller's Return to State Hospital

John Miller is mentally ill and has been so diagnosed by several psychiatrists. For the past three years, this 21-year-old young adult has been living at home with his elderly parents. He can take care of his own minimal needs, but he has no interest whatsoever in any personal contact. He spends most of the day sitting in the living room, staring either into empty space or at the TV. His parents dare not leave him home alone. They have approached you, John's social worker, requesting that you make arrangements to have him returned to the state hospital since they feel that they can no longer give him the care he needs. You appreciate their situation, but you also know that returning John to a state hospital may harm him.

You know that it is unethical to deprive anyone, even a mentally ill person, of his freedom except under certain clearly specified circumstances. What are the circumstances that would warrant a social worker's considering involuntary hospitalization? John Miller's behavior has not been dangerous to himself or others, regardless of the strain on his parents. Suppose in an isolated area there are no alternative treatment possibilities, what should the social worker do if John is unwilling to alter his life? Is it ethical for a social worker to interfere in John's life if he does not want to change his situation? Is it ethical to accept his decision or should one attempt to change his mind? Is the parents' request sufficient? Is the fact they are elderly and tired sufficient for the social worker to attempt to find alternative arrangements for John? How can a social worker choose between the needs of the parents and John's needs? How would this social worker's dilemma differ if the psychiatric diagnosis indicated that sooner or later John would inflict serious harm on others or to himself, even though he has been entirely harmless until now? Where in the *Code* can a social worker find guidance as to whose needs take priority?

A BRIEF HISTORY OF CODES OF PROFESSIONAL ETHICS

All modern professions have developed codes of professional ethics. These became common only in the past century, but their long and checkered history goes back to antiquity. More than two thousand years ago, Hippocrates (c. 460–377 B.C.) demanded that all Greek physicians pledge themselves to a high level of professional and ethical conduct. There is no record of similar codes for theologians and lawyers, the only other professions in the ancient world. The Hippocratic Oath became a guide, informing medical doctors in many parts of the ancient and medieval world of correct professional behavior.

Just as medicine was the first profession in the ancient world to develop a code of ethics, so did it lead the way in modern times. Dr. Thomas Percival of England is credited with writing the first of the modern professional codes of ethics in 1803. The first American code was promulgated by the American Medical Association in 1847 and was modeled on Percival's code. Pharmacists followed a few years later with their own code. Contemporary accounts suggest that pharmacists wrote this code because they wanted the public to know that their professional conduct differed from that of physicians, who in those days did not have a good reputation.

For most American occupational groups, the development of a code of ethics coincided, more or less, with the decision to formalize the transformation of the occupation into a profession. Social workers, for example, were aware that a code of ethics was one of the prerequisites for professional recognition long before the appearance of Greenwood's important article on the attributes of a profession (1957). They tried to draft codes of professional ethics soon after Flexner (1915) told them that social work was not yet a profession. An experimental draft code of ethics for social case workers, printed in 1920, has been attributed to Mary Richmond (Pumphrey, 1959).

The prestigious *Annals of the American Society for Political and Social Sciences* devoted its entire May 1922 issue to ethical codes in the professions and in business. Contemporary observers viewed the appearance of this journal issue as crucial to the emerging interest in such codes. In the *Annals* article on social work ethics, Mary Van Kleeck and Graham R. Taylor, two veteran social workers, wrote that social work did not have a written code of professional ethics but that social work practice was ethical because practitioners were guided by the ideal of service and not by any thought of financial gain. Several local and national groups developed draft codes during the 1920s. The American Association for Organizing Family Social Work prepared, but did not adopt, a detailed draft code in 1923. Many of the 38 paragraphs of that draft still sound relevant today.

The American Association of Social Workers (AASW), the largest organization of professional social workers of that day, endorsed the need for a code of professional ethics. An editorial in the April 1924 issue of *The Compass,* the official journal of the AASW, came out in favor of a code of professional ethics and asked, "Hasn't the public a right to know how the ordinary social worker is likely to act under ordinary circumstances?" The Research Committee of the AASW tried to identify common problems of ethical practice. The AASW Executive Committee appointed a National Committee on Professional Ethics even before this study was completed. This action spurred many local chapters to discuss the need for a code. Several chapters tried to produce draft documents. The Toledo (Ohio) chapter reportedly was the first local AASW chapter to publicize a draft code. Though that draft was limited to a few general ethical principles, it inspired other chapters to try their hand at preparing their own draft code of professional ethics. However, despite much interest, the adoption of a nationwide professional code had to await further organizational developments. It was only in 1951 that the AASW Delegate Assembly adopted a code of ethics.

When the historic merger of all major professional social work organizations took place in the mid-1950s, work on drafting a new code of professional ethics was started almost immediately, but the NASW Delegate Assembly adopted a code of ethics only in 1960. Seven years later, this code was amended to include a nondiscrimination paragraph. The absence of such a provision from earlier codes tells much about the change in the moral climate of the country and in the profession.

Before long, many social workers called for a complete revision of the code in order to produce a document that would provide clearer guidance for practitioners and that would be more in tune with the realities of contemporary practice. A completely new code was adopted by the 1979 NASW Delegate Assembly. Soon it became evident that this code did not yet provide sufficient guidance for social work practitioners who sought help when facing difficult ethical issues. In an early discussion of the draft code, one prominent social worker noted that its usefulness was limited because of "its high level of abstraction and lack of practice utility" (McCann, 1977, p. 18).

The revised NASW *Code of Ethics* placed a much greater emphasis on the welfare of individuals than did the earlier 1967 document. This change may be considered problematic because it tends to shift the focus away from the common welfare. At that time, one analysis of different codes of professional ethics found that all other helping professions (with the exception of medicine) placed a greater emphasis on the common welfare than did social work (Howe, 1980).

Several groups of social workers have prepared codes. For example, social workers affiliated with the National Association of Black Social Workers prepared a code of ethics that gives expression to their belief that individual welfare can be served best by promoting the common welfare of all African-American people. Social workers in clinical practice adopted a code of ethics that reflects their special concerns. The Code of Ethics of the Canadian Association of Social Workers reflects some of the special concerns of Canadian society. A Feminist Therapy Code of Ethics is based upon feminist philosophy, psychological theory and practice, as well as political theory. In recent years, the NASW *Code* was revised several times in rapid succession (1993, 1996, 1999) in an attempt to assist social workers to deal better with evolving problems. Web sites where these codes are located can be found at the end of Chapter 1.

EXERCISES

1. Ethical principles and rules are derived from societal values. Identify the relevant social work ethical rules for the following societal values:

   cultural diversity   equality   freedom   integrity
   knowledge building   privacy   social justice

   You can find in Chapter 1 the Web addresses for several professional associations' codes of ethics. Can you identify differences in the ethical rules offered in the several codes of ethics?
2. Discuss in small groups whether it is possible and desirable for a social worker to remain neutral and keep her own values from influencing clients.
3. As a social worker, if you had to choose between a child's right to confidentiality and a parent's right to know things that affect the child, how would you go about making this decision? What factors would influence your decision?
4. Look on the Web for the Feminist Therapy Code of Ethics. When you compare that code or guidelines with the NASW *Code,* can you identify themes not emphasized in the NASW *Code* but that are found in the Feminist code? Are there any standards that conflict? How congruent are the political stances of the NASW *Code* and the Feminist Codes? Discuss in small groups whether it is preferable that social workers work only with clients whose values are similar to their own. Are there any potential ethical positives to such a decision? If not, what are the potential ethical negatives of such a decision?
5. Discuss in small groups whether the NASW *Code of Ethics* should apply to *all* social workers, regardless of whether they belong to NASW or not.
6. Most professional associations (i.e., physicians, engineers, lawyers) have codes of ethics available on their Web sites. Do an Internet search for the code of ethics of a profession other than those listed in Chapter 1. Compare that code with the NASW *Code* in terms of specificity and usefulness.

SUGGESTIONS FOR ADDITIONAL READINGS

McGowan (1995) examines how values shape professional decision making as well as the history of shifts in social work value preferences and ethical concerns. Reamer (1998) traces the evolution of social work ethical norms, principles, and standards. Excellent introductions to the place of moral philosophy in social work practice can be found in Siporin (1982), Goldstein (1987, 1998), and Manning and Gaul (1997). Conrad (1988); Walden, Wolock, and Demone (1990); Kugelman (1992); Proctor, Morrow-Howell, and Lett (1993); Dolgoff and Skolnik (1996); Regehr and Antle (1997); and Healy (1998) report on research on the ethical aspects of social work practice in various settings. Barker (1988b) raises a question that faces social workers who are members of several professional associations. Which code of ethics should they follow?

3 CHAPTER | Guidelines for Ethical Decision Making

Concepts, Approaches, and Values

Social workers must make ethical choices every day. A client tells her social worker that she is planning to commit suicide. A group member who has been unemployed for the past nine months asks his social worker not to tell a prospective employer about his criminal past so that he can get the job, which he needs desperately. Another client has been telling his worker that he embezzled funds from his employer in order to pay for his son's graduate school tuition. A young man threatens to harm a fellow worker who he believes has caused his fiancée to lose her job. Each of these situations confronts the social worker with one or more ethical dilemmas because they involve conflicting obligations. What are a social worker's obligations toward her clients? Toward others who may be harmed or benefited by what the client did or will do? Toward society? Toward her own values?

A better understanding of the philosophical and practical components of ethical decision making is desirable in order to encourage ethical behavior among social work practitioners. An analysis of a practice situation, the Exemplar 3.1, will illustrate this approach.

❖ 3.1 Serena Adams Has Herpes

In the Jeanette April residential treatment center for teenagers with emotional problems, the staff has become aware that Serena Adams, a 15-year-old female has herpes. Herpes is an incurable, non–life threatening disease that lies dormant but is easy to transmit when active at the time of intercourse, and sometimes when no symptoms are present. Serena has been sending notes to Donnie, an 18-year-old male resident, suggesting dates for sex. The fact that Serena is infected is known only to the staff members and to Serena. Serena has complained from time to time of itching and sores in her groin and burning sensations while urinating. Although not life threatening, genital herpes can affect one's life by making one more susceptible to HIV infection; newborn babies can be infected if herpes is active in the mother at the time of birth; and one may have to explain the disease's presence to future partners. The treatment team, after discussing this development, asked Jackie LaMartine, Serena's social worker, to speak to her and explore the situation with her. She should try to convince Serena to avoid any sexual relations with Donnie, or at the least to make sure they use safe sex methods. She said she didn't mind speaking to Serena but feels someone should inform Donnie of Serena's herpes. Ms. LaMartine thought that not telling Donnie prevents him from making an informed choice, even to assure his use of a condom. When Ms. LaMartine spoke to Serena, she told her that she knows she loves Donnie and that she feels Serena would want to protect him and herself. Serena refused to cooperate, arguing that the information must be kept confidential, that she and Donnie love each other, and that how they have sex is their own business. She demanded that no one tell Donnie of her illness. The team members are split as to what to do now. The facts seem fairly clear, as are several of the ethical dilemmas that face Ms. LaMartine and the team. There are many questions that arise out of the social worker's professional knowledge and experience, among them:

1. Should Ms. LaMartine and the team leave Serena and Donnie to make their own decisions despite the risks to them both? Is the duty to protect Donnie more important than the maintenance of confidentiality for Serena? If Ms. LaMartine tells Donnie the facts, she will interfere with Serena's self-determination and freedom; but if she doesn't tell him, she exposes him to potential infection. Is the social worker ethically justified to discuss the situation with Donnie without Serena's agreement?

2. What is the social worker's duty to protect in this situation and who should she try to protect?

What are the long-term potential costs for Serena and Donnie if the team accedes to Serena's request? Are the costs to the agency, to these two residents, as well as to other residents, worth an effort to prevent a sexual relationship—which may not be preventable in any case?

Ethical decision making does not involve the automatic application of arbitrary rules. What MacIver wrote more than 80 years ago is still relevant today: "ethics cannot be summed up in a series of inviolate rules or commandments which can be applied everywhere and always without regard to circumstances, thought of consequences, or comprehension of the ends to be attained"

(1922, p. 7). If this were the situation, social workers would find it easier to deal with the ethical problems they encounter.

Social work professionals, like other professionals, make many ethical judgments every day with confidence. They do not think that such judgments are difficult or controversial. The professional *Code of Ethics* and common sense provides them with sufficient guidance to cope with many of these dilemmas (Beyerstein, 1993). Social workers, however, do not always face "simple" choices between one good option and one bad option. Instead, they are often confronted by a number of choices, each one of which contains both positive and negative features, as in Exemplar 3.1. In such situations, the skilled worker must assess and weigh all options and outcomes and then select the one that appears to be the most ethical. How does a social worker know which option is "the most ethical"?

FOUNDATIONS FOR ETHICAL DECISION MAKING

Decisions about ethical questions are rarely idiosyncratic and usually follow an individual's consistent behavior patterns. Since such decisions involve questions of right and wrong, they are deeply rooted in that value system which is most important to the decision maker. Though philosophy has had a major impact on the development of ethics, there have also been other influences. Frankena (1980) made reference to traditional, political, religious, racial, and gender influences on the development of contemporary ethics. Essentially, ethical systems are derived in two ways: (1) **autonomous ethics** includes those systems in which humans determine the moral rules; (2) **heteronomous ethics** ethical systems derive moral rules from nonhuman sources. For example, when religious philosophers teach that moral rules are of divine origin, they are referring to heteronomous systems.

Contemporary philosophers have identified two major theories that encompass most approaches to ethical decision making. These two theories are generally known as (1) ethical absolutism and (2) ethical relativism.

Ethical Relativism

Ethical relativists reject fixed moral rules. They justify ethical decisions on the basis of the context in which they are made or on the basis of the consequences that result. An option is chosen because it will lead to desired results or is rejected because it will lead to results that are not wanted. The amount of good that is produced or the balance of good over evil (not any absolute standard) serves as the major criterion for reaching an ethical decision.

Ethical relativists differ when it comes to identifying the target or the intended beneficiary of the planned decision. Ethical egoists believe that one should always maximize what is good for oneself, no matter what the consequences for others. Ethical utilitarians, on the other hand, argue that the most important thing is to seek the greatest good for the largest number of persons.

(consequences)

Ethical relativism is not a recent invention but was already known in ancient Greece. Among its early followers were the sophists and Herodotus. In more recent times, John Stuart Mill, Jeremy Bentham, and Sigmund Freud were among those who followed this approach. All three taught that ethical decisions should be made on the basis of maximizing pleasure and avoiding pain.

There are those who are highly critical of ethical relativism, suggesting that this approach to practice is essentially asocial and perhaps even amoral because it assumes that individual satisfaction is the primary value. Others fault ethical relativists because they say that the only thing that matters is the result. Is this position always defensible? Is there really no difference between an armed robber who kills a bystander during a bank holdup, a soldier who kills an enemy in combat, and a social worker who, by following the provisions of the child welfare code and not removing a youngster from his abusive parents, contributes to the death of a child? Different motivations and differing activities lead to the "same" results, but are they really the same?

The search for certainty, a rational and definable truth, is questioned by many persons and even discredited. Some believe there are no universal "truths" and absolute rules are unacceptable, while various "isms" (postmodernism, deconstructionism, social constructionism) claim that situations, including those that require ethical decision making, are best viewed from their "more truthful" perspectives. Because postmodernists believe there are no independent standards of objectivity, no universal "truths," and no absolute rules (Rothstein, 2002), they are included here as a subset of ethical relativism.

(context may change)

According to some persons, our era is a postmodernist age, that is "the point at which modern untying (dis-embedding, disencumbering) of tied (embedded, situated) identities reaches its completion; it is now all too easy to choose identity, but no longer possible to hold it" (Ulrich & Beck-Gemsheim, 1996, p. 24). Necessity and certainty are being replaced by contingencies. The certainties of God, nature, truth, science, technology, morality, love, and marriage are being turned into "precarious freedoms" in which "nothing that has been binds the present while the present has but a feeble hold on the future" (Bauman, 1996, p. 51).

Ethical Absolutism

(Rules are going to hold)

Ethical absolutism stresses the overriding importance of fixed moral rules. Philosophers who hold this approach teach that an action is inherently right or wrong, apart from any consequences that might result from it. A specific action or practice is morally right or wrong not because of its consequences or the circumstances but "because of some feature intrinsic to the act or practice itself" (Callahan, 1988, p. 20). Ethical absolutists maintain that ethical rules can be formulated and that these should hold under all circumstances. For example, they will argue that the rule, "A social worker shall tell the truth to her client," is always correct and applies in every situation, no matter how much damage may be caused by telling the truth in any particular situation. Philosophers such as Plato and certain religious philosophers who follow this theory are known as **deontologists.** Immanuel Kant (1724–1804) was the first modern philosopher to adopt deontological concepts. He insisted that categorical imperatives are morally necessary and obligatory under all circumstances. Jeremy Bentham (1748–1832), one of the earliest exponents of English utilitarianism, accepted "the greatest good for the greatest number" as a binding principle that applies in every situation. Some modern philosophers who are committed to situation ethics argue that "love" is the principle that should guide all human behavior (Fletcher, 1966; Lyden, 1998). On the other hand, many ethical absolutists, even those who teach a heteronomous ethics, allow for situations where the fixed rules do not apply. Many theologians have accepted the argument, first proposed by the Dutch jurist, Hugo Grotius (1583–1645), that one must always tell the truth and never lie, but that it is permissible to speak falsely to thieves because no one owes them the truth. However, there is an important difference between not applying a rule in an exceptional situation and deciding each situation as if there were no rules (Diggs, 1970).

Practitioners may not be aware of these efforts by professional philosophers. Neither do they always know which ethical theory they follow when making ethical decisions. This is especially true because the differences between the major theories frequently are not as clear in practice as they are on the printed page. These theoretical approaches often seem to merge in practice, but it does make a difference in ethical decision making whether a social worker follows one or the other theory, as the following analysis will illustrate.

Different Approaches of Two Social Workers

We will examine how two social workers—Ruth, an ethical relativist, and Anne, an ethical absolutist—might approach the ethical aspects of Serena's situation (Exemplar 3.1). Our focus will be on learning how these differences might lead to different considerations and decisions.

Serena demanded that her social worker keep her Herpes status confidential. Social worker Anne believes that every person has an absolute right to make decisions about himself or herself, even if the consequences of those decisions might harm another person. She also believes that confidentiality is a first-order professional value that social workers must follow at all times. Anne, therefore, has no hesitation about respecting Serena's demand since to her violating the confidential relationship is ethically wrong and also will destroy the trust that a client must have in her social worker. After all, Serena is in the residence because of her serious emotional problems. This "practical" consideration, however, is not the crucial ethical criterion for Anne's decision. No doubt Anne would agree that it is desirable to help Serena see the long-range advantages of either avoiding sex with Donnie or informing him of her condition. However, as far as social worker Anne is concerned, the principles of confidentiality and client autonomy are absolute, no matter who the client or what the situation.

For the time being, we have proposed that social worker Anne has elevated confidentiality and client autonomy to absolute rules, regardless of situations. Later in this chapter, we will introduce an approach to setting priorities in ethical decision making. When we do so, we will note that confidentiality and client autonomy are two important values but are not the highest on our ethical principles screen. When it comes to Herpes and sex, there are values higher than confidentiality and client autonomy. Since the value of life and health have a much higher priority, social worker Anne's professional decisions would be quite different. The protection of life and health is an absolute value of the highest order, superior to confidentiality and client autonomy. She will now do everything possible to help Donnie protect his health, even if this means violating a lower level value, such as confidentiality or client autonomy.

Social worker Ruth views the ethical aspects of Serena's situation in an entirely different light. Being an ethical relativist, she assesses the consequences of respecting Serena's request for confidentiality against the consequences of not informing Donnie. She concludes that protecting Serena's privacy can have very serious immediate and long-term consequences for Donnie's life and, potentially, also for Serena's life and emotional health. If they have unprotected sex and he discovers later that he has contracted herpes, Serena's actions will have given Donnie a heavy burden, he may become violent, and their relationship may be destroyed. She tells Serena that either Serena herself or the worker must without delay inform Donnie of the risks of having sex with Serena. If Serena is unwilling or unable to inform Donnie, social worker Ruth will do so, waving aside client autonomy and confidentiality issues in order to prevent harmful consequences.

The two decision-making scenarios just described illustrate ethical absolutist and ethical relativist decision making. The decisions made by social workers Anne and Ruth are in each case only one of many different scenarios they could choose. The scenarios presented previously illustrate the general decision-making patterns (absolute rules or weighing the results of actions or omitted actions) connected with each philosophy.

The answer to what is the best course of action in this situation depends upon the social worker's philosophy of life, her values, her commitment to ethical relativism or ethical absolutism, and the degree of immediate and direct danger to Donnie's life. It also depends on the influences of the worker's peer group, family, professional group, neighborhood, and society. The situation, as with all ethical dilemmas, touches on the question of priorities. What is best for Serena and what is best for Donnie? Donnie's health and, perhaps, life are at risk, whereas Serena's health is already at risk, and reducing her privacy may be considered a lesser priority than endangering Donnie's health.

Furthermore, the impact of any decision involving Donnie and Serena must also take into consideration other participants in this situation, including the agency, the society that pays for the care being (or to be) provided, the families of the two actors who will be affected by any negative consequences, and other persons that may be involved.

Not all deontologists follow identical ethical rules with respect to any given problem. Identification of the relevant rules is, therefore, of the greatest importance. For example, some ethical systems consider abortion to be the same as murder and prohibit it altogether, no matter what the circumstances; others permit abortions under specified conditions, such as danger to the mother's life.

Still other ethical systems are mute on this issue, leaving any decision to the individual involved. Social worker Anne may face other ethical dilemmas after she has identified the relevant moral rules. One dilemma arises out of a conflict between two categorical imperatives—the professional value and standard that calls for client self-determination and her own value system that may assign the highest priority to the protection of life. There is also another conflict between two competing professional values, confidentiality and client decision making based on full information. Here are situations where the social worker cannot honor both categorical imperatives, but must make a choice about which one to follow. The problems involved in making such choices will be discussed later in this chapter.

CONTEMPORARY APPROACHES TO ETHICAL DECISION MAKING

Philosophers have identified ethical absolutism and ethical relativism as two major ethical theories. Yet these theories are usually presented at so generalized or abstract a level that people do not always find them helpful when coping with the ethical issues they face. In the past, conscience was often suggested as the key to ethical decision making. Some contemporary philosophers have substituted guilt feelings for the older concept, and others have added "feeling good," "democracy," and "empowerment" as current keys.

Conscience or guilt feelings are too idiosyncratic to serve social work professionals as guides for ethical decision making. One person's conscience will not be the same as another's. Professional ethics are common to the entire professional group and should, therefore, be relevant to every member of that profession. What a social worker needs are tools of analysis that will permit a more systematic and rational consideration of the ethical aspects of social work intervention. The *Code* of the professional association helps social workers handle clear and obvious ethical choices that arise in practice; states the standards of ethical practice by which professional conduct can be evaluated; and promulgates the ethical principles of the profession, all the while assuming there is consensus within the profession about the standards (Beyerstein, 1993). Such models must include knowledge elements, but ethical decision making cannot be based on knowledge alone because ethics deal principally with what ought to be and not with what is. Before presenting our ethical decision making models, we will discuss various approaches that other social workers have found useful in making ethical decisions.

Clinical Pragmatism

Many social workers indicate that they are neither philosophers nor specialists in solving ethical problems. Instead, they believe that their primary responsibility is to deliver a high level of professional service. Perhaps they agree with Jim Casey, who, in John Steinbeck's *Grapes of Wrath,* said, "There ain't no sin *values aren't absolute based on society.*

and there ain't no virtue, there is just stuff people do." They are sure that they will not become entangled in ethical problems if they concentrate their efforts on improving practice. In addition, they suggest that the type of service provided, the nature of the problems dealt with, and the modes of intervention used are determined in the first instance by society so that a worker's personal ethical stance is far less important than societal ethics. Social workers who follow this approach focus on implementing the values of the society that sanctions their activities. For example, one of the functions of social workers in contemporary American society is to help individuals and groups who face various kinds of emotional disturbances and crises. These social workers use societal values as the only criterion to identity the types of behavior that require professional intervention. They try to resolve any value conflicts that may arise in the practice context by considering the value priorities of the group in which they work.

While this approach seems simple, straightforward, and even supportive of scientific practice, it has a conservative tinge. Radical writers, such as Thomas Szasz (1994) and Ivan Illich (1977), have criticized this approach as unethical because these social workers tend to act as agents of social control on behalf of dominating and exploiting societal institutions. Social workers who follow this approach rarely question society's ethics or its norms (as they understand them). Their practice supports the status quo. These social workers rarely encourage the autonomous development of alternate lifestyles, nor will they be found among those who challenge society's values in other ways. These social workers should remember that social workers have the responsibility and ethical imperative to "not practice, condone, facilitate or collaborate with any form of discrimination on the basis of race, ethnicity, national origin, color, sex, sexual orientation, age, marital status, political belief, religion, or mental or physical disability" (NASW *Code*, 1999, 4.02). Furthermore, social workers "should advocate for living conditions conducive to the fulfillment of basic human needs . . . and . . . the realization of social justice" (NASW *Code*, 1999, 6.01). The questions are whether those who follow this approach are aware of the implications of what they are doing. They must seriously consider whether they are in compliance with the professional ethics cited.

Humanistic Ethics

what's good for the client.

Many practitioners have found the humanistic ethical approach attractive because it combines a strong idealism with opportunities for individual choices. An idealistic view of human nature as essentially positive, together with an optimistic stance toward the future, provides the basis for this approach. The focus is on causal rather than on moralistic explanations of human behavior. This approach stresses the capacity, opportunity, and responsibility of every person to make choices that make sense to him or her. The individual client or group, rather than any institution or ideology, occupies the center of attention. Such an approach appears to be particularly suited to contemporary America, with its emphasis on individualism and pluralism.

individual responsibility

Self-realization has been at the center of the humanistic theories of Abraham Maslow, Erich Fromm, and other existentialists. Human beings are believed to be innately good and to have the ability to behave ethically. The inner core of the human personality is intrinsically ethical. Individual freedom and responsibility form the basis of social life. Self-expression and self-actualization are postulated as the desired outcome of mature development. Personal identity is defined by each individual according to self-chosen values that are derived, we hope, rationally. The priority of professional intervention at the individual level and group level will be to help people achieve self-actualization, rather than to help them to learn how to adjust to the existing social order. On the societal level, social workers following this approach will intervene to change those social institutions that inhibit the growth and self-realization of individuals.

Practitioners following this approach can be found in the forefront of many causes that promote freedom and equality. Some oppose stable social authority structures (Rogers, 1977); others emphasize hedonistic rather than traditional values (Orovwuje, 2001). All followers of this approach feel that they have minimized the ethical dilemmas they face. By clearly identifying value priorities, they feel that they can cope with the ethical aspects of most practice problems. More important, by emphasizing individual responsibility, the major burden for ethical decision making is shifted from the practitioner to the client.

The selection of humanistic ethics as the major approach to ethical decision making can be criticized on several grounds, primarily because such a choice does not reduce but increases the necessity for dealing with dilemmas. Not everyone comes to social workers seeking help for self-actualization, and the fact is that one person's individual self-realization may very well interfere with another person's self-realization, including the social worker's aims. Conflicts generated by individual self-realization and clashes of will can exist between the client, practitioner, agency, community, profession, and society—all of which will require means of dealing with the dilemmas that arise out of the conflicts.

There is yet another criticism of this perspective. Is it better for social workers as a profession to encourage individualism and hedonism, which in many ways fragment and undermine the social work aim to build a sense of community and alter societal structures so they are more enhancing of people? Such a question raises the reality of conflicts between individuals and professions and society. After all, few, if any, clients or social worker behaviors are devoid of moral questions and considerations in their lives. The chief criticisms of self-realization are that not everyone is innately good, one person's or group's fulfillment can clash with other persons and groups, and self-realization without boundaries and responsibility can lead to destructive as well as constructive actions.

Situational Ethics

Situational ethics claims that there are no ethical laws. Ethical decisions should be influenced only by the norm of love. Situational ethics became popular during the 1960s, the era when all types of authority were questioned. Without general rules, the social worker must evaluate what is the right thing to do in

By '60's! Joseph Fletcher.

every situation and try to choose a course of action that demonstrates the most love for all those concerned. Thus, situational ethics would allow one to lie to save a life or to prevent harm to others. Situational ethics was originally promulgated as a Christian ethic. Critics suggest that love is of primary concern for Christian believers, but they point out that in the church this love is subject to rules and laws and is not just the result of individual intuition. Situational ethics affirmed personal judgment in an era when all authority and institutions were being challenged. Other critics thought that this approach to ethical decision making was overly simplified (Lyden, 1998).

Nevertheless, situational ethics found a widespread response. The secularization of modern life encouraged the abandonment of absolute rules and universal criteria. At a time when a plurality of ethical rules has emerged it is arguable that no one is able or willing to say that any one rule is correct or applicable in every situation. As a result, many deal with ethical dilemmas on a case-by-case basis, preferring to use "fragmentary moral rules as a substitute for universal rules" (Carlton, 1978, p. 2).

Though situation ethics "emerged" in the 1960s, it has had many forerunners. The Danish philosopher Soren Kierkegaard (1813–1855) insisted that truth is subjective, while the French philosopher Jean Paul Sartre (1905–1980) taught that ethical decisions can be made only in the light of the prevailing situation, since each case is unique and unlike every other case. Different and changing situations call for different ethical criteria and decisions. As one reflective thinker wrote, "The good differs from culture to culture, and there is no objective way . . . of verifying one [culture's good] as better than another" (Shirk, 1965, p. 58). Environment, circumstance, and context shape human behavior as well as the criteria for ethical conduct. What might be considered correct or proper in one sphere will be incorrect in another. A social worker may be ethically justified to intervene in one situation, even while a similar intervention in another situation might be ethically questionable. Any given activity itself is neither ethical nor unethical. It is the situation in which it takes place that defines its ethical dimension.

The critical importance of the context was experimentally demonstrated in what is known as the "simulated prison experiment." College students who volunteered to participate in this experiment were randomly assigned roles of prisoners or guards. Those who became "guards" had little notion that within less than twenty-four hours they would behave in a very authoritarian and very punitive manner. Prior to the experiment, all of these students had used very different ethical criteria, but the experimental context invited ethical considerations that the participants believed to be appropriate to the prison setting. In the words of the senior experimenter, "evil acts are not necessarily the deeds of evil men, but may be attributable to the operation of powerful social sources" (Haney, Banks, & Zimbardo, 1973, p. 90).

Social workers who use situational ethics do not have any fixed rules that help them make decisions about the ethical aspects of practice problems. Because of this, they need even more support systems and guides for making such decisions than do most other social workers.

Religious Ethics

Religious ethics presuppose a belief in the existence of God. While secularist philosophers teach that men and women are the creators of their own values, religious philosophers maintain that there is a set of divine values that humans must try to discover. Unlike those who deny the existence of absolute truth and absolute ethical rules, those who follow religious ethics declare that there are eternal rules that give direction for correct behaviors at all times. Believers are convinced that religious faith and ethical morality are two sides of the same coin. They cannot conceive of the long-term effectiveness of ethical principles that come from a source other than the divine will. The ethical aspects of interpersonal relations can exist only if one accepts the authority of God. They agree with Ivan in Dostoyevsky's *The Brothers Karamazov* when he said, "If there is no God, everything is permissible."

Jacques Maritain, a Christian philosopher, argued that a secular ethics in which the individual becomes the ultimate goal does not deify the person but degrades him or her because "the greatness of man consists in the fact that his sole end is the uncreated Good" (1934, p. 269). For believers, the search for divine meaning is meaningful, while nonbelievers consider this search futile.

One of the consequences of accepting the religious approach is that ethics and law merge into one comprehensive, interrelated system. Because ethical principles are usually stated on a very generalized and abstract level, the authorized interpreters of religious law deduce specific applications to daily problems. These deductions become precedence or law. When this occurs, law is no longer "divorced from ethics but serves as a means to implement ethical principles in the every-day life of society" (Kurzweil, 1980, p. 71). This approach provides those who follow it with a powerful tool that helps them cope with many of the ethical issues encountered in social work practice. On the other hand, they face a very serious problem when applying this approach because they practice in what is essentially a secular society.

Feminist Ethics

Traditional Western approaches to ethics are criticized by feminist ethicists. Feminists raise questions about Western ethics and view traditional ethics as reflecting masculine culture and masculine ways of reasoning. According to this view, traditional ethical decision making emphasizes universality and impartiality over "culturally feminine ways of moral reasoning that emphasize relationships, particularity, and partiality" (Tong, 1998, p. 261). Much emphasis is placed by feminist ethics on an ethic of caring that views individuals as "existing and flourishing only within networks of care . . . networks of relationships, practices, values, and ways of life" (Manning, 1992, p. 163).

Among the aspects of feminist theory that have importance for professional ethics are the following:

1. The critique of domination and the concomitant articulation of the value of reciprocity, balancing traditional power differences

2. The recognition of the distinctive individuality of the other
3. A commitment to an ideal of caring
4. A rejection of abstract universality and a model of reasoning that is concerned with context

Because domination and oppression in any form are considered morally wrong, feminist ethics are concerned with both particularities of individual situations *and* a concern with social structural conditions such as racism, classism, and sexism. In ethical decision making, private troubles are viewed within the context of public issues. Personal situations and societal contexts should not be viewed separately (Abramson,1996).

However, there is no one feminist approach to ethical decision making, and different models have been developed, including maternal, political, and lesbian. Furthermore, as Glassman suggests, feminists also will find that "their feminist beliefs come into serious conflict with other deeply respected social work traditions, values, and principles" (1992, p. 161). Can social workers respect the cultural values and customs of some ethnic groups without accommodating and perpetuating oppression? What should social workers do who are respectful of self-determination when clients accept patriarchal or other communal values?

Perhaps over time as these newly developed approaches find means of dealing with various ethical dilemmas, they may challenge and alter more traditional ethical decision-making patterns in social work practice. Just as clinical pragmatism, humanistic, situational, and religious ethics, among other perspectives, have had their particular impact on ethical decision making in social work, so feminist ethics may also contribute to contemporary ethical decision making, although its impact is not clear.

PERSONAL, GROUP, SOCIETAL, AND PROFESSIONAL VALUES

Values, are a key element in the ethical decision-making process. No wonder Levy (1976b) called ethics "values in action." The purpose of clarifying one's personal and group values, as well as societal and professional values, is to increase one's awareness of the potential conflicts among them and the potential impact these conflicts can have on ethical decision making. Recognition of our own values and those of clients, agencies, communities, and other people—including professionals—involved in various practice situations is an important step in preparation for ethical decision making. Ethical decision making requires being alert to the impact of values in order to reduce conflicts and to assist social workers in making ethical decisions based on client needs and the maintenance of one's own ethical integrity.

Before clarifying the relationship between values and ethics, it may be helpful to differentiate between different levels of values:

1. *Individual or personal values* are values held by one person but not necessarily by others.

2. *Group values* are values held by subgroups within a society—such as religious groups, ethnic groups, and so forth.
3. *Societal values* are those values that are recognized by major portions of the entire social system or, at least, by the leading members or spokespersons of that system.
4. *Professional values* are those values proclaimed by a professional group, such as social workers.

Generally, these four value sets are complementary or reciprocal, although at times they may be in conflict. Most of the time and in most places, discord among the different level value sets is infrequent, though differences in interpretation, priority, and intensity are not uncommon.

Clarifying Personal Values

Some social workers question or denigrate the importance of personal values for professional practice. They suggest that a social worker must suspend or neutralize her personal values when serving clients. Charles Levy, who chaired the NASW committee that drafted an earlier *Code of Ethics,* said: "To be a professional practitioner is to give up some of one's autonomy and to relinquish some of one's right as a freely functioning being" (1976a, p. 113). However, the conflict between personal and professional values is rarely as unambiguous as this. The desirability of professional social workers suppressing their personal values in many situations, although perhaps possible, remains an ambitious, problematic, and very difficult task.

Others suggest that personal values have relatively little influence on ethical professional behaviors. They claim that social workers know instinctively or intuitively what is the right thing to do. Admittedly, feelings and instincts are important and do influence behavioral choices. However, having a strong feeling for something does not necessarily make for an ethical choice. A worker may feel that she wants to have sex with or befriend a client, but this instinctive feeling, strong as it may be, does not make this behavior ethically correct.

Frankena (1980) indicated that a person's cultural experiences and background, including personal values, implicitly direct the ethical decision-making process of that person. Unless these become explicit, however, there is danger that biases and stereotypes, rather than professional values and ethics, will shape professional behaviors. For example, Garb (1994) reports recent research findings showing the existence of gender biases in personality assessment for both male and female clinicians. Siporin (1985b) noted the difficulty that many social workers have when it comes to making ethical decisions. He suggests that in view of the contemporary libertarian and relativist moral climate it has become increasingly difficult for many persons to be clear about their own values. Even when personal values have been identified, making ethical choices on the basis of these values is often difficult, as Coughlin noted when he said that "in a society that is philosophically, culturally, politically, and religiously pluralistic, making value choices is no way to win friends" (1966, p. 97).

Shakespeare gave sound advice when he wrote: "This above all, to thine own self be true. . . . Thou canst not then be false to any man" (*Hamlet,* 1, 3, 78–80). This same advice may also help social workers when they consider their personal values that are relevant for ethical decision making. No matter what approach social workers use, it is essential that they clarify and make explicit their own personal values. Those who agree with Siporin that "there is a moral and ethical imperative that social workers act as moral agents" (1985b, p. 20) know the importance of holding clear, unambiguous, and specific personal and professional values. Only such values are effective in influencing and guiding behavior. In no other way can a social worker be true "to thine own self" and not act as a "hired gun" for a client, an agency, or even the state. It just will not do to speak in generalities. Instead, a social worker must carefully scrutinize and define her values.

It is not enough for a social worker to say that she favors (or opposes) assisted suicide. She must be able to define her values about assisted suicide clearly. Does she believe a person has a right to doctor-assisted suicide if death is expected in the next six months and the person is found by a psychiatrist not to be depressed? Or does she believe that, with palliative care, all terminally ill persons can take advantage of the dying process to search for important values, to reconcile with families, and make some valued use of the time? Does she dismiss assisted suicide under any circumstances and opt for life despite the difficulty of the last days? These questions are raised here to emphasize that social workers must first clarify their own value stance in relation to value-laden issues they meet in practice situations if they want to be true to themselves and to their profession. In the section Clarifying Professional Values, found later in this chapter, this theme of clarification, differentiation, and integration of personal, group, professional, and societal values will be discussed further.

Clarifying Group Values

Social workers, like all other people, belong to more than one group and derive their values from those of their family, community, as well as from professional, religious, and other groups with which they are in contact. Part of analyzing one's value system is clarifying the values of those reference groups with which one identifies. Group membership and context are powerful and often decisive value forces. Like everyone else, social workers act in ways that they might not have chosen except for the influence of groups.

Most Americans grow up valuing a sense of independence. There, however, is a growing diversity of group values and cultural standards that social workers encounter and/or hold. Some groups favor strong interdependence among their members (loyalty, dependence, and connection to the group) and others foster independence (move out, do not be dependent, and steer your own course). Some of these may be contrary to those held by mainstream America. Independent decision making is valued by Americans in general, but some groups may hold other values. For instance, persons with Pacific Island backgrounds (among other groups) attach a greater value to group-oriented decisions than to individual self-determination (Ewalt & Mokuau, 1995). Without considering those population groups that value group decisions above individual-oriented values, the NASW *Code* (1999,1.02) prioritizes self-determination among the ethical responsibilities of social workers when it encourages social workers to respect and promote this right among clients (Ewalt & Mokuau, 1995), except when clients' actions or potential actions pose a serious, foreseeable, and imminent risk to themselves or others.

Immigrants often share their residence with relatives or other families because their cultures emphasize family closeness and interdependence or for economic reasons. This group value is foreign to many Americans who are raised and live in one-family apartments and homes, valuing their privacy. Many social workers may come from groups that do not value such living arrangements. Similarly, a professional may be unhappy when immigrants turn for help to kin and hometown networks rather than to the organizations in which social workers are employed, despite their effectiveness as informal helpers (Padilla, 1997; Chow, 1999).

Just as assumptions cannot be made by social workers about their own group values, it is often difficult to offer generalizations about the values of particular client groups. Social workers should keep the following in mind:

1. Among possible conflicts between the social worker's values and client values, in some instances the difference may be based on the client's membership in a particular group.
2. There are limits to the generalizations that can be made about groups, and social workers must take care to avoid the use of stereotypes. Clients may have values that differ from others in their *own* cultural group by date of immigration, whether American born, education level, geographic origin, social class, and even language (Agbayani-Siewert, 1994). Differences within a group may be greater than differences between two groups.
3. Professional social workers should not assume their clients will necessarily reflect or follow the values of their group.

Social workers who understand and clarify their values and the connection of those values to the groups that affect them and their clients have a better chance of identifying and handling value conflicts in ethical decision making.

Clarifying Societal Values

In the United States, it grows more and more difficult for social workers to identify and use societal values as ethical guidelines in a multicultural, multireligious, multivalues society. The influx of persons and families from so many different cultures and nations has created an expanded pluralism of values. To the extent that ethical behavior in general reflects what society values, nevertheless, a social worker must have accurate knowledge of the current various societal value stances and take them into consideration when assessing a problem situation and when making her decisions. There, however, may be situations when a social worker is justified, even obligated, to act in ways that are contrary to perceived societal norms. However, in every instance, the worker first has an obligation to clarify the relevant societal values.

The application of societal norms may become problematic when a society accepts values that previously were disvalued, especially when the adoption of the new value occurs unevenly among different groups within society. For example, today many but not all Americans accept the value that one may choose one's lifestyle freely, particularly if this does not impinge on the lives of others. Other issues such as school prayer, abortion, and assisted suicide, however, still divide Americans because the acceptance of these new values has not been uniform across American society.

Clarifying Professional Values

Social work professional ethics are based on "social work's core values of service, social justice, dignity and worth of the person, importance of human relationships, integrity, and competence. The profession expresses its values through its primary mission to enhance human well-being and help meet the basic human needs of all people, with particular attention to the needs and empowerment of people who are vulnerable, oppressed, and living in poverty" (NASW *Code*, 1999, Preamble). Essentially, the social work value system reflects a democratic *ethos* that provides for individual and group fulfillment. It calls for respect of individuals and their differences, while at the same time recognizing the need for mutual aid and societal supports so that all persons can attain their maximum potential.

Finding the correct balance between the rights of the group or community and the rights of the individual is often not an easy matter and is a challenge not unique to social work. Such choices present serious dilemmas for which there are few guidelines. Within this balance, however, ethical decisions clearly require adherence to a democratic *ethos*.

Social work practice always involves ethical decision making. Assumptions about morals and values are basic to social workers' theories, policies, and practice decisions. Ethical dilemmas may arise when there is a conflict between the social worker's personal, group, societal, and professional values that are relevant in a given situation. The "absence" of conflict for the social worker may indicate either that the social worker is unconscious of the moral nature of the choices she faces or that the social worker is so clear about her values and societal priorities that the choice is *prima facie* correct. Another explanation may be that making the decision is not problematic for this worker because such decisions are routine (Fleck-Henderson, 1991). This does not imply that decisions made in such situations will be ethically correct. When decisions become so routine that they do not cause the social worker second thoughts, the time may have arrived for taking extra care in regard to ethical decision making.

EXERCISES

1. Social workers deal with varied situations, which may be congruent or dissonant with their personal values. Can you identify what your

personal values are re the following: abortion, genetic screening, religious beliefs or their absence, personal and family responsibility, family planning and contraception, sexual intercourse before marriage, and pornography? From where did you derive your personal values? Can you identify how your values play a part in your personal life and how they might play a part in your professional life?

2. The legislature of your state has been alarmed by a sharp rise in the number of children born to young adults with mental retardation. Even when these infants are healthy, many of the parents with retardation are not able to give their children the care that they need. As a result, most of these children must be placed in foster homes at great expense to the public. A bill has been introduced by a group of powerful state senators calling for mandatory sterilization of all men and women with mental retardation. The senators argue that this is an effective, efficient, and painless way of taking care of this problem. You have been asked by your local NASW chapter to prepare testimony in opposition to this bill. In your testimony you should be mindful that considerations of efficiency and effectiveness cannot be dismissed out of hand in these days of tight budgets. Yet you might argue that ethical considerations are sometimes even more important. Remember, however, that you are trying to convince legislators, not social workers.

3. Organize a class debate on the proposition: "A true professional must be willing to give up some of his autonomy and some of his rights as a freely functioning individual, especially when there is a conflict between personal and professional values."

4. Tonight's forecast is for below-freezing temperatures. The mayor has ordered the police to pick up all homeless persons and to deliver them to the city shelter. The police have asked the shelter social workers to help them to locate the homeless and to persuade them to come to the shelter. You are one of the shelter social workers and know that many homeless persons will refuse to go to the shelter. What are the ethical implications of this request? What should you do as a professional social worker?

SUGGESTIONS FOR ADDITIONAL READINGS

Fleck-Henderson (1991) draws on social psychological research on moral reasoning and behavior and applies it to moral reasoning in clinical practice. In "Religious Denominational Policies on Sexuality," Bullis and Harrigan (1992) describe how the religious values and beliefs of clients and social workers in relation to sexuality can impact the therapeutic process. Loewenberg (1992) illustrates some potential conflicts between personal and professional values. Brill's "Looking at the Social Work Profession through the Eye of the NASW *Code*" (2001) provides one view of social work practice and the ethics of the profession.

Guidelines for Ethical Decision Making

CHAPTER 4

The Decision-Making Process and Tools

In the previous chapter, we examined the philosophical components, contemporary approaches, and values as background for ethical decision making. In this chapter, we turn to the practical components of decision making itself. A social worker can realize instantaneously that an ethical decision must be made. Typically, it is a process or series of thoughts and activities that occur over time and that result in a person or group acting (or not acting) in a particular manner. Since the process need not be conscious, it always precedes making the ethical decision itself. Decisions will be better, more effective, and more ethical to the extent that the process becomes conscious.

Decisions can be approached step by step so that one moves gradually through a series of stages until, at the end of the process, one makes the decision. It is erroneous to assume that only one person, the decision maker, participates in this process. There may be many participants in the decision-making process, but there is only one responsible decision maker. Many different persons present information, react to assessments, introduce additional options, or make changes in the environment; these, in turn, change the nature of the data on which the decision is based or the nature of the decision that is made.

Observing decision making is like watching ocean waves approach the shore. Choices are always influenced by previous decisions that lead to new directions. Ethical decision making is far too complex to permit the development of a simple "how-to" problem-solving model. Some model, however, is necessary if we are to understand what decision making is all about. A simpler model of decision making may help social workers understand what is involved in ethical decision making. Such a model, like all models in science, will simplify reality by focusing on only one decision. A model is a permissible didactic device as long as it is understood that in real life every decision is preceded and followed by other decisions, many of which have a direct bearing on the matter under consideration.

In Figure 4.1, we present one such general model for decision making. As a general model, it is applicable to many different situations and is not limited to ethical decisions. This model is based on the assumption that social workers can plan rationally what is needed for intervention in human situations and that they want to minimize the irrational, the impulsive, and the unplanned consequences of purposeful actions.

ETHICAL ASSESSMENT SCREEN

The social worker who is alert to the ethical aspects of practice will examine and assess the available options and alternatives somewhat differently than her colleague who is not as concerned with the ethical aspects of practice. This becomes clear when we consider various assessment criteria. In Figure 4.2, we present an ethical assessment screen designed to help social workers further clarify and integrate the ethical aspects of decision making in social work practice.

Protection of Clients' Rights and Welfare

The definition of rights and privileges changes over time. What is thought to be a right at one time may not be so defined in another era. These changes may create ethical problems. Social workers were once expected to protect confidentiality, no matter what the obstacles. Today, because of changes in laws; court decisions; the introduction of various technologies; managed care and administrative record keeping required by funding and accrediting organizations; participation and consultation with team members, including those from other disciplines; and responsibility to supervisors and courts, social workers remain concerned but may have much less control over potential breaches of confidentiality. In a later chapter, new privacy regulations required by the Health Insurance Portability and Accountability Act (1996) that became effective in 2003 will be discussed.

Changing definitions of what constitutes rights may also create ethical problems for social workers. Consider the ethical problems faced by social workers in the adoption field as the right of adopted persons to information about their biological parents is becoming recognized in more and more jurisdictions. At one time, the biological and adoptive parents were assured that such information would remain confidential and would never be shared with the adoptee. Now, when court decisions or legislative enactments in some

Figure 4.1 | A General Decision-Making Model

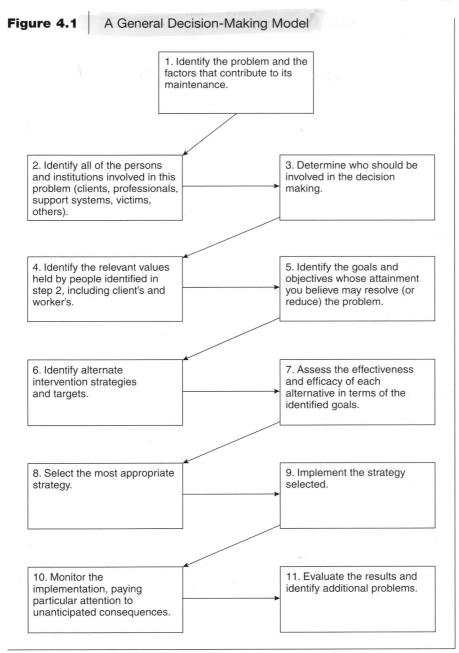

1. Identify the problem and the factors that contribute to its maintenance.

2. Identify all of the persons and institutions involved in this problem (clients, professionals, support systems, victims, others).

3. Determine who should be involved in the decision making.

4. Identify the relevant values held by people identified in step 2, including client's and worker's.

5. Identify the goals and objectives whose attainment you believe may resolve (or reduce) the problem.

6. Identify alternate intervention strategies and targets.

7. Assess the effectiveness and efficacy of each alternative in terms of the identified goals.

8. Select the most appropriate strategy.

9. Implement the strategy selected.

10. Monitor the implementation, paying particular attention to unanticipated consequences.

11. Evaluate the results and identify additional problems.

Figure 4.2 | Ethical Assessment Screen

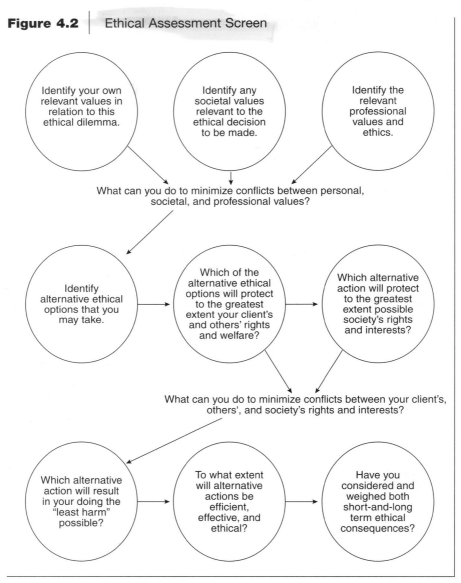

states support the right of adopted persons to this information, social workers in these jurisdictions have little choice but to reveal it. However, is it ethical for other social workers to continue to tell biological and adoptive parents that this information will always remain confidential when they have no way of ensuring this promise? This problem is not limited to courts and adoptees. No social worker can ever assure complete confidentiality because the social worker often does not control the data received.

Protection of Society's Interests

Sometimes it is difficult to balance society's interests with a client's interests. If a client tells his social worker that he has committed a property crime, the social worker must weigh her obligations to the client against her obligations to society. Social control is one of the functions of every social worker, but so is the maintenance of a helping relationship. To which function should the practitioner give priority if she cannot pursue both at the same time? Would the same considerations apply if the client were a part-time prostitute in a town where prostitution was prohibited by law? Can lawbreaking be overlooked when a client makes progress toward attaining identified and constructive intervention goals? Does it matter whether the law violation harms another person? Keep these questions in mind as you assess the ethical dilemmas posed in Exemplar 4.1.

❖ 4.1 Security or Protection?

John Newton was a likable young man—22 years old, not steadily employed, but always willing to help. Even before Ray Dunkirk, the community worker, had arrived on the scene, Newton had organized a number of young adults into a club. This club was well known in the neighborhood for the many helpful services it provided. The community's elderly population was especially appreciative of the security services that the group gave them. Thefts and holdups of older people had ceased ever since this club began to operate in the community.

Dunkirk also became aware that Newton has intimidated local store owners and has obtained regular payoffs from them in return for promising them "protection."

What was Ray Dunkirk to do? He considered various options, including the following:

1. He could overlook Newton's protection racket in view of the many positive things he was doing that were benefiting the community.
2. He could report Newton's protection racket to the police, since illegal activities should never be condoned.
3. He could strengthen his relations with Newton with the view of helping to guide him away from the illegal activity; in the meantime, he would not report the law violation to the police.

What are the ethical aspects in choosing the best option? One ethical dilemma is how to balance the best interests of the various publics involved: older persons, storekeepers, the community, the larger society, and others. Another question concerns the ethics of doing something that might result in the return of violence against the older people of this community. The following discussion is intended to help social workers cope with these conflicts and to find answers to these questions.

The "Least Harm" Principle

Sometimes social workers are confronted by problems for which there are no positive choices. Regardless of the option chosen by the client and/or the worker, some harm will come to one person or another, perhaps even to the client or to the social worker. What is the ethical choice in such situations? The "least harm" rule suggests choosing the option that will result in the least harm, the least permanent harm, or the most easily reversible harm. These are not always simple decisions. In some cases, there are complex considerations. A social worker has to consider "the least harm to whom." A given choice may result in the least harm to one person but major harm to another person.

Consider the options facing Morgana Elam, the social worker who has to consider the options in the Guevara family situation (Exemplar 1.1). Does the least harm principle offer guidance in choosing the most ethical alternative? How?

Some have suggested that the routine application of the least harm principle may diminish the possibility of choosing the most effective intervention technique. There may be times when it is justified to use an option that has great risks but enhances the likelihood of a successful outcome. However, such a choice should be made only with the full consent and agreement of the client.

Efficiency and Effectiveness

Many people think that *efficiency* and *effectiveness* are synonyms, but there are important differences between the two terms, especially when it comes to ethical decision making. The **efficiency criterion** is concerned with the relative cost (including budget, staff time, agency, and community resources) of achieving a stated objective. Whenever two options will lead to the same result, the one that requires less budget, less staff, and less time is the more efficient one. The **effectiveness criterion,** on the other hand, relates to the degree to which the desired outcome is achieved. When the implementation of one option results in halving the number of poor people in a county, while the second option reduces the poverty population by 80%, the latter option is the more effective one—but its cost may be so high that it is considered inefficient.

Difficult choices arise when the more efficient option is the less effective one, or vice versa. Making decisions on the basis of only efficiency and effectiveness criteria may result in unethical decisions. At times, the most efficient or the most effective option must be rejected because of its ethical implications. Cuba as early as 1975 tracked down Cubans who spent time in Africa and tested them for diseases. Cuban officials also committed people to sanitariums when they tested HIV positive, where they were forced to remain, despite human rights complaints by Cuban and other persons. Later, some HIV-positive men and women were allowed to leave if their condom use and hygiene were approved (Aguilera, 2003). In the United States, these actions may be highly effective at controlling the transmission of HIV but may also be questionable from an ethical point of view. For example, sending poor people or people with chronic mental illness to another city or deporting them to another country may be the most effective and the most efficient way of eliminating poverty or the expense of long-term hospitalization, but such decisions must be dismissed out of hand by anyone who is concerned with the ethical implications of these proposed plans.

More often, the ethical assessment of an option is not as clear as in these examples, so a social worker may find it difficult to make a decision. For example, what are the ethical implications of forcing poor people to work? Work is highly valued in our society, but *force* means limiting a person's freedom, another important value in our society. The ethical assessment, in this case, demands that we assess work and independence against the loss of freedom. In the past, social work ideology rejected out of hand the various "workfare" programs that forced poor people to work. With the implementation of Temporary Assistance for Needy Families (TANF), apparently a change in societal and social work ideology and values may be taking place. However, there are no widely accepted assessment procedures that can help a social worker weigh the ethical aspects of each of the many state workfare options. Once workfare is the law, the profession and individual social workers must make an ethical assessment of the law (Dolgoff, 2002). Of course, there are assessment procedures that can be used in these cases; we are offering some in this book. What is lacking is a professional consensus on the issue.

Another kind of ethical quandary arises out of the continuing efforts to deinstitutionalize patients of mental hospitals. When this policy was first proposed some years ago, certain professionals supported and implemented the program because they thought it would right a wrong. In some instances, the option of releasing mentally ill patients from hospitals was adopted even though it was known that most communities lacked adequate resources for caring for these people. Many state governments were unable to help communities with the problem because they themselves were facing major budget cuts. How ethical was it to institute a strategy that might result in some long-range improvements, but in the short run might harm many fragile people? Was it ethical to do so without first ensuring the availability of adequate community resources? Consider this question by using the ethical assessment screen (Figure 4.2).

The ethical assessment screen in Figure 4.2 provides a sequence of questions to be answered systematically that takes a person through the important variables to consider in order to arrive at a thoughtful and careful ethical decision.

RANK-ORDERING ETHICAL PRINCIPLES

In the preceding sections we discussed a number of ethical criteria that some social workers have found helpful when assessing decision alternatives. These criteria have not been arranged in any order of priority. More specific guides are needed whenever two or more of these criteria point toward different alternatives.

Figure 4.3 | Ethical Rules Screen (ERS)

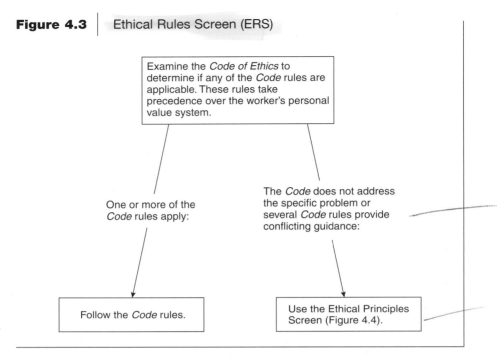

Examine the *Code of Ethics* to determine if any of the *Code* rules are applicable. These rules take precedence over the worker's personal value system.

One or more of the *Code* rules apply:

The *Code* does not address the specific problem or several *Code* rules provide conflicting guidance:

Follow the *Code* rules.

Use the Ethical Principles Screen (Figure 4.4).

Even though some social workers disagree, we believe that the preferred way of resolving such conflicts among ethical principles is a lexical ordering of these principles—that is, rank-ordering them from the most important to the least important. Such ordering is necessary even though "ordering principles is not an easy task" (Christensen, 1986, p. 82).

A lexical ordering of ethical principles can provide social workers with a guide, but such a guide is not meant to be a magic formula that can be applied blindly. As Baier (1958) suggested, the principle of priority should be used when two or more moral rules (standards) conflict. Based on the earlier work of a number of authors including Baier (1958), Kitchner (1984), Joseph (1985), Lewis (1984), Reamer (1983), Siporin (1983), and Zygmond and Boorhem (1989), we have prepared guides for ethical decision making. Social workers rarely make direct use of theoretical knowledge or philosophical principles when making practice decisions. Instead, they have integrated knowledge and values into a set of practice principles, and these are what social workers use at the critical points in the decision-making process.

We have used the work of the authors mentioned, as well as additional sources and our own practice experience, to prepare the following two guides or screens that we believe will be helpful in making ethical decisions. We call these guides the **ethical rules screen (ERS)** and the **ethical principles screen (EPS)** (see Figures 4.3 and 4.4). These guides are meant to be tools; they should not be applied blindly.

Figure 4.4 | Ethical Principles Screen (EPS)

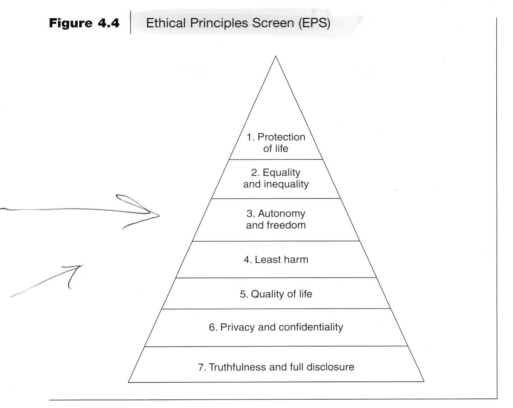

1. Protection of life

2. Equality and inequality

3. Autonomy and freedom

4. Least harm

5. Quality of life

6. Privacy and confidentiality

7. Truthfulness and full disclosure

The ERS should always be used first. Only when this screen does not provide any satisfactory guidance should the social worker use the EPS. To be useful, a guide for rank-ordering ethical principles must clearly indicate the order of priority of such principles. Once such a priority list has been established, the operating rule is that the satisfaction of a higher-order principle takes precedence over the satisfaction of a lower-order principle. Even though there is not yet any general agreement on the rank order of professional ethical principles, we have developed the EPS on the basis of our perception of what might be the consensus among social workers. All ethical principles are important. When more than one ethical principle is relevant in the analysis of a set of practice options and each of these principles leads to a different outcome, the rank order suggested in the EPS should be used to make a decision. In other words, an assessment based on Ethical Principle 1 is more compelling than one using Ethical Principles 2 or 3. For example, if both confidentiality (Principle 6) and full disclosure (Principle 7) apply, the ethical principle of confidentiality should receive priority. Since the EPS is the key ethical assessment tool for resolving ethical practice dilemmas, we will comment in detail on several of these principles.

Ethical Principle 1   The *protection of human life* applies to all persons, both to the life of a client and to the lives of all others. This principle takes precedence over every other obligation. "The right to life is the most basic of all rights, for if one's right to life is violated one cannot enjoy any other rights" (Kuhse & Singer, 1985, p. 509).

Most physicians follow this principle of saving and prolonging human life, regardless of the resulting quality of life or the economic costs involved. This life-sustaining principle received wide publicity through the case of Karen Ann Quinlan, whose physicians refused to withdraw life-support systems, even though this patient had been unconscious for many years and there was no further hope for any positive change. Today, physicians keep many Americans "alive" through the use of high-tech life-sustaining instruments. Social workers, on the other hand, tend to place more emphasis on improving the quality of life for individuals, groups, and communities. Most of the time, social workers are not aware of any conflict between the biophysical principle of sustaining life and the psychosocial principle of improving life. At times, however, there is conflict. One example is the case of a middle-aged man with marked hypertension. The medication that brought down his life-threatening blood pressure also caused sexual impotence (Roberts, 1989). Is it ethical for a social worker to support this client's decision to stop taking the medication so that he can once again enjoy sexual relations? Such a decision may lead to an improvement in the quality of his life (Ethical Principle 5), but it may also contribute to shortening his life span(Ethical Principle 1).

Ethical Principle 2   The *principle of equality and inequality* suggests that all persons in the same circumstances should be treated in the same way; that is, persons in equivalent situations have the right to be treated equally. At the same time, persons in different situations have the right to be treated differently if the inequality is relevant to the issue in question. Unequal treatment can be justified when other considerations such as beneficence outweigh the equality principle or on the ground that such unequal treatment will promote greater equality (Frankena, 1973, p. 52). This principle was formulated by Kitchner (1984) and is based on the seminal work of Rawls (1971). Kitchner specifically applied this principle to ethics. She taught that a principle can suggest an obligation, but if there are special circumstances or when there are conflicting and stronger obligations, one should always act on the basis of the obligations derived from the higher principle.

Examples in which this principle apply occur in situations that involve child abuse or elder abuse. Since the abused child (or elder) and the abuser are not in an "equal" position, the principles of confidentiality and autonomy with respect to the abusing adult are of a lower rank order than the obligation to protect the child or old person, even when it is not a question of life and death. Another situation in which this principle applies occurs when several families apply for certain resources (e.g., provision of shelter after a flood or fire may not be equal but differ because of the number of people in families). Should their prior lifestyles be taken into consideration? In situations where one family is demonstrably nearer nutritional or other disaster, the ethical principle permits or even requires the unequal allocation of scarce resources.

Ethical Principle 3   A social worker should make practice decisions that *foster a person's self-determination, autonomy, independence, and freedom.* Freedom, though highly important, does not override the right to life or survival of the person him- or herself or of others. A person does not have the right to decide to harm him- or herself or anyone else on the grounds that the right to make such a decision is his or her autonomous right. When a person is about to make such a decision, the social worker is obligated to intervene since Ethical Principle 1 takes precedence.

The risk/benefit ratio may also help determine when the autonomy principle applies and when it is ethical to ignore a client's "decision." If the condition facing a client is life threatening and if the risk of intervention is minimal (while the potential benefit of the intervention is great), the social worker may consider proceeding even without a client's consent. In this situation, the client's refusal should be considered an indication of his lack of competency. On the other hand, if the risk is great and the potential benefit minimal, the client's refusal is logical and should be accepted.

Ethical Principle 4   The *least harm principle* holds that when faced with dilemmas that have the potential for causing harm, a social worker should attempt to avoid or prevent such harm. When a harm must be done to one involved party or another, a social worker should always choose the option that will cause the least harm, the least permanent harm, and/or the most easily reversible harm. If harm has been done, the social worker should attempt where possible to repair the harm done.

Ethical Principle 5   A social worker should choose the option that promotes a better quality of life for all people, for the individual as well as for the community. Consistent with the *Code of Ethics,* "social workers should promote the general welfare of society, from local to global levels, and the development of people, their communities, and their environments" (NASW *Code,* 1999, 6.01).

Ethical Principle 6   A social worker should make practice decisions that strengthen every person's *right to privacy and confidentiality.* Keeping confidential information inviolate is a direct derivative of this obligation. Professionals have a duty to protect the privacy of clients and groups to the greatest extent possible consistent with laws and the will and agreement of the clients. Confidentiality, however, is not sacrosanct when the social worker can prevent violence or harm of a serious nature to others.

Ethical Principle 7   A social worker should make practice decisions that permit her to speak the truth and to *fully disclose all relevant information* to her client and to others. Social and professional relationships require trust in order to function well, and trust, in turn, is based on honest dealing that minimizes surprises so that mutual expectations are generally fulfilled.

Application of Ethical Decision-Making Screens

Let us try to apply these two ethical decision-making screens to analyze Exemplars 4.2 and 4.3.

❖ 4.2 What Will Happen to Jimmy Prego?

Jimmy Prego is a passive, deeply disturbed early adolescent who lives in a therapeutic home where he has sometimes had to be protected from other residents. He is now ready to be moved to a less restrictive environment but clearly needs a therapeutic foster home, something your supervisor originally suggested.

You have contacted such a home and begun plans to move Jimmy in about two weeks. When you inform your supervisor that you have initiated the move and that everything is proceeding as usual, he tells you that space has become available in an even less restricted group home run by your agency and that it would be appropriate to move him to the group home instead of the therapeutic foster home.

You tell your supervisor that you will check it out, but he seems a little uncomfortable. When you check out the group home, you discover the residents are older, bigger, and more aggressive than Jimmy. You do not agree that the group home is appropriate for Jimmy who has had difficulty defending himself where he currently resides. Also, you learn that the agency has placed pressure on the supervisors to boost the group-home's census, an action related to agency financial considerations. Jimmy's mother is unable to assist in making the decision because of overwhelming personal and mental health problems. Jimmy's problems and his youth make him incapable of making the decision. Mrs. Prego insists that she trusts you and that you will do what is best for Jimmy.

Several issues are involved in this exemplar. First, whose best interest takes priority—the client, agency, or worker? What is best for Jimmy and his mother? When you examine the *Code of Ethics* for applicable standards, you find that your "primary responsibility is to promote the well-being of clients" (NASW *Code,* 1999, 1.01). To whom do you owe loyalty as you make your decision about what the correct thing is to do? To Jimmy? His mother? Your supervisor? Your agency? Yourself? Some social workers might argue that Ethical Principle 5 is relevant because the worker wants to promote a better quality of life for Jimmy Prego and the right treatment situation will support that outcome. Will the least harm (Ethical Principle 4) be done by confronting your supervisor and—even in a small way—reducing the agency income when that is what the agency needs, but perhaps succeeding in obtaining the placement in the therapeutic home? Will Ethical Principle 4 be fulfilled by not confronting your supervisor, placing Jimmy in the group home, and increasing agency income? If you don't go along with the supervisor, harm may come to you, your supervisor, and the agency.

Second, who is competent to make decisions? When clients lack "the capacity to provide informed consent, social workers should protect clients' interests by seeking permission from an appropriate third party" (NASW *Code*, 1999, 1.03c). Jimmy is not capable of making an informed choice. Mrs. Prego trusts the social worker and wants her to make the best decision for her son. Is your supervisor an appropriate third party? He is placing the agency needs before those of Jimmy. In addition, "social workers should not allow an employing organization's policies, procedures, regulations, or administrative orders to interfere with their ethical practice of social work" (NASW *Code*, 1999, 3.09d).

You, the social worker, are the only one in this situation who is competent to make decisions for the best interest and protection of Jimmy and to advocate for the right treatment plan. Jimmy's needs take priority over the supervisor's, the agency's, and your own needs.

Let's look again at the ethical dilemma that the social worker for Serena Adams (Exemplar 3.1) faced. This social worker, you may recall, had to decide whether or not to inform Donnie that Serena has herpes, even though Serena demanded that confidentiality be respected. Several *Code of Ethics* standards are directly applicable to this dilemma. "Social workers should respect clients' right to privacy" (NASW *Code*, 1999, 1.07a); "Social workers should protect the confidentiality of all information obtained in the course of professional service, except for compelling professional reasons. The general expectation that social workers will keep information confidential does not apply when disclosure is necessary to prevent serious, foreseeable, and imminent harm to a client." (NASW *Code*, 1999, 1.07c).

Because the *Code* standards conflict, we will use the EPS. Ethical Principle 6 indicates that a social worker should not invade a person's privacy by involving others without that person's consent. Ethical Principle 3 stresses the ethical requirement to foster a person's autonomy. Both of these ethical principles direct the social worker to respect Serena's demand to refrain from informing Donnie. Ethical Principle 1, however, requires decisions that protect a person's life and survival. This social worker felt that Serena will find ways to have sex with Donnie, placing his health and welfare in danger. Since Ethical Principle 1 has the highest priority, overriding any decisions required by lower-ranked principles, she decides that she must inform Donnie. Do you agree with this worker's decision? If not, what would you do and on what basis would you decide? Exemplar 4.3 provides another example.

❖ 4.3 Starting in Private Practice

Cliff Baxter is an experienced social worker who recently resigned his agency job in order to devote all of his time to private practice. Before Cliff left the agency, Dennis Norton, a colleague in the agency, told him that he would be willing to refer clients to him for a "finder's fee." As in many beginnings, Cliff is having a difficult time making ends meet. His income last month was not even sufficient to pay the rent for the office. Should he give Dennis a call?

We will use the ERS and examine the NASW *Code of Ethics* to determine if there are any rules relevant to this situation. The NASW *Code* (2.06c) states: "Social workers are prohibited from giving or receiving payment for a referral when no professional service is provided by the referring social worker." This rule provides such clear and unambiguous guidance that no further screening seems necessary. Cliff should not call Dennis to take advantage of his offer.

In Exemplar 4.4, we will apply the EPS.

❖ 4.4 The Wrong Man Sits in Prison

Raul Lovaas has been enrolled in a drug rehabilitation program in order to break his cocaine addiction. The program's treatment routine includes pharmacological treatment, group therapy, and individual therapy. You are his social worker. You have succeeded in establishing a positive and meaningful relationship with Raul in the daily treatment sessions. One morning Raul tells you that, some years ago, he accidentally injured a bank guard during a holdup. He was never caught by the police, but another man was convicted for this crime and now sits in prison on a lengthy sentence. For several days you have been trying to convince Raul that he should talk to the police in order to free an innocent man from prison. Raul not only refused to listen to your suggestion but has told you that he expects you to keep in complete confidence what he has told you. What should you do?

These are some of the thoughts that you have:

1. Raul has neither a legal nor a moral right to have another man serve a lengthy sentence for a crime that Raul committed.
2. The "wrong" that you may cause by breaking confidentiality is hardly of the same importance as the wrong inflicted on an innocent person who is now imprisoned.
3. The effectiveness of the entire program may be compromised if it becomes known that social workers do not always keep confidential the information they receive from clients.
4. On the other hand, your whistle-blowing can cause the release of the wrongly convicted person.

We will focus our analysis on the latter two considerations since the first point, though obvious, does not relate directly to what you, the social worker, should do, but rather to what the client is ethically required to do.

At least two ethical principles are involved in the second consideration: Ethical Principle 3, the principle of autonomy and freedom, specifically the freedom of an innocent man who is now imprisoned; and Ethical Principle 6, the principle of confidentiality, specifically respecting the confidence of the information that your client, Raul Lovaas, gave you.

Some may also base their decision on Ethical Principle 2, the principle of equality and inequality. An innocent man in prison is obviously not in an equal situation and requires additional resources in order to regain access to equal opportunities.

Since Ethical Principle 6 (principle of confidentiality) is of a lower order than both Ethical Principles 3 and 2, the second consideration leads to the decision that this social worker is ethically justified in breaking confidence and reporting to the police what she has learned from Raul.

From a practice point of view, the third consideration may be especially important since in most situations we would hesitate to do anything that might impede the effectiveness of an intervention. It might be argued that a program that can improve the quality of life (Ethical Principle 5) of many addicts should receive preference over the quality of life of one individual, even if that person is falsely imprisoned. It is likely, however, that such reasoning involves a number of fallacies, including the following:

1. We have no information on the effectiveness of this rehabilitation program. How effective is it in improving the quality of life of all/most/some participants?
2. We do not know what impact, if any, breaking confidentiality will have on the effectiveness of the program. It may well be that other participants will be happy that the worker was instrumental in freeing an innocent person from prison.
3. Statistical probabilities are never a permissible substitute for ethical screening.

In other words, the quality of life principle (Ethical Principle 5) is not relevant in this situation, but even if it were, it would be of a lower order than Ethical Principles 3 and 2. Consideration 3 is, therefore, not relevant and should be ignored in making an ethical decision. We would, therefore, conclude that the social worker is obligated to inform the police if she is unable to convince Raul to do so himself.

In this chapter, we have examined a series of guidelines and decision-making processes that social workers can use when making ethical decisions. We noted that every social worker is confronted by ethical dilemmas and that these always require choices that must be made before action can be taken. Iserson (1986) suggested that we ask three questions as a final "check out" before moving to the action phase of ethical decision making.

1. *Impartiality* Would you be willing to act the way you have chosen if you were in the other person's place? This question asks the social worker to consider the effect her action would have if she or a member of her family or other loved ones were the recipients of the action. The purpose of this question is to correct for partiality and self-interest and to minimize or prevent the possibility they will play too dominant a part in the decision.
2. *Generalization* Are you willing to undertake this action in similar circumstances? Generalizing a particular decision may reduce bias and partiality,

but it also may blind one to the unique qualities of a situation that demands a unique response, one that would not generally be used in many other situations. When one evaluates a particular action in light of its general applicability to similar situations, one is concerned with both the breadth and range of effects and the short- and long-range consequences. The purpose of this question is to make the social worker think of the consequences of an action beyond the short term and to consider it not as a particular instance but as a justified general practice in similar circumstances.

3. *Justifiability* Can you explain and justify your decision to others? The purpose of this question is to make certain that you have, in the available time, consciously and planfully considered the options and have made certain the client's rights and best interests are served by your professional actions in the context of the values and standards of the profession.

EXERCISES

1. Ruth and Anne, social workers, approached Serena Adams' demand for confidentiality from different perspectives. The discussion of their approaches illustrated some of the differences that arise when a social worker follows one or the other ethical approach. These are not the only differences. Can you identify others that result from the two different approaches?
2. Examine the ethical principles screen (EPS). Would you order the principles in the same way? What, if any, principles would you add or delete?
3. Identify two ethical decisions you recently made or learned of that took place in social work practice. On the basis of the Ethical Assessment Screen and the Ethical Principles Screen (EPS), would you change your or the other social worker's ethical decision?
4. If when you read the NASW *Code of Ethics,* you believe the *Code* assumes that one particular ethical standard is the highest priority for social workers' ethical behavior, which standard do you think it is?

SUGGESTIONS FOR ADDITIONAL READINGS

Glassman (1992) presents a series of personal and professional dilemmas that emerge when social workers attempt to implement feminist values in a practice setting. Dean (1998) describes her view of "The Primacy of the Ethical Aim in Clinical Social Work: Its Relationship to Social Justice and Mental Health." Horner and Whitbeck (1991) in "Personal versus Professional Values in Social Work" suggest their view of the differences between social workers and the general population, including personal relationships, service to others, open-mindedness, and self-concepts.

Confidentiality and Informed Consent

A person's right to privacy is a first-order value in our culture. Every person has a right to determine *when, how,* and to *what* extent he or she wants to share (or have shared) personal information with others. Even though the Constitution does not explicitly mention a right to privacy, Chief Justice Richard B. Hughes of the New Jersey Supreme Court wrote, "Supreme Court decisions have recognized that a right of personal privacy exists and that certain areas of privacy are guaranteed under the Constitution" (*In re Quinlan,* 170 NJ 10, 1976). Privacy is protected under the Constitution in certain circumstances, including, for example, distribution of contraceptives to married adults (*Griswold v. Connecticut,* 1965), unmarried adults (*Eisenstadt v. Baird,* 1972), and persons under 16 years of age (*Carey v. Population Planning International,* 1977), and abortions during the first trimester (*Roe v. Wade,* 1973).

Privacy was found not to be a fundamental right in cases of consensual homosexual sex in a home (*Bowers v. Hardwick,* 1986) and for houseguests not staying overnight (*Minnesota v. Carter,* 1998). In *Lawrence v. Texas* (2003), the Supreme Court overruled a Texas sodomy law. It also overturned *Bowers v. Hardwick,* in effect, apologizing for its earlier decision. The Texas case concerned two men arrested in a Houston-area apartment following the police responding to a false report of a "weapons disturbance" in the apartment. The men, charged under a "homosexual conduct" law that criminalized sexual intercourse with an individual of the same sex, were held overnight in jail and each was fined $200. The reporting neighbor was later convicted of filing a false report. The ruling struck down 13 states' sodomy laws (four applied only to same sex partners and nine applied to partners of the same sex and opposite sex.).

Privacy of school records is limited, and individuals have no right to sue a school for releasing records covered by the Family Educational Rights and Privacy Act (*Gonzaga v. Doe*, 2002). Recently, the U.S.A. Patriot Act (2001) served to diminish privacy rights as antiterrorist legislation made it easier for law enforcement persons to conduct electronic surveillance. Privacy is a protected value but with some limitations.

The professional ethical principle of confidentiality is derived from the privacy societal value. This principle is not a modern invention but was already recognized in ancient times by Hippocrates. The physician's oath that is attributed to him states, "What I may see or hear in the course of treatment . . . I will keep to myself, holding such things shameful to be spoken about" (Van Hoose & Kottler, 1985, p. 7). In the NASW *Code of Ethics* this principle appears as a major standard:

> Social workers should respect clients' right to privacy. Social workers should not solicit private information from clients unless it is essential to providing services or conducting social work evaluation or research. Once private information is shared, standards of confidentiality apply (NASW *Code*, 1999, 1.07a).

Seventeen other paragraphs (1.07b through 1.07r) provide additional explanations and limitations. For example, valid consent is required before social workers can disclose confidential information (107b), and clients should be informed to the extent possible of disclosure of confidential information and the potential consequences of such disclosure (1.07d). However, information may be disclosed if compelling professional reasons exist, such as imminent harm to a client. Where disclosure is required, only the minimal amount of information necessary to achieve the goals should be shared (1.07c). Social workers should discuss with clients and other interested parties the nature and limitations of their right to confidentiality (1.07e).

In addition, social workers providing services to couples, families, or other groups "should seek agreement among the parties involved concerning each individual's right to confidentiality and obligation to preserve the confidentiality of information shared by others" (1.07f); they should also inform clients of policies "concerning . . . disclosure of confidential information among the parties involved in the counseling" (1.07g).

Social workers "should not disclose identifying information when discussing clients for teaching or training purposes unless the client has consented to disclosure of confidential information" (1.07p) or with consultants unless the client has consented to disclosure or there is a compelling need for such disclosure (1.07q). Confidential information should not be discussed in public areas (1.07i) and client records, including electronic files, should be stored in a secure location (1.07l). In addition, "reasonable precautions [should be taken] to protect client confidentiality in the event of the social worker's termination of practice, incapacitation, or death" (1.07o).

PRIVACY AND CONFIDENTIALITY

Confidentiality means that a social worker will not reveal to anyone information that she has received from a client without the client's informed consent. However, it is not always easy or possible for a social worker to implement this rule. The *Code* itself recognizes the possibility that "compelling professional reasons" (NASW *Code*, 1.07c) may require a social worker to reveal information received in confidence "when disclosure is necessary to prevent serious, foreseeable, and imminent harm to a client or other identifiable person" (1.07c). The nature of some of these compelling reasons will be discussed later in this chapter under the section on Duty to Warn. Even those who are committed to practicing in an ethical manner and who want to observe confidentiality face ethical dilemmas. No social worker can guarantee that information received by her will always remain confidential because of the duty to warn, interdisciplinary team practice requiring sharing information between professionals, demonstrating outcomes for accountability, and meeting requirements of third party payers.

Confidentiality is an ethical principle rather than a legal one. It affirms the explicit promise or contract to reveal nothing about an individual except under conditions known and agreed to by the client, with the exception of these which require disclosure for "compelling professional reasons." Social workers and clients may differ in their perceptions of this issue. Millstein (2000) found in a study of experienced social work practitioners that almost three-quarters of them strongly agreed that confidentiality is necessary to maintain therapeutic relationships; however, less than half believe that clients expect that confidentiality will be maintained. An ethical dilemma occurs whenever a practitioner has to choose among conflicting claims that may be equally meritorious, such as choosing between a client's right to privacy and the right of other people and of society to certain information.

It is generally assumed that a client's reliance on confidentiality promotes trust in the social worker. Many think that this relationship with the professional would be harmed if clients were aware that there are limits to confidentiality. They believe that the confidentiality principle is crucial for maintaining an effective professional relationship. Without observing confidentiality, it is thought there is a risk of the following:

1. People who need professional help may be deterred from requesting this help.
2. People who have already begun a relationship with a social worker may not fully engage.
3. The trust relationship that has already been developed may be destroyed; clients who have disclosed confidential information may feel betrayed by the professional whom they trusted (Edward, 1999).

Empirical studies do not support the assumption that limiting confidentiality necessarily endangers the client-social worker relationship. Steinberg, Levine, and Doueck (1997) found that only 27% of clients of psychotherapists withdrew from treatment immediately or shortly after the therapist made a mandated child abuse report. Retention in treatment was higher when the informed consent procedure was more explicit and when the reported perpetrator was a third party uninvolved in the treatment. Similarly, Weinstein and colleagues (2000) found that when mental health professionals reported suspected child abuse and maltreatment, the relationship for three-quarters of the patients was not disrupted, and in many cases, the therapeutic process was enhanced.

Confidentiality is an especially problematic issue because this ethical principle is based on an oversimplified practice model that includes only the social worker and the client. The reality, however, is much more complex because most often there are many more parties than, for example, merely the abuser and the abused child. Among the parties included may be parents and other siblings, "society" and its agents (police, courts), participants, other social workers, colleagues from other fields, administrative personnel, insurance companies and third-party payers, relatives, and the client. Each of these parties may make conflicting demands for confidential information. The ethical considerations for sharing confidential information with each of these participants may differ because the obligations to share may differ.

Other Social Workers

Often we do not give sufficient thought to the ethical implications of sharing confidential information with other social workers. We are not referring here to small talk at a cocktail party (which is clearly against the ethical rule of confidentiality), but to formal or informal consultations with colleagues or supervisors, as well as to the transmission of such information to other social workers who have a professional interest in the information (such as a social worker who is working with other members of the same family, the social worker who will take over the case while the worker is on vacation, and so on). This type of information transmission is intended to be for the client's benefit because it is meant to assure more effective service, but is it ethical to provide this information to others without the client's consent? In many cases, a general informed consent agreement will suffice, but special situations may require revisiting the issue of confidentiality and informed consent.

The 1999 *Code of Ethics* provides some guidance on this issue. In addition to discussing the limitations of confidentiality with clients (1.07e), "social workers should take reasonable steps to ensure that clients' records are stored in a secure location and that clients' records are not available to others who are not authorized to have access" (1.07l). Social workers should not disclose "identifying information when discussing clients for teaching or training purposes unless the client has consented to disclosure of confidential information" (1.07p). Finally, "if a new client has been served by another agency or colleague, social workers should discuss with the client whether consultation with the previous service provider is in the client's best interest" (3.06b). These sections of the *Code* suggest that it is generally not ethical to share information about the client with other social workers without the client's prior consent.

However, the social worker should also consider the possible harm that may be caused by not providing vital information to colleagues who are in a position to be helpful to the client. It is this consideration that led Taylor and Adelman (1989) to conclude that "keeping information confidential can seriously hamper an intervener's efforts to help" (p. 80).

Colleagues from Other Fields

Many social workers practice on multidisciplinary teams or in settings where information must be shared with colleagues from other professions whose confidentiality practices may differ from those of social workers. To what extent is it ethical for hospital social workers to reveal confidential information to physicians or nurses? Is it ethical for a school social worker to share with a teacher confidential information about a child and his family, knowing that this information may be entered into the child's permanent school record and thus be read by many others?

Some social workers are required to share information with others because of the type of position they occupy. For example, those who provide case management services are obligated to share information about the client. However, the client must consent to what information will be shared with which agencies before the social worker shares confidential information. According to Galambos (1997), "information provided to the client should include the essentials of when, where, why, and how information will be shared with others" (p. 63).

Administrative Records

Social agencies and other employing organizations need information about clients and client contacts for administrative and accountability reasons. The initial request to supply these data may be entirely proper, but once the requested data have been transmitted, the practitioner is no longer able to protect their confidentiality. According to Davidson and Davidson (1996), "it appears that information, once passed from the social worker to a managed care service and logged into the medical database of a third-party insurance payer, may be as accessible as credit card information or mortgage payment records" (p. 209). As the use of computerized records becomes more common in social agencies, this aspect of the confidentiality issue has become even more crucial. For example, a California court ruled that social workers cannot refuse on legal grounds to enter confidential information about welfare recipients into the agency's computerized record system (*Belmont v. California State Personnel Board*, 35 Ca. App. 3d 518, 1974).

The 1999 *Code of Ethics* specifically addresses these issues, requiring social workers to "take precautions to ensure and maintain the confidentiality of information transmitted to other parties through the use of computers, electronic mail, facsimile machines, telephones and telephone answering machines, and other electronic or computer technology. Disclosure of identifying information should be avoided wherever possible" (1.07m). Unfortunately, once the social worker transmits the information, she may not be able to control further dissemination of the data. Davidson and Davidson (1996) recommend that "social workers, individually and in consortium, need to negotiate with managed care policymakers and government regulators to develop new mechanisms to protect client information" (p. 208). Health Insurance Portability and Accountability Act (HIPAA) (1996) requirements may be helpful in this area as health care agencies are required to develop procedures to protect the confidentiality of client information. It is not simply the electronic transmission of data, however, that requires precautions. Today, computers are also used to store case and process records, all of which require ensuring security.

Insurance Companies and Third-Party Payers

New dimensions have been added to the problem of confidentiality as more and more social workers are required to report diagnoses to insurance companies or other third-party payers in order to qualify clients for reimbursement. While clients may consent to sharing this information because they are interested in having a third party pay for part or all of the services they receive from a social worker, they are not always aware of the diagnosis reported. In addition to the issue of confidentiality, the severity of the diagnosis may be overstated in order to qualify clients for reimbursement (Jayaratne, Croxton, & Mattison, 1997). This problem will be discussed in greater length in Chapter 11.

Once clients are aware that third-party payers may share confidential information with others, such as their employers and future service providers, they may prefer to pay for the services of the social worker out of their own pocket. The 1999 *Code of Ethics* specifically states that "social workers should not disclose confidential information to third-party payers unless clients have authorized such disclosure" (1.07h).

Police

In many states, the law requires that social workers, as well as other professional practitioners, inform the police whenever they acquire information about criminal activities that have taken place or that are being planned. For example, a social worker who is present when an adolescent street gang plans a holdup should have no ethical qualms about reporting the gang's intentions to the police. When a third party (such as a parent or neighbor) tells her about such a plan, she must ask herself several questions: How reliable is the report? Can the information be used without revealing the source? How might such revelation affect the helping relationship? What harm can be prevented or result by informing the police? The situation has legal and ethical elements. To whom does the social worker owe loyalty—the gang, parent or neighbor, the police, and society? What harm could be prevented. All of these and other questions have factual, professional, and ethical implications. Often it is difficult to separate these aspects.

Many social workers are perplexed by ethical dilemmas arising out of various other kinds of law violations, particularly delinquent acts that do not seem to harm others. Exemplar 5.1 describes one such situation that raises a number of ethical questions.

❖ 5.1 Fraud and an Aging Mother

Social worker Jean Fisher is a marriage counselor and family therapist in the Old Town Family Consultation Center, a nonsectarian United Way agency. Sue and Dean Kern have been coming to her for marital therapy once a week for the past two months. Though their problem is not critical, they came to seek help while their marriage was still salvageable. They have made good progress toward reaching their goal.

During today's session Dean Kern mentioned that he has continued to receive supplemental security income (SSI) payments for his aged mother, who lived with them until she moved overseas two years ago. She now makes her home with his sister, who lives in England.

Should Ms. Fisher report this case for possible fraud? Does client/worker confidentiality cover this communication? According to the *Code*, disclosure required by law or regulations is a compelling reason to break confidentiality with certain cautions (1999, 1.07e); therefore, it is important for social workers to know what the reporting regulations are in their jurisdiction and to act accordingly.

If Ms. Fisher is not required by law to report this case, then several other issues should be addressed. For example, what will happen to the client/therapist relationship if Ms. Fisher does reveal what she learned? Should she consider the possible consequences of the treatment before she decides what to do? Should she discuss the possible consequences of their activities with the clients in an attempt to persuade them to change their behavior? What other criteria should she use to resolve the ethical issues posed here?

What would Ms. Fisher's obligation be if she had learned that Dean Kern had escaped from prison several years ago? Or that Sue Kern was pushing drugs? Does the seriousness of the offense change the ethical considerations? Does the degree of harm to the client or someone else make a difference?

Relatives

Are the relatives of a client entitled to confidential information that might affect them? What should the social worker do if a son asks whether his father is dying when that father who is terminally ill has specifically asked that none of his relatives be told how ill he is? How does the social worker decide whether to keep the confidence or tell the truth? Do the relatives of a person living with HIV have the right to know about the person's HIV status? Does the type of relationship matter (e.g., a spouse or a sibling)? This is a type of ethical dilemma that may be especially acute for social workers who are engaged in settings such as health care and genetic counseling and who are privy to medical and or genetic information that may affect the health of other relatives (Freedman, 1998).

Are parents entitled to confidential information about their children? Does the age of the child make a difference? For example, Planned Parenthood researchers in Wisconsin found that most girls under 18 would stop or limit their use of health services at family planning clinics if their parents had to be told they were seeking prescribed contraceptives (Flaherty, 2002). Consider the following exemplar on confidentiality in a school setting:

❖ 5.2 Debbie Roberts Is Pregnant

Debbie Roberts is a 12-year-old sixth grader who is 10 weeks pregnant. She has been a good student, and her teacher reports that she has never had any problems with Debbie.

The school nurse referred Debbie to the school social worker because Debbie refused to discuss her condition with the nurse. At first, Debbie also refused to speak to the social worker, but later she told her that she did not want to have an abortion. Debbie asked the social worker to make arrangements so that she could carry to full term; she repeatedly emphasized that she did not want her parents to know that she was pregnant. Debbie will not reveal who the father is, and the social worker suspects that Debbie may have been sexually abused.

Should Debbie's parents be told about their daughter's pregnancy? Should Child Protective Services be told about the situation? What is the ethical decision in this ambiguous situation? Should the social worker respond differently if Debbie is older, if she is 16 or 18 years of age and is willing to identify the father of the baby?

Clients

What are a social worker's obligations when a client wants information about himself, such as wanting to read his own case record? According to the *Code of Ethics,* "social workers should provide clients with reasonable access to records concerning the clients . . . Social workers should limit clients' access to their records, or portions of their records, only in exceptional circumstances when there is compelling evidence that such access would cause serious harm to the client" (1999, 1.08a). However, questions may still remain about what constitutes "reasonable access," "exceptional circumstances," or "serious harm."

There are several possible arguments against sharing confidential information with the client, especially against granting him unlimited access to his own record:

1. The case record may contain information supplied on a confidential basis by a third party, such as another social worker, teacher, neighbor, or

relative. According to the *Code of Ethics*, "when providing clients with access to their records, social workers should take steps to protect the confidentiality of other individuals identified or discussed in such records" (1999, 1.08b). This suggests that while the social worker needs to protect the confidentiality of others mentioned in the client's record, it is not sufficient reason to deny the client access to his records.

2. The case record may contain "raw data" that have not yet been checked or evaluated, or test results or other data that may be misinterpreted by a lay person. The *Code of Ethics* requires social workers to "provide assistance in interpreting the records and consultation with the client regarding the records" (1999, 1.08a). Therefore, this may not be a sufficient argument for denying access to client records.

3. The social worker may use the case record to explore various options or to ask herself questions that need further clarification; when the client reads such material, his trust in the worker may be impaired. In this situation, the social worker will need to assess the potential for serious harm to the client to be caused by reading the record; if such potential exists, then access may be limited or denied (*Code of Ethics*, 1999, 1.08a).

4. Reading or hearing negative information about himself may hurt the client. Again, if the potential for serious harm exists, then access may be denied. Whenever the social worker denies access to the record, "clients' requests and the rationale for withholding some or all of the record(s) should be documented in clients' files" (*Code of Ethics*, 1999, 1.08b).

There are also several arguments in favor of giving clients access to their own case records:

1. Reading the information gives the client an opportunity to correct mistakes.

2. A client can give informed consent to share information with others only if he knows what this information is.

3. Knowledge of information may lead to change, while ignorance will result in only maintaining the present unsatisfactory situation.

4. Opening the case record will demonstrate the efficacy of client/worker cooperation and may be followed by even greater client participation in the social work process.

We have presented several arguments for and against opening case records to clients in order to help social workers arrive at an ethical decision. Admittedly, this is a decision that few social workers employed in agencies have to make alone because, generally, agency policy and directives on this point are specific and clear. However, if you were asked to present to an agency board of directors on the issue of client access to records, what would your recommendation(s) be? If you were in private practice what policies would you decide on regarding client access to records?

Clearly, there are limits to confidentiality. In one of the first meetings between the client and the social worker, the nature of confidentiality should be explained to clients and other interested parties, including the limitations of the clients' right to confidentiality. This information may need to be revisited throughout the professional relationship (NASW *Code of Ethics*, 1999, 1.07e). However, in what detail should these limits be discussed?

Weinstein et al. (2000) found that about 40% of experienced mental health practitioners *did not* inform clients about the limits of confidentiality until information that legally should be reported to the authorities came up. The study also found that informing clients about the limits of confidentiality did not deter them from entering treatment.

HEALTH INSURANCE PORTABILITY AND ACCOUNTABILITY ACT (1996, HIPAA)

Social workers and others (health plans, health care clearinghouses, and health care providers who transmit health information electronically) are expected to be in compliance with HIPAA requirements. The Department of Health and Human Services (DHHS) established a standardized electronic format for eight common health care transactions: claims payment and remittance advice, coordination of benefits, eligibility for a health plan, enrollment and disenrollment in a health plan, health care claim status, premium payments, and referral certification and authorization.

Consent for sharing data about *routine* health care purposes (treatment, payment, and health care operations) is optional. Covered entities are *required* to provide patients with notice of their rights and the practices of their organization but are not required to have a signed consent form from the client to disclose client health information for purposes of treatment, payment, and health care operations. However, direct treatment providers are required to make a good-faith effort to obtain the client's written acknowledgment of receipt of the notice of privacy rights and practices. The rule does not preclude social workers from obtaining a written consent prior to release of information for treatment and payment. Providers are still required to have a separate written authorization from the client for each *nonroutine* use and disclosure of health information.

In states where minors can give consent to health care treatments, they also have the right to make their own decisions about the release of protected health information. In those states, their parents are not considered to be their personal representatives for this purpose. In some states, minors are permitted to consent to drug and alcohol counseling, mental health treatment, or health care regarding pregnancy without parental consent. In these states, social workers may exercise their discretion to deny or provide access to the records by a parent. If a parent voluntarily consents to a confidentiality agreement between the minor and the social worker, the minor can also make individual decisions about the use and disclosure of their own protected health information. If a state law has specific provisions that grant or deny access by the parents to minors' health information, the state law applies (NASW, October 1, 2002). HIPAA was passed in 1996, but not fully implemented until April 2003. Like any new law or policy that has the potential to have a major impact on social work practice, social workers are encouraged to stay updated on this issue. (For additional details, see http://www.hhs.gov/news/press/2002pres/20020809.html.)

CHILD ABUSE AND CONFIDENTIALITY

Social workers and other professionals are required by law to report all cases of suspected child abuse and neglect to the child protective services agency or other designated authority. Although details vary from state to state, such reporting is required in every jurisdiction in the United States and in many other countries. There is less concern with the ethics of breaking confidentiality in cases of child abuse and neglect; instead, the ethical concerns focus on ways to assure the safety of the maltreated child. In 1997 in the United States, more than 3 million children were reported for child abuse and neglect. The actual number of abused and neglected children is much larger. Community-based incidence studies estimate that reported child abuse cases include about 40% of all actual cases (Kalichman, 1999). In the Third National Incidence Study of Child Abuse and Neglect, it was found that Child Protective Services (CPS) had investigated less than one-half of children identified as maltreated (NIS-III, Sedlak & Broadhurst, 1996). This suggests that many children who were identified as experiencing child abuse and/or neglect were not reported to CPS. Surveys repeatedly have found that one in three professionals have had contact with at least one case of suspected child abuse that they have declined to report, and they reported only about one-third of the abuse cases they suspected (Kalichman, 1999). When a report is made to CPS, a child protective services worker is required to investigate the reported maltreatment and is required to take any necessary action to protect the child.

Social workers who continue to be uneasy about the ethical and practice implications of reporting suspected child abuse that involves one of their clients might want to consider the following when the need to report arises:

1. Working with the client to help him make the report himself; the social worker should follow up with the client to make sure that the report was made.
2. Discussing with the family why a report needs to be made, what the potential benefits and risks to the family are, what procedures will be followed during the investigation, and if the report is substantiated or indicated, what some of the treatment options are likely to be. The social worker should be aware of the procedures followed in her area so that she can accurately inform clients about what to expect.
3. Sometimes it is appropriate to report without notifying the family if not doing so would place the child at immediate risk.

PRIVILEGED COMMUNICATIONS

Privileged communication is a legal right granted by legislative statute. It guarantees that certain information will not be revealed in court without the consent of the person who originated the communication. Privileged communication is a rule of evidence that allows one party in a legal proceeding (in this case, the client) to limit the admissibility of statements originally communicated in confidence, thus rendering the witness (that is, the social worker) "incompetent" to testify regarding a particular matter.

The common law principle that the public has a right to every person's evidence is followed in the absence of a statute of privilege. No person can refuse to testify in court when called to do so. Persons reluctant to testify can be subpoenaed or commanded to testify by the court; failure to appear and testify in response to a subpoena can result in a citation for contempt of court. Historically, privileged relationships have been limited to husband/wife, attorney/client, and priest-confessor/worshipper. Any other relationship is privileged only when so defined by a statute enacted by a state legislature.

Wigmore's (1961, vol. 8, p. 52) criteria for privileged communications are generally used to determine whether the privilege should apply. Wigmore believed that a privilege status exists only when all four of the following criteria are met:

1. The communication must originate in the belief that it will not be disclosed.
2. The inviolability of the confidence must be essential to achieve the purpose of the relationship.
3. The relationship must be one that society should foster.
4. The expected injury to the relationship through disclosure of the confidential information must be greater than the expected benefit to justice if the witness were forced to testify.

The physician/patient relationship, according to Wigmore, does not qualify because it does not meet the fourth criterion. Social workers who practice psychotherapy appear to meet all four of Wigmore's criteria for privileged communications, but it is doubtful whether social workers practicing in other areas, such as community organization and social planning, do so. However, statutes generally cover an entire profession no matter what specific activities any one practitioner performs (VandeCreek, Knapp, & Herzog, 1988). All 50 states and the District of Columbia have enacted laws concerning privileged communications. Special attention must be paid to this issue by social workers because the specifics of the privilege differ from state to state.

"Every U.S. jurisdiction has recognized some form of evidentiary privilege for statements made by a patient to a psychotherapist for the purpose of obtaining treatment" (Harris, 1999). On the federal level, the U.S. Supreme Court established the psychotherapist–patient privilege in the federal courts with its ruling in *Jaffee v. Redmond* (1996). The Court had not previously addressed this issue, but did so in a case involving a licensed clinical social worker, simultaneously establishing the principle for psychiatrists and psychologists. For practical purposes, the Supreme Court ruling extends the privilege to civil actions in federal courts, thus institutionalizing recognition of psychotherapist-patient privilege. The exact dimensions of the privilege will evolve through case decisions as they unfold. For example, in *United States v. Chase,* the United States 9th Circuit Court of Appeals ruled in August 2002 that there *is* a dangerous patient exception to the *Jaffee* privilege, a ruling opposite to a position taken by the 6th Circuit in *United States v. Hayes.* During 2001 the 9th Circuit ruled that communications between an unlicensed EAP counselor and a patient are protected from compelled disclosure by the privilege established by *Jaffee.* The privilege belongs to the client, not to the social worker. When a client waives the privilege, the social worker must testify in court even if the client does not know or is not certain what information is included in his case record and even if this testimony may harm him. Other interested persons do not control the privilege. For example, a father or husband cannot suppress or waive testimony of a social worker who is treating his child or wife, even when he pays for the treatment (VandeCreek et al., 1988).

The privilege is not applicable and ceases to exist in a number of situations, including the following (this list is not exhaustive and may differ from state to state):

1. When the client consents to disclosure.
2. When the law requires reporting of certain information.
3. When reimbursement or legal rules require disclosure.
4. When the client is dangerous and plans to harm another person or himself.
5. When there is a serious risk of suicide or other danger to the client's life.
6. When there is serious suspicion of child abuse or neglect.
7. When a social worker is appointed by a court to make an assessment (however, if one of the attorneys requests a pretrial examination by a social worker, then that social worker is covered by attorney/client privilege).
8. When the client plans to commit a crime.
9. When the social worker determines the client is in need of hospitalization for a mental or psychological disorder.
10. When the client sues the social worker for malpractice.
11. In child custody cases, because the interest of the child is considered paramount.
12. When the client has already introduced privileged material into the litigation.
13. When the client threatens to harm the social worker.
14. When a social worker needs a court order to collect fees for professional services rendered.

In many states, the privilege ceases to exist if a third party was present at the time that the client communicated the confidential information to the social worker. However, some state laws specifically extend the privilege of communications to situations that involve group, marital, and family therapy—that is, to situations where third parties are present (VandeCreek et al., 1988). In other states, the courts decide whether the rule of privilege applies, but no clear trend has evolved regarding communications in the presence of third parties. The Minnesota Superior Court addressed this question in *Minnesota v. Andring* (10 FLR 1206, 1984) and ruled:

> The participants in group psychotherapy sessions are not casual persons who are strangers. . . . Rather, every participant has such a relationship with the attending professional, and in the group setting, the participants actually become part of the diagnostic and therapeutic process for coparticipants.
>
> An interpretation which excluded group therapy from the scope of the psychotherapist-patient [privileged communication rule] would seriously limit the effectiveness of group psychotherapy as a therapeutic device. . . . [T]he confidentiality of communications made during group therapy is essential in maintaining its effectiveness as a therapeutic tool. . . .

In the absence of a privilege statute, a social worker who voluntarily testifies about confidential information that she has received from a client may face a double bind—if she testifies, she may be sued by the client for revealing confidential information; if she refuses to testify, she may be cited for contempt of court.

Privileged communication is a legal and not an ethical concept. Questions arising out of privileged communications require legal consultation.

INFORMED CONSENT

The professional ethics rule of **informed consent** is derived from the moral principle of autonomy, that is, moral agents have the capacity for self-government and that capacity must be respected. Informed consent is a relatively new concept. The first use of the term only dates to 1947 (Moreno, Caplan, & Wolpe, 1998). Informed consent means that a social worker or another professional will not intervene in a client's life or release confidential information about him unless the client has consented. Informed consent involves issues of disclosure of information, voluntariness, and competence (Grisso & Appelbaum, 1998). Problems involving any one or all of these issues make for difficult ethical dilemmas in social work practice.

It is generally agreed that confidential information should be released only with the consent of the person who supplied the information. The problem arises most often when another agency needs information originally supplied (directly or indirectly) by the client. Generally, social work agencies require the client's written consent before they will release such information. In order not to delay the transmission of vital information, some agencies routinely ask clients to sign a release form at intake. While observing the technicalities of consent, such a routine does negate the concept of informed consent. Often clients do not understand what they are signing, nor is their signature always voluntary, because they are left with the impression that signing the form is a condition for receiving service. This is especially true when the routine forms used by many social agencies require a college reading level in order to understand them (Wagner, Davis, & Handelsman, 1998). Wagner and colleagues found that personalizing informed consent forms and making them easier to read increased participants' perception of the helpfulness of the helping process.

The problem may be that many forms in use today were designed primarily to protect the agency and the worker from malpractice suits rather than to guarantee the client's informed consent. While some social workers believe they are legally protected by formal consent agreements, ethical problems involving informed consent are not avoided in this manner (Davidson & Davidson, 1996). The challenge facing ethical social workers is to develop forms that are both readable and sufficiently specific, but do not scare the client. In addition, informed consent needs to be viewed as a *process* in which adequate information is provided in an ongoing manner as the client's needs and/or treatment progresses (Manning & Gaul, 1997; Wineburgh, 1998). Consent needs to be obtained at the time of treatment, and it cannot be assumed that because the client consented to the same treatment in the past he will again consent. (Manning & Gaul, 1997). According to the NASW *Code of Ethics,* "social workers should provide services to clients only in the context of a professional relationship based, when appropriate, on valid informed consent. Social workers should use clear and understandable language to inform clients of the purpose of the services, risks related to the services, limits to services because of requirements of a third-party payer, relevant costs, reasonable alternatives, clients' right to refuse or withdraw consent, and the time frame covered by the consent. Social workers should provide clients with an opportunity to ask questions" (1999, 1.03a). If a client is not capable of providing informed consent, then permission should be sought from an appropriate third party (1999, 1.03c). If a social worker is serving involuntary clients, then she "should provide information about the nature and extent of services and about the extent of clients' right to refuse service" (1.03d).

Ethical problems around informed consent are often difficult to resolve, as will become evident when we consider Exemplar 5.3.

❖ 5.3 Archie Walker's Golden Years

Muriel Palmieri is an outreach worker for the Downtown Elderly Program (DEP). She has organized a group of volunteers who regularly visit with homebound older people. These volunteers have been trained to identify older people who need additional help so that they can report their names to the DEP. One of the volunteers recently told Ms. Palmieri that she had discovered a bedridden older man in a cold and dirty fourth-floor walk-up apartment.

Archie Walker was probably not as old or as feeble as he appeared, but the volunteer thought that he required more care than the occasional help provided by his 79-year-old neighbor, who brought him food whenever he thought of it. When this neighbor forgot to come, as happened not infrequently, Mr. Walker subsisted for days on cold water and bread. It had been years since Mr. Walker last saw a doctor. He seemed delighted with the volunteer's visit and begged her to come again soon.

Ms. Palmieri told the volunteer that she would see what could be done to make Mr. Walker more comfortable. When Ms. Palmieri visited Mr. Walker, he welcomed her warmly and she was able to verify the volunteer's observations. Mr. Walker seemed relatively alert. Ms. Palmieri thought that his dissatisfaction with his present condition was realistic and a hopeful sign, indicative of a capacity to participate in developing plans for the future. Mr. Walker explained that his only income came from Social Security. He had never heard of the federal Supplemental Security Income (SSI) program.

Ms. Palmieri suspected that he would qualify for SSI. Mr. Walker said that he could not afford to move to another apartment, but he insisted that he did not want to go to an "old folks'" home.

Ms. Palmieri explained to Mr. Walker about many of the programs that were available to help persons in his situation. She listed the advantages and disadvantages of each and indicated the time it might take before each program or service would start for him. She also noted how she could help him qualify. Among the programs they discussed were SSI, Meals-on-Wheels, health visitors, homemakers, Title 8 housing, and the Manor Apartments.

Mr. Walker seemed bewildered by the many programs from which he could choose and by the many decisions he had to make. He asked Ms. Palmieri to do whatever was best for him.

If you were in Ms. Palmieri's place, what would you have done? Here are some of the ethical issues that may arise in trying to help Mr. Walker

1. What did Mr. Walker mean when he told her to do whatever was best for him? Does this mean that he gave his consent for her to make arrangements on his behalf? Is this a satisfactory way of giving informed consent? If not, in what ways does it fall short?

2. Instead of overwhelming Mr. Walker with so many choices, should Ms. Palmieri have simplified the decisions he has to make by presenting only a few options at a time? Perhaps it would have been better to have Mr. Walker decide first whether he really wanted to stay in his present apartment or move somewhere else. Can he make this decision without having a full knowledge of all options? Do social work ethics require that a client have full knowledge of *all* the relevant options?

3. Ms. Palmieri tried to present all of the advantages of every option. Did she really know *all* of the consequences? Does Mr. Walker really care about *all* of the consequences? Is he not much more interested in what will happen to him in the next few months? How much knowledge must a client have before the social worker can be sure that she has met the demands of the *Code of Ethics?*

4. Would it be ethical for Ms. Palmieri to design a package of relevant services on the basis of her assessment and on the basis of Mr. Walker's wishes—and then ask Mr. Walker whether this package was acceptable?

Additional questions could be asked, but it is already clear that in social work practice informed consent is beset with many difficulties and that these difficulties often lead to ethical dilemmas.

Disclosure of Information, Voluntariness, and Competence

The three issues of informed consent are (1) disclosure of information, (2) voluntariness, and (3) competency (Grisso & Appelbaum, 1998; Moreno, Caplan, & Wolpe, 1998). We will discuss briefly the ethical aspects of each of these issues.

Disclosure of Information   A person can be considered sufficiently informed to give consent only if he knows what will occur during the intervention or treatment, what the results of the intervention will be, and what will happen if consent to the intervention is not given. He should know how much better (or worse) he will be if he agrees to the intervention than he will be if he does not agree. He should also have full knowledge about alternate options and their associated risks and benefits. In situations in which the client is being asked to consent to the disclosure of confidential information to a third party, he should know what information will be released, to whom, for what purposes, and with what consequences. Finally, the disclosure of information must be done in a clear and understandable manner (Grisso & Appelbaum, 1998). In some cases, fundamental problems of communication may exist when attempting to communicate technical and value-laden information, particularly to those who are in stressful situations. For example, some persons may have difficulty understanding the idea of probability or different styles of communication may be intimidating to some clients (Moreno, et al., 1998).

Much of the required information can be provided by the social worker, but even she may not be cognizant of many of the possible outcomes. In fact, the nature and consequences of any option are never entirely clear and may be interpreted differently by different experts. Ms. Palmieri might explain to Mr. Walker how Meals-on-Wheels operates, the type of food this program provides, and how much it costs. However, she does not know whether this program will survive the next budget cuts. In fact, Mr. Walker may lose the help of his neighbor (inadequate as it is) if he joins Meals-on-Wheels and be in a worse position if that program is terminated. Ms. Palmieri might point out all the benefits and risks, but there are always secondary and unanticipated consequences which, though unpredictable, may be equally if not more important.

There is also evidence that people often do not pay attention or fully comprehend information presented to them no matter how carefully the details and possible risks are explained to them. Whether this is a case of selective listening or of suppressing unpleasant information is not always clear. In a study of patient-physician communication following general exams, the patients could not remember almost 70% of the problems physicians diagnosed (American College of Physicians Observer, 1997). There are estimates that only 20% of adult Americans have the ability to read, understand, and act on health care information (*Dent*, 2000). Other patients simply do not want to know what might go wrong or have hearing difficulties.

Social workers differ in many ways from physicians, but many social workers also report that their clients really do not want to know all the details. They have a problem and want help from an expert whom they trust. Yet, the social worker is ethically committed to the principle of informed consent. One of the ethical dilemmas of informed consent occurs when a social worker does not want to overwhelm the client with too much information, but does want to provide sufficient information so that the client can make a meaningful decision. Should the worker proceed when the client gives permission, even though the social worker suspects that this client does not fully understand the information and its meaning. Or should the social worker delay help in order to give the client additional information?

Voluntariness   Consent is meaningful only when it is uncoerced and given freely. Though there is wide agreement with this ethical rule, some social workers practice in settings where the client has little or no freedom. Prisoners and hospitalized persons with mental illnesses are classic examples of involuntary clients. When working with court-mandated clients, there are three barriers to informed consent. First, the risks and benefits of the court-ordered assessment cannot be fully anticipated. Second, the power imbalance results in client vulnerability that undermines voluntariness of consent. Third, while the "ability to form a therapeutic alliance and obtain relevant information is valued by the court, the therapeutic alliance may not always serve the best interest of the client, who may not be aware of the complexity of the relationship" (Regehr & Antle, 1997, p. 301).

Consent may also be less than voluntary in some settings. Voluntariness is often presented as a dichotomous value—a decision either is or is not voluntary. However, closer inspection will suggest that there is a wide range of possibilities between the two absolutes. For example, how voluntary is the consent of a "voluntary" client who believes it is important to gain the worker's goodwill? A destitute single mother may agree with almost everything her social worker suggests because she desperately wants to qualify for assistance. The man who is eager for reconciliation with his estranged wife may agree with everything his social worker mentions because he believes that in this way he may be able to salvage his marriage. These people are not forced to come to a social agency or to agree with the social worker, but is their consent fully voluntary?

Social workers often work in settings in which clients' participation is non-voluntary. Such settings include corrections, juvenile justice, child protection, involuntary commitments for mental health treatment, and court-ordered treatment for substance abuse. There may also be subtle coercion for employees to obtain specific services. In addition to issues of voluntariness, other issues that may arise include those of trust, privacy, relationship, and the efficacy of treatment.

Social workers have reported mixed effectiveness for individual interventions with those involved in the criminal justice system (Ivanoff, Blythe, & Tripodi,

1994). Another review of the literature on the effectiveness of social work interventions with legally mandated clients found that clients can have more successful results than had earlier been thought to be the case. These positive results, however, also suggested that coerced intervention often produces *time-limited* benefits that do not last beyond the use of external pressure (Rooney, 1992). In addition to the long-standing belief that successful mental health treatment must be voluntary and uncoerced, the use of involuntary treatment modalities also raises many ethical questions that social workers must face.

Another ethical dilemma facing social workers arises out of the desirability of client trust. Research has shown that trust or faith in the practitioner is a key component in effecting change. Yet frequently, faith or trust results in a surrender of decision-making participation. Instead of giving voluntary consent, the client who has blind faith will agree to everything his worker says. Developing and encouraging trust, while strengthening voluntary consent, is a challenge for every social worker. Grisso and Appelbaum (1998) comment that "encouraging patients to pursue a particular option is not coercion, unless unfair threats are involved. Clinicians need not simply lay out the alternatives for patients. They can distinguish among the options they consider more or less viable" (p. 9).

The problem of involuntary consent takes on special significance when a client wants to harm himself, either by wishing to commit suicide or by wanting to engage in other self-destructive behaviors. There are those who have argued that a social worker has no right to interfere with a person who really wants to harm himself, that self-determination is the highest social work value. They argue that every person has a right to make decisions that affect only him- or herself. There are others, however, who have suggested that intervention, at least temporary intervention, may be justified in order to determine whether the contemplated action is fully voluntary and whether the decision maker is indeed knowledgeable and competent. Gewirth held that "the conditions of voluntary consent are never fulfilled in such cases [because] only abysmal ignorance or deep emotional trauma can lead persons to extreme measures like these" (1978, p. 264). He no doubt would suggest that a social worker must always intervene in cases of threatened suicide or other self-destructive behavior in order to protect that person's welfare. According to the Ethical Principles Screen in Chapter 4, the protection of life takes precedence over every other obligation.

Competence   Informed consent presupposes that the person who gives consent is competent to do so. However, many social work clients are less than fully competent. Young children, persons with dementia, Alzheimer's disease or mental retardation, and the seriously emotionally disturbed may not be competent to give informed consent for some or all decisions. However, Robertson (1985) notes that even though "competence appears to be a binary process . . . on closer examination its binariness dissolves and vanishes" (p. 555). In other words, it is not a question of classifying clients as those who are competent and those who are not. Instead, persons will be located along a continuum, ranging from those completely competent, to others who are somewhat competent, to still others who are barely competent or not at all competent. Furthermore, persons may be quite competent in one area and less than competent in another. This conceptualization has many implications when we consider professional ethics and practice.

Only a court of law can declare a person incompetent, but there are many situations in which a social worker must make an informal assessment of a person's competency to participate in decision making. The ethical problem is complicated because ostensibly the issue of competency is raised only when a client disagrees with his social worker's recommendation. Rarely do we consider him incompetent if he agrees. Ethical problems arising out of the issue of competence are well known to social workers in many situations, especially those who are working with adoption, foster placement, custody, abortion, contraception, and end-of-life decisions.

The social worker's dilemma may become a difficult one, particularly when young children are involved. While there isn't agreement about how old a child must be before he or she is considered competent, everyone agrees that an infant is not competent to make decisions. Children, like adults, may not always mean what they say or say what they mean. Stated preferences may not reflect actual preferences.

The decision to intervene in a person's life must never be taken lightly. To limit a person's freedom by removing him from his home and placing him in an institution is a very serious decision, which ordinarily should not be made without the person's consent. At the same time, it may be a mistake to always accept a client's consent or refusal at face value. A client may be temporarily depressed, may change his mind upon further reflection, or may be reacting to a situational fear or misunderstanding. Robertson (1985) warned "the alacrity [to accept the first response] may stem from a superficial sense of legal and ethical duty" (p. 569).

The issue of informed consent takes on a special significance when the client is a community or neighborhood. A social worker involved in a neighborhood renewal program must consider whether the elected representatives really represent all residents. Does their informed consent suffice, or must every resident consent? What is the situation when the initiative for intervention comes from the outside? It will not be possible to obtain informed consent if the social worker's first objective is to raise the residents' consciousness to the fact that there is a problem. Requiring every person's consent in this latter situation may be tantamount to ruling out any intervention activity, yet intervening without informed consent is a violation of professional ethics. What should a social worker do in these circumstances?

Ways of Consenting

Oliver Goldsmith (1764) wrote that "silence gives consent," but social workers have learned that silence and other nonverbal signals, such as a nod, or even a verbal yes may be deceptive and may indicate something other than consent. Clients may be ashamed to withhold consent or simply not understand what they have been asked to agree to. A social worker is obligated to offer a full explanation of what the intervention involves, what the projected benefits and risks will be, what other options may be available, and what might happen if the client does not consent. All this must be presented in a language that the client can understand. Language per se is important but even more so may be how the social worker presents the information. Many clients have short attention spans. Exceeding that time span may mean "turning the client off," even if the language is simple.

Aside from questions of disclosure of information, voluntariness, and competency, the various forms of consent also make for ethical problems. Consider the following possibilities:

1. *Direct or tacit.* *Direct* refers to the client's verbal response, while *tacit* means that the client remained silent. Is it ethical for the social worker to assume that the client agrees when he does not respond to her suggestion?
2. *Oral or written.* Written consent is often preferred, but is the use of oral consent necessarily unethical? Does using written consent forms automatically eliminate all unethical dilemmas? Should services that are typically provided via telephone (e.g., suicide hotlines) be withheld until written consent can be obtained? Can other forms of documentation that consent was obtained (e.g., audio recordings of the verbal consent or copies of e-mail messages) substitute for written consent?
3. *Past/present.* Does current dissent invalidate all past consents? Is this a case of change of mind, diminished competence, situational fear, or something else? To state this dilemma differently, how much credence should a social worker give to a person's change of mind when she knows that in the past he consistently expressed a contrary view?
4. *Present/future.* Can a social worker assume that the client would (or will) agree with her decision if he were (or when he becomes) more aware of what is involved? Can a social worker wait to obtain informed consent until the client and the process is far enough along so the client understands fully the consequences of the decision?
5. *Forced consent.* One way to obtain a client's consent is to frame options in such a way that the client will consent, no matter what the response. For example, the social worker may ask: Do you want to move to the nursing home this week or next? Is this an ethical way of obtaining consent? Another form of "forced consent" is by threatening undesirable consequences unless the client consents. Clearly, everybody agrees that this is not ethical. What if the agency provides only one kind of service—and if the client does not agree, he cannot be served. Is a "threat" of no-service-unless-you-agree ethical?

As we have already said, each of these forms of consent presents ethical problems and dilemmas that require resolution. However, one thing is certain: Involving the client in providing informed consent is not a one-time activity but an ongoing process.

Some have suggested that good clinical practice will resolve all of the problems around informed consent. If a client is fully involved in the decision-making process, questions of consent will not arise. It is a fact, however, that even formal contracting does not resolve all the problems involved in obtaining informed consent. The power gap between client and worker often results in contract negotiations between unequals. Some unintended coercion may be brought into play, and this may lead the client to agree to choices that are not entirely of his choosing.

DUTY TO WARN

The ground rules that govern how all mental health professionals, including social workers, must deal with violent or potentially violent clients were changed by a landmark legal case in California (*Tarasoff v. The Regents of the University of California*). This ruling, which is known as the *Tarasoff* rule, has aroused a great deal of anxiety among professional workers. Many feared that this decision would destroy the confidential relationship that is basic to any helping process. The landmark legal case in California started when a murder took place in 1969. The case changed the ground rules for mental health professionals when dealing with violent or potentially violent clients and stimulated anxiety among mental health professionals. Major concerns were expressed at the time by many professionals who feared the decision would undermine the practice of therapy by destroying the confidential nature of therapy. A young man—Prosenjit Poddar—who was a voluntary out-patient at the student health service at the University of California (Berkeley) told his therapist that he intended to kill his former girlfriend just as soon as she returned from an out-of-town trip. Shortly thereafter, the young woman— Tatiana Tarasoff—was killed by the young man. The young woman's parents, subsequently, charged the therapist with neglect. The therapist argued that he was not guilty because his relationship with the young client/killer was confidential. However, the judge held that:

> Public policy favoring protection of the confidential character of patient-psychotherapist relationship must yield in instances in which disclosure is essential to avert danger to others; the protective privilege ends where the public peril begins.
> When a therapist determines, or should determine, that his patient presents a serious danger of violence to another, *he incurs an obligation to use reasonable care to protect the intended victim* against such danger. This duty may call for him (1) to warn the intended victim or (2) [to inform] others likely to apprise the victim of the danger, (3) to notify the police, or (4) to take whatever other steps are reasonably necessary under the circumstances (*Tarasoff v. Regents of the University of California*, 1976, 551 P 2d 334 at 340; emphasis added).

We have cited at length from the *Tarasoff* ruling because it has become very important for all mental health professionals, including social workers. Although it was a California court case, this case has had a nationwide impact. Since 1976, mental health practitioners have been required to take reasonable measures to protect potential victims from a client's foreseeable violent acts. Subsequent court decisions further defined the *Tarasoff* doctrine. One decision explained that under the *Tarasoff* doctrine, a social worker or other professional (1) must be able to predict "pursuant to the standards of his profession" that the client is violently dangerous and (2) must be able to specify one or more clearly identifiable victims (*Brady v. Hopper,* 1983, 751 F2d 329).

In another decision, the California Supreme Court extended the *Tarasoff* doctrine beyond the identified intended victim to others who also might be in danger. In this latter case, the victim's minor children were murdered, and their father successfully sued. In the same decision, the court ruled that a therapist's failure to use reasonable care to protect a third party from harm constituted "professional negligence," rather than "ordinary negligence." This definition allows suits to be initiated for up to three years after the injury occurred, rather than the usual one-year limitation (Butz, 1985, p. 87, citing *Hedlund v. Superior Court,* 1983, 669, P 2d 41).

In recent years, the duty to warn has been further interpreted, but its practice applications still are not always entirely clear. New decisions by various courts clarify some questions. For example, a 1994 "California appellate court case, *Gross v. Allen* expands the Tarasoff duty to include suicide threats. It also makes explicit that a psychotherapist's 'duty to warn' includes informing a subsequent therapist about a patient's known dangerousness" (Meyers, 1997, p. 365).

Yet other important issues remain open, undecided, or ambiguous (Almason, 1997). Social workers must become aware of and remain up to date on the current laws in their states. In *Rost v. State Board of Psychology,* a Pennsylvania court held that ignorance of the law is not a sufficient defense for not protecting confidential records. The court stated that "a psychologist cannot claim ignorance of the ethical obligations of her profession, and if there was a conflict between her ethical duty to maintain confidentiality and the subpoena, she should have sought legal advice" (Beck, 1998, p. 378). Although this case deals with confidentiality, rather than duty to warn, it suggests that ignorance of ethical or legal responsibilities is not a defense for unethical or illegal actions.

The duty to warn varies from state to state (Beck, 1998) and may be ill defined in states where laws regulating professions do not define the *Tarasoff* duty. Some states have enacted *Tarasoff* legislation and others have not. Some states have adopted and extended the *Tarasoff* principle; others have "contained" third party liability within the context of the state's protective disclosure law yet other states found there is no duty to warn, including Florida, Mississippi, and Texas. Still other states acknowledged circumscribed duties to warn or protect (Felthous & Kachigian, 2001). Even the state of California in a criminal case (*People v. Felix,* Court of Appeals, 2001) revisited these issues and tested the limits of the duty to warn. This court held that applying the duty to warn principle would mean those who need therapy for homicidal thoughts would not seek it because they would view therapy as self-incriminating. While mental health professionals praised the ruling, law enforcement personnel claimed it undermined the rights and safety of potential victims (Ewing, 2002).

Social workers should be alert to the legal dimensions regarding the duty to warn because the complexities differ from state to state and from profession to profession. Some professions may receive the benefit of immunity from liability for breaches of confidentiality while others do not. Some state laws create legal confidentiality as a right of the client but do not provide liability waivers for mental health practitioners who warn a potential victim. There is no wide agreement on what is meant by "serious threat of physical violence," nor on the meaning of "intended" or "capable of being carried out." However, "most state statutes require an actual or serious threat; thus therapists in these jurisdictions no longer have to attempt to predict dangerousness" (Almason, 1997, p. 481).

Different states also vary in their requirements in regard to how the warning duty may be discharged: warning the potential victim or someone close to the victim, notifying the police, starting commitment proceedings, or informing mental health evaluators of the nature of the threat. Each of the alternatives may present new ethical dilemmas. Reporting to the police, for example, may fulfill the duty to warn, but the police may have different values in regard to the uses of this information (Egley, 1992). What if a social worker practices in a state without a legal duty to warn in certain situations? Does she have an ethical responsibility to do so? This issue will also be addressed in Chapter 12 concerning persons with HIV.

In addition to varying state legislation and court decisions concerning the duty to warn, a fundamental issue of concern is the assessment of the probability of violence. For example, consider the following situation:

❖ 5.4 An Idle or Serious Threat?

Mr. Rufus Hall is seeking help with his four-year marriage. According to Mr. Hall, his wife, Sara, refuses to come to counseling with him and has been threatening to get a divorce. Mr. Hall reports that on occasion he gets very angry with his wife and has "slapped" her once or twice. During one session, he said that he loves his wife and would kill her if she goes through with her threat to get a divorce.

His social worker, Jillian Adams, who lives in the same community as Mr. and Mrs. Hall, knows that Mrs. Hall recently saw a lawyer about a divorce. To date, Mr. Hall has only spoken of a couple of "slaps," but Ms. Adams is uncertain how to respond to his comment that he would kill her if she divorces him.

Should Ms. Adams report the husband's comment as a threat? If yes, to whom? How can she assess the seriousness of this random comment? Would it matter if you knew his "slaps" had been more violent than he reported? What information would be helpful in deciding whether the threat to Mrs. Hall's safety is real and should be reported?

Admittedly, the prediction of violence is not a hard science. While some personality characteristics have been found related to a higher probability of violent behavior, potential violence cannot be predicted with any certainty.

A study of the predictive accuracy by clinicians of almost 2,500 patients in an emergency psychiatric department over a two year period found that (1) higher levels of violence occurred than were expected; (2) clinicians were found to be relatively inaccurate predictors of violence; (3) judgments about male patients had modest clinical utility; and (4) clinicians had great difficulty predicting violence in women (Lidz, Mulvey, & Gardner, 1993). In some cases, short-term hospitalization or other interventions seem justified based on assessments of potential danger (Newhill, 1992). Beck (1998) comments on the difficulty of predicting violent behavior, especially for clients who are likely to be impulsive, such as those with certain mental disorders. So far, "when violence appears to be impulsive for whatever reason, courts are reluctant to find the defendants negligent" for not warning a potential victim (Beck, p. 381).

Certain additional ethical problems arise in regard to the *Tarasoff* duty, the answers to which are not readily found in the NASW *Code of Ethics*. A social worker should reveal a confidence only "for compelling professional reasons. The general expectation that social workers will keep information confidential does not apply when disclosure is necessary to prevent serious, foreseeable, and imminent harm to a client or other identifiable person" (1999, 1.07c). However, there remains much ambiguity about the definition of threats to injure.

The *Tarasoff* decision has not only produced new ethical dilemmas but has also led to changes in practice and to new ways in which professional organizations deal with clients. Clients are now routinely informed about the limits of confidentiality so they may decide what to disclose and not to disclose. Some practitioners and agencies may avoid accepting potentially dangerous clients because of the possible liability problems that may arise. Some may not sufficiently explore issues of dangerous intent so that charges of negligence can be avoided when no stated specific threat was actually heard. Others have used mental hospitals as a principal means of protecting the public from potentially violent persons through preventive detention, at times appropriately and at others inappropriately. Such defensive practices may be considered safe because they may help the social worker avoid legal problems, but are such practices ethical? Are there more appropriate ways to comply with the *Tarasoff* decision?

Currently, there is no statute or model law that provides a complete definition of all the components of the duty to warn. The major question is whether social workers have a duty to protect potential victims. Because there is so much activity in this area of the law, even social workers who practice in states where there is no clear precedent would be well advised to proceed as if they have such a duty (Egley, 1992; Kopels & Kagle, 1993).

There are those who hold that the *Tarasoff* doctrine should not present social workers with any new ethical problems because the requirement to break confidentiality and warn the intended victim applies only in specific instances. Beck (1998, p. 375) suggests that the legal and ethical issues surrounding the duty to warn are "remarkably congruent with good clinical practice." When the duty to warn does apply, the ethical decision screens provide clear guidance because saving human life from direct and immediate danger is a higher-order ethical principle than confidentiality. The ethical issue becomes problematic only when the risk to life is ambiguous.

Since the initial establishment of a clinician's duty to warn in order to protect third parties from violence, courts adopted and expanded *Tarasoff*-like duties. However, gradually, limits have been placed by courts on this duty by clinicians. The establishment of limits on the duty has been accompanied concurrently by the establishment of state statutes that explicitly codify the *Tarasoff* duty and the discharge of the duty. Given the "mixed" and changing legal definition of the duty to warn, social workers should be certain they know the law in their state and weigh carefully through professional supervision and legal consultation appropriate actions (Walcott, Cerundolo, & Beck, 2001).

EXERCISES

1. Investigate the laws in your state (or of neighboring states or of your home state) concerning confidentiality, privileged communication, and the duty to warn, as they apply to social workers.

2. Prepare a brief to be presented to your state legislature, urging that the privileged communication rule be extended to the client-social worker relationship and that it include group, couple, and family therapy.

3. Divide the class into groups of two. In each small group, have one person assume the role of the social worker and the other the role of an applicant who is seeking help for coping with an alcoholic and physically abusive significant other. The specific task is for the social worker to inform the applicant/client of the limits of confidentiality. Students should try several different approaches and report to the class the one that they think is most effective and best meets the demands of the *Code of Ethics*.

4. Divide the class into groups of two. In each small group, have one person assume the role of the social worker and the other the role of an applicant who is seeking help with parenting issues. The specific task is for the social worker to inform the applicant/client of the limits of confidentiality, especially given the possibility of the need to report child maltreatment to the appropriate agency. Students should try several different approaches and report to the class the one that they think is most effective and best meets the demands of the *Code of Ethics*.

5. Your agency is reviewing its policy on giving clients access to their case records. Almost all staff members agree to abide by the *Code of Ethics*, but there is a difference of opinion on how to define "reasonable access" and "exceptional circumstances when there is compelling evidence that such access would cause serious harm to the client" (1.08a). Try to define these in ways that are congruent with both professional ethics and clients' rights. If there are differences of opinion in your class, organize a discussion to examine the strengths and weaknesses of each position. Can the class reach consensus on how to best define these issues?

SUGGESTIONS FOR ADDITIONAL READINGS

Roberts, Battaglia, and Epstein (1999) discuss the unique ethical issues related to mental health care in rural communities. Royce, Dhooper, and Rompf (1999) discuss confidentiality and other legal and ethical considerations for field instruction of social work students. Conte, Fisher, Callahan, and Roffman (1996) describe a procedure for obtaining informed consent via telephone. Schlossberger and Hecker (1996) discuss the *Tarasoff* ruling as it relates to family therapists working with clients who are HIV-positive. Beck (1998) discusses the *Tarasoff* duty as it relates to work with impulsively violent clients, and Meyers (1997) discusses the *Tarasoff* duty to subsequent caregivers. Harris (1999) discusses the *Tarasoff* duty and the *Jaffee* decision on psychotherapist-client privilege. Strom-Gottfried (1998a) examines informed consent in relationship to managed care.

6 CHAPTER | Client Rights and Professional Expertise

An ethical dilemma arises out of a conflict between two guides: (1) the self-determination or autonomy guide, which states that the person most affected by a decision should make that decision, and (2) the benefit guide, which posits that the professional social worker has the knowledge and skill necessary to best assure a positive outcome and is, therefore, responsible for making the decision that will secure the optimum benefit for the client.

Social workers believe that every person has a right to make his or her own decisions. Veteran social worker Charlotte Towle (1896–1966) noted that "a person has a right to manage his own affairs" (1987, p. 15). A client's right to self-determination was one of the first, if not the first, principle social workers proclaimed. Similarly, the NASW *Code of Ethics* states, "Social workers respect and promote the right of clients to self-determination and assist clients in their efforts to identify and clarify their goals." (NASW *Code*, 1999, 1.02). This rule seems clear and unambiguous. The *Code* also states "social workers may limit clients' rights to self-determination when, in the social workers' professional judgment, clients' actions or potential actions pose a serious, foreseeable, and imminent risk to themselves or others" (NASW *Code*, 1999, 1.02). The *Code of Ethics* states, "Social workers practice within their areas of competence and develop and enhance their professional expertise. Social workers continually strive to increase their professional knowledge and skills and to apply them in practice" (NASW *Code*, 1999, Ethical Principles). It is assumed that the social worker should serve clients with the maximum application of professional skill and competence.

At one time, this ethical problem was less severe because there was a great deal of uncertainty about the adequacy of social work knowledge and about the effectiveness of social work intervention. In more recent years, studies by deSmidt and Gorey (1997), Reid (1997), Gorey, Thyer, and Pawluck (1998), and Lee and Gaucher (2000) and others have shown that the application of professional knowledge and appropriate professional skills can result in positive client outcomes. The practice problem with potentially critical ethical implications is how to combine client self-determination with the use of professional knowledge and skill. Is it ethical for a social worker to refrain from using professional knowledge if the client chooses an option with which the social worker cannot concur?

The issue is not so much that the social worker does not concur with the client's decision but rather that in some cases the social worker *knows* with a high degree of certainty that the client's choice will result in harm to others. The practitioner's ability to help will be severely limited when the client makes decisions that are contrary to the strategy suggested on the basis of professional knowledge. The social worker may know what strategy will best achieve the objectives that the client has chosen. Is it ethical for the social worker to implement this more effective strategy when the client prefers another? The social worker may understand what it is that the client needs or wants even before the client is aware of this. Again, the ethical question arises: May the social worker follow the strategy suggested by her knowledge and insight when the client has made another, less beneficial decision based on ignorance or partial knowledge?

Some social workers do not hesitate to give priority to their professional knowledge and skill even when this means ignoring a client's input. Halmos observed that a therapist cannot be helpful "unless we mean therapy to be therapeutic and, therefore, determining and directing in important ways" (1965, p. 92). This view follows the tradition that professionals "profess to know better than . . . their clients what ails them . . ." (Hughes, 1965, p. 2). Others hold that a social worker should never make decisions for a client, even if the client's decision does not seem as congruent with the worker's knowledge. This position is based on a number of principles, including (1) the primacy of the client self-determination rule, (2) the philosophical principle that no one but that person himself or herself can change a person, and (3) the practice principle that change efforts without the participation of the person to be changed will not be effective.

Often a social worker can follow the best of practice knowledge and professional skills and still respect a client's right to self-determination. One of the reasons for this is that social workers believe not only in the right but also in the therapeutic effectiveness of client participation in all phases of the social work process. Almost all professionals have moved a long way from the traditionally negative attitude toward clients, such as the one expressed by the 1847 *Code of Ethics* of the American Medical Association, which declared that professionals have "a right to expect and require that their patients should entertain a just sense of duties which they owe to their medical attendants."

Early social workers may not have been as blatant in their public statements, but they, too, expected that clients follow their good advice without asking too many questions.

The conflict between client self-determination and the worker's use of her professional knowledge and skills need not result from any Machiavellian desires. Even when a social worker cares about her client's interests and rights, this ethical problem becomes a critical one in many practice situations. Connected to the issues of client self-determination and the worker's use of knowledge and skills, however, is the question as to who is the client for whom knowledge and skills will be applied. We will turn now to consider this question.

WHO IS THE CLIENT?

The question "Who is the client?" may be the source of several ethical dilemmas. Traditionally, a client was defined as the person(s) who engaged the practitioner and paid her a fee. Alternately, the client is the person (or the system) whose behavior is to be modified or changed by the professional's intervention. However, these definitions may not be entirely appropriate for most social workers, especially for those who are employed by an organization, such as a social agency, a department of government, or an institution. According to the first definition, the organization that pays the social worker's salary should be considered the client. Is the school really the client of the school social worker? Is the prison the client of the correctional social worker? Nowadays, the traditional definition may be too narrow, since it was originally devised for clients of independent professional practitioners in private practice.

The alternate definition also is problematic because it is not always correct to say that the client is the person or system whose behavior needs to be changed. Often social work intervention involves changes in systems other than the client system. When a social worker helps a recently widowed woman complete an application for Social Security benefits, the worker does not intend to change the widow, but instead helps the client to gain access to resources in her environment. Until not too long ago, a physician was certain that the sick person who came to his office was his patient, just as the social worker automatically considered the person(s) who applied for help as her client(s). Today, neither physician nor social worker is certain that the answer to the question "Who is the client?" is quite so simple, as Exemplars 6.1 and 6.2 illustrate.

❖ 6.1 Arlene Johnson's Abortion

Arlene Johnson, 18 years old and single, is nearly six months pregnant. Yesterday, she came to the Women's Counseling Center to request help in getting an abortion. At the time of the procedure, the fetus was considered viable and was placed in the neonatal intensive care unit as a high-risk premature baby.

Arlene was most upset when she learned that the "abortion" had resulted in a live infant. She refused to look at the baby or take care of it. Instead, she threatened to sue the doctor and the hospital if the infant survived despite her expressed wish for an abortion.

Arlene asked Robin Osborn, the hospital social worker, to make sure that the baby not be given intensive care, but rather be left alone so that it would die quickly.

Who is Robin Osborn's client? Arlene Johnson? The premature infant? Whose interests should be accorded priority? The Exemplar 6.2 is entirely different, but it raises similar questions.

❖ 6.2 Mrs. Linden's Classroom

Mrs. Linden is a fifth-grade teacher in the Abraham Lincoln Elementary School. The school is located in a neighborhood into which a large number of Central American families have moved recently. Mrs. Joan Ramirez is the social worker assigned to this school.

Yesterday, Mrs. Linden asked Mrs. Ramirez for help in keeping her pupils quietly in their seats. She told Mrs. Ramirez that never in her 20 years as a teacher has she had as much trouble as this year. She thought that her troubles were caused by the many children who recently transferred from foreign schools and do not speak English well. Surely Mrs. Ramirez could advise her how to handle these children so that they would be quiet and stay in their seats.

Again, who is the client? Mrs. Linden? The pupils? Their parents? The school? Whose interests should be accorded priority? What if Mrs. Ramirez believes the problem stems from a different source such as racism or inflexibility? The two problem situations seem quite different, but in each case the request made by the applicant for service creates for the social worker a dilemma that has ethical implications. Arlene Johnson does not want to have a baby, but once a live infant had been born, her expectations of the obstetrician (and request she made to the social worker) conflict sharply with the rights of the infant and with what society expects from these professionals. Similarly, Mrs. Linden's expectations are different from those of her students. Both teacher and students (and their parents) have different expectations from those of Mrs. Ramirez. The social worker is not at all sure that the problem is with the pupils; perhaps the teacher is the real problem.

One of the reasons why the "Who is the client?" question causes so many ethical dilemmas is that the question itself is based on an oversimplified and not entirely accurate model of the professional relationship. The traditional model included only the practitioner and the client. An updated model should include the applicant, client, target, beneficiary, practitioner, agency, community, and others. Each of the four positions noted in Figure 6.1 can be occupied by one or

Figure 6.1 | Some Participants in the Social Work Process

Applicant   The person(s) or system that requests help with a defined or
                felt problem

Client   The applicant who enters into a formal, contractual, goal-focused
                relationship with a social worker

Target   The person(s) or system(s) that must be modified in order to achieve
                the desired outcome to which client and worker have agreed

Beneficiary   The person(s) or system(s) that will benefit from successful goal
                achievement

more persons or institutions. Sometimes the same person is the applicant as well as the client, target, and beneficiary. At other times or in other situations, different persons occupy each of these positions. The applicant may not be the client (a mother applying for her child) and the client need not be the target (the target may be, for example, an employer or school principal), nor is the client necessarily the beneficiary of the intervention. When different persons occupy these positions or roles, we can be almost certain that each one will have slightly different expectations, problem definitions, demands, and goals. Often these differing expectations are in conflict with each other, thus creating an ethical dilemma for the social worker. When there is a conflict of expectations, whose expectations should receive priority attention? Arlene Johnson and Mrs. Linden are the applicants, and their requests are important. However, both Robin Osborn, the hospital social worker, and Joan Ramirez, the school social worker, must deal with the question of identifying the primary client, target, and beneficiary. Here are the seeds for ethical dilemmas.

Social workers who engage in genetic counseling are constantly faced by difficult problems that involve ethical issues. Modern medical procedures such as amniocentesis and chorionic villus sampling make it possible to detect hundreds of different genetic disorders. When there are positive findings, the social worker must help parents think through all of the implications so that they can make the best decision for them. However, some physicians expect the social worker to persuade the pregnant mother to abort. Others may expect the social worker to persuade the mother not to abort based on religious or other principles whenever there are indications of a genetically defective fetus. Should the best interest of the as-yet-unborn child play a part in the decision? What is the best interest? Should the social worker stress arguments in favor of abortion, even if it is evident that the parents do not want to terminate this pregnancy? What is the ethical stance that the social worker should adopt? Should the decision of the social worker depend on knowledge of more or less certainty of the predicted consequences of genetic effects, that is, mild or severe effects leading to a degree of independence or to the need for constant care and assistance?

Social workers in the criminal justice system face similar ethical issues. In the probation service, social workers regularly prepare reports for the court judge. The judge takes these reports into consideration when making a final disposition of the case. The ethical dilemma here is that the social worker is both helper and judicial fact finder. The client/worker helping relationship starts during the first contact with the juvenile, long before the social worker has completed her evaluative assessment or presented her report to the judge. To whom does the social worker owe priority consideration—to the juvenile detainee or to the judge? Who is her client? Note that in the criminal justice system social workers will often face situations in which the resolution of the ethical issues may not fully coincide with the legal requirements. Does the social worker in these settings need to explain her court responsibilities to the client?

SELF-DETERMINATION

Immanuel Kant, one of the early giants of modern philosophy, insisted that a person's right to determine his or her own destiny is an unconditional right. He taught that persons are always ends in themselves and should never be treated as means, that is, the social worker is to provide professional services for the client and not take advantage of the client, not the client serve the social worker. Self-determination is also a first-order principle in American society. Though not specifically mentioned in the Constitution, the U.S. Supreme Court, in a series of due-process cases, equal protection cases, and privacy cases, developed the position that self-determination is a fundamental right that is protected by the Ninth and Fourteenth Amendments. Supreme Court Justice Brandeis (Brandeis & Warren, 1890, p. 1) suggested over a century ago that a fundamental right is "the right to be left alone."

A person's right to make his or her own decisions is the source for the social work value of self-determination. Many hold that self-determination is an absolute right, yet most social workers would agree with Rothman (1989) that when used as a practice principle, its application is limited. Bernstein (1960) writes that self-determination is "not supreme, but supremely important," while Perlman (1965) suggests that self-determination, though important, is nine-tenths illusion. No wonder that Rothman states "self-determination is accorded utmost esteem in the profession [but] its meaning and application are clouded" (1989, p. 598). The right of self-determination has become the source for "one of the most common and most perplexing dilemmas for social workers" (Abramson, 1985, p. 387). How can a practitioner respect and uphold client self-determination when working with a client whose conception of what is good for him or her differs from that of the social worker? Or differs from the conception of those who will be affected by the client's decision?

These ethical dilemmas become more frequent and increasingly perplexing as more and more major decisions about life involve highly technical and specialized considerations that often are beyond the comprehension of lay people. Reliance on professionals who have the necessary expertise has become increasingly common. Under these circumstances, directiveness as a helping technique seems to have become more acceptable. There is a need to reexamine issues of self-determination and autonomy as social workers respond to new mandates and demands concerning persons with disabilities and those who are especially vulnerable (Murdach, 1996). In some cases, clients are unable to fend for themselves, causing social workers to intervene protectively, despite the client's objections. For example, a suicidal client requires hospitalization, but he does not want to be admitted to the hospital. The use of directive methods raises an ethical question as to whether the ends ever justify the means. Should a client be pressured into doing things he does not want to do even when his social worker is certain that this will contribute to solving or reducing his problem? Is it ethical for a social worker to deceive a client in order to have him participate in a treatment that he would reject if he knew all the facts? The issue can be identified not as directiveness by the social worker but as who decides that a client cannot manage for himself? Some persons say that social workers are interested parties in making such decisions and, therefore, should not make the decision alone.

Some professionals do not hesitate to use their superior knowledge and power to move the client in the "right" direction. Thus Gillis writes that "all modern psychotherapists, whether they know it or not, engage in maneuvers and manipulations that add to their power over the patient" (1974, p. 91). Dworkin (1985) adds that control of the client by the worker occurs in all professional relationships, no matter what theoretical framework is used. Usually, this control is not manifest but occurs in an implicit or unconscious way. Dworkin suggests that it would be better if this control were acknowledged and exercised in a systematic and explicit way.

Control and manipulation are concepts that social workers avoid and are not acceptable professional methods. Nevertheless, social workers often must reassess the meaning and practice of client self-determination. What are the ethical considerations that should guide a social worker who is convinced that an older adult client (who can no longer cope alone at home) should enter an assisted-living facility very soon, but who knows from past experience with this client that every worker suggestion elicits a "no" response? If this client has close relatives, should they be asked to make the decision? If there are no close relatives, should the worker make the decision without fully involving the client? To do so limits the client's freedom of choice. On the other hand, an aging person in a nursing home who is physically disabled, confined to a wheelchair, incontinent, and eating poorly but also has been fiercely independent through her life wants to return to her home, although she will need special care for medications and because of her physical limitations. Her aging sister says she will be able to care for her at home. Although this resident has law on her side (The Patient Self-Determination Act and the Uniform Health Care Decisions Act), her social worker could oppose her self-determined discharge because it appears to be life-threatening (Sasson, 2000). Such interventions in the life of the client can range from limited to extensive involvement and must be related to the degree of rational impairment or incapacity for decision making demonstrated by the client, as well as the amount of risk or danger present in the situation.

Stereotypes about age, for example, should never be used to limit client self-determination. There is some evidence that class-related or age-related criteria are sometimes used to assess the capacity of different client groups to make autonomous decisions. Those who work with aged clients are very much aware of this problem, but this ethical quandary is not limited to the aged. Stereotypes exist about teenagers, racial and ethnic groups, genders, rich and poor, and other groups as well. For instance, it is commonly thought that poor persons have fewer problem-solving skills, have different cognitive styles, are lazy, lack effort, have low intelligence, and therefore, cannot be expected to make autonomous decisions (Lott & Bulluck, 2001).

A situation, involving both the problem of "Who is the client?" and the problem of self-determination is illustrated in Exemplar 6.3.

❖ 6.3 Should Eleanor Pomer Come Home?

Eleanor Pomer is eight years old, the youngest of six siblings. She has been a resident in a special school for the last three years because of a diagnosis of Down's syndrome. According to her cottage parents, psychologist, teacher, and social worker, she functions on a moderate level but needs assistance with certain daily activities.

Both of Eleanor's parents are employed. They rent the downstairs apartment of a two-family home in a working-class neighborhood about one hour's drive from Eleanor's school. The Pomers visit Eleanor once a month. For the past year, Eleanor has also spent one weekend a month at home. Eleanor's home visits have been successful. Both Eleanor and her family look forward to these monthly visits.

The school's staff feels that Eleanor now is ready to leave the school and live again at home. The social worker has acquainted Eleanor's parents with this staff assessment, has told them about the community resources that are available in their city, and has urged them to take Eleanor home. However, the Pomers do not agree with this recommendation. They are satisfied with the present arrangement; they feel that it would be too much of a strain on their other children if Eleanor again lived at home. The social worker is convinced that it would be best for Eleanor to leave the school and resume a more normal home life. Eleanor is excited about the possibility of again living with her parents and brothers and sisters.

The ethical problem in this situation arises out of the conflict between applying professional knowledge and respecting the client's right to make decisions. How much weight must the social worker give to the Pomers' wishes? To Eleanor's wish? Should the most important criterion in reaching a decision be what is best for Eleanor? Who decides what is best for Eleanor? What about the welfare of the other Pomer children? Does the social worker have an ethical right to manipulate the environment (for example, by raising the tuition fee) in order to "help" the Pomers reach the decision that staff thinks is best for Eleanor? Are there standards in the *Code* that will help you decide what is the correct decision? Does the Ethical Principles Screen in Chapter 4 provide any guidance?

Another basic ethical dilemma in social work practice arises out of two—at times contradictory—professional principles that all social workers have accepted. These are (1) the principle to provide professional help when needed or requested by a client in order to assure or improve that person's welfare, and (2) the principle not to interfere with a person's freedom. These two professional principles are almost identical with Gewirth's basic or generic rights of "well-being" and "freedom" (1978, p. 64). Ideally, a social worker should not experience any conflict between these two rights (or principles). What if a person's well-being can be achieved only at the expense of his or her freedom? Who defines well-being? Who defines the need for professional help? Who can legitimately request professional help for another person?

Unless there are serious indications to the contrary, no social worker will want to interfere with another person's freedom, even if that person is her client. It is, however, generally agreed that there are occasions when intervention becomes necessary even if it is at the expense of freedom. Most people agree that a person's right to self-determination should be limited when its exercise will result in harm to another person, but what if the harm is only to the person himself or herself? This is why Abramson suggests that "paternalism takes precedence over autonomy" whenever the value of client autonomy comes into conflict with the value of securing a client's safety (1989, p. 105).

Though the conditions that justify intervention may seem clear, a social worker will discover many ambiguities. What is *clear and present danger?* How can it be demonstrated? When is harm sufficiently grave to warrant coercion? Who may coerce? How certain must the social worker be that her intervention will prevent the harm before she is justified in curtailing a person's freedom? Consider the following situation in Exemplar 6.4.

❖ 6.4 How Immediate Is the Danger?

Social worker Maria Espinosa has been working for one month with Allison Bode, an extremely thin, almost gaunt, reserved 17-year-old college freshman. Allison was referred to the Family Counseling Center by her pastor after she told him of her loneliness and obsessive thoughts. She came for help with the agreement and support of her parents. Allison is doing passing work academically but has been unsuccessful making friends at school. This afternoon, Allison told Ms. Espinosa that her menstrual cycle stopped. When Ms. Espinosa explored the situation, she learned that Allison is on a diet and exercises two to three hours a day to lose weight. She is slightly depressed but still able to concentrate on her school work and reports she is seldom irritable. Based on all of this information, Ms. Espinosa is quite certain that Allison has anorexia and suggests she go to the college health service to consult with a physician. As soon as Allison heard the suggestion, she rejected it. Is this a case of clear and present danger that requires immediate action? What harm would be done if a few more weekly sessions are used to help Allison act to protect her health and her visit to a physician delayed? What is the ethically correct choice?

More crucial than the type of problem or the chances of rehabilitation or recovery is the question of the client's capacity to make decisions. As long as he can make informed decisions, the social worker has no mandate to interfere, unless it is a question of life and death, or the duty to warn because of danger to self or others. The social worker's mandate is to enable the client, to the maximum extent possible, to make an informed decision.

An additional dimension of this ethical problem arises from the social worker's obligation to do more than merely observe the negative injunction of not interfering with a person's freedom. This obligation demands positive action designed to strengthen or promote the client's freedom. If promoting and not interfering with a client's freedom is to be more than empty rhetoric, social workers must understand that a person is truly autonomous only when all of the following conditions prevail:

1. The environment provides more than one option from which a person can make choices.
2. There is no coercion on the person from any source to choose one or another option.
3. The person is aware of all the available options.
4. The person has accurate information about the cost and consequences of each option so that he can assess them realistically.
5. The person has the capacity and/or initiative to make a decision on the basis of this assessment.
6. The person has an opportunity to act on the basis of his or her choice.

No extensive research is needed to discover that the freedom of most social work clients is quite limited. Though these limitations usually do not result from practitioner activities, social workers must be concerned when anybody's freedom is limited. Americans enjoy more freedom than the citizens of many other countries, but the social and economic conditions of most contemporary societies limit some of the freedom of most people. This is especially blatant with respect to those conditions that reinforce inequality, racism, sexism, and ageism. As Stevens reminds us, the freedom to choose and the right to make decisions are profoundly cherished rights; however, "self-determination is grievously restrained when opportunities for social mobility are blocked" (1998, p. 294).

Social workers are committed to use their professional skill and know-how to help all people gain full freedom. This ethical commitment may explain why many social workers have been in the forefront of struggles for more freedom and greater equality for all people. This ethical concern for greater autonomy must also find expression in the day-by-day practice of social workers.

Access to self-determination also varies with the dependency of the client on the benefits he receives from his social worker. The more essential and valuable the goods or services received, the greater the client's feelings of dependency on the worker and the less likely it is that he will choose an option that he believes his social worker will disapprove. Among those receiving public assistance, those persons who believed themselves to be personally responsible for being on "welfare" were less assertive about their rights as public assistance clients and were least likely to have disagreed with a caseworker or appealed a decision. Stigma, loss of self-esteem, psychological and economic hardship, and a lack of options undermine the ability to be self-determining (Goodban, 1985). This shortage of options continues to be true. For example, there is no "exit" option for public assistance clients enrolled in welfare to work programs, other than exiting the program and losing needed benefits. As a result, to avoid losing benefits, the only possible protest strategies are to fail to comply—to the extent possible—with objectionable program practices or staff behaviors (Hasenfeld & Weaver, 1996).

The limited knowledge and/or capacity of many clients to engage in autonomous decision making places a particular ethical obligation on the social worker to help them make reasoned choices so that they can maximize their benefits, even with unrealistic goals. In the final analysis, however, the center of gravity in the helping process remains with the professional. As Rothman stated, "The prime responsibility for making professional decisions about means of helping the client falls to the practitioners" (1989, p.608).

AMBIGUITY AND UNCERTAINTY

The degree of ambiguity and uncertainty encountered in practice situations can increase the probability of ethical dilemmas. Professional decisions to ignore or countermand client rights in order to assure a higher value, such as the protection of life, depend on the information available. Three types of ambiguity and uncertainty make for ethical problems in social work practice: (1) uncertainty about values and goals, (2) uncertainty about scientific knowledge and about the facts relevant to any specific situation, and (3) uncertainty about the consequences of the intervention.

These uncertainties occur in a world characterized by a general disillusionment with authority. The previously infallible guides and granite virtues have been discarded. Even faith in science and progress, characteristic of the belief system of previous generations, has been replaced by a pervasive sense of uncertainty. For many, the pursuit of personal happiness and individual fulfillment has become more important than following imperatives. It has become more and more difficult to know what is right. As a result, some have suggested that right is whatever one thinks is good. Even those who accept this approach, however, find that they must cope with ambiguity and uncertainty, just as their colleagues have to do who are still searching for ethical imperatives relevant to modern society.

Ambiguity may be more critical a problem for social workers than for many other professional practitioners. The reasons for this include the following:

1. The issues with which social workers deal are often nonspecific.
2. Social workers generally have less control over the outcome of their intervention than do practitioners in many other professional fields.

So many different factors impinge simultaneously on a person that it is often difficult for a social worker to assess the specific impact of her intervention. An unsuccessful outcome may be (but need not be) due to something that the social worker did or did not do. The same intervention activity in two seemingly identical problem situations may lead to two entirely different outcomes because of factors over which the social worker has no control. Nor will any member of any profession ever know what might have happened had she not intervened or used a different strategy.

For example, in a case of suspected child abuse, a social worker cannot predict with certainty what will happen if the child continues to stay with his parents, nor will the worker know for certain what might happen if the child is forcibly removed. Similarly, no social worker can predict with any accuracy whether helping a neighborhood council obtain a grant for restoring dilapidated houses is the best or the worst help that she can offer.

One such situation with many ambiguities is explored in Exemplar 6.5.

❖ 6.5 A Victim of Child Abuse

Several months ago, Ms. Gillis told her public welfare social worker that she suspected that an upstairs neighbor, Mr. Hill, regularly and brutally beat his two-year-old son, Leroy. She heard the most frightful noises several evenings each week. When she saw the boy at rare intervals, he always wore bandages and looked so sad. The worker noted these remarks in her case report, but took no further action.

Last month, Mrs. Hill brought Leroy to Lakeside General Hospital emergency room. Leroy suffered from multiple fractures, which according to his mother, occurred when he fell down the front stairs. The attending physician did not believe her story since the X ray revealed a large number of previous fractures in addition to the current ones. As required by law, he notified the public welfare department that he suspected child abuse.

Andre Conti, an experienced child protection social worker, was sent to the Hill home to investigate. He talked at length with both parents. They admitted beating Leroy occasionally when he misbehaved. This, they explained, was their way of disciplining him. Mr. Conti suggested that there were other ways to teach a boy to behave properly but concluded that the boy was in no immediate danger. Two weeks later, another social worker made a follow-up visit to the Hill home. This worker, Millie Walker, agreed with Mr. Conti's assessment that for the time being there was no need to remove Leroy from his home.

Ten days after Ms. Walker's visit, Mrs. Hill called for an ambulance, saying that her son was having difficulty breathing. When the ambulance crew arrived, they found Leroy unconscious. Twelve hours after he was brought to the hospital, he was pronounced dead. He had not recovered consciousness. The postmortem confirmed that death was caused by a severe beating with a blunt instrument.

This exemplar gives rise to a number of questions with ethical implications, including the following: Did Ms. Gillis's social worker pay sufficient attention to the report of child abuse? Are a neighbor's suspicions sufficient cause to warrant interfering in the Hill family? How can Mr. Conti or any social worker know for certain that "a clear and present danger" exists for Leroy's life? When does parental discipline become child abuse? Under what conditions is the removal of a child from his family justified? How certain must a social worker be of the consequences before deciding to leave an endangered child with his family?

It should be noted that there are three sets of ambiguities in the Leroy Hill exemplar: (1) ambiguities resulting from a lack of clarity of societal norms (e.g., What are the limits of parental discipline?), (2) ambiguities resulting from a lack of knowledge (e.g., What evidence is sufficient to warrant intervention?), and (3) ambiguities resulting from an inability to know what the future will bring (e.g., What will be the consequences of intervention?). The social workers involved in this case made professional judgments that Leroy was not at risk. As a consequence of their mistaken judgment, Leroy is now dead. The mistake could also have gone the other way—identifying a risk when there is no danger to the child's welfare and thus removing the boy from his home needlessly. Every social worker in this situation faces a critical ethical dilemma because both types of mistakes cannot be avoided at the same time. Ambiguities and uncertainties are endemic conditions in social work practice. Neither the social worker, nor anyone else, can know for certain that a given parental behavior will lead to the child's death. The test of an effective social worker is that she should retain the ability to function even while coping with the ethical dilemmas that result from ambiguity and uncertainty.

EXERCISES

1. Role-play the situation described earlier in this chapter where the social worker has determined that her older adult client is no longer able to live alone in his home. We know that this client responds negatively to every worker suggestion. Try various approaches to this problem situation. Keep in mind the ethical aspects.
2. Rothman (1989) and others have stated that the primary responsibility for making professional decisions falls on the social work practitioner. On the other hand, many social workers argue that the client has the

exclusive right to make decisions about his life. Organize a debate around these two professional positions.

3. Assume that you are the child protection social worker sent to investigate the report of Leroy Hill's abuse (Exemplar 6.5). What criteria would you use to arrive at a decision to remove or not to remove Leroy from his parental home? Keep in mind the ethical aspects.

4. Review the material in Chapter 5 on informed consent and ways of obtaining consent. How does this material relate to issues of self-determination? If you did the role play suggested in Exercise 1, did the social worker resort to using coercive ways of obtaining consent? How else could she have addressed the issue with the client? Is coerced consent ever appropriate?

SUGGESTIONS FOR ADDITIONAL READINGS

Sasson (2000) examines the dilemmas of social workers regarding beneficence and respect for autonomy with aging persons. How can a social worker encourage self-determination and at the same time take full responsibility for delivering the professional services that the client needs? Freedberg (1989) and Rothman (1989) review the development of the self-determination principle in social work practice and its impact on practitioners. Murdach (1996) reexamines issues of autonomy and self-determination raised by new mandates concerning disabled persons and vulnerable individuals. Bernstein (1993) explores self-determination in group practice. Jayaratne et al. (1997) reported on advice-giving behavior by social workers.

7 CHAPTER | **Value Neutrality and Imposing Values**

In today's world, many scientists try to avoid all questions of values and morals because they are committed to deriving knowledge only from empirical data. One of the traditional expectations of professional social workers is that they not impose their personal values on clients and that they suspend judgment about clients' behavior and actions even when their own values or societal values demand a judgment. In the real world of social work practice, however, things are not always so simple. The *Code of Ethics* (NASW, 1999, Purpose) recognizes that social workers "should be aware of the impact on ethical decision making of their clients' and their own personal values and cultural and religious beliefs and practices. They should be aware of any conflicts between personal and professional values and deal with them responsibly." Crucial professional decisions always involve value choices—if not worker values, then values of clients or of society. Professional decisions "are not simple choices of technical means to ends, and even choices of means have a value component" (Bayles, 1981, p. 67).

VALUE NEUTRALITY

For many years, the practice principle of value neutrality found wide acceptance among social workers. In an attempt to gain scientific credibility, psychotherapy "has moved towards being 'value free'" (Parrott, 1999, p. 1). Some clinicians view the requirement of neutrality as a fundamental clinical and ethical principle (Simon & Gutheil, 1997). One observer suggested that professional practice requires listening to what the client is really saying "without imposing one's own values, beliefs or judgments" (Weick, 1999, p. 331). Several writers, for example, urged social workers who work with pregnant teenagers to maintain a neutral position about the girls' behavior in order for the worker to be really helpful (Cain, 1979; Cervera, 1993). One reason for suspending value judgments, according to many, is that in our pluralistic society there is no longer any absolute right or wrong. What might seem wrong to me will seem right to the next person. What is right today may be wrong tomorrow. Sophie Freud pointed out that even the concept of normality "has become so fuzzy to the point of making the very word *normal* a problematic word. . . . We can no longer agree on our values" (Freud, 1999, p. 338). Do we encourage an elderly couple to divorce or not or a young couple to favor abortion or not?

There also are critical questions about this value-neutral stance that must be considered. Many have asked whether value neutrality or value suspension is a realistic option for social workers. They point out that social workers are human beings, not robots. Turner (2002, p. 61) suggests "it is impossible to interact with another human being . . . without making a series of judgments and observations about them that shape our responses to them." What are they to do with the values they hold when working with clients who hold contrary values? Can they really avoid introducing or imposing their own values by subtle or nonverbal communications?

Even though there are no easy answers, these questions must be considered by every practitioner. Many believe that suspension of judgment, a basic concept in social work, has been so misinterpreted that it has caused rather than prevented much unethical professional behavior. Siporin writes that "in being of help to people, there is need to make moral ethical judgments, and to help clients do so as well" (1985a, p. 202). Goldstein (1998) suggested that social work should not be concerned only with what works (without a moral orientation). For Goldstein, the situations and problems of social work practice present difficult moral dilemmas for social workers, and they have a moral obligation to act as moral agents, not ignoring what is good and ethically correct, what is "right" and "wrong." There is no escaping moral and ethical issues at each step of social work processes. Maslow indicates that a science that is "morally neutral, value free, value neutral is not only wrong, but extremely dangerous" (1969, p. 724).

Value neutrality may actually cause damage in the following situations:

1. Attention is not paid to potentially self-destructive or other destructive acts.
2. Social workers fail to distinguish between what is functional or dysfunctional, normative or pathological behavior.
3. Failing to challenge a client's behavior may result in that client thinking that she approves of what he does. The worker may intend her silence to be an expression of value neutrality, but her silence may be interpreted as a signal of acceptance of that behavior.

Value neutrality is itself a value. Sometimes social workers do not acknowledge their own moral judgments. The contemporary social worker who bases her practice on value neutrality may be evading moral dilemmas through a more complete acceptance of client self-determination. Value suspension became a professional response to the moralistic paternalism of the Friendly Visitors, the volunteers who preceded professional social workers in the last decades of the nineteenth century. Originally, suspension of judgment meant that the social worker related to the whole person and to his strengths, instead of only to his weaknesses and problems. It meant trying to understand this person in terms of his personal history, environment, culture, and community. If the client's behavior was problematic, then the social worker was ready to help him change that behavior without condemning him. This was often expressed by, "I accept you, but not your behavior." More recently this stance has been changed so that now many social workers seem to say, "I love you and your behavior, no matter what you have done." Can we honestly say that we do not care what a client does? Can we accept child molestation, neglect, violence, cheating, stealing, or lying? Dare social workers not condemn physical and sexual abuse, rape and beatings, irresponsible sexual activities, and similar antisocial behaviors?

In today's practice context, social workers have to balance the notion of the client's right to self-determination against being directive. There is more clarity about directiveness or paternalism when clients do not have the capacity to make informed decisions and in the face of potential harm and danger to the client and others. More directiveness by practitioners may be forced by managed care, pressures to maintain agency funding or income, and productivity measures.

Rothman and colleagues (1996) found that social workers, including those using psychodynamic as well as cognitive-behavioral, task-centered, and brief treatment focuses, used a broad range of directiveness modalities in their practices. Although the directiveness modalities they used were influenced by specific contextual factors, they avoided either extreme—paternalism or client self-determination—as their one confirmed practice pattern. However, this flexibility and consistency reflects one of the practical limitations to social worker neutrality, in that it discounts the social worker's ethical and legal responsibility to protect the welfare of clients (Woody, 1990).

As economic factors have assumed greater roles in the practice of social work, practice situations have become increasingly dominated by managed care. Limitations placed on social workers and human service agencies by third-party payers increasingly determine the length of treatment in many settings, in turn placing limits on the self-determination options available to both social worker and client (Reid, 1997).

IMPOSING VALUES

Much of what social workers do involves helping people choose between available options; ethical principles are one important consideration in this choice. Can a social worker provide this help without imposing her values? This question takes on special urgency because social workers often grapple with strategies that are designed to modify or change the beliefs and values of clients.

Some approaches to helping people with problems hold that it is desirable to systematically change their values and thought patterns and substitute more sensible and rational thoughts and values, such as those held by social workers. The rational/emotive therapy (RET) developed by Ellis is one school of therapy that urges this view. The therapist's values always influence client values. For example, RET "shares the views of ethical humanism by *encouraging* people to emphasize human interest (self and social) over the interests of deities, material objects, and lower animals" (Dryden & Ellis, 1988, p. 232, emphasis added). While those following this school suggest that these values be used in a conscious and controlled manner (Frank, 1991), many others disagree with the attempt to impose values.

A social worker may actually impose her own values when she tries to "suspend" value judgments and offer instead a range of value choices. Covert value messages are often more powerful than overt ones. A social worker may define the goals and outcomes of the treatment without once saying what it is that she deems appropriate. How can one ethically justify such unilateral worker control? Some have suggested that an explicit communication of the social worker's values would safeguard the client against any potential misuse of power by the worker (Lewis & Walsh, 1980). Sophie Freud (1999, p. 338) went so far as to suggest "it might even be best to admit our own biases to our clients and engage in honest debates with them. . . . " Such self-disclosure of the worker's values may enhance the client's comfort with and sense of trust in the practitioner. Value self-disclosure may also be harmful when used inappropriately or at the wrong time, especially early in the professional relationship. Doing so may suggest to the client that he then has the "right to know" other personal information and could use personal questions for the social worker as a tactic in order to avoid dealing with his own issues. Spero (1990) and Strean (1997) concluded that any short-term advantages of a worker's value disclosure may be cancelled by long-term harmful effects.

The problem facing the social worker of Bess and Todd Moore illustrates the range of ethical dilemmas around the issue of imposing values.

❖ 7.1 Saving a Marriage

Bess and Todd Moore have agreed to seek help to "rescue" their marriage. Bess recently discovered that Todd has been having sex with several other women over the past few years. Todd has told the social worker that his sexual relations with other women are only physical. Since he has greater sexual needs than Bess, he cannot give up these relations. Yet he loves his wife and wants to continue this marriage. Bess is ready to forgive the past, but cannot bring herself to live with Todd, knowing that at the same time he has sex with other women.

Different social workers hold different values about marriage and extramarital relations. Should the social worker keep her own values to herself so that she will not influence the decision of the Moores? Is this possible? Or should the social worker openly state her own values and then let Bess and Todd work on a solution to their problem? Which is the more ethical approach?

Do social workers have a responsibility to examine together with the client the ethical nature and quality of the problems that people bring to them? Or is it more helpful to overlook the moral aspects of the situation? Society, with near unanimity, condemns child sexual abuse and incest. Should a social worker assume a value-free stance and listen to her client's report of what could be incestuous behavior with the same equanimity as she would to any other problem he may raise? Should she communicate the community's valuation of incest? Does it make a difference whether the abuser or the victim is the worker's client? Are there cultural factors that might make a difference in assessing the ethical implications of this type of behavior? What if the client's ethnic culture does not proscribe father/daughter relations that do not involve penetration? What if the incestuous relations occur between consenting adults?

The three types of behavior (value neutrality, value imposition, client-worker value gap) that have been discussed in this section form a matrix of ethical intensity. The discussion suggests that beyond a certain point most social workers will abandon any attempt to maintain a value-free stance. But the ethical dilemma is more serious than these "unusual" examples suggest because, in fact, ethical quandaries involving the social worker's judgment occur at every step of the social work process. The social worker who "suspends" her judgment when a client relates a promiscuous episode or an aggressive behavior incident may be as judgmental as her colleague who does not hesitate to indicate disapproval. When a client feels guilty about a certain behavior but the worker addresses only the problem of guilt, the client may conclude that the worker considers such behavior acceptable. One psychiatrist summed up this latter point of view when he stated, "I'm a shrink, so I'm more interested in his motivation than his morality" (Lipsyte, 2002, p. 5).

It has been suggested that in these and similar situations a social worker can avoid making judgments by letting the client decide what he wants; whether he wants help with his "guilt" or with the "deviant" behavior. At first glance this appeal to the principle of client self-determination seems to solve all ethical problems. On second thought it may turn out that this is an irresponsible and perhaps even an unethical response to a client who desperately seeks help. Even when the client's request for help is specific, the worker may have a societal responsibility that she dare not shirk. Should a social worker help a client reduce his guilt so he can continue an extramarital affair?

As the population of the United States grows more diverse through changing patterns of immigration, social workers are faced more frequently with behaviors that generally lie outside the experiences of American-born and raised social workers. Consider the following case situation.

❖ 7.2 Loyalty to Self or Family?

Mrs. Arriga, a social worker at a Family Service agency, has seen Ms. Salima, a recent immigrant, for three sessions because she has been depressed and experiencing much conflict at home with her parents and other relatives and much anxiety on her job as a packer. All family members, including Ms. Salima, must work because everyone's paycheck is necessary to maintain a marginal existence. Her supervisor, who likes her, referred her to the agency for help. Ms. Salima told Mrs. Arriga with some ambivalence that her family will not allow her to have a normal American social life. Her parents want to arrange a marriage for her and do not allow her to date. She cannot leave home because her earnings are insufficient to support herself, and her English and other skills are not developed enough for a better job.

Ms. Salima vascillates between love for her family, pride at doing what is expected in her family's culture, and becoming more Americanized by dating and deciding for herself whom she should marry.

What should Mrs. Arriga do? Should she support loyalty to Ms. Salima's family? After all, they are all dependent on each other, and they are her only relatives in the United States. Should she support Ms. Salima's struggle toward more independent values? Is a social life possible other than through dating? If Ms. Salima has the possibility of living with extended family members or friends she knows from her past, should she be encouraged to leave home and live with them? How should a social worker who is a feminist respond to this situation? What if Mrs. Arriga is from the same culture as Ms. Salima's family and is known in their community? Will that make a difference?

It seems that suspension of judgment is an impossible demand. The *Code of Ethics* and social work practice stress self-determination, but doesn't Ms. Salima have some obligation to her family and group? Some try to avoid the ethical dilemma by suggesting to a client that they approve or disapprove only of a specific behavior, but not of the client. This is a fine, almost legalistic distinction that may seem to avoid the ethical issues posed here. Such a solution, however, creates other practice problems and does not really avoid the ethical issues raised. Perhaps a more realistic way of phrasing this ethical obligation is to demand that the social worker's own value judgment, probably reflective of her own American value system, never become the sole criterion for making a decision. There is no relationship that is free of values. At the same time, we must remember that it is the client's responsibility to identify the values that will guide his behavioral choices; the social worker can never assume this responsibility (Franki, 1968).

CLIENT–WORKER VALUE GAP

A significant gap between worker values and those of social work clients is common. For example, the personal value systems of social workers were found to distinguish them from those of the general population. Social workers assign more importance to personal relationships, service to others, and open-mindedness. Social workers' views of the values of the profession also differ from the values of other Americans in the importance they assign to equality (equal opportunity for all), helpfulness (working for the welfare of others), and being broadminded (open-mindedness) (Horner & Whitbeck, 1991). This gap is another potential source for several ethical problems and dilemmas.

In addition, a major discrepancy between the religious beliefs and practices of many clients and the nonreligious values held by many mental health professionals has been noted by Siporin and Glasser (1986), Loewenberg (1988), and Hodge (2002). Hodge, in particular, contrasts the belief in a personal God held by large proportions of the general American population and the large percentages of social workers who reject a belief in a personal God. He points out that Evangelical Christians, Catholics, Religious Jews, Muslims, Mormons, Hindus, and Sikhs among other religious groups hold many different values from the majority of social work practitioners. These issues have become more problematic for social workers since the advent of the war on terrorism.

Practitioners need information about their clients' participation in any religious group. The degree of religiosity and strength of a client's knowledge of, and commitment to, specific religious values can influence the worker's choice of interventions. When sexuality (abortion, adultery, homosexuality, premarital sex) issues arise in therapy, there may be value conflicts between the worker's values and those of the client (Bullis & Harrigan, 1992). These differences in religious values are only one area of value discrepancy, reflective of the discrepancies that exist in many other value areas.

Unless the worker or the client is blinded from recognizing real problems by their common values, shared values may optimize the chances for successful outcomes. Goldstein writes that "the initiation of any substantial relationship (including the helping relationship) depends on the extent to which its members can share, complement, or otherwise resolve their moral differences" (1987, p. 181). Though matching of client and worker values may be desirable, this is not always possible in the world of practice. Various problems can arise when there is a significant client–worker gap, but here our concern will be limited to the ethical aspects of these problems. These relate primarily to the possibility of value imposition when there is a major difference between client and worker values. Because of the power imbalance between client and worker, this ethical problem is often very real.

Typical of the client–worker gap is Exemplar 7.3.

❖ 7.3 A Drug Addict Has a Baby

Jeff Butz, public welfare worker, received a call from the Community Hospital social worker. Mona Koss, a single mother with a drug addiction, gave birth to a baby girl two days ago. Mother and baby are due to be discharged tomorrow, but the hospital social worker does not think that the infant will be safe if she goes home with her mother. As far as is known, Mona Koss has no permanent home. Currently, she shares a bed with a drug pusher who has been involved in the past in physical and sexual abuse situations.

The world of Jeff Butz is as far from Mona Koss's world as the North Pole is from the South Pole. Their values are diametrically opposed. This, incidentally, is a situation in which value matching is neither possible nor desirable. One way for social worker Butz to respond to the telephone call he received is to initiate legal proceedings designed to remove the infant from her mother. This may seem congruent with his own personal values and with what he believes to be societal expectations. Mona Koss, though a drug addict, is also a human being with her own personal values, however, can these be ignored? What is best for the newborn infant? Jeff Butz feels that he should explore these questions with Mona Koss before making any decision.

In this case, as in many others, a client–worker value gap is often unavoidable. Social workers must, therefore, develop ways to deal with these value differences. Some have found the following approach useful:

1. During the intake/assessment/diagnostic stage the social worker should determine if there is a relationship between the value differences and the presenting problem. The marital problem for which Bess and Todd Moore sought help (Exemplar 7.1) may very well be related to value differences between themselves and their social worker.
2. The social worker should discuss her finding with the clients if they are able to participate in determining whether these differences might complicate the social work process. No prior assumption should be made that a client is not ready and able to participate in such joint decision making. Though Mona Koss holds values that are quite different, Butz must not assume that she cannot participate in making decisions for herself and her newborn baby.
3. A joint decision should be made whether to continue the social work process or whether to refer the client to another social worker with more congruent values, if such a worker is available.

Some have suggested that the social worker should always disclose her own values during the first session so that the client can protect himself against overt and covert value imposition. Raines (1996) considered therapist self-disclosure appropriate at the beginning of the treatment process because the therapist should have an underlying ethic of selfless love devoted to the welfare of the client. Routine disclosure of the worker's values too early in the social work process, however, may actually harm clients since they may feel that the worker is challenging their own values even before a working relationship has been established between them (Anderson & Mandell, 1989; Beit-Hallahmi, 1975; Spero, 1990). Strean concluded that such questions should not be answered but turned back to the client to explore underlying anxieties because the problem "in answering personal questions at the beginning of treatment is that the client then has the 'right to know' encores" (1997, p. 366). Goldstein also defended the right of therapists to "feel free to not self-disclose to patients. Therapists and those close to them personally do have rights to their privacy and therapists can have limitations about what they can deal with in the therapeutic process at certain times" (1997, p. 56).

THE INEVITABILITY OF VALUES

In this chapter, we have included sections on value neutrality, the imposition of values, and client–worker value gaps. One must remember that practice should reflect the value principles of the social work profession expressed in the *Code of Ethics.*

Goldstein (1998, p. 246) describes the ethically grounded social worker as "alert and responsive to questions of moral choice, social justice, prevailing moral codes of conduct, and, not the least, personal accountability whether she is doing research, applying theory, planning, or engaging in practice—any professional activity, that impinges on the life and well-being of others."

Ethical decisions by social workers have importance at every level from individual case to social and political action. One means of selecting from the multitude of ethical issues for clients and oneself in practice is through a screening device. Behavior can be considered along a continuum (see Figure 7.1). Knowing where one falls on this continuum can help in deciding when one can anticipate value conflicts.

Situations as described in this chapter may present painful dilemmas for both clients and social workers but—for example—neglect, abuse, and violence also raise questions as to who the social worker represents, whose welfare is at stake, and social worker's roles as moral agents. The *Code of Ethics* states that "social workers should promote the general welfare of society. . . . " (NASW *Code,* 1999, 6.01) and "social workers should act to expand choice and opportunity for all people, with special regard for vulnerable, disadvantaged, oppressed, and exploited people and groups" (NASW *Code,* 1999, 6.04b).

Figure 7.1 | Continuum of Worker Values

| Ethical behaviors—those that the worker believes are *ethically right* (e.g., protecting human life): The worker may find it difficult to work with clients or an agency with opposing values (e.g., an agency that provides adults with information on assisted suicide). | Behaviors that the worker believes are neither inherently right or wrong—those that the worker does not have strong personal values about: The worker could support agency or client values as long as they are not in conflict. | Unethical behaviors— those that the worker believes are *ethically wrong* (e.g., abortion): The worker may find it difficult to work with clients or an agency with opposing values (e.g., a family planning or pro-choice clinic). |

EXERCISES

1. It has been said that even when a social worker does not declare her values publicly, her lifestyle and her nonverbal communications will usually indicate the values that she holds. Identify how your own lifestyle and nonverbal messages will inform a client of the values you hold. What problems might this create for maintaining a professional relationship?

2. The risk of being HIV-positive and contracting AIDS from sexual activities has been compared with the risk of fatal automobile accidents (Gochros, 1988). Does such a comparison communicate a value, or is it an example of value neutrality? Defend your answer.

3. Your client feels very guilty about engaging in certain behavior. Assume that this behavior is not illegal. He asks your help, but he does not specify whether he wants help (1) in dealing with his guilt, or (2) in extinguishing the behavior. Discuss the ethical implications of choosing either approach. Will the specific behavior make a difference in your ethical assessment? Try to assess the two approaches with the following types of behavior: overeating, smoking, gambling, masturbation, eating foods his physician suggested he avoid for medical reasons, having an extramarital affair, or taking the time to work out for an hour five times a week.

4. How would you respond to the telephone call that Jeff Butz received (Exemplar 7.3)?

5. There are social workers who support a person's right to commit suicide or to commit adultery. There may even be others on the "fringe" of the profession who support the right to incest under certain circumstances, use of drugs, and other behaviors. Some persons believe these positions are derived from a value-free approach. Others believe they prove the impossibility of a value-free approach. The question becomes: What values and whose values will prevail? In group discussions, decide which view is right, and identify the implications of each approach for ethical decision making.

SUGGESTIONS FOR ADDITIONAL READINGS

Siporin (1985b) and Goldstein (1998) suggest that the place of values in social work practice is crucial, and social workers have to be moral agents. Simon and Gutheil (1997) defend the duty of neutrality for therapists. Rothman et al. (1996) report on the directiveness of social workers in practice. Jayaratne, Croxton, and Mattison (1997) report social workers' reported behaviors and perceived appropriateness regarding recommending a religious form of healing and giving legal advice other than referral to a lawyer. Raines (1996), Strean (1997), and Goldstein (1997) approach therapist self-disclosure from different perspectives and place quite different limits on it.

8 CHAPTER | Equality, Inequality, Limited Resources, and Advocacy

Every person has an equal right to obtain social benefits and an equal duty to carry social burdens. This principle is based on the first-order societal value of equity (Frankena, 1973; Rawls, 1971). From this societal value, social workers have derived the professional rule that obligates them to distribute available resources on an equal basis to all clients.

COMMITMENT TO EQUALITY

An ethical problem occurs when available resources are so limited that an equal distribution is not possible. For example, when a county has only 20 beds for chronically ill older people, these cannot be distributed on an equal basis to 30 clients who need this service. The equity value may create ethical problems even with respect to goods and services that lend themselves to an equal division (such as the social worker's time or the department's budget), because another rule obligates a practitioner to meet the specific needs of each client.

Time

Time is a very limited and precious resource in the social work process. For example, a social worker in a family agency may be available 30 hours a week for direct service to clients. Is each of her 30 clients entitled to a one-hour interview every week? For some clients, an hour a week may be more than they need, while for others it may not be sufficient. Client Peter Barr needs many hours of counseling this week to help him cope with an unexpected and sudden family crisis, but his social worker can meet this need only if she allots less time to other clients. Is such an unequal division of time ethical? Many treatment strategies are ruled out because sufficient staff time to implement them is not available. Many social workers recall situations when a client could have received more effective service if only there had been more time available. Ethical dilemmas can occur both in regard to fairness (equity) and equality (equally situated persons receiving what is needed). For example, the attempt to observe equity in the allocation of time to clients results in several ethical dilemmas, one of which is illustrated in Exemplar 8.1.

❖ 8.1 Incest in the Schild Family

Doreen Schild is a cute 13 year old with a history of school truancy, alcohol and drug experimentation, and several attempts at running away from home. Her parents appear warm and accepting, but the family agency worker who has been meeting with Doreen for the past four weeks suspects that the real problem is Doreen's home life.

Today was the fifth session with Doreen. The conversation was routine, and little of significance was said until three minutes before the next client's scheduled appointment. Suddenly, Doreen started to relate some very important and emotionally charged material. Both her father and older brother have tried repeatedly to have sexual relations with her, but thus far she has not let them go all the way. When she told her mother about this, she was told to forget it had ever happened. As Doreen related this information, she became noticeably more upset.

The social worker realized that this interview could not be terminated just because time was up now, but how long could she keep the next client waiting? Doreen could easily use all of the next client's hour, but that would not be fair to the other clients scheduled for today. Who knows what difficulties they are dealing with? Furthermore, if Doreen was not exaggerating, immediate arrangements would have to be made to remove her from her home. This might take many additional hours of the worker's time, hours already scheduled for other urgent assignments.

What would you do? What other ethical issues, in addition to the equity issue, does this worker face? What are the social worker's obligations to Doreen? To her parents? To other clients with whom she has appointments scheduled? To the community?

Inequality

Americans have accepted as a self-evident truth that all persons are created equal. From this first-order value, social workers have derived the ethical rules of "equal distribution of resources" and "equal access to opportunities."

Equality is popularly equated with democracy. Those raised in this tradition often find it difficult to understand how some people can raise questions about it. They are upset when it is suggested that an equal distribution of resources is not always ethical and may lead to injustices. Some have asked whether it is right that medical resources, especially scarce and expensive life-extending technologies and instruments, are distributed equally, regardless of a patient's age. Daniel Callahan, a philosopher and medical ethicist, does not seem to think that such an approach is ethical. He writes that medicine should "resist the tendency to provide to the aged life-extending capabilities developed primarily to help younger people avoid premature and untimely death" (1987, p. 24). He suggests that age be used as a decision criterion for allocating life-extending therapies. What does this mean? Does this mean that open-heart surgery should be available only to people under a given age, such as 80? Is not the life of an 84-year-old person as important and valuable as that of a 74-year-old person? Some would argue that the chances of a successful operation decrease rapidly as people grow older. Others avoid this statistical argument by noting that it is preferable to use limited resources to add 20 years of life rather than one or two years. This is particularly so when the younger person can still make a contribution to society, while the aging person may be entirely dependent on the efforts of others. In recent years, a variant of this problem has occurred in the State of Oregon, which uses a prioritized list of health services for its Medicaid program. Services are listed from most important to least important for their comparative benefit to the population served. Health services are thus rationed based on the funds available and the fact one is poor and on Medicaid (Oregon Health Services Commission, 2003).

Deciding for and against the allocation of societal resources on the basis of possible returns gives rise to other serious ethical problems. The social contribution of high-intelligence people may be more valuable than that of people with a lower intelligence and perhaps more significant than that of persons with mental retardation. Does this give society the ethical right to limit open-heart surgery to people whose IQ is above 150? Or above 98? Or to people with a college degree? Or with a certain income? This diabolic argument can be pushed even further by arguing for the "elimination" of all undesirables, a policy implemented by Nazi Germany in the 1940s. While few will maintain that the "final solution" was ethical or moral, the implication of this approach for the unequal distribution of resources demands further careful thought. These examples come from the health field. Have you encountered parallel problems in social work situations?

It is a fact that many social work resources are not distributed equally. There are disparities in mental health care for minorities. According to former Surgeon General David Sacher, members of minority groups suffer disproportionately from mental illness because they often lack access to services, receive lower quality care, and are less likely to seek help when in distress (Goode, 2001). Similarly, when child welfare research was reviewed, it was found that "children of color and their families experience poorer outcomes and receive fewer services than their Caucasian counterparts" (Courtney et al., 1996, p. 99). It is urgent that, wherever such unequal distribution of resources exists, this issue be reexamined and, if necessary, corrected.

The establishment of unequal treatment can be overt but—often—it occurs in social agencies in more subtle and less formal ways. The Exemplar 8.2 illustrates how unequal treatment can take place informally.

❖ 8.2 A Friend in Need Is a Friend Indeed

Latoya Jefferson is a volunteer social worker in an emergency food pantry where persons come to obtain needed food for themselves and their families. The only requirement is that people answer several questions: name, household size, and source of income, not subject to verification. No one asks about living situations (a place to cook, ages of children, or special dietary needs). There are not enough paid staff and volunteers to run the pantry as well as is needed.

Because of the shortage of supplies, families can only receive food once a month. The staff and volunteers get to know individuals and their situations. Ms. Jefferson recently discovered that Keisha Attlee, another volunteer social worker favors some clients over others. She chooses "favorites" who are especially friendly or who have well disciplined and "cute" children with them. She also identifies those who according to her "abuse" the system. When food is in short supply, she refers the "abusers" to another pantry while assisting her "favorites." When Ms. Jefferson complained to Ms. Attlee about her discriminating so that some get needed supplies and others are referred elsewhere, Ms. Attlee replied that "I am a volunteer. In my view I am giving food to those who are most needy and cooperative. Aren't they entitled to the help? Because they have it 'together' I know they will make good use of the food. Those I refer elsewhere may be selling the food and buying beer and whiskey. Furthermore, as a volunteer I don't want to be 'supervised.' If you keep bothering me, I will just leave and you can do the job."

What should Ms. Jefferson do? If she "bothers" Ms. Attlee, the pantry loses a volunteer worker when they are short of staff. Do the "abusers" actually misuse the food? Does it make a difference if they do so? If she keeps quiet, some families receive supplies while others don't. As it is now, who gets food often depends on who the volunteer is and only the "luck of the draw" determines who gets what.

As noted in Chapter 4, there is another side to inequality. Those who are not equal should receive special (and therefore "unequal") help (both services and resources) in order to gain equal access to life opportunities. It is this consideration that often justifies the unequal allocation of resources. Children with disabilities, for example, may receive more attention and greater resources than other children in order to compensate for disabilities. A blind child will not have the same access to education as a sighted child unless we provide the blind child with extra resources, including talking books and/or a reader.

RACISM

Despite the efforts of many social workers and other citizens, racism contin-ues to exist in America. In what has become increasingly a multiracial, multi-ethnic society, competition for various resources undoubtedly exacerbates conflicts between groups, especially during times of recession, economic changes, and increased international economic competition.

For social workers, racism is a societal problem that directly affects their practice, the availability of resources, and the delivery of social services. A content analysis of social work articles on Asian Americans, African Americans, Latinos, and Native Americans published in the 1980s found that most of the literature on social work practice and minorities "portrays the social work profession as naive and superficial in its antiracist practice" (McMahon & Allen-Meares, 1992, p. 537). According to the authors, minor-ity clients are viewed out of the racist context in which they live, proposed changes have to do with changes in the awareness of social workers, and the literature seems to accept the status quo by focusing on individual change. More recently, a large number of social work texts contained no chapters on multicultural issues or paid minimal attention to African Americans, Latinos, Asian Americans, and Native Americans. These trends have continued (Court-ney et al., 1996; Lum, 2000).

Social workers must do more than they are doing now to prevent and oppose racism. Racism is inconsistent with the ethical standards of the pro-fession, and social workers cannot achieve their aims where racism interferes. The ethical principles enunciated in the NASW *Code of Ethics* (1999) call on social workers "to help people in need and to address social problems," to "pursue social change, particularly with and on behalf of vulnerable and oppressed individuals and groups of people," to be "mindful of individual dif-ferences and cultural and ethnic diversity," and to "promote, restore, main-tain, and enhance the well-being of individuals, families, social groups, organ-izations, and communities." There is a whole range of activities that are necessary, ranging from individual interactions to confrontation of institu-tional and societal racism. Indicative of such efforts are those of the Council on Social Work Education over several decades to minimize racism and sex-ism in Schools of Social Work (Trolander, 1997) and the efforts of all schools to become antiracist institutions.

Some have suggested that one must differentiate between the individual social worker's obligation to fight racism and the obligation of the profession to fight racism. These two aspects are interrelated, but they are not the same (Bayles, 1981). The *Code of Ethics* makes explicit its ethical stance toward racism when it states "social workers should not practice, condone, facilitate, or collaborate with any form of discrimination on the basis of race, ethnicity, national origin, color, sex, sexual orientation, age, marital status, political belief, religion, or mental or physical disability" (*Code,* 1999, 4.02) and "Social workers should act to prevent and eliminate . . . discrimination against any person, group, or class on the basis of race, ethnicity, national origin, color, sex, sexual orientation, age, marital status, political belief, religion, or mental or physical disability" (*Code,* 1999, 6.04d).

Individual social workers have an ethical responsibility to work toward the elimination of discrimination in their practice, employment, and in society. Also, the National Association of Social Workers and other social work professional organizations have responsibilities to eliminate racial and other discriminations through advocacy, social action, legal, and other efforts within their organizations and in society. Racism in society and the profession makes it difficult to achieve social work's goals and ethical aims of equal access—equitable services and resources—for the fulfillment of individuals and the society.

Earlier in this chapter, we reviewed reports that suggest discrimination exists in mental health and child welfare. To the extent that these conclusions are warranted, there is the suggestion that some social workers have been guilty of serious ethical breaches. Even though they did not necessarily engage in deliberate unethical activities, their behavior was unethical when they remained silent in the face of systematic institutional racism. The single child welfare worker may not have been able to change the entire system, but this is hardly an acceptable excuse to avoid attempts to change as much of one's local system as possible. What are the ethical obligations of social workers who encounter such ethics violations by systems or institutions? As background, see the NASW *Code of Ethics* (1999, 3.07b, 3.09d, 4.02, and 6.04).

Dilemmas about race and racism occur in different situations, not always as serious as the system problems in child welfare and mental health previously noted. For example, what should be done in the following situation?

❖ 8.3 Al Tabrizzi Makes a Racist Comment

You are a clinical social worker seeing Al Tabrizzi, an elderly, somewhat irrational, and very depressed client in a family service agency. This client has been making progress on dealing with a number of tasks—getting out of his apartment, seeking social life, improving his eating habits, and taking care of his affairs—but he has much further to go. Often he has spoken to you about how comfortable he feels with you as his worker and how he has been growing more trustful of your relationship because you have been so fully accepting of him and not judging him. In today's session, he has made racist comments about Latinos.

Mr. Tabrizzi is "somewhat" irrational and clinically depressed. Is this the first time he has made such comments? How much control does he have over his remarks at this point? Are these slurs related to situational events or a sign of his failing health? If he is aware of his comments, he may be reflecting the culture in which he has lived his entire life, or he may be testing you. In that case, should you confront him about his slurs directed at another group? If his remarks are the result of physical problems, should you ignore them? Would it make a difference if you are a Latino social worker? Why or why not? Does the *Code of Ethics* require questioning racism in all circumstances? How much change is Mr. Tabrizzi able to make in his values and behaviors? What is the ethical thing to do? What if the person making these remarks was a co-worker, your supervisor, or a friend? Would you still respond in the same way as you would with Mr. Tabrizzi?

Should your response change if it is an agency issue? For example, what do you do if you are on the staff of a training program for young adults whose funding will be cut unless the program serves both White and African American persons? At present few Whites are enrolled. In order to meet the demands of the funding agency, the staff is making strenuous efforts to recruit qualified White applicants, even though there is a waiting list of qualified African American candidates. In these circumstances, should you condone giving preference to Whites? Is this ethical? Weigh the alternatives. If you report the situation publicly, the program will lose its major funding base. If you do not serve more White young adults, funding will stop, and no one—neither White nor African American young adults—will receive the service they now receive. If you do comply and recruit more White participants, the result will be that the program will serve fewer African American young adults. What is the ethical thing to do?

LIMITED RESOURCES

The ethical problems resulting from the equality-and-inequality rule are often aggravated by limited resources. If they were unlimited, there would be no problem in providing all persons with the help they need. In the real world, there are never enough resources for everything that should be done. Life is like a zero-sum game. Allocating a scarce resource to one person means that another will not receive it. The concept of limited resources, however, may be a manipulation of language used to conceal certain decisions. Often it may mean that available resources have been allocated elsewhere or that commitments or priorities have been shifted. For example, at the beginning of the 1960s, decision makers in Washington decided to give highest priority to landing a person on the moon by 1970, no matter what the cost. While there undoubtedly was a great deal of waste and even loss of life in pursuing this goal, the first astronaut did land on the moon in the summer of 1969. More recently, tax cuts and the "war on terrorism" have become top priorities. The successful moon landing was made possible and success in the war on terrorism will come only by assigning a lower priority and by making fewer resources available to other important programs, including social programs to eradicate poverty, eliminate discrimination, and improve Medicare. In other words, even while overall societal resources are limited, it is possible to assign vast resources to one particular program if such a policy decision is made at the highest level and if there is a wide consensus that this program deserves the highest priority, even at the expense of limiting allocations for other important projects.

If this is the meaning of limited resources, the focus of ethical decision making shifts from the micro to the macro, from the specific case to societal allocations. On one level, the ethical problem facing the social work practitioner will be how to allocate the resources she controls. On another level, the profession as an organized group, as well as individual social workers as citizens, has an ethical responsibility to become involved in the societal allocation process, that is, the political process. For example, home health care, a major segment of community-based long-term care, is especially important for frail elderly persons. When budgets for this program are cut back because of soaring costs, many of these elderly people are pushed into nursing homes and hospitals, even though this type of care creates unnecessary dependency and is more costly. Social workers have a responsibility on ethical and other grounds to advocate for continued home health care services (Beder, 1998).

Much of what social workers can and cannot do is determined by political decision makers. When the legislature passes budgets, it determines to a large extent the resources available both for public and voluntary agencies and institutions. Other political decisions have a major impact on the nation's economic health, rate of economic growth, availability of jobs, and so forth. Are social workers merely passive observers of these political processes? Or is there an "ethic of responsibility" that obligates social workers to take an active part in these societal processes?

We agree with Siporin (1985b) and Goldstein (1998) that social workers are moral agents who have a responsibility to influence organizations and communities. Priorities and commitments determine resource allocations. Significant resources have been allocated to drug "wars" and rehabilitation programs, while considerably less money has been allocated to solve the problems of the homeless. What are the ethical implications of such decisions?

Ethical Problems in Allocating Limited Resources

Many allocation decisions are made at the highest political level in Washington or at a state capitol, settings in which most social workers do not feel at home. However, at other times such decisions are made much closer to home. Consider the decision facing the social workers of the Centro Latino, a United Way agency in Westport, a community that has always had a large concentration of Spanish-speaking immigrants. Centro Latino was started as an indigenous self-help group in the 1960s by immigrants from Latin America. Today, its budget is met largely by the United Way and supplemented at times by specific state and federal grants. Though volunteers are still used, most assignments are now handled by professional staff members. The decision-making powers are vested in the agency's board of directors, made up largely of veteran Spanish-speaking residents of the community. At a recent staff meeting, the staff discussed an issue (Exemplar 8.4) that many felt had ethical implications.

❖ 8.4 Refugees in Westport

Early last year, more than 400 new Central American refugee families arrived in Westport. Centro Latino was able to generate a special one-time $100,000 grant to help in the adjustment of these refugees. The board of directors decided after lengthy discussion to allocate 20% of this grant to employ two more part-time social workers and to distribute the remaining funds directly to families to help them in their adjustment. The detailed rules for distributing these funds were to be developed by the agency's staff.

The current staff meeting was devoted to developing criteria for distributing the funds. The agency's director, Sandra Lopez, argued that equity demanded that each of the families receive an equal cash grant of approximately $190, which each family could use as it wished. Several staff members agreed with Ms. Lopez. But others urged that the limited funds be used where they could do the most good. Since the basic needs of these families were already met, the new monies should be earmarked for special needs where an intensive use of resources could best achieve the desired objective. Each staff group believed that its proposal was supported by the professional ethics code.

If you had been participating in this staff meeting, which position would you have supported? Look at the NASW *Code of Ethics*. Do you find guidance there for your proposal? Following your review of the *Code*, look at the ethical principles screen in Chapter 4. What ethical considerations, including those of equity and equality, should be weighed before making a decision? What would you say is the ethically correct decision? Why?

ETHICAL DILEMMAS IN ADVOCACY

The NASW *Code of Ethics* supports the obligation of social workers to "advocate for living conditions conducive to the fulfillment of basic human needs and . . . promote social, economic, political, and cultural values and institutions that are compatible with the realization of social justice" (NASW *Code*, 6.01). A social work advocate "identifies with the plight of the disadvantaged. He sees as his primary responsibility the tough-minded and partisan representation of their interests, and this supersedes his fealty to others" (Brager, 1968, p. 6). The objective on a case level is to intervene to obtain a needed resource or service for individuals, or on a class level to alter the environment through social policy change or concessions from resistant or unresponsive systems (Mickelson, 1995).

The Ethical Principle of Equality and Inequality provides the ethical justification for engaging in the advocacy role. Empowerment techniques are necessary in order to give deprived groups and individuals a chance for equal access to life opportunities. However, this ethical justification does not mean that social worker advocates can avoid all ethical dilemmas. Suppose there is only one bed available in the only home for the senior citizens in your community. Your client needs to enter this institution because he no longer can cope at home. You also know that there are other elderly people (not your clients) whose situation is even more desperate. Should you become an aggressive partisan on behalf of your client, knowing that, if you are successful, his admission will be at the expense of other people who need this service? Should you advocate his admission even if you are fairly sure that your success will cause irreversible harm to others? How do the "who is your client" considerations discussed in earlier chapters affect your decision? In what other ways can you meet your ethical obligation to all the elderly persons who need this service?

Another ethical dilemma a social worker advocate may encounter is illustrated by Exemplar 8.5.

❖ 8.5 No Winter Clothing

Three children in a family receiving public aid are sent home from school because they are not adequately dressed. There is no money available at home because their mother has used every last cent she has to pay off more pressing bills. You, the family's social worker, have no emergency funds available for such purposes.

What should you do? Should you become an advocate to press for institutional changes, such as more adequate public welfare allowances or special clothing allowances? Should you mobilize your volunteer network to locate suitable clothing donations so that the children can return to school as quickly as possible, or should you do both?

What are the ethical implications of causing short-run harm to your client (by ignoring a client's request for immediate help) in order to gain an uncertain ultimate benefit? This situation is complicated by the fact that in one strategy the cost is certain (not attending school), while the benefit is uncertain but possibly would help many people (modification of policy). The immediate strategy may result in early benefits for your clients, but other children most probably will face the same problem sooner or later.

Social worker advocates will encounter many ethical problems when their practice role is not fully supported by the employing agency. The case of the Apple Hill Young Adult Social Club (Exemplar 10.7) provides one example of this problem. Exemplar 8.6 provides another illustration.

❖ 8.6 Traffic in Shady Hill

Shady Hill was a quiet residential neighborhood until last year, when a new expressway exit brought a great amount of traffic onto its streets. As a result, there are now several very dangerous intersections. Last month, three children on their way to school were seriously injured crossing one of these intersections.

Parents and neighborhood residents are enraged and have demanded that the city close the exit or put up traffic lights. A meeting with the mayor has led to no results.

Lou Seward is the neighborhood worker who for the past two years has been staffing the Shady Hill Neighborhood Council. Since his arrival, the council has undertaken several projects to improve the quality of life in the neighborhood. Everyone has been happy with what these projects have achieved. Since the current problem has become acute, Seward has helped council officers organize a coalition of all neighborhood groups interested in the problem, including the PTA, churches, and fraternal organizations.

At last night's meeting of the coalition, it was agreed that ways must be found to put additional pressure on City Hall. It was decided to call a news conference tomorrow morning in order to announce that a protest rally would be held across the street from City Hall next Monday afternoon. If no positive response is received, the residents plan to block the exit the following week. Seward participated in last night's meeting by raising a number of questions, encouraging the group, and by providing technical information and advice.

In this morning's conference with his supervisor, Seward reviewed the Shady Hill situation to see if there were additional ways he could be helpful. His supervisor thought that Seward had not done enough to calm the neighborhood. Though the problem demanded attention, his supervisor did not think that an aggressive conflict strategy was helpful. He and the agency expected Seward to use his influence to keep the neighborhood quiet. That, after all, was the major reason why the city allocated monies to this department. The message was clear and so was the problem.

To whom does Lou Seward owe loyalty? To the Neighborhood Council that has successfully improved life in the neighborhood? To his supervisor and the agency? (After all, they have been in the neighborhood and accomplished much good and will still be there after he leaves.) To himself as a professional who wants to place service to clients as his highest priority or to himself as a social worker who wants to retain his job?

EXERCISES

1. What would you do if you were the neighborhood worker in Shady Hill (Exemplar 8.6)? What are the ethical problems this neighborhood worker faces? How would you resolve them? Do you think that the supervisor's comments are in accord with the *Code of Ethics*? What are the supervisor's ethical dilemmas, and what would you do if you were the agency director?

2. The director of a drug addiction rehabilitation program faces a difficult budget allocation decision. He has sufficient budget to mount only one

of the two programs his agency would like to offer. Program A is geared to elementary school students. It will serve 500 children from some of the city's most troubled neighborhoods. Past experience has shown that without such a program 200 children will be addicted by the time they are 16 years old. With such a program, it is expected that no more than 50 will become addicted. Program B focuses on the rehabilitation of adolescent drug addicts. Fifty teens can be served each year. The success rate of this program is 60 percent. What ethical considerations should the director examine? What ethical rules and ethical principles can he use to help him make a decision? How does the availability of the outcome data provided affect the decision-making process?

3. The East Side Neighborhood Council has received a small grant to mount an educational program for Central American refugees now settling in large numbers on the East Side. The board is considering two projects: one would fund supplementary classes in local schools, the other would establish English classes for adult refugees. There is a need for both projects, but there is barely enough money to mount one. What ethical considerations should the board members keep in mind? Does the social worker who staffs the board have a responsibility to acquaint board members with the relevant professional ethics? Suggest ways this social worker can reach an ethically correct decision.

4. The racist situations described earlier in this chapter in Exemplar 8.3 and by Courtney et al. (1996) are situated at direct practice and organizational levels in social work practice. What would you do in these cases?

SUGGESTIONS FOR ADDITIONAL READINGS

Schools of Social Work and the Council on Social Work Education (Trolander, 1997) have made strenuous efforts to eradicate racism in individual schools and in social work education. See Basham, Donner, Killough, and Rozas (1997) who describe the efforts and process by which the Smith College School of Social Work moved to become an antiracist institution. McMahon and Allen-Meares (1992) use publication as an advocacy technique in regard to antiracist practice. Courtney and colleagues (1996) report on discrimination in child welfare and its effects. Robert Sunley (1997) describes advocacy required of social workers in an era of managed care.

9 CHAPTER | The Professional Relationship: Limits, Dilemmas, and Problems

Social work practice is based on the relationships between social workers and clients, and these relationships—in turn—require trust, an essential element. Trust is an interactional phenomenon, and helping relationships require that the client be able to trust the social worker and, often, that the social worker trust the clients. For the client, as Pellegrino (1991, p. 69) suggests, "to trust is to become vulnerable and dependent on the good will and motivations of those we trust." Going to a social worker or other professional for help requires an act of faith that the professional will act morally, will perform professional functions competently, and will be concerned about the problems the client brings to the situation.

The client is dependent upon the prudence of the professional. In order for the client to receive any service, it is often necessary that he remove the protective cover and privacy that he normally uses. The client does so with the expectation that the professional will use her good judgment and skill for the client's good.

The "relationship between the professional and the client is a professional relationship. The client trusts the professional and entrusts himself or herself—not just his or her possessions to the professional" (Sokolowski, 1991, p. 31). The professional presents herself as trustworthy because she is certified as a professional, and she is obligated both to the client and to the profession. In turn, clients actually place their trust in the reputation of the employing agency. For example, we don't check out personally every airplane pilot or railroad engineer with whom we travel. We depend on the employer to select qualified professionals. Similarly, we trust that our vulnerability will not be exploited by the professional for her own purposes such as power, profit, or pleasure.

The social work professional's relationship with the client assumes special duties that arise because of the trust or confidence the client places in the social worker. The professional also has special knowledge and powers that can dominate and influence the client as a result of the relationship. As a result, the social worker must act in the best interest of the client and not take advantage of the client to promote her own interests. Several important concepts derive from the professional relationship. The professional role introduces a power imbalance—a relationship in which the client has certain needs and the social worker has various powers. The confidentiality and informed consent obligations are intended to prevent the abuse of power by the professional agent. Social worker honesty is required to build trust, which is integral to the relationship. It is important for social workers to recognize the ethical nature of the professional relationship and the limits it places on social workers in their dealings with clients—ethical duties that are reflected in the *Code of Ethics* and can lead to conflicts of interest (Kutchins, 1991).

Many social workers assume clients trust them as well as the agencies that employ them, although there is an *ethos* of distrust of professionals and of many social agencies. Many people are cautious about placing their trust in professionals, including social workers. Trust, while necessary, is not enforceable. Clients cannot be made to trust a worker or a social agency even when they have no choice about the service they need. It is also true that social workers cannot be forced to trust clients, even when practice theory demands they do so.

Until recently, the lack of trust in clients was an individual worker's ethical problem just as the client's lack of trust in a worker was that worker's problem alone. Today, the caution of clients may reflect not only their own questions but also the skepticism and climate of distrust found throughout society. Several additional factors have affected the trust relationship, including deprofessionalization, and democratization and the rights revolution.

Deprofessionalization

The advent of managed care and privatization of health and mental health services, where specialized skills and professional judgment are required, has tended to deprofessionalize or undermine the professional authority and powers of clinicians and others by limiting their control over treatment choices, instituting productivity reporting systems that intrude upon professional decision making, and skewing treatment choices and options (Dumont, 1996). Clients do not know who is making decisions—the clinician or someone at the insurance company.

Democratization and the Rights Revolution

The consumer rights revolution is part of the civil rights movement and legislation, the development of self-help organizations, demedicalization and self-care, deinstitutionalization of the mentally ill population, and the independent living movement of physically disabled people (Tower, 1994). These consumer movements often criticized professionals. Two aspects of these criticisms are (1) a desire by consumers to affect the quality of services they receive and (2) their desire to participate in gaining some control over standards by exerting political power. Previously, human service systems and professionals were less accountable to clients and could more easily hide errors. As a result of the rights revolution, professionals are now charged to explain to clients how they can help, how long it will take, and what the expected outcomes will be of their services. Decisions and notes previously not shared with clients are now open to inspection by clients and others. These changes empower clients and democratize to a greater extent the delivery of services.

For every change, however, there is a cost. The question is how this greater accountability affects the client, the worker, or the effectiveness of the helping system. These accountability systems are interpreted by many professionals as indicating a lack of trust in their judgment, while the social worker's caution about what to place in a record and hesitation about opening records may be viewed by clients as a lack of trust. Furthermore, because of managed care, social workers often cannot make decisions about what services they can provide, thus conveying to the client the existence of a hidden, unapproachable, and unaccountable presence affecting his life.

LIMITS OF THE PROFESSIONAL RELATIONSHIP

The client-social worker relationship is not a primary relationship. Primary relationships, especially those within the family or between friends, have few limits. The professional relationship, on the other hand, is focused on a problem for which help is sought. The professional assumes responsibility for helping the client with his problem(s). Traditionally, the relationship terminates once these objectives have been achieved. It is a limited relationship in contrast to the broad primary relations most people treasure.

We will not explore here the practice problems that occur because many clients misunderstand the friendliness and informality that characterize their contacts with a social worker. These practice problems arise because most people have become accustomed to a greater degree of formality, impersonality, and even indifference from their previous contacts with other professional practitioners. We will focus instead on the ethical problems and dilemmas that social workers face because of their commitment to certain values within the professional relationship.

One of the major causes for ethical problems in this area arises whenever a social worker determines that the help a client needs requires a relationship that goes beyond what the traditional definition of the limited professional relationship allows. As the discussion in this chapter will show, however, this is only one cause; there are others that create equally perplexing ethical dilemmas.

Anomie is a core problem in the contemporary world. Many people have become rootless; they have lost all connections with their personal roots, as well as with their fellow human beings. The psychosocial symptoms reflecting anomie are well known and need not be repeated here. Practitioners realize that often they treat only these symptoms without resolving the core problem. In order to strike at the roots of the problem, it is necessary to establish or reestablish more meaningful interpersonal relationships. Some have suggested that the social worker-client relationship serve as a model for this more meaningful relationship. How can a client learn a new interaction pattern if the limited professional connection does not permit the social worker to fully invest in this relationship?

Some social workers hide behind the limited professional relationship because they are uncomfortable with their clients' lifestyles and cultures. Many more social workers want to identify with their clients by expressing empathy with their fate. Without wanting to imitate a lifestyle not authentic for them, they want to learn about and participate more fully in their clients' lives. They know that they cannot be effective and helpful without such knowledge. This type of relationship cannot be limited to the 9 A.M. to 5 P.M., Monday-through-Friday workweek. The conscientious social worker often is not entirely clear about what the correct professional conduct is. Is it ethical for a social worker to accept an invitation for Sunday dinner in the client's home or to join the client on Friday evening in the local bar? May a social worker reciprocate and invite a client for supper at her home or in a restaurant? Is it appropriate for a social worker who wants to learn about a particular culture to accept an invitation from a client to explore the client's ethnic neighborhood with him so as to understand better the culture from which he has come? Practice wisdom has given fairly clear and generally negative answers to all of these questions, but increasingly, social workers express discomfort with the barriers erected between them and their clients.

Though the relationship is supposed to be a limited one, social workers often have an emotional reaction to their clients. Such feelings may be natural, but the consequent worker behavior may cause ethical problems. When a worker's own needs become entangled with the professional relationship, emotional feelings may become destructive. In such situations, the social worker may lose her sense of objectivity; instead of helping the client, she may cause harm.

CLIENT INTERESTS VERSUS WORKER INTERESTS

Giving priority to a client's interests is one of the cornerstones of every professional code of ethics. The *Code of Ethics* expresses this professional obligation as follows: "Commitment to Clients: Social workers' primary responsibility is to promote the well-being of clients. In general, clients' interests are primary. However, social workers' responsibility to the larger society or specific legal obligations may on limited occasions supersede the loyalty owed clients. . . . " (NASW *Code*, 1999, 1.01).

This ethical rule is meant to safeguard the client from exploitation, since most clients can neither control nor evaluate practitioner activities. Unnecessary treatment is one widely known violation of this ethical principle, but some members of every profession have at one time or another ignored this rule by placing their own interests ahead of those of their clients. From time to time, professionals (psychiatrists, social workers, and others) as well as social agencies and institutions are charged with unnecessarily extending the period of service or providing uncustomary services for financial or other reasons. Some hold that this is hardly an ethical problem for the majority of social workers who are employed by social agencies since they do not gain any economic advantage by ignoring this ethical rule. Perhaps an occasional social worker in private practice may be tempted to place financial gain above client interests, but do agency-employed social workers face this dilemma? However, this problem touches every social worker when the issue is self-preservation and survival, rather than financial gain. Must a social worker give priority to client interests, even when this may result in physical injury to the worker or her family? Do considerations of self-preservation and survival legitimize actions that ordinarily might be considered unethical?

There are other ethical dilemmas of this kind that do not involve a threat to life. A social worker is in the middle of preparing supper for her family when she receives an emergency call for help from one of her clients. Should she drop everything and rush out to help her client, even if this means that her family will once again have a cold supper? Another social worker has a very important date whom she is to meet within the hour when she is notified that one of "her" foster children has run away. What should she do? What is the ethical thing to do?

Gewirth's Principle of Generic Consistency may be helpful when considering these problems. He stated, "Act in accord with the generic right of your recipients (that is your clients) *as well as yourself*" (1978, p. 135, emphasis added). Gewirth suggests that there is no need for the worker to abdicate the right to her own welfare, even when this right conflicts with the client's right to professional services. Since Gewirth's principle was not developed to guide professional activities, some people argue that it does not apply to professional practitioners. Instead, they hold that a professional should always be guided by the ethical obligation to give priority to a client's interests, no matter what the consequences to herself.

Those who would follow Gewirth's lead must consider whether ethics are relative. Do ethical obligations change according to their consequences? What must be the degree of potential harm before it is permissible to disregard the ethical rule that demands giving priority to a client's interests? Must social workers serve their clients' interests at all times, regardless of the consequences? Is it ethical for them to declare that under certain unusual circumstances the professional obligation to serve their clients' interests is no longer primary? How did you respond to Exemplar 1.3, where the social worker is asked to leave her family in a potentially dangerous situation so she can respond to clients' needs? Would you still give the same response now? Consider Diggs's observation that "there is an important difference between interpreting a rule or violating it in *special circumstances,* and deciding each individual case just as if there were no rules" (1970, p. 267). This formulation permits retention of the client-priority ethical rule except in special circumstances, such as when the life of the worker is threatened. In such a case, complete allegiance to the rule (client's interests above all) would be unrealistic and unwise.

In the next section, we will examine issues related to dual role relationships. Please keep in mind there are differences between conflicts of interest and dual roles. A conflict of interest occurs when a social worker advances her own interests or the interests of others in ways detrimental to clients' or others' interests. The *Code* (NASW, 1.06 b) cautions against taking unfair advantage of any professional relationship to exploit others in order to further one's personal, religious, political, or business interests. Of course, dual-role relationships do not have to be exploitive and conflicts of interest.

DUAL ROLES WITHIN
THE PROFESSIONAL RELATIONSHIP

Professionals may fill more than one role concurrently or in serial fashion with clients. It is possible that a social worker, because of the nature of the community in which she resides and practices, may have social, business, financial, religious, or other roles in addition to her professional role with a client. While this possibility may be minimized in large urban areas, those who practice in smaller towns and rural areas may encounter the problem more frequently, as may those in particular smaller subcommunities such as religious, political, sexual orientation, and new immigrant groups. Here are some examples of dual-role relationships:

1. You discover that your client Bertha Martins is your dentist's mother.
2. Ms. Olds, your daughter's new teacher, is the mother of Tom Olds, a troubled teenager whom you have been treating for the last year.
3. Mrs. Simkins, the wife of Al Simkins, stockbroker, is your client and inadvertently discloses insider information about local businesses in which you own stock.
4. Your client, Cynthia Goddard, joins a recreational basketball league, and her assigned team plays regularly against the team to which you belong.

In such dual-role situations, it is always possible for a client to be confused by the circumstances, for the professional to exploit or harm the client in some manner, or for the additional role to interfere with the professional relationship. The *Code of Ethics* states "social workers should not engage in dual or multiple relationships with clients or former clients in which there is a risk of exploitation or potential harm to the client. In instances when dual or multiple relationships are unavoidable, social workers should take steps to protect clients and are responsible for setting clear, appropriate, and culturally sensitive boundaries" (NASW *Code,* 1999, 1.06c). "Social workers who provide supervision or consultation are responsible for setting clear, appropriate, and culturally sensitive boundaries" (NASW *Code,* 1999, 3.01b), and "Social workers should not engage in any dual or multiple relationships with supervisees in which there is a risk of exploitation of or potential harm to the supervisee" (NASW, *Code,* 1999, 3.01c). Also, "Social workers who function as educators or field instructors for students should not engage in any dual or multiple relationships with students in which there is a risk of exploitation or potential harm to the students" (NASW *Code,* 1999, 3.02d).

These standards highlight the issue of dual-role relationships so that social workers may take steps to set limits on such relationships or to avoid them wherever possible and in this way avoid actions detrimental to clients, supervisees, and students. The avoidance of exploitation of or of harm to clients, former clients, supervisees, and students, among others, is the major focus of these standards.

Must dual-role relationships necessarily interfere with professional relationships or be conflictual? In modern society, everyone fills multiple roles, and there are many opportunities for social workers and clients to participate in dual or multiple relationships. Both may be members of the same political party, church, mosque, or synagogue, or their children may attend the same schools or be classmates. There is no reason for a social worker to withdraw from these activities simply because the client also engages in them. The issue is to separate the professional relationship from other relationships. Among the relationships with clients that should be avoided are dating, bartering services, buying, investing work or money in businesses, and endorsing or recommending a client's business to potential buyers. For example, the used car salesman who is a client may offer to sell you a car at a discount. Don't accept his offer, no matter how good it is!

Questions have been raised about social workers in health care and other settings who receive gifts from representatives of insurance companies, medical equipment companies, and nursing homes. The vendors expect "gratitude" for their gifts. A number of issues are raised by the gifts. The cost of the gifts is passed on to patients and others. The best interests of the patient may become secondary to those of the vendors. A social worker's decisions may become biased as a result of one's "gratitude." The acceptance of the gift creates a dual-role relationship between the social worker and the donor, a relationship that suggests an obligation for reciprocity. Social workers are in a position to reciprocate through referral of patients who pay either personally or through insurance. As a result, social workers can become enmeshed in a dual-role relationship that is not known to patients but has the power to influence what happens to the client. Is there a difference between the acceptance of gifts for oneself or for patients? Are gifts given to the social work department different from those provided to individual social workers? Do all gifts carry attached strings deserving of reciprocation? Since patients are unaware of these relationships, is the acceptance of gifts consistent with fully informed consent (Ross, 1992)?

Reconsidering and Further Defining Dual Relationships

Essentially, dual relationships are problematic because they lead to ethical dilemmas. Recently, questions have been raised about rigidly prohibiting dual relationships. Zur and Lazarus (2002) offered arguments for and against dual relationships with clients or patients, thus implying there are inevitable dual relationships, especially when the social worker is in private practice or in a denominational or special-group agency. First, they argue that boundary violations may be harmful and exploitative but also constructive (e.g., a home visit to a bedridden client or attending a family event such as a wedding). Rigid boundaries can reflect distance and coldness. Second, there is no reason to assume that a hug, home visit, or acceptance of a gift will lead to sexual contact. Third, not all relationships in which persons have differential powers are misused or exploitative. Social workers, according to this argument, can abuse or use their power. Depicting clients as weak and defenseless perhaps suggests a disempowerment of clients rather than their empowerment. Fourth, there are communities (e.g., rural, religious, feminist, gay, and ethnic minorities) in which it is neither feasible nor desirable to maintain rigid separations from dual relationships. Fifth, rather than foremost considering risk management and legal issues, social workers should implement treatment plans based on the client's personality, situation, gender, culture, and ability to function, that is, not base their interventions on defensive actions for legal reasons but instead on sound treatment plans. Finally, there may be very good reasons for informal encounters, such as eating a meal with an anorexic client, visiting a community center or library with an agoraphobic client, attending a dramatic performance or sport event in which a client who has been fearful of such activities participates, and interaction in common living situations such as rural, college, military, disabled, or other overlapping relationships in small communities. (See Exemplars 9.5 and 9.6 later in this chapter for dual-role problems related to a supervisor who is a friend.)

SEXUAL RELATIONS WITH CLIENTS

There are many "gray" areas in regard to social workers and their social, non-sexual relationships with clients. Undoubtedly, there are many qualifications, contextual factors, and motivations which need to be considered for many such relationships. The *Code*, however, is quite clear that "social workers should under no circumstances engage in sexual activities or sexual contact with current clients, whether such contact is consensual or forced" (NASW *Code*, 1999, 1.09a). This ethical rule is found in the codes of ethics of most professions. In addition, similar standards are stated for such activities "with clients' relatives or other individuals with whom clients maintain a close personal relationship when there is a risk of exploitation or potential harm to the client" (NASW *Code*, 1999,1.09b), "with former clients because of the potential for harm to the client" (NASW *Code*, 1999, 1.09c), and "should not provide clinical services to individuals with whom they have had a prior sexual relationship" (NASW *Code*, 1999, 1.09d).

In regard to sexual relations with a former client, it is at least arguable that an act that is unethical today continues to be unethical at a later date. Does sex with a client or former client model for the client the idea that sexual relationships might be expected in subsequent psychotherapy? For those social workers who engage in sexual relationships with former clients or claim that an exception to the prohibition is warranted, the burden is on them to demonstrate "that the former client has not been exploited, coerced, or manipulated, intentionally or unintentionally" (NASW *Code*, 1999, 1.09c).

A study of 654 NASW members' definitions of who is a client found that approximately half of them believe "clienthood" ends when service is terminated, while the other half believe once a client, always a client. Others believed various time periods following service defined whether a former client remained a client. A definite lack of consensus was found among MSWs regarding the definition of former client and what is appropriate behavior at what times regarding various dual relationships (Mattison, Jayaratne, & Croxton, 2002).

Sexual intimacy between professional social workers and clients is not simply an ethical breach. Such intimacy with clients is also grounds for legal action in all 50 states where the social worker may be sued for battery, malpractice, intentional and negligent infliction of emotional distress, and sexual abuse. Some states have defined sexual exploitation of a client as a crime (Kagle & Giebelhausen, 1994).

In some states, potential legal action against the practitioner is not avoided by the formal termination of the treatment relationship. In a number of states, sexual contact following the termination of client status is illegal for one-, two-, or three-year periods (Perry & Kuruk, 1993). Current as well as past clients are dependent on the social worker; exploiting this dependency for personal gain, sexual or nonsexual, is unethical, illegal, and unprofessional, regardless of whether the social worker's action affects the therapeutic or other outcome.

To be sure, some social workers have questioned these rules, pointing out that many problems brought to their attention involve problems of sexual dysfunction. The professional intervention, they argue, might include sexual techniques and activities. There have been therapists who believe and practice the notion that sexual involvement with a client is beneficial. They suggest that this is not a new helping technique; Freud's colleague Sandor Ferenczi "helped" his clients express their physical affections toward him as a way of compensating for their childhood deprivations (Van Hoose & Kottler, 1985). One finding of a study of a sample of NASW members in direct service positions found only a small 1.1% acknowledging having sex with a former client. (No questions were asked about intimate relationships with clients.) However, almost 5% saw nothing professionally inappropriate in such behavior (Jayaratne, Croxton, & Mattison, 1997). Berkman and colleagues (2000) studied the attitudes of 349 final semester MSW students about sexual contact with clients. They found a relatively high approval level by the students of sexual contact between social workers and clients in certain circumstances. These circumstances included sexual contacts following terminated professional relationships, brief treatment, and relationships that only involved social workers helping clients to obtain concrete services such as gaining entry into a hospital or applying for Supplemental Security Income.

Those who say there is no problem when sex takes place between social work professionals and their clients are underestimating the impact of such behavior both on professional relationships and on the lives of their clients. These relationships between social workers and clients are quite serious because of the consequences for the persons involved. Pope and Bouthoutsos (1986) reported that 90% of the 559 clients they studied, all of whom were sexually involved with their therapists, had adverse effects and suffered some kind of damage. The consequences of therapist-client sex take several forms: ambivalence, guilt, emptiness and isolation, sexual confusion, impaired ability to trust, confused roles and boundaries, emotional lability, suppressed rage, increased suicidal risk, and problems in cognitive functioning, including concentration and memory, flashbacks, intrusive thoughts, unbidden images, and nightmares (Pope & Vasquez, 1998).

There is some evidence that those most vulnerable to sexual exploitation by their therapists are those who have been sexually abused in the past (Coleman & Schaefer, 1986). However, Bates and Brodsky (1989) suggest that instead of the personal history or characteristics of the client, the most effective predictor of whether a client will become sexually involved with a therapist is whether the therapist has previously engaged in sex with a client.

Sexual relationships between social work students and their field instructors also injure and have the potential for imitative behavior by the student. Such sexual relationships can be replicated and reinforced in subsequent work with clients. A national study of 481 psychologists found that a student's engagement in a sexual relationship with a supervisor is statistically linked to the likelihood that this pattern will repeat itself with future clients, students, and supervisees (Barnett-Queens, 1999). Of those who reported sexual contact with an instructor, almost one in four (23%) reported subsequent engagement in sex with a client compared to only 6% of those who while students had no sexual experiences with their teachers (Pope, Levenson, & Schover, 1979; Glaser & Thorpe, 1986; Ryder & Hepworth, 1990; Bonosky, 1995).

How frequently does this problem occur in social work practice? A review of eight national self-report anonymous surveys of mental health practitioners (psychiatrists, psychologists, and social workers) found that 4.4% of the therapists reported becoming sexually involved with a client. There are significant gender differences as 6.8% of male therapists reported such behavior but only 1.6% of female therapists reported engaging in sex with a client. This data was supplemented by a national survey of patients who had been sexually involved with a therapist. In one study, slightly over 2% of the men and about 4.6% of the women reported having been sexually involved with their own therapists

(Pope & Feldman-Summers, 1992). A national survey of clinical social workers reported numbers of them experience sexual attraction and sexual fantasies about clients; 3.6% of the male therapists and 0.5% of the female therapists reported having actual sex with a client (Bernsen, Tabachnik, & Pope, 1994). These results were similar to those reported in a review of seven national surveys of mental health practitioners (Kagle & Giebelhausen, 1994). Overall, male therapists are most often involved; female patients are most often the objects; therapists who ignore sexual boundaries are likely to repeat the behavior; and no differences are found among the behaviors of psychiatrists, psychologists, and social workers (Pope & Vasquez, 1998).

Sexual behavior with clients is the most frequently reported ethical violation in the social work profession. Although it is probable that some inappropriate sexual behavior goes unreported, malpractice suits for sexual misconduct are increasing despite the prohibition in licensing laws, professional standards, and the *Code of Ethics* (Houston-Vega et al., 1997, p. 72). Furthermore, incorrect treatment and sexual misconduct together accounted for the largest percentage of malpractice suits (NASW, 1995b).

Attitudes of almost all practitioners about having sex with clients are changing. Among psychologists it was reported in 1977 that 5.5% of male psychologists and 0.6% of female psychologists had sexual intercourse with patients (Holroyd & Brodsky, 1977). A decade later, Borys and Pope (1989) reported that only 1.3% of therapists reported sexual involvements with clients. Each year there are about 10% fewer self-reports of patient-therapist sex than the prior year, regardless of the mental health profession (Pope & Vasquez, 1998). It may be that this marked drop in reported sexual activity reflects a broad acceptance of the ethical rule prohibiting sexual relations with clients. What is not entirely clear from the data is whether therapists now refrain from having sex with their clients, whether they are less willing to admit that they behave in unethical ways, or that this behavior pattern has become more accepted despite the legal and professional sanctions against it.

Jayaratne, Croxton, and Mattison (1997) studied six domains of social work practice: intimate relationships, dual role relationships, mixed modalities, advice giving, boundary behaviors, and financial transactions. The study was based on a large sample of the membership of the Michigan Chapter of NASW. Some of their findings are summarized in Table 9.1. While only a small number of practitioners report they have dated a former client, over 6% think it appropriate to do so. Similarly, a small number report they have had sex with a former client, while almost 5% believe that such behavior is appropriate. Very large percentages report they have dual-role relationships with clients (e.g., friendship; serving on the same boards or committees). Only a few social workers use massage in their practices, however, more than one in eight believe to do so is appropriate; almost 40% believe it is appropriate to touch a client as a regular part of the therapy process.

Exemplar 9.1 raises a number of ethical issues to which all social workers must pay attention.

Table 9.1 | Frequency and Percentages of Incidents and Perceived Appropriateness of Behavior of Social Work Professionals

Behavior	Done		Perceived as Appropriate	
	N	%	N	%
Go on a date with a former client	7	0.8	53	6.4
Have sex with a former client	9	1.1	37	4.6
Develop a friendship with a client	174	21.2	170	21.0
Have clients with whom you have another relationship	185	22.5	270	33.5
Serve on community boards or committees with clients	187	22.6	471	58.7
Use massage	15	1.8	107	13.7
Touch a client as a regular part of therapy process	253	31.2	319	39.9
Give financial investment advice	37	4.5	64	7.7
Advise clients to do something that may be illegal	25	3.1	30	3.7

Source: Adapted from S. Jayaratne, T. Croxton, and D. Mattison (1997), "Social Work Professional Standards: An Exploratory Study," *Social Work* 42, 187–198.

❖ 9.1 Treatment of an Inferiority Complex

Jill Jordan, a 35-year-old divorcee, has been a client of The Family Consultation Center for a number of months. Her presenting problem is that she feels inadequate, unattractive, and stymied in her career. She feels her negative self-image contributed to her divorce and has become a barrier to advancement on the job. She feels that her career and more fulfilling relationships depend on her being more positive about herself and being more optimistic.

Bob Temple, an experienced social worker, was assigned as her therapist. A contract was established with the presenting problem as the focus. During the course of treatment, Bob was very understanding and warmly responsive to Jordan. His objective was to restore Jill's faith in herself. As treatment proceeded, Jill became more and more openly admiring of Bob. At the end of one session, she spontaneously hugged him and said how appreciative she was for all his help. As she experienced more successes in her life, she would ask for a hug as a sign of his support for her. Still later, she made it evident that she was attracted to Bob and would not reject his interest in her. Bob was also attracted to Jill. He very much wanted to further express his feelings toward her and have sexual relations with her, but he knew that the professional ethics demanded that he not do so. What is the most ethical way of handling this problem?

1. Is it best that he deny his feelings and continue treatment but discontinue the hugs; chances are that these emotions, if controlled, will not interfere with the treatment.
2. He can maintain a professional relationship in the office and join her church, where there will be opportunities for them to meet after hours, outside the office.
3. He can accept his emotional attraction to Jill, but at the same time realize that a professional social worker cannot have a personal relationship with a client. Next time Jill broaches the subject, he should tell her that he likes her and that if he were not her social worker he might become involved with her. Since he is her social worker, his task is to help her professionally; no other relationship is possible.
4. He realizes that he cannot control his emotions. Therefore, it is best to terminate the relationship and refer Jill to another social worker.
5. He realizes that he cannot control his emotions. Therefore, it is best not to deny his attraction for Jill and instead do what comes naturally, that is, have sex with her; at the same time, he can continue to be her social worker.

Option 5 is clearly not acceptable. In most jurisdictions this behavior is judged as illegal, even criminal. The NASW *Code of Ethics* prohibits it, as do the ethical codes of all other professions. Though there is no ethical or professional justification for this choice, we mention it because we are aware that a small number of our colleagues do engage in such behavior, a behavior that is blatantly unprofessional and unethical. Obviously, some of the other options are also unethical and/or go against the *Code.* Use the two ethical decision screens to determine which might be the preferred approach in the situation facing Bob Temple.

According to Schoener (1995), sexual misconduct and other boundary violations by professionals (other than court decisions) are dealt with through combinations of reprimands or temporary privilege suspension followed by personal therapy and possibly some sort of supervision. Rarely are there independent, formal evaluations or planned rehabilitation efforts. There are occasions when the distress experienced by the colleague associated with being charged or prosecuted has been the focus of the therapy rather than the misconduct or boundary transgression. The following questions have been suggested when a rehabilitation provider and practitioner are considering whether a practitioner's rehabilitation has been complete: (1) To a reasonable degree of psychiatric or psychological certainty have the problems being treated been fixed or resolved? (2) Would you have any qualms whatsoever if your spouse or child went to see this person for individual therapy?

TOUCHING

Touching became a popular practice technique during the late sixties and early seventies as a result of the popularity of the encounter movement. Clients "touched" by their therapist evaluated counseling more positively than those not touched, particularly if the touching was done by a therapist of the opposite sex (Algana et al., 1979). Some have questioned the ethical propriety of touching, believing that such behavior is only a first step that will inevitably lead to full sexual relations. Others reject this assumption. The available research evidence is contradictory and does not provide an unambiguous answer (Bogodanoff & Elbaum, 1978; Borenzweig, 1983; DeYoung, 1988; Willis, 1987). Nevertheless, the *Code* provides for physical contact but "Social workers should not engage in physical contact with clients when there is a possibility of psychological harm to the client as a result of the contact (such as cradling or caressing clients). Social workers who engage in appropriate physical contact with clients are responsible for setting clear, appropriate, and culturally sensitive boundaries that govern such physical contact" (NASW *Code*, 1999, 1.10).

NONSEXUAL SOCIAL RELATIONS

While almost all social workers agree that it is unethical to engage in sexual activities with clients, there is less agreement about the ethical propriety of engaging in different social relations. One can note in Table 9.1 the lack of agreement that exists among professional social workers as to what are appropriate professional behaviors. Some of the results highlight the lack of consensus about which social relations are deemed unethical. Although not identified in the table, large percentages think it appropriate to hug or embrace a client (see NASW *Code*, 1999, 1.10), pray with a client, recommend a religious form of healing, comment to clients about their physical attractiveness, discuss one's religious beliefs, or accept goods or services from clients instead of money (see NASW *Code*, 1999, 1.13).

Informal Settings

Social workers who do not practice psychotherapy may have somewhat different views about the ethical implications of some of the behaviors studied by Jayaratne, Croxton, and Mattison (1997). Group workers, community organizers, and social planners may have no compunctions about going to the local diner or coffeehouse with a group of clients after a session, but they may (or may not) draw the line when it comes to doing the same thing with an individual client. (See Chapter 13 for a discussion of ethics and social work with groups and macro social work.) Some social work administrators report that their most important contacts with board members occur in social settings. Obviously, the definition of who is a client and the purpose of the professional relationship are two factors that affect the ethical assessment of such professional behaviors.

As long as social workers think there is no conflict between agency interests and client interests, dual-role relationship (client/agency) ethical problems do not exist for them. Usually, it is suggested that the agency is committed to what is best for the client. If we examine this proposition objectively, however, we must realize that this is only the social work version of "What is good for General Motors is good for the country!"

In fact, organizational survival interests often do not coincide with what is best for the client. Sometimes ethical dilemmas occur when social workers must choose between their agency's interest and their client's interest. The ethical issue of the dual relationship dilemma may arise out of a social worker's attempt to serve at the same time both the best interest of the client and the best interest of the employing agency or institution. This ethical problem is familiar to hospital social workers. Hospital policy (often as a result of requirements by the government or insurance companies that reimburse hospitalization expenses) is to send patients home at the earliest possible time, even if this is not in a patient's best interest. In this instance, a social worker who is the "agent" of both the hospital and the patient cannot meet the best interests of both. Such pressures can result in social workers rushing the caretakers of those to be discharged from hospitals. A study of perceptions by discharge planners in an urban hospital and family caregivers found that planners overrated the amount and adequacy of information provided about posthospital care, the choice of discharge to home or nursing facility, and the need for decision-making time by the caregivers (Clemens, 1995). Similar problems are faced by social workers in the armed forces, police, prisons, mental hospitals, and schools. Increasingly, this problem is faced also by social workers employed in industrial settings and in social agencies. (See Exemplar 1.2, "Blanca Gabelli Costs Too Much," for another example of this problem.)

A somewhat different version of this ethical dilemma is faced by social workers who employ various group strategies: How can they simultaneously serve the best interest of every participant? If the focus is on strengthening the group or family, one or the other participant may not receive the maximum benefit. On the other hand, if the group is the vehicle to help one or more group members with their problems, there may be other group participants who will not obtain any significant benefit. Dolgoff and Skolnik (1996) found when they studied ethical decision making by social workers with groups that the social workers, when asked to make group records available to a court so that one member could obtain child visitation rights, sided in 84% of the cases with the group members that did not want to release the records.

TRUTHTELLING AND MISREPRESENTATION

The NASW *Code of Ethics* states that "social workers should not participate in, condone, or be associated with dishonesty, fraud, or deception" (NASW *Code*, 1999, 4.04). Telling the truth and avoiding deceptions are basic ethical obligations. Every human interaction is based on the premise that each side in the interaction intends to tell the truth. Deceiving—that is, deliberately misrepresenting facts in order to make another person believe what is not true—violates the respect to which everyone is entitled. Telling the truth to a client is an even stronger professional obligation than the generalized obligation of truth telling. This professional ethic is anchored in the specialized client/practitioner relationship and in the obligations that a practitioner owes to her clients.

Some practitioners may believe that dishonesty that serves the client is ethical, but such a stance requires further thought before it can be accepted. For example, is it ethical for a social worker to assign a wrong diagnosis so as to provide service that otherwise would be unavailable, or otherwise be dishonest to the benefit of the client?

Bayles concluded that the obligation to be honest with clients does not require honesty toward others when acting on a client's behalf (1981, p. 71). Is honesty always the best policy for a social worker? Expressing such a view is, of course, a little bit like attacking home and mother. Haley raises a number of questions about the efficacy of always being honest (1976, p. 208). These include:

1. Some social work professional situations are not honest human experiences, but paid relationships. Do social workers (therapists and nontherapists) have an ethical obligation to be honest in their professional relationships?
2. Can any therapist, no matter what her orientation, claim that she is willing to share with a client all of her observations and understandings?
3. Must a therapist answer all questions that a client has about the therapy that will be used? Will this patient be better able to achieve autonomy when he fully understands the theory used by the therapist?
4. Will an "honest sharing" of understanding solve the problems for which the patient is paying his money to get help?

Haley presents one point of view, but not everyone agrees. In addition to Haley's questions, there are a number of ethical dilemmas that may arise out of the attempt to tell the truth. Consider the ethical problems facing Gail's social worker in Exemplar 9.2.

❖ 9.2 Gail Finds a Job

Gail Silva is a single parent; she is raising two daughters, ages seven and six. She has been trying to find a part-time job to supplement her meager child support income ever since her younger daughter started kindergarten. She has been repeatedly refused a job because she has had no prior employed work experience. By now she has become very frustrated and has developed a very negative self-image. She believes that nobody wants her—neither as a spouse nor as a worker. This morning she told you excitedly that she thinks she has found a job. As she describes the job, you realize that she is telling you about an employer who is known to exploit his workers and who pays below the minimum wage, when he pays at all. Should you tell Gail the truth about her prospective employer? Or should you share her enthusiasm, hoping that things will work out? What is the ethical thing to do?

Deception has become so common in our world that we hardly pay attention to the little lies and half-truths that everyone uses and knows how to justify. Nyberg (1996, p. 187) suggested that deception is a necessary part of our world: ". . . deception is not merely to be tolerated as an occasionally prudent aberration in a world of truth telling; it is rather an essential component of our ability to organize and shape the world, to resolve problems of coordination among individuals who differ, to cope with uncertainty and pain, to be civil and to achieve privacy as needed, to survive as a species, and to flourish as persons." Or, as he suggests: "to live decently with one another we do not need moral purity, we need discretion—which means tact in regard to truth" (p. 202).

What are the ethical implications for a social worker who uses "lies"? What is the ethical question involved in telling another person a bit less than the full truth? When a social worker decides to withhold the truth from a client or to deceive him, she usually thinks that she is doing so for the client's benefit. Whether this is really so is subject to empirical assessment. Whether her decision was ethically justified cannot be assessed empirically.

Are there reasons why a social worker might deceive her client or not tell him the full truth? Are the following reasons for dishonesty ethical?

- To make a client-selected goal less desirable
- To create new goals
- To obscure options
- To increase options
- To change the cost/benefit estimate for one or more options
- To increase or decrease client uncertainty
- To increase or decrease client anxiety
- To protect the client from "damaging" truth
- To protect the effectiveness of the current intervention strategy
- To obtain the client's "informed" consent
  To protect confidential information received from a third party
- To strengthen the relationship with a client by lying at his request to a third party
- To increase the worker's power over a client by withholding information
- To make the worker look good by "papering over" mistakes she has made

Which of these reasons may be applicable in Exemplars 9.3 and 9.4?

❖ 9.3 A Growth on the Foot

Art Elder, age 34, is a high school teacher. At present he is a patient in University Hospital because he has a growth on his foot. His physician told him that there are two ways of treating this problem. Both involve some risks. When Art asked what he would advise, he suggested surgery.

Sally Brown is the social worker in the surgical department. From her discussion with the resident, she learned that Dr. Kutner, the physician, did not tell the patient all the available choices and that he withheld information about the option with the least risk. Evidently, he weighted his presentation in favor of the experimental treatment method that he is just now developing.

Here we are not concerned with Dr. Kutner, but with Sally Brown. Should she tell Mr. Elder the truth? Should she mind her own business and leave the giving of medical information to the medical staff? Should she suggest that Mr. Elder get a second opinion? It may be that such behaviors by physicians is less common than it once was but Sally Brown still faces an ethical dilemma. On what basis can she decide what the ethical course of action is?

Social workers in direct practice are not the only ones who may have ethical problems with truthtelling. An exemplar from the field of social work administration also raises questions about the ethics of truthtelling.

❖ 9.4 The Frans Music Appreciation Room

The Frans family contributed a considerable sum of money to the Uptown Community Center to furnish and equip a music appreciation room in memory of their mother. An appropriate plaque marks the room. Since the center accepted the contribution, the neighborhood has experienced a large influx of immigrants from Southeast Asia. Because of their needs, the room is now used for purposes other than those designated by the donors.

You are the center's associate director. You know how important the music appreciation room is to the family. There is a good possibility of obtaining additional donations for other projects from this family, but if the family discovers that their room is no longer used for music appreciation activities, they may lose interest in Uptown Community Center. At the monthly meeting of the United Way Board of Directors, you meet Mr. Frans. He asks you how the music appreciation room is doing. How should you reply? Do you tell the truth? Do you try to avoid the issue by shifting the conversation to another area? Do you tell a little untruth, such as "the immigrants love music"? Or not? What is the ethically correct response? How do you decide?

Social workers at every level sometimes have to choose between loyalty to a friend or colleague and telling the truth. In Exemplar 9.5, a supervisor has to make a choice concerning truthfulness.

❖ 9.5 A Supervisor Decides

Karl Samil is a supervisor in a large Department of Social Services where it is difficult for anyone to know all members of the staff because of their large number and the fact that many work at satellite locations. Roger Lewis, a colleague, applied for promotion. Samil is one of those asked for his opinion; he is aware of earlier instances when Lewis acted in ways that were harmful to the agency, including inappropriately criticizing the agency at several interagency committee meetings, which may have injured the reputation of the agency's elder-abuse team. For over a year, Samil has noted that Lewis has been distracted and jumpy about his current job responsibilities. Most of his local colleagues have been aware of his behavior but out of loyalty have kept quiet and have often covered for him. To confuse matters further, Samil and Lewis have played cards together in a weekly game since they graduated college. Even there, Lewis's behavior has been somewhat erratic. When Samil spoke to Lewis to say he seemed unusually upset and distracted, Lewis brushed it off. If promoted, Lewis will move to another part of the agency.

Should Samil because of personal loyalty give a positive reference, thereby passing Roger Lewis on to another setting without letting them know of his limitations? Should he risk his own reputation if the promotion is gained but Roger does poorly at the job? What about loyalty to himself and family? Should he turn his back on the agency and the profession? Or, should he speak to Roger again and suggest that Roger defer promotion and take care of his own problems?

Table 9.2	Intentions and Facts	
The statement is factually	The speaker intends to be truthful	The speaker intends to be deceptive
True	The speaker intended to tell the truth and did so.	The speaker intended to deceive, but unknowingly spoke the truth. While her intentions were not ethical, her actual behavior does not raise any ethical issues.
False	The speaker intended to tell the truth but failed to do so because she did not have the correct information. The problem here may be lack of competence or lack of skill, or both, which *although unintentional, may be unethical.*	The speaker intended to deceive and did lie. *This situation involves questions of unethical behavior.*

The question of truth or deception involves the intention of the speaker and not the factual accuracy of the statement. Knowing the truth does not necessarily result in telling the truth, while not knowing the truth does not always result in a deception. The relations between the objective situation and a speaker's intentions are summarized in Table 9.2.

Some practitioners who abhor lying have suggested that it is possible to deceive without lying by exaggerating or manipulating. One social worker, for example, wanted to dissuade a client from placing his daughter with mental retardation in an institution. She arranged for the father to visit the worst possible institution but did not mention the availability of other alternatives. This social worker would never lie, but did she tell the truth? A social work administrator exaggerates the benefits that may result from a new program so that the agency will receive a larger budget allocation next year. Are these social workers acting ethically? Or is this yet another version of the ends-justifying-the-means quandary?

PRACTITIONER IMPAIRMENT

The personal and professional abilities of a social worker can be damaged, diminished, and impaired by extreme mental or physical health difficulties, overwhelming personal/familial problems, psychosocial distress, or substance abuse. These problems can affect a social worker, her family and friends, and colleagues, and may result in a social worker's inability to provide professionally competent services. Social workers are thought to have about the same rates of alcohol and substance abuse problems as members of other stressful health professions. The New York City Chapter of NASW reported that 43% of the respondents to a study knew at least one social worker with a drug or alcohol problem. A survey of all Indiana Chapter members reported that 53% knew a social worker whose performance was affected by emotional or mental health problems, substance abuse, burnout, or sexual misconduct (Hiratsuka, 1994).

Among the ethical issues for the profession is the assurance that all professional social workers are able to provide quality professional services and that such a standard is maintained while respecting all other ethical norms, including confidentiality. Impaired social workers may act in undisciplined, insensitive, erratic, unprofessional, and unethical ways. Sometimes they use inappropriate language or behavior with clients and colleagues, pay haphazard attention to job requirements, fail to follow through on assignments, or engage in excessive absenteeism. Impairments can lead to inadequate and even unethical behaviors, which can lower the public's estimate of and trust of the profession, result in actions detrimental to clients and others, and present ethical problems for other social workers.

The *Code of Ethics* includes four standards directly related to the impairment of professional social workers, referred to as colleagues. Those who have direct knowledge of such impairment should consult with the colleague and, where the colleague has not taken adequate steps to address the impairment, are expected to take action through appropriate channels (NASW *Code*, 1999, 2.09a, b). Similarly, where social workers have direct knowledge of a colleague's incompetence, they are expected to consult with the practitioner. Where the practitioner does not take adequate steps to address the incompetence, action should be taken through appropriate channels (NASW *Code*, 1999, 2.10a, b).

Clarification of the responsibility does not provide answers for all the dilemmas that exist in this area. Consider the following situation in Exemplar 9.6.

❖ 9.6 My Friend, Mentor, Supervisor, and Alcohol

You are a social worker assigned to a satellite unit of a family service agency with Davis Jones, your supervisor, the only other social worker who works in that office. Your relationship with Davis goes back at least 15 years, and he has been very important in your life at several junctions. He helped you get into social work school; he recommended you for an advanced treatment institute; and once when your child was ill, he helped you obtain medical care from the best specialist in town. Recently, however, Davis, who also evaluates you for pay and possible promotions, has been late arriving for work and has missed some meetings. You have had to cover for him more than a few times with his clients. You are still somewhat in awe of Davis and owe him a lot. He has helped you out of many a difficult situation. You feel that his current erratic behavior is related to alcohol and family difficulties.

Consider the ethical implications for each of the following options the worker may select.

1. Encourage one of his clients for whom you have had to replace him for several sessions to register a complaint with the agency.
2. Call in sick one day and ask for a substitute to cover cases so that another social worker discovers the problem.
3. Ignore the situation. Wait for someone else to "blow the whistle." Meanwhile, cover his cases.
4. Ask a mutual friend to call him and say that he has heard about his behavior on the job and suggest that it is important that he do something about his problems.
5. Report the situation to a high-level agency administrator.
6. Speak to Davis Jones directly. State that you will keep quiet about the situation but he must go for help.

So far Davis has done little if any harm. At what point must you act? Earlier or later? What about loyalty to a mentor, friend, and colleague from whom you have learned much? What about loyalty to yourself, your career, and your family? What about the risks you expose yourself to by acting? What should you do? Which options would be ethical?

Sources of Help

Social Workers Helping Social Workers (SWHSW), founded in 1980, is a national association that provides confidential assistance to colleagues primarily through e-mail, listserves, and by telephone. Social workers can contact SWHSW at (773) 493-6940 (confidential) or swhswil@aol.com. In 1995, NASW published a *Chapter Guide for Colleague Assistance for Impaired Social Workers*. NASW and some chapters offer materials on helping social workers identify colleagues with chemical dependency problems and ways to intervene with these colleagues.

PSYCHOLOGICAL INDIFFERENCE AS AN ETHICAL LIMITATION

Today, almost everyone experiences sensory overload. Information comes at us constantly by word of mouth, pagers, cellular phones, computers, television, radio, and other technologies. We live in an era of sound bites, brief messages intended to convey complex information. Social workers, along with other human service workers, also experience stress on the job, stress in their personal lives, and pressures to be productive, along with a myriad of other stressors. In many cases, burnout—both as personal alienation and as a coping mechanism in response to stress—is a defense against the invasion of our personal and professional spaces. Social workers upon occasion can tune out, deal only with the surface of things, experience a sense of impotence, and distance themselves from clients, colleagues, and their work (Powell, 1994; Soderfeldt, Soderfeldt, & Warg, 1995).

One possible result of psychological distancing is paying less attention to the ethical dilemmas that one encounters in practice, Hannah Arendt in *Eichmann in Jerusalem* characterized this human ability as leading to "the banality of evil." Americans learned about the potential insidious impact of this kind of banality at My Lai in Vietnam. Such psychological distancing can lead a social worker through acts of commission to avoid responsibility by distancing herself from clients, to treat clients with less individualization and dignity, and to serve the organization or society when the right action is to serve the individual; or by acts of omission that avoid doing the right thing in professional service. What should the administrator in Exemplar 9.7 do?

❖ 9.7 An Administrator Decides What to Do

Joseph Parocha is the overworked and stressed-out executive director of a Meals-on-Wheels program. Drivers recently have begun reporting seeing longer and longer lines at several soup kitchens as they travel to deliver meals to shut-in elderly people. Also, drivers have discovered mothers with young children without sufficient food at several of the houses where they deliver meals. In speaking to the president of the board, Haakon Query, Mr. Parocha suggested that the agency has a responsibility to also try to help these other people. After all, their job is helping feed people who are hungry. Mr. Query responded sharply that the agency has trouble enough maintaining itself and that he and others on the board would oppose any attempt to assist either the soup kitchens or the young families. The homeless and the young parents are the responsibility of other agencies. The agency should focus on its primary mission. Mr. Parocha was torn by his feeling that something should be done, and he knew that the staff could be doing more, although he personally didn't need any more pressures. When he talked it over with his wife, she reminded him that his health is also important, their son is to start college this fall, and their daughter needs braces. Mr. Parocha was upset but eventually decided that it was better not to confuse the mission of the agency by trying to move it in new directions and that there was little else he could do.

Is Mr. Parocha's decision a result of self and family protection, burnout, or a pragmatic decision? What should Mr. Parocha have done? After all, he doesn't know the people whose problems are being reported to him by staff members and volunteers, nor is it his responsibility to help support all other social agencies. In fact, he understood his situation in terms of his role as executive director and told himself: "Anyone in my position would do the same thing." Was his decision correct?

Mr. Parocha was confronted with a situation in which he decided to tolerate inadequate situations for young women and their families and the homeless while working hard to maintain the Meals-on-Wheels program and to protect his family. To whom does he owe loyalty? His agency? The president and board members? The soup kitchens? The homeless? The young women and their families? Himself? His family?

EXERCISES

1. If there is an NASW chapter in your area, invite the chair of the Chapter Committee on Inquiry to discuss with your class how complaints about ethical misconduct are handled. You might want to examine with the chair how effective these procedures are.

2. Sexual activities with clients are prohibited by the NASW *Code of Ethics* (1999, 1.09). Some social workers have argued that there is no scientific evidence that such activities are necessarily harmful. They say that a rule of this kind is no longer relevant in a society that permits a wide variety of lifestyles. Present arguments both for changing and for keeping this rule.

3. The "limited professional relationship" characteristic of the client-social worker relationship baffles many clients. It is a relationship that is quite unlike the formal, bureaucratic relationships with which they are familiar, yet it is also different from the informal relations they maintain with friends and relatives. How important is this principle from an ethical point of view?

4. In teams of two, develop two lists: (1) social relations with clients that are ethical and permissible, and (2) social relations with clients that are definitely unethical and, therefore, prohibited. Compare your lists with those of other teams. Discuss those areas where you find disagreement. Are there cultural issues that influence what is considered acceptable and what is considered unethical?

SUGGESTIONS FOR ADDITIONAL READINGS

The conflict between workers' and clients' interests in a hospital strike situation is examined by Fisher (1987). Kagle and Giebelhausen (1994) examine sexual and nonsexual dual-role relationships between social workers and their clients, including ethical, legal, and practice issues. Clemens (1995) illustrates a dual-role dilemma for a hospital social worker. Sloan, Edmond, Rubin, and Doughty (1998) report findings from a survey of licensed social workers in Texas on their knowledge of and experience with sexual exploitation by psychotherapists. Jayaratne et al. (1997) report on research on dual-role and intimate relationships and on boundary behaviors.

10 CHAPTER | Bureaucratic and Work Relationships

So far, our discussion has focused on ethical problems and ethical dilemmas occurring in the professional relationship between social workers and clients. In this chapter, our attention will be directed to ethical issues arising out of the relationship among social work colleagues and between social workers and their employers, agencies, supervisors, and administrators.

We noted earlier in Chapter 2 that one of the functions of professional codes of ethics is to permit colleagues to work together in harmony. The *Code* "informs other professionals with whom the professional must work about the kind of cooperation they have a right to expect from the professional and the limits to the cooperation that a professional ought to give" (Beyerstein, 1993, p. 420). This information reduces bickering and infighting that might lead to professional self-destruction. One section of the NASW *Code of Ethics* deals with the social worker's ethical responsibilities toward colleagues, and another section with her ethical responsibilities to employers and practice settings. Several additional ethical rules dealing with relationships with colleagues are found in the section devoted to ethical responsibilities toward the profession.

Strom-Gottfried (2003) examined 894 ethics complaints filed with NASW for the years 1986 to 1997. Of the 894 cases, 93 (10.4%) were filed against persons identified in the study as colleagues; an additional 40 (4.4%) complaints were filed against an employer or supervisor; and 174 (19.4%) complaints were filed against employees or supervisees. Thus, 34% (307) were filed against colleagues, employers or supervisors, all of whom are work associates.

The most commonly occurring violation concerned poor supervision—involving failure to maintain or share performance standards with workers, using insufficient investigation and documentation in performance review processes, not holding regular supervisory sessions, or holding sessions that were unclear and ineffective. The second most common violation involved employee dismissals that were judged to have been based on insufficient or absent personnel policies, or which diverged from accepted processes of progressive discipline, such as counseling or disciplinary actions (Strom-Gottfried, 1999). The number of complaints may represent only the tip of the proverbial iceberg because many unethical behaviors of this type are not brought to the local NASW committee but are handled in other ways, as will be discussed later in this chapter and in Chapter 14.

RELATIONS WITH PROFESSIONAL COLLEAGUES

What is a social worker to do when she discovers that a colleague engages in unethical or unprofessional conduct? How should she respond when she realizes that a fellow worker provides poor quality client services? What are her obligations when she believes that another social worker harms a client? What is her responsibility when she discovers that another worker engages in activities prohibited by their agency? What are her responsibilities when she learns that a colleague has violated the *Code of Ethics?*

The ethical rule obligating social workers to treat colleagues with respect (NASW *Code*, 1999, 2.01a) is one of those rules that ordinarily do not create an ethical quandary. Most people understand that the members of a club do not "wash their dirty linen" in public. Goffman wrote about the backstage area, access to which is restricted to colleagues (1959, pp. 106–140). Whatever happens in this area may not be revealed to those who are not members of the profession. It should remain forever a secret among those who work backstage.

Social workers faced relatively few ethical problems as long as the rules governing relations with professional colleagues were unambiguous and not challenged by other ethical rules. As accountability to clients and others became more important, the rule to "protect your own" became increasingly problematic. Some examples of unethical behavior are (a) having sexual relations with a client or a supervisee; (b) knowing a colleague is an alcoholic and is berating some clients; (c) sharing confidential information about a colleague with other colleagues; and (d) "bad mouthing" a team leader after failing to convince an interdisciplinary team to proceed with a particular treatment plan.

Today, most social workers are no longer willing to overlook their colleagues' unethical behavior, but it is not always clear what should be done. On learning that a colleague has engaged in unethical behavior, a social worker may choose one or more of the following options:

Option A. Not reporting the violating behavior. Reporting it may be too troublesome. Or past experience suggests that nothing will be done about it, even if it is reported. Or the conduct thought to be in violation of the

Code may be so widespread that it is unlikely that anyone will take the complaint seriously.

Option B. An informal approach to the colleague may resolve the problematic behavior, especially if the violation is of a minor or technical nature or appears to be the result of lack of experience or knowledge. The situation differs if your colleague is a peer or a supervisee or a supervisor.

Option C. If the alleged unethical conduct also violates agency rules, it may be brought to the attention of one's supervisor or it may be raised formally by using agency procedures established for this purpose.

Option D. The alleged unethical behavior may be brought to the attention of the NASW Committee on Inquiry. In order to use this procedure, the colleague who allegedly engaged in the unethical behavior must have been an NASW member at the time of the alleged violation, the complaint must charge a specific violation of the *Code of Ethics,* the complainant must have personal knowledge about the alleged behavior, and the complainant must be able and willing to provide the Committee on Inquiry with relevant and reliable testimony (NASW Procedures for Professional Review, 2001). The National Committee on Inquiry has primary administrative responsibility in all professional review matters. The NASW professional review procedures will be discussed in more detail in Chapter 14.

Option E. In states where a state licensing board regulates social work practice, unethical conduct harmful to clients can be reported to the board.

Option F. The unethical conduct may be brought to the attention of the general public (whistle-blowing), with the expectation that an aroused public will demand appropriate action to bring an end to the violation.

There are a number of possible alternatives within each option. Option A is problematic. Options B, C, D, and E are sanctioned by the *Code of Ethics.* Are there times and occasions when "going public" is the only way to proceed (Option F)? However, the decision to "go public" should never be a routine one and should be taken only after careful consideration of all possibilities.

Before choosing which option to follow, the social worker should attempt to clarify what she hopes to achieve by the action she intends to initiate. Loewenberg (1987) suggests the following as possible objectives:

1. Discontinuance of the unethical behavior.
2. Punish the offending social worker.
3. Identify the unethical practitioner so that potential clients and/or employers will avoid this person and turn to another, more ethical practitioner.
4. Prevent others from engaging in this behavior by warning them that it is unethical and will result in sanctions against the practitioner.
5. Protect the "good name" of the profession by declaring publicly that the unethical behavior is not approved by the profession.

Exemplars 10.1 and 10.2 will highlight some of the problems involved in this ethical issue.

❖ 10.1 Sex with Clients

Your colleague Mitchell Moore has been hospitalized quite suddenly. While he is on sick leave, you have been assigned to cover some of his cases. You learn from one of his clients that Mitch has been having sexual relations with her. She says that she was uncomfortable but felt something bad would happen if she had objected. She also asks you to protect her confidentiality and that she will handle the situation when he returns. This behavior is clearly in violation of the *Code* which states, "Social workers should under no circumstances engage in sexual activities or sexual contact with current clients, whether such contact is consensual or forced" (NASW *Code,* 1999, 1.09a).

The violation of the *Code of Ethics* as reported is obvious, but what you should do is not clear because there are many conflicting demands on you. Your most serious consideration is: How trustworthy is this client's report? Can you/should you act if you have questions about what happened? However, assuming you believe the client's report, let us examine these claims, one by one, but not in any order of priority. The references are to the relevant paragraphs of the *Code of Ethics* (NASW *Code*, 1999).

1. Your obligation to promote the well-being of clients (NASW *Code,* 1999, 1.01).
2. Your obligation to respect confidential material received in the course of the professional relationship, except for compelling professional reasons. (NASW *Code,* 1999, 1.07c).
3. Sex and touch therapy may be modes of practice, but social workers are cautioned by the *Code* that they "should not engage in physical contact with clients when there is a possibility of psychological harm to the client as a result of the contact . . ." and if they do so they "are responsible for setting clear, appropriate, and culturally sensitive boundaries that govern such physical contact" (NASW *Code,* 1999, 1.10).
4. Your obligation to "take adequate measures to discourage, prevent, expose, and correct the unethical conduct of colleagues" (NASW *Code,* 1999, 2.11a).
5. Further, "social workers should base practice on recognized knowledge, including empirically based knowledge, relevant to social work and social work ethics" (NASW *Code,* 1999, 4.01). In regard to the utility of therapeutic touch, experienced therapeutic touch practitioners who claimed to treat conditions by using their hands to manipulate a "human energy field" perceptible above the patient's skin were unable to detect "energy fields" (Rosa, Rosa, Samer, & Barrett, 1998, p. 1005), casting doubt on this type of treatment.
6. Your obligation to uphold the values, ethics, knowledge, and mission of the profession (NASW *Code,* 1999, 5.01b).

7. Rumor has it that a number of other social workers also engage in this type of behavior. Making a fuss about it will only result in making you look ridiculous.

These latter considerations argue against your taking any action (Option A—Not report), while the earlier considerations suggest a more active response (perhaps Option B—Informal approach; Option C—Use agency procedures; Option D—NASW and professional review; or even Option E—Report to the State Licensing Board). (See pages 161–162 for descriptions of options.) How can a social worker prioritize these considerations by importance? Does the ethical principles screen (EPS) help you in unraveling this conundrum? Which is the priority ethical obligation?

Let us consider another situation that presents the social worker with ethical quandaries in her relation to colleagues in Exemplar 10.2.

❖ 10.2 Failure to Report a Case of Child Abuse

Jake Dember, a frail five-year-old, was brought to the Emergency Room of Mt. Ebal Hospital unconscious, covered with blood from head to toe, with serious internal injuries. His father, Hiram, said that Jake fell from their second-floor apartment and landed headfirst on the cement sidewalk. The medical team was able to save Jake's life, though serious brain damage could not be reversed. Now, two weeks later, Jake is still in the hospital's critical care unit. The attending physicians are determined to report this as a case of child abuse. Before doing so, they have asked the hospital social worker, Josie Perry, to pull together all the relevant information they possess so that it can be provided to CPS at the time of the report.

Erica Dember, Jake's mother, did not want to talk to Josie. She said that she and her husband were already in family therapy at the Family Service Agency, if Josie wanted to know anything about them, she should talk to their therapist, Ed Custer.

Josie arranged to meet with Ed Custer on the following afternoon. Ed was willing to share his assessment of the Dember family since both parents had signed the customary consent forms when Jake was admitted to the hospital. In the course of their conversation, Ed acknowledged that he had been aware of ongoing child abuse in this family, but since he thought that it was not too serious, he did not file a report. He feared that such a report would have interfered with the therapeutic relationship that he was trying to develop with this family.

There are similarities and differences between this exemplar and the previous one. In both cases, one social worker became aware that another social worker may have violated ethical standards. In the first case, continuation of the unethical behavior (sexual relations with a client) might result in further harm to the client. In the present case, the harm to Jake had already been done and perhaps will not be repeated with Jake, but Ed Custer's criminal conduct and his failure to report other cases of child abuse may cause harm to other clients. Are the conflicting claims on Josie Perry similar to those that faced Mitch Moore's colleague? How valid is Custer's fear that reporting a client's child abuse may interfere with the therapeutic relationship, especially when there are data suggesting that such fears may be overstated.

Research findings do *not* support the claim that reporting child abuse interferes with maintaining a therapeutic relationship. A national survey of psychologists who are psychotherapists and who had filed at least one mandated child abuse report found that clients remained in treatment when such reports were made, especially when certain factors were present. Important for maintaining this relationship was the explicit involvement of the client in the informed consent procedures. It was also important that the limits of confidentiality were fully discussed with the client. Moreover, clients were more likely to continue when there were positive therapeutic relationships prior to the report and when the perpetrator was a third party (someone not engaged directly in the treatment). Most surprising, clients reacted more positively when sexual abuse—rather than other forms of abuse—was reported (Steinberg, Levine, & Doueck, 1997). How should Josie Perry resolve the ethical dilemma facing her? Should she report Ed's negligence to the NASW chapter? Ignore it? Choose another action?

So far, our consideration of the ethical quandaries arising out of this issue has focused on relations with social work colleagues. Social workers also interact with practitioners from other professions and with nonprofessional human service workers. Although the nature of these relations may be different, the NASW *Code of Ethics* states that the same respect and cooperation that is extended to social work colleagues should also be extended to colleagues of other professions (NASW *Code*, 1999, 2.01a). In one sense, the ethical problems arising out of these relationships will be the same as those that occur in relationships with social work colleagues. In other ways, the ethical dilemma may be more critical because these non–social work colleagues are not subject to the provisions of the NASW *Code of Ethics*. They may follow other norms of confidentiality or may routinely engage in behaviors that professional social workers define as unethical. What should social workers do if their values and ethics are in conflict with the values and ethics of team members from other professions when the respective ethical obligations have not been clearly established as suggested by the *Code* (1999, 2.03a) or the disagreement cannot be resolved through appropriate channels (1999, 2.03b)? Which other avenues should be pursued to address their concerns consistent with client well-being?

If a social worker learns of the incompetence of a team member from another discipline, what is one's ethical responsibility? What if social workers are working in cooperation with educators, psychologists, lawyers, physicians, or other disciplines? Is the ethical responsibility of the social worker always the same in whatever setting concerning abuse, confidentiality, sexual impropriety, inadequate professional performance, conflicts of interest, and the like? In face of the conflicts and obligations, to whom does the social worker owe responsibility—the client or patient, the team, herself, the social work profession, the other involved professions, or society (Abramson, 1984)?

ADHERENCE TO AGENCY POLICIES AND REGULATIONS

The fact that most social workers are employed by bureaucratic organizations makes for another set of ethical dilemmas. Every organization has rules and policies. Those individuals who accept employment voluntarily agree to abide by these regulations. The NASW *Code of Ethics* considers this commitment to the employing organization a basic ethical obligation: "Social workers generally should adhere to commitments made to employers and employing organizations" (NASW *Code*, 1999, 3.09a). The goals and objectives of some organizations, even of some social service agencies, however, are not always congruent with the values of the social work profession. Organization maintenance and survival demands may result in rules that contradict the primary obligation of social workers to give priority to their clients' interests. Efficiency measures may limit intervention options so that the most effective option for a given client may not be available. Budgetary considerations may result in service cutbacks that will not be in the client's best interest. This is the type of ethical dilemma that is especially demanding for social work administrators. They must resolve a critical ethical dilemma—whether to give priority to adherence to agency rules or to service to clients.

One response to these situations is collusion with clients to violate agency policies. This approach is often rationalized by the social worker by defining her activities as promoting the client's welfare or contributing fairness and social justice. Is it ever ethical to violate agency policies? For example, what should a social worker do upon learning that a client has occasional additional income, which she is supposed to report to her public assistance worker so that part of this income can be deducted from the following month's welfare check? Or, a Social Security beneficiary is working "off the books" and not reporting the extra income, which is above the legal limits either for Social Security or income tax purposes? If the social worker does not report this income, all of the extra money will be available to the clients. In the first case, the additional cash may help her to return to employment and independence and, in the second case, enable the Social Security beneficiary to live at a minimal subsistence level. Keeping quiet may be in the best interest of both clients. Does the amount and the regularity of the extra income make a difference? In each case, what about the worker's obligations to the law, her employer, and society?

A particularly difficult ethical dilemma is faced by social workers when they discover that their agency's policies or regulations are unethical. For example, a hospital social worker discovers soon after employment that it is hospital policy to pressure social workers to encourage mentally competent patients to move into nursing homes. Intended to counter excessive concern by the hospital staff about patient safety following discharge, these actions override patients' rights to autonomy and self-determination (Clemens, 1995). As another example, what if the administrator of a child protective agency hires inadequately trained paraprofessional workers to investigate complaints of child abuse because of insufficient funds to hire professionally trained workers, even though this assignment requires a particularly high skill level.

The examples in the previous paragraph present a question as to what are ethical responses to budget cuts for the administrator and direct practitioner? Exemplar 10.3 provides another example where the purposes of the staff are served without due consideration of the needs of the client.

❖ 10.3 Pregnant Women Need Support

Terry Newton is a social worker in a private organization, Upward Strivers, that performs contract work for a local Department of Social Services (DSS). The clients receive public assistance under the Temporary Assistance to Needy Families (TANF) program as long as they are enrolled and active in a program that is designed to prepare them for regular employment through job readiness training. When needed, clients also receive GED preparation or literacy classes. After completing the three weeks of job readiness, those clients not enrolled in training programs must begin job searches with the help of a placement specialist and may be enrolled part time in GED preparation or literacy training. The Department of Social Services frequently refers pregnant women to the job readiness program. None of these women are able to find employment following the training because most employers won't hire pregnant women. The pregnant women are enrolled in GED preparation in order to avoid the loss of their financial support. Both Upward Strivers and the DSS created this informal policy, which enables both DSS and Upward Strivers to receive payments from the State.

The purposes of these informal policies are to maintain payments for the client, the Upward Strivers, and for the DSS. The client needs financial support as do the two agencies, both of which are engaged in many important and constructive activities. If you were a social worker who discovered this pattern of behavior, where would you look in the *Code of Ethics* for guidance on how to choose among the clients and their needs, Upward Strivers, and the DSS, in an ethical manner? To which persons, organizations, or institutions, do you have an ethical commitment? How would you implement your ethical decision?

A different aspect of the conflict between agency interests and client interests that results in ethical quandaries is illustrated by Exemplar 10.4.

❖ 10.4 Case of a Hyperactive Boy

David is a hyperactive child in a residential institution. In the last few weeks, he has become very disruptive. He frequently tosses food during meals with other children, "short sheets" other children's beds, turns on fire alarms, arrives late wherever he is expected, throws pencils in class, and other such behaviors. Although he is not physically harmful to himself or others, he has been highly disruptive of the institution's daily routine. The consulting physician has prescribed large doses of a tranquilizer to calm the child and manage him better, but the cottage social worker has refused on ethical grounds to administer this medicine to David. She feels strongly that such pharmaceutical control will interfere with the child's welfare and freedom and will be counter-productive in any therapy attempted. Her social work supervisor has supported this decision. The physician insists the medication pre-scribed be given to David. The institution's director, a psychologist, supports the doctor against the decision of the social worker.

The agency executive requires an institution that runs smoothly. He also needs a physician who is willing to cooperate with the institution's staff. The social workers in this case argue that David has engaged in some asocial behavior—behavior they believe can be controlled more productively in other ways. Whose welfare takes priority? Is their responsibility to David and their own treatment plans, the executive director, the physician, or to the other chil-dren in the institution who also have rights the social workers are obligated to support?

Non–Social Work Employers

When a social worker is employed by an organization outside the human services field, she may face even more perplexing ethical problems. Today, social workers are employed by hospitals, industry, police, prisons, the mili-tary, colleges, long-term care facilities, and a variety of other organizations that are not social work oriented. To whom do these social workers owe their *primary* loyalty? Who is the "client" of these social workers? For example, the employees of a large manufacturer may consult about personal problems with the social worker whom their employer has hired. Should the employer be informed when a worker's problems may affect the production schedule of a factory or that may have security implications? Should detectives have access to confidential information that a prison social worker has obtained from her contacts with prisoners?

The problem of identifying who is the client may be especially difficult for social workers in military service. Consider Exemplar 10.5.

❖ 10.5 A Colonel Outranks a Captain

Pfc. Richard Mozart recently discussed some personal difficulties with Capt. Emilio Pacifico, a social worker on an air force base. Mozart is very concerned about his aged parents, who live in a distant state and who find it increasingly difficult to cope by themselves. He has been so worried about this situation that he has started to use drugs intermit-tently. He told Capt. Pacifico about this in confidence.

Recently, because of some physical complaints, Mozart took a number of tests at the base hospital, including a urinalysis. The results of this test confirmed his use of drugs, but Pfc. Mozart is not aware of this finding.

On this base, the commander does not have access to the medical files of servicemen, but social workers, psychologists, nurses, and physicians have ready access. Yesterday, the base commander, Col. Benjamin Brown, discussed with Capt. Pacifico his concerns about Pfc. Mozart. His work has been less than satisfactory; his behavior suggests that he has serious problems and that he may be on drugs. Col. Brown asked Capt. Pacifico to check out the situation and let him know whether Mozart uses drugs.

Capt. Pacifico is troubled by this request. Must he comply with the order issued by his commanding officer and disclose the results of the medical test or information that he has received on a confidential basis from his client? Should he refuse and claim privileged communications? What is the ethical behavior expected of him?

The Exemplar 10.6 describes an ethical dilemma that a social worker involved in international service may encounter, but it has implications for workers in many other settings.

❖ 10.6 Serving Only the Good People or . . . ?

Amanda Frankel is a social worker for an international aid organization in a war zone. The forces of one side of the conflict are particularly cruel, attacking civilians, raping young girls and older women, and murdering groups of men and burying their bodies to do away with evidence. Until yesterday, Ms. Frankel was happy and proud to serve those in need who were being attacked. Then her supervisor sent a message that she was going to be transferred to the other side to serve the people there. Just as here, she would serve all people, including military and paramilitary personnel. She was awake all night considering what she should do. What is the ethically correct choice in this situation?

In what way is Ethical Principle 2 (equality and inequality) relevant to Ms. Frankel's situation and dilemma? In what ways do her personal values conflict with her employing agency's values and requirements? Does the *Code of Ethics* suggest there is a correct choice for Ms. Frankel? Can you identify in your local community situations in which social workers might have their personal values challenged by similar decisions by the agencies for which they work?

Ethical problems arising out of adherence to agency policies occur in all settings. Some of our illustrations are taken from non–social work settings because there the ethical dilemmas may be more evident. Social workers employed by social agencies, however should not think that these problems cannot happen to them, as Exemplar 10.7 illustrates.

❖ 10.7 Apple Hill Young Adult Social Club

The Apple Hill Community Center is a group service and recreation agency in a changing neighborhood. When it was established almost 50 years ago, it served an immigrant population and was instrumental in the Americanization of many thousands of newcomers. It now sees "character building" and "strengthening democratic decision making" as its major contribution to the community. As a matter of policy, it avoids all political activities. Neither staff nor groups affiliated with the center are allowed to take a public stand on controversial issues.

Otto Zupan, a social group worker, staffs the Young Adult Social Club. This group is composed of 25 young men, ages 18 to 21, almost all of whom are high school graduates. They spend much time at the community center because most of them are unemployed. Lately, they have talked a lot about why there are no jobs for them. Some thought that the recession was to blame; others felt it was because they were African Americans. Otto urged them to do some research and see if they could come up with some answers to their question. The results of their field study left little doubt that they were the victims of discriminatory hiring practices. Otto urged them to go public because discrimination in hiring was against the law. Letting the public know about their findings might help them get a better break when applying for the next job. They thought that Otto's idea was great and decided to call a news conference. They asked Otto to arrange for a room at the center for the news conference.

When Otto talked over their plan with the center's director, he was rebuffed flatly. Not only could they not have a room for the news conference, but as a center social club they could not engage at all in this type of action program. Furthermore, Otto must do everything to bring the group back to its original objectives as a social club. The center director added that if he could not do this, he should ask for another assignment.

Loyalty to agency rules or meeting client needs—these are two conflicting professional obligations that create a serious ethical problem for social worker Otto Zupan. Is it ethical for him to abide by the agency's directives and abandon the young adults at this critical point in their development? Should he ignore his obligations to his employer and help group members organize outside the center? What is the ethical stance demanded of a social worker who faces this situation?

Another type of ethical dilemma occurs when an agency channels clients into programs that are not beneficial for them. For example, what are the ethical issues faced by social workers when a large number of unskilled men and women are directed into job-training programs that lead only to dead-end or nonexistent jobs? Should social workers act against agency policy and tell their clients all that they know about these programs? Is it more ethical to follow organizational directives and keep quiet? How does a social worker make ethical decisions of this type?

What are the ethical implications when a social agency engages in discriminatory practices? There was a time when such practices were blatant and open; now they are less obvious but may be equally damaging. One child welfare agency places white children in adoptive homes and minority children in institutions "because there are no adoptive homes for them." In another agency, homosexual AIDS patients receive one type of service, while heterosexual AIDS patients receive another type of service. Whatever the reason, discriminatory practices never benefit the client who is being discriminated against. The *Code of Ethics* clearly states, "Social workers should not practice, condone, facilitate, or collaborate with any form of discrimination on the basis of race, ethnicity, national origin, color, sex, sexual orientation, age, marital status, political belief, religion, or mental or physical disability" (NASW *Code,* 1999, 4.02). What does this mean in practice? Should a social worker refuse to accept employment in an agency that practices discrimination? Must she resign when she discovers such practices? Should she ignore such agency policies and, whenever possible, not follow them? Or should she accept a job with the intention to change the agency? Consider Exemplar 10.8. What would you do if you had Dale Jenkins's job?

❖ 10.8 Social Work in a Bank

Social worker Dale Jenkins is employed by a large bank as a community representative in a minority neighborhood. Jenkins is African American. Part of his assignment is to be visible and become accepted in the community. He has been very successful in meeting this objective. He is accepted by the neighborhood's residents and is liked by nearly everyone. In the past year, he has been able to help a number of residents qualify for business loans and mortgages. Mr. Stamos, vice president of the bank to whom he reports, recently told Jenkins that the bank has decided to direct less money and services to this neighborhood, but his job is safe. Stamos implied that in a few years the bank might again direct monies to this neighborhood. In the meantime, Jenkins should be more selective in referring residents to the bank for loans and mortgages.

Jenkins understood this message as meaning that the bank no longer would give mortgages to minority group applicants.

He considered the options he had, including the following:

1. Making sure that he had understood correctly. If he didn't, then he could discuss with Mr. Stamos how the misunderstanding had occurred and how to avoid it in the future. However, if he did understand correctly, then he could consider other options, such as:
2. Try to persuade Mr. Stamos and other bank officials to change the new and discriminating policy.

3. Ignore the new policy and operate as he had in the past.
4. Tell community leaders about the new policy and encourage them to apply political pressure on the bank to change its policy.

What are the ethical implications of each of the options that Jenkins is considering?

ETHICAL DILEMMAS IN SOCIAL WORK ADMINISTRATION AND SUPERVISION

Social work administrators and supervisors have an ethical responsibility to protect clients' rights and to foster an atmosphere in which workers will do the same. At the same time, they are accountable to the agency's sponsors for productivity and for operating within the authorized budget. With diminishing budgets and rising demands, this can be a most difficult task. In addition to ethical obligations toward the agency, an administrator also has responsibilities toward his or her employees.

Many administrators think that the line between ethical and unethical behavior is crossed only when their activities result in personal gain. They feel that it is ethical to do whatever is necessary as long as their activities benefit clients or the agency. If a government contract provides money for staff training but not for staff supervision, they do not hesitate to "redefine" supervision as training. Recreation services are renamed "respite services" if government funding for recreation is dropped (Bernstein, 1990). In such cases, an illusion of compliance is achieved by playing semantic games, but is this ethical?

Another ethical dilemma that some administrators face occurs when there is a conflict between their responsibility for organizational maintenance, on the one hand, and professional or communal responsibility, on the other hand. Take the case of the director of a children's home that for decades has provided institutional care for infants aged three days to one year. From a professional point of view, there is no longer any justification for continuing this service, yet the director has responsibilities to the sponsors, to staff, and to others for ensuring that the agency continues to function. How would you respond to the ethical dilemma facing this social work administrator?

A dilemma of a different nature is presented in Exemplar 10.9.

❖ 10.9 The Good of the Agency, Community, or the Staff?

John Meenaghan is a social planner in a United Way community fundraising and social planning agency. Over lunch, Melissa Bridgewater, a longtime friend and a member of the executive staff, told him that the executive director—who is not a social worker—and several favored members of his personal staff have been living lavishly on their expense accounts and padding their expenses. All the information she provided in the past has been completely accurate. The executive director is tyrannical and punitive but has been extremely creative and improved productivity many times over. The fund drive has reached new heights. Later, in his office, Meenaghan spent almost an hour contemplating why Ms. Bridgewater shared this information with him. Why doesn't she go public herself? What should he *do,* if anything?

John Meenaghan understands that "whistle-blowing" can do good as well as harm. If he goes public with the information about agency corruption, he could do much harm to the agency and undermine its fund-raising capacity for some time into the future. Alternately, if he goes public with the information (for which he has no direct evidence), he could perform a public service, protecting the community's resources while ensuring that funds will be spent on the problems for which they were intended. At the same time, the element of trust that generally exists in the agency will be destroyed. The authority structure of the agency will be damaged, at least for a time, thus potentially creating havoc in the administration. If he reports the problem to his supervisor or to a member of the board of directors, he might further his good relations with some superiors and colleagues, and perhaps with members of the board, but the executive director and others will be angry and will be liable to legal actions. Finding successful executive directors is not an easy task.

A number of standards in the *Code* are relevant to this situation: "Social workers' primary responsibility is to promote the well-being of clients" (NASW *Code,* 1999, 1.01); "Social workers should treat colleagues with respect and should represent accurately and fairly the qualifications, views, and obligations of colleagues" (NASW *Code,* 1999, 2.01a, c). In addition, "social workers should take adequate measures to discourage, prevent, expose, and correct the unethical conduct of colleagues" (NASW *Code,* 1999, 2.11a, b, c, d); "social work administrators should take reasonable steps to ensure that the working environment for which they are responsible is consistent with and encourages compliance with the NASW *Code of Ethics.* Social work administrators should take reasonable steps to eliminate any conditions in their organizations that violate, interfere with, or discourage compliance with the *Code*" (NASW *Code,* 1999, 3.07d); and "social workers should be diligent stewards of the resources of their employing organizations, wisely conserving funds where appropriate and never misappropriating funds or using them for unintended purposes" (NASW *Code,* 1999, 3.09g).

Who is the client or what is the priority in this situation? Ms. Bridgewater, who shared the information? The executive director, who has done an outstanding job for the agency, maintaining the viability of the United Way? The community agencies that benefit from the United Way? Those being served by communal agencies? What does John Meenaghan owe Melissa Bridgewater? Lacking detailed information about the improprieties, would he be treating any of his colleagues with respect if he were to move forward? Does he have the right to correct a non–social worker, someone who is not bound by the *Code?* What would you advise John Meenaghan to do?

More generally, both supervisors and administrators have a responsibility to support workers' ethical behaviors and to stop workers' unethical behaviors. They must remember, however, that workers (as well as clients) are human beings, not robots.

Dual-Role Relations

Supervisors and agency administrators are powerful persons because they have considerable influence over the social workers and students whom they employ or supervise. They make assignments, evaluate their work, decide on promotions, and at times terminate their employment. They are obligated to use this power in ethical ways. This rule has a number of implications.

Any relationship with employees or students in which an administrator/supervisor takes advantage, exploits, or harms persons with less power is unethical, even if the initiative comes from the employee or supervisee. This holds not only for sexual relations but also for other types of relations that create bonds that may negatively affect the professional relationship. Several standards in the *Code of Ethics* provide clearer guidance for social workers in regard to dual/multiple relationships. This area of unethical behavior has received increased attention in recent years. Here we wish to highlight the need for social workers to consider seriously the ethical problems that may arise in work settings among persons with different degrees of power.

How would you assess the following supervisory situations:

- Your supervisee's husband is an insurance broker. She tells you that her husband will give you a large discount on your automobile insurance. Will you avoid the dual relationship problem if you place your insurance with him but pay the full insurance rate?
- Your supervisee, a BSW social worker, just enrolled in a graduate school of social work. The school is ready to appoint you as a field instructor and have you supervise your employee's field instruction.
- Your agency is employing your wife as a caseworker and assigns you to work on a team with her.
- Your supervisee has a summer home in the mountains. She invites you and your children to use it this summer while she and her husband are vacationing elsewhere.

In each of these situations, there is a potential for an ethical difficulty. Do the standards give clear answers to these problems?

Other Conflicting Obligations

Social work supervisors are often in the position of the person "in between" with multiple pressures and obligations, as Exemplars 10.10, 10.11, and 10.12 illustrate.

Supervisors have many roles and obligations in social agencies. In addition to their primary responsibility to ensure the delivery of high-quality services. Their responsibilities include committee meetings, assignments representing the agency in the community, phone calls, emergencies, and other demands on their time and energy.

❖ 10.10 Friend, Self, Family, Agency—Loyalty to Whom?

Thomas Kinane recently was promoted to supervisor, a job that pays much more than his prior position. His teenage daughter has been in therapy, and he feels lucky because the money is arriving just when the family needs it. He is responsible for supervision of 12 workers who are on a task force to implement a new service in Gordonsville, a satellite location. He has an enormous amount of record keeping and report writing to do. Because of demands of the job on his time, both in Gordonsville and central headquarters, he frequently has to cancel supervisory sessions with individual workers, yet he does not feel ready to use group supervision—which would help him to better control his time.

Thomas Kinane's situation is not unusual. He wants to succeed in his job, needs the money, and has a responsibility to his employer. But he also has a responsibility to his supervisees' clients, to his family, and to his supervisees. How would you choose among these conflicting obligations? What would you choose to do?

❖ 10.11 The Ethics of Moonlighting

The employment contract of the Bay City Department of Human Services (DHS) states: "Social workers may not work for another employer in their professional social work capacity, even outside of their regular working hours." Every new social work employee in the department is made aware of this provision and acknowledges her agreement to it in writing. The other evening, Ellen and Bill Stock rushed their infant daughter Sharon to the hospital because she had a very high fever. While Ellen stayed with the baby in the emergency room, Bill handled the admission routines.

Later on, Bill told Ellen that among the people with whom he had to speak in the admissions office was a social worker. He had been very impressed by her warm and sympathetic interest in their sick child. Ellen asked Bill if he recalled the worker's name and was surprised to learn that it was Joan Gilligan, one of the social workers she supervises at DHS.

On the way out of the hospital, Ellen peeked into the admissions office to make sure that this was the same social worker she supervises. It was. Since Ellen did not use her husband's name at work, she was sure that Joan did not realize that she had been helping her supervisor's husband.

Ellen did not know what she should do about her discovery. On the one hand, Joan's moonlighting was in violation of the commitment that she, like all DHS social workers, had made to the agency. The *Code of Ethics* states clearly, "Social workers generally should adhere to commitments made to employers and employing organizations" (NASW *Code*, 1999, 3.09a). On the other hand, Joan's moonlighting did not harm anyone. As a matter of fact, her presence in the hospital admissions office benefits many patients at a time when they are in a state of crisis. What about Ellen's obligations to her employer? To her colleague? To the profession? Are there other ways to address this dilemma, such as working to change the agency policy?

Exemplar 10.12 deals with yet another work-related issue.

❖ 10.12 A Caribbean Cruise

Wilma Stevens supervises a unit of six social workers, of whom Carla Bick is the most qualified and most effective. Last week, Carla was not at work. Her boyfriend called in to say that Carla had a bad case of the flu and would probably be out all week. Today, she returned to work, bringing a note from her doctor stating that she had been sick all week. Aside from the note, there was no evidence of her having been sick. She explained that yesterday she went to the beach; this accounted for her suntan.

Wilma's cousin had been on a Caribbean cruise all of last week. When they had supper together, her cousin told Wilma all about the trip and about the many interesting people she met on board the cruise ship. One of those people was a young social worker, Carla Bick. The cousin wondered whether Wilma happened to know her.

As Wilma thought about Carla's absence from work last week, she noted the following points:

1. Carla's absence was not authorized and was in violation of agency policy.
2. Carla's behavior was unethical and unprofessional.
3. Carla harmed her clients by failing to provide them with regular service.
4. Carla had not told the truth when she claimed that she had been sick.
5. Carla was her best worker and Wilma did not want to lose her.

Other workers probably also misused sick leave but were not caught. Would making an example of Carla persuade others to desist from this unethical behavior? If Wilma does so, what will be the cost? Would making an example of Carla be unethical since her privacy and respect would be violated?

It will be difficult to differentiate between Wilma's administrative/supervisory responsibilities and her professional social work responsibilities. Any decision that she will reach will necessarily include both aspects. Whatever her decision, it will have ethical implications.

One of the assignments of an agency director is to "staff" the board of directors, the agency's policy-making group. Establishing a good working relationship with board members is essential for every successful agency director. At times, the agency director will encounter ethical dilemmas because of conflicting ethical principles. Consider Exemplar 10.13.

❖ 10.13 The Board of Directors of the Alzheimer's Association

The Alzheimer's Association is a local, voluntary United Fund agency established about 10 years ago to provide a wide range of community services to families of Alzheimer's patients. At last night's meeting, the board of directors voted to eliminate all homemaker services because the insurance carrier had again raised the premium for liability insurance that homemakers must carry.

You, the agency director, know that the demand for homemaker services has always exceeded the staff available. It is not only a popular service, but a resource that has enabled many families to keep their Alzheimer's patient at home instead of placing him or her in an institutional facility.

You know that the agency provides other services for which there are fewer demands; reducing these services could pay for the higher insurance premiums. These other services, however, are of special interest to several board members; they will do anything to protect their favorite services.

What are the ethical problems that this exemplar raises? For example, to whom does the director owe loyalty?

Supervisor Ethics and Liabilities

Ethics complaints and legal actions can be brought by clients and employees against supervisors that allege ethical breaches or negligence by the supervisors and by those whom they supervise. Supervisors are affected by two types of liability. *Direct liability* may be charged when harm is caused by the supervisor's acts of omission or commission, such as when the supervisee is assigned duties for which the supervisee is inadequately trained or experienced, or when supervisors do not follow supervision guidelines promulgated by their state boards and/or professional associations.

Supervisors may also be charged when the supervisee makes mistakes. Some claims may implicate supervisors under the legal doctrine of *respondeat superior* that is "let the master respond." This doctrine—also known as *vicarious liability*—means a supervisor is responsible for the actions of a supervisee that were conducted during the course of employment, training, or field instruction, including potential ethical lapses.

The *Code of Ethics* expects social workers to provide competent service, that is, with the skill and care of the ordinary competent practitioner. This standard of care is established by professional practice, and courts have accepted the "community" or "locality" rule when defining what is meant by the standard of care in social work and other human service professions (Nurcombe & Partlett, 1994). The standard of care is the benchmark used by courts and others to judge whether or not the professional services performed by a practitioner compare with those of other professionals of similar training and experience in their locale.

ADVERTISEMENTS AND SOLICITATION

As of 1988, NASW members are free to *truthfully* and *nondeceptively* advertise and market their services. Payment to a referral service is allowed. Prospective clients can be solicited among clients receiving similar services from another professional.

A number of ethical standards in the *Code* are intended to deal with issues related to these problems (1999, 4.06c, 4.07a, b).

The *Code* makes some things clear, while others remain ambiguous. What is truthful, nondeceptive advertising and marketing? How much training, education, and experience entitle one to claim expertise in a particular therapeutic method? Who is vulnerable to undue influence, manipulation, or coercion? What is unwarranted solicitation of potential clients? Aren't most—if not all—social work clients under stress? How much real choice does a potential client under stress actually possess? Do such stressful situations allow for truly informed consent in which the liberty and autonomy of the potential client are assured?

Social workers are not to give or receive payment for a referral when no professional service is provided by the referring social worker (NASW *Code*, 1999, 2.06c). Can referral services always be distinguished from other on-going services being provided? Is referral itself a professional service, entitling the referring social worker to receive a payment? Are personal gifts—donations to organizations or political campaigns supported by a social worker who refers cases to you—"payments"? At what point would a "gift" clearly be a payment? What about the payment or receipt of referral fees by organizations? Is there a double standard?

❖ 10.14 Payment for Referrals in an Employee Assistance Program

Libby Rudo is a social worker in the employee assistance program (EAP) of the Colonel Electric Company. The company administration worked out an arrangement with one agency—the Central City Services Group—so that they will pay the Colonel Electric Company a fee for every case referred to them. They also established a policy that the EAP staff will refer employees to Central City Services only when longer-term treatment is needed by employees than is provided by the EAP. Ms. Rudo is certain that Mrs. Quarles, who is in her office consulting her about a family problem, requires a kind of treatment that is not available at Central City Services but that is the only acceptable treatment agency where employees can be referred. What is the ethical thing for Ms. Rudo to do?

May a social worker solicit payments for referrals so that they are paid not to her but to a nonprofit agency or department? If a social worker is a member of a for-profit group, may the group receive payment for referrals and include the payments in the overall income of the group to be distributed to the members as part of their earnings? When a business firm provides free or discounted service for one of your poor clients because of other referrals you have sent to the firm, is this "payment" a fee for referrals in the same way that it would be if you received it directly?

In this chapter, we examined ethical dilemmas that develop in relationship to colleagues, agencies, employers, dual relationships, and advertisement and solicitation of clients. These ethical dilemmas are complex and raise difficult issues for practitioners whose ethical actions may require "taking on" one's employer, colleagues with whom one has a long positive history, and others. Although we have focused mainly on the dilemmas that confront direct practitioners, we introduced some of the dilemmas that may face administrators and supervisors as well.

EXERCISES

1. Consider the ethical dilemmas facing social worker Timothy Land (Exemplar A.5 in Appendix A). How would you resolve the ethical problems that he faces?
2. Some employment situations make demands that may force social workers to violate professional ethics (if they do not want to look for another job). Exemplar A.1 (in Appendix A) presents such a dilemma. How would you respond to this ethical challenge?
3. Does your state have a list of unethical professional behaviors that are actionable by your state social work licensing authority? What are the unethical professional behaviors on the authority's promulgated list? Are there actions that you would add to the list? What sanctions or punishments are available to this authority? Are there other sanctions that you would like to add?
4. Review the employee handbook for the agency where you are employed or in field instruction. Are any of the agency policies inconsistent with the *Code of Ethics?* How would you address these inconsistencies?
5. In a community organization, you are a member of the staff at a staff meeting when several employees advocate that only African American professionals should work with African American groups and neighborhoods and that only lesbian and gay persons can be successful in working with lesbian and gay communities (Shillington, Dotson, & Faulkner, 1994; Tully, Craig, & Nugent, 1994). However, the *Code* states "social workers should not practice, condone, facilitate, or collaborate with any form of discrimination on the basis of race, ethnicity, national origin, color, sex, sexual orientation, age, marital status, political belief, religion, or mental or physical disability" (NASW *Code*, 1999, 4.02). What should you do?

SUGGESTIONS FOR ADDITIONAL READINGS

See Berman-Rossi and Rossi (1990) for an exploration of problems facing social workers in schools in regard to childrens' self-determination and autonomy. Verschelden (1993) argues that social work values and ethics suggest social workers should be pacifists. Do you join Verschelden in the belief that social work ethics require a social worker to be a pacifist? Loewenberg (1987) analyzes how a social worker might respond to a colleague's unethical behavior. Ethical decision making by social work supervisors is examined by Congress (1992). Steinberg, Levine, and Doueck (1997) report on the effects of legally mandated child-abuse reports on therapeutic relationships.

11 CHAPTER | **Private Practice Social Work**

A number of ethical problems and dilemmas faced by private practitioners will be discussed in this chapter. Some of these problems (such as misdiagnosis) are also encountered by social workers in agency practice but are discussed here because practitioners in private practice come upon these problems and dilemmas more often and more acutely than their colleagues who practice in social work agencies. Many of the ethical problems discussed in this chapter are problems faced not only by social workers but by all private practitioners, regardless of their professional affiliation.

In 1995, of the employed NASW members surveyed, 14% of the respondents indicated private solo practices as their primary practice setting. Another 31.9% indicated private solo practices as their secondary practice setting. Thus, a large number and percentage of employed NASW members in 1995 were in private practice, either on a full-time or part-time basis (Gibelman & Schervish, 1997). This pattern, undoubtedly, continues.

When the NASW Delegate Assembly officially recognized private practice in 1964, few thought that so many social workers would choose to practice outside the traditional agency setting. The thinking of the delegates on this question is clear from the 1964 decision, which states specifically that "practice within socially sponsored organization structures must remain the primary avenue for the implementation of goals of the profession" (Golton, 1971, p. 950). The recognition of private practice by the professional association, along with their view that socially sponsored, organization-based social work would remain the predominant emphasis, must be viewed within a historical context. The creation of private practice social work is the reverse of the evolutionary pattern of the development of professions in general. Toren (1972) makes the point that the classic professions (medicine, law, clergy) grew out of individual, solo practice. Social work reversed this evolutionary pattern by first being organization-based, a factor that influences social work's commitments, professional conduct, degree of public recognition, theoretical study and technical skills, and its focus on supervision.

Because many social workers engage in private practice, moving away from nonprofit and governmental auspices, there is concern among some social workers about changing attitudes and behaviors that may no longer be in consonance with the profession's ethics. This concern was expressed by Specht and Courtney (1994), as well as others, who suggested that one consequence of such a shift is a diminishment of social work's historic mission to help the poor and oppressed, those who are the most vulnerable in our society. This charge has been made of the profession as a whole, and particularly of social agencies. The problem is especially critical when social workers opt for private practice in order to gain status, prestige, and higher incomes. Gibelman and Schervish (1997, p. 164) ask: "How do private practitioners honor a professional code of ethics that not only requires services to individuals but delineates social workers' responsibility to make larger social systems more responsive to the needs of individuals?" One conclusion of a national survey of the NASW Register of Clinical Social Workers was that "private practitioners concentrate their work on the 'haves' of society, rather than the 'have nots'" (Strom, 1994, p. 87). Many practitioners were found to have a "bottom line" orientation as reflected in the level of fees and the limited amount of free care provided. When this happens, some professional ethics concerns (e.g., social responsibility) may become secondary considerations.

Private practice is consistent with the capitalist and free enterprise system. Furthermore, American values stress freedom and autonomy. The freedom of social workers as private entrepreneurs to enter into contractual relationships with those persons who seek assistance is consistent with American values. Is there an ethical problem when some people go without services while others who are able to pay receive the assistance they need? Does the *Code* or the ethical principles screen (Chapter 4) provide sufficient guidance for social workers who want to decide whether to engage in full-time or part-time private practice? Whether to serve clients who are unable to pay?

FEES

Social workers must make sure that the fees they charge "are fair, reasonable, and commensurate with the services performed. Consideration should be given to clients' ability to pay" (NASW *Code*, 1999, 1.13a). Some private practitioners do not know what "due regard for the client's ability to pay" means. Does it require a sliding scale? Does it mean that varying rates should be charged for the same service, depending on the financial resources of the

client? Or is a "reasonable fee" the fee that most private practice social workers in a specific locality charge?

Only sparse attention has been paid in social work literature to fees, but
issues of fee payment have increased in number as more social workers enter
private practice and as private practices (and agencies) are increasingly
affected by managed care and insurance reimbursement. There are numerous
ethical dilemmas that confront a private practitioner around fee setting and
collection. A fundamental issue is the balance between the practitioner's
income needs and the client's interests. Seeking a balance between priorities
can be difficult. Among these dilemmas are what should one do about clients
who are financially limited? For those whose income goes up or down signif-
icantly? What is an adequate income for a social work practitioner? Are there
any conflicts in the *Code* with social workers as entrepreneurs in private practice (Wolfson, 1999)?

There are other questions concerning fees. For example, one of the ethical
principles of the NASW *Code of Ethics* states that "Social workers are encouraged to volunteer some portion of their professional skills with no expectation
of significant financial return (pro bono service)" (NASW *Code*, 1999, Ethical
Principles). Does this principle require that social workers in private practice
take some clients who are unable to pay? What if you and your family are
experiencing financial pressures?

Client Dumping

What is the ethical thing to do when, during the course of treatment, a client's
situation changes and he can no longer pay the fee? Consider the situation of
Larry Firth in Exemplar 11.1.

❖ 11.1 A Difficult Family Situation

Larry Firth came to consult with you about a "difficult family situation."
His wife has left him and their two sons in order to live with her
boyfriend. He himself has formed a satisfactory relationship with a married neighbor. However, he is concerned what his teenage sons will say
and do when they find out the truth about their parents.

You are making good progress in helping Larry Firth come to grips
with his problem. Today, however, Larry tells you that he has lost his job
and that he can no longer afford your fee. You are not yet sufficiently
well established to carry "free" cases. There is no family service agency
in the town that provides services free of charge. What should you do?

"Dumping the client" is one way that some practitioners have responded
to clients who can no longer pay the fee. There are various ways to dump a
client. A worker may tell a client that his problem has been solved successfully
(when it has not yet been solved) or that no more can be done for him (when,
in fact, the worker could still be helpful). The worker may cancel appointments
so frequently that the client loses interest, or the worker may refer a client who

no longer can afford his services to a public or private not-for-profit agency. No matter what technique is used, in *some cases,* the worker's objective is to get rid of the client who can no longer pay. In other cases, referral to an agency may not be "dumping" but the most helpful thing to do. Barker (1992, p. 110) suggests that private practitioners "are far more likely to engage in the unethical behavior of premature or precipitous termination than are agency-based professionals." What can an ethical practitioner do when this situation arises? As insurance companies place limits on the number of sessions that they will cover, how should a social worker address problems that she feels will require more sessions than the insurance company will pay for? Should she do the best she can in the number of sessions allowed, work with the client to establish treatment goals that can be achieved in that time frame, or provide free or reduced cost services after the insurance coverage ends?

A national survey of experienced and well-established psychotherapists (psychologists) found that most continued care when insurance coverage ended. They chose the following options in descending order: (1) advocate for more benefits; (2) patient pays out of his or her own pocket; (3) reduce the fee for patient who continues on a self-paying basis; (4) treat the person on a pro bono basis; (5) make a proper referral to an agency for continued treatment; (6) terminate treatment; and (7) alter the diagnosis so treatment would be covered (Murphy, DeBernardo, & Shoemaker, 1998). Another available option a social worker should consider is that the client will pay when his financial situation improves. None of these options is without problems, but each—with the exception of termination—may be viewed as ethical. In the case of termination, much would depend on the state of the person, the nature of the problem, how close the client is to attainment of the goals of treatment, the number of persons being seen by the social worker, and other such variables.

Double Billing

Double billing occurs when a service provider bills a third party, such as an insurance company or a governmental program, for services not provided or for services already billed to another party. This practice usually occurs without the client's knowledge. It is both unethical and illegal. If detected, the practitioner is liable to criminal prosecution and to malpractice litigation.

DIAGNOSIS AND MISDIAGNOSIS

The controversy about the place of diagnosis in social work practice, which will be discussed, has a number of ethical aspects. Many social workers believe that diagnosis is an essential element in every professional intervention, but others reject its use because they consider it an inappropriate application of the medical model to social work practice. Some point to psychologist Carl Rogers, who consistently argued against the use of any psychodiagnosis because he thought that such a procedure interfered with a client's need to experience himself subjectively. Diagnosis, according to Rogers (1951), substitutes an external definition about the problem at a time when it is most crucial that the client gain greater subjective clarity about his situation. Psychiatrist R.D. Laing (1967) also criticized traditional diagnostics because it often leads to a self-fulfilling prophecy. If certain behaviors are expected, chances are that the client will perform them and/or that the worker will detect them.

For many, the problem of diagnostics has become even more critical in recent years as use of the *Diagnostic and Statistical Manual of Mental Disorders,* (DSM-IV-TR) of the American Psychiatric Association (APA, 2000) has spread rapidly among social workers. Many social workers are required to use the DSM-IV-TR even though they do not think that it is an appropriate diagnostic instrument for social work practice because many government programs (which authorize service or reimburse for service rendered only on the basis of an appropriate DSM-IV-TR diagnosis) and by insurance companies (which require such a diagnosis before they will authorize third-party payments) (Schamess, 1996). Often, authorization and reimbursements are limited to certain diagnostic categories; in other instances, the amount of reimbursement (or the length of treatment authorized) depends on the diagnosis submitted. All of these requirements put pressure on social workers to use this diagnostic instrument. Some engage in deliberate misdiagnosis in order to meet the stated requirements for reimbursable social work treatment. Exemplar 11.2 illustrates one of the ethical problems that this creates.

❖ 11.2 Let the Insurance Company Pay the Bill

When Christine Sales saw her private practice social worker last week at their initial session, she mentioned that she hoped her insurance company would reimburse her for these sessions. Today, Christine brought in the insurance company forms and asked her social worker to complete them. The social worker, who was familiar with the requirements of this insurance company, realized right away that she would have to report a more "serious" diagnosis than was clinically indicated if she were to qualify the client for insurance reimbursement.

Under what circumstances is it ethical for a social worker to lie about a diagnosis? What are the potential risks for both the client and the social worker? What is the ethical thing to do if the only way the person will receive services is for the social worker to "fudge" the diagnosis?

While some social workers will report a more serious diagnosis to obtain third-party payments, others may will report less serious diagnoses and justify it as harmless or in the client's best interest. Generally, social workers use "the least noxious diagnosis" (also known as the mercy diagnosis). Reasons for deliberate misdiagnosis include the following:

1. It minimizes the communication of damaging and confidential information to nonsocial workers, especially to insurance companies and others.
2. It avoids the labeling effects of a more severe diagnosis.
3. It limits the adverse impact on a client's self-esteem if the client should become aware of the diagnosis.

4. It can protect the future employment prospects (and possibly protect a current job) for the client, as well as the potential for future insurance coverage.

These reasons are used to justify underdiagnosis by suggesting that it is in the client's interest. Some social workers admit to deliberate underdiagnosis at some time. For example, they might use the category adjustment disorders when a more serious diagnosis would have been more accurate. Others may use overdiagnosis, that is, they report a more severe diagnosis than the actual diagnosis. They may use an Axis I diagnosis when this is not warranted in order to qualify a client for insurance reimbursement. Though claiming that overdiagnosis is done for the client's benefit, the real beneficiary may be the social worker whose payments are now guaranteed by a third party.

Misdiagnosis of any type may be one result of managed care and third-party payers and their intrusion into the professional relationship. While managed care may provoke such responses in some cases, the misdiagnoses are the responsibility of the social workers who make or report the incorrect diagnosis. However, not all misdiagnoses are the result of a tactic to gain benefits for the client; some misdiagnoses are the result of practitioner incompetence, the ambiguity of some diagnostic categories, failure to consider biological and physical factors, or failure to ensure medical review when indicated. Competency in all aspects of the social worker's practice is an expected ethical norm.

Another ethical problem arises when a social worker reports a diagnosis for one individual when the primary problem is located in the family system. Since DSM-IV-TR allows only the diagnosis of problems of an individual, this deliberate misdiagnosis is usually used to get insurance reimbursement.

Even under the best of circumstances, social workers, like many other professionals, will make mistakes and err in their diagnosis. Mistakes are unfortunate and regrettable, but probably inevitable. Among the mistakes in diagnostics that have ethical implications are the following:

1. Lack of sufficient knowledge in using diagnostic instruments such as DSM-IV-TR
2. Poor professional judgment
3. Deliberate misdiagnosis, often in connection with third-party insurance reimbursement claims and/or reimbursement by government programs

Mistakes such as these may involve both illegal and unethical behaviors. Even though diagnosis and assessment are often viewed as professional techniques that are based solely on skill and knowledge, they always involve ethical considerations. Examine Exemplar 11.3 and consider the ethical aspects involved in arriving at a diagnosis.

❖ 11.3 Barry Has a Learning Problem

Barry is a first-grader. He has two older brothers, ages eight and ten. His oldest brother is doing very well in school, but his middle brother has been identified as a "slow learner" and is in a special education class. Barry's teacher reports that Barry also has some learning problems, and he finds it difficult to keep up with the rest of his class.

The school social worker and the educational psychologist have been discussing what to do with Barry. His tests indicate a relatively low score but within the "normal" range. The social worker knows that Barry would benefit from special attention that his regular classroom teacher cannot give him. However, sending Barry to an ungraded class might label him for the rest of his life, result in his being stigmatized, perhaps being insufficiently challenged, and potentially placing real limits on what is possible for his future.

In this situation, as in many others, the "simple" technical task of diagnosis has a number of ethical aspects that every thoughtful social worker must consider seriously before arriving at a decision.

OTHER ETHICAL ISSUES

Fitting Diagnosis to Treatment

An ethical problem occurs whenever a social worker tries to fit the diagnosis to the treatment she plans to use, rather than select a treatment that is appropriate for the identified problem. This ethical problem occurs in various guises. One such version is illustrated by Exemplar 11.4.

❖ 11.4 Individual or Family Therapy?

The parents and adolescent children in the Martin family have been having their problems. There has been a series of incidents in which everyone involved has been shouting at each other, calling each other names, or not talking to each other for days.

Ms. Martin feels that she has failed as a mother. She has asked Ms. Aberdeen, a private social worker, to help her cope with her feelings. After talking with Ms. Martin, the worker felt that the problem went beyond Ms. Martin's feelings and that family therapy was indicated. Even though Ms. Aberdeen is a competent social worker, she has had no experience in providing family therapy. However, there are no family therapists in this rural county. Ms. Aberdeen, therefore, diagnoses the problem in such a way that individual therapy intervention is appropriate.

Is it ethical for Ms. Aberdeen to define the problem in a way that makes it possible for her to help Ms. Martin but not directly intervene with the family as a unit? From an ethical point of view, would it make a difference if this situation had occurred in a city where there were a number of family therapists? There are other ethical aspects to this issue. Professional ethics demand that the intervention method be selected on the basis of the social worker's best professional judgment. Using other criteria may be unethical. For example, long-term therapy may be indicated for a given case, but social workers may be required to indicate short-term treatment to comply with the requirements of a third-party payer. This may be done to maintain one's position on the insurer's professional panel of approved therapists. Kutchins and Kirk (1997) suggest that clinicians routinely try to fit their clinical diagnoses to the complexities of the DSM and to the requirements of managed care corporations. They refer to this as "an ethically challenged game of cat and mouse among therapists, clients, and payers" (p. 256).

Social workers in both private and agency-sponsored practice often have to use the DSM. Kutchins and Kirk (1997) raise additional questions about the ethics of its use. According to these authors, DSM "sweeps increasing numbers of human problems into the realm of psychiatric disorder and medical jurisdiction" (p. 16) on the basis of fragile scientific evidence, political advocacy, and pathologizing "those in our society who are undesirable and powerless" (p. 16). No claim is made that DSM is a valid classification system, and according to these authors, evidence is lacking for reliability claims.

There is another ethical conundrum for social workers related to DSM use. The use of DSM requires a medicalization of human or social situations. Trouble at school becomes "oppositional defiant behavior." Other human problems are translated into medical and stigmatizing terms; for example, not sleeping becomes "major depressive disorder," or bearing grudges becomes "paranoid personality disorder," etc. Developed under a grant from the National Association of Social Workers, the PIE (person-in-environment) system describes, classifies, and codes the problems of clients. It, however, does so in such a way that it clarifies aspects of the client's problems that are in the domain of social work and facilitates work with clients (Karis & Wandrei, 1992). Is the use of DSM instead of PIE ethical? Does the NASW *Code* provide guidance on these issues, or are these simply practical issues for those engaged in private practice? Is this an issue of pragmatism that requires an advocacy agenda by the profession of social work until the reimbursement system is less oriented toward the disease and medical model?

Supervision and Consultation

While social workers hold various views about the need for traditional supervision, there is a general consensus that an ethical social worker does not practice without availing herself of consultation. Consultation, however, costs money; skipping supervision may be one way to save money in private or agency practice. Does the NASW *Code* (1999) suggest implications for private practitioners (see sections 2.05a, b, c)?

Misrepresentation

The NASW *Code of Ethics* specifically states: "Social workers should ensure that their representations to clients, agencies, and the public of professional qualification, credentials, education, competence, affiliations, services provided, or results to be achieved are accurate" (NASW, 1999, 4.06c). What seems like a simple ethical rule gives rise to a number of questions, including the following:

1. Is it ethical for a social worker to identify herself as something other than a social worker (such as a marriage counselor or psychotherapist)?
2. Is it ethical for a social worker to call herself "Doctor" when she has not earned this degree?
3. Must a student social worker always identify herself as a student in field instruction placements, or can she present herself as "your social worker"?

Those who engage in one of these practices claim that they do so to give clients greater confidence in their worker and thus increase the chances for a successful outcome. Is this ethical?

Promises

Reamer (1995) studied 634 malpractice claims against social workers filed between 1969 and 1990, a period in which malpractice claims became increasingly frequent. The largest percentage filed was for incorrect treatment, including failure to introduce appropriate therapeutic interventions or to apply treatment techniques appropriately.

Myers and Thyer (1997) argue that social work clients have a right to receive effective, empirically validated treatment. The *Code of Ethics,* they suggest, should place an emphasis on the client's right to effective treatment but currently only requires a social worker to "strive to become and remain proficient in professional practice and the performance of professional functions" (NASW *Code,* 1999, 4.01b). Myers and Thyer call on NASW to include in the *Code* requirements that (1) encourage ever more responsible professional behavior by social workers and (2) empirically proven interventions as the *first* treatment choices by practitioners. Reflecting this point of view, Howard and Jenson (1999) advocate for guidelines to direct practice in the most effective and proven ways, faulting the professional association for failing to implement practice guidelines. Others argue that solving human problems through the use of an "approved list" of techniques would violate the richness and dignity of human struggles and triumphs. Social workers "deal with enormously complex and difficult issues. To do this well, they must be analytical, reflective, and compassionate in their approach to human suffering. They must recognize that they often know very little about the lives of those they serve and that, therefore, they must listen and learn from them" (Witkin, 1998, pp. 79–80).

Does the *Code* provide guidance for a social worker in regard to the promise to be helpful in regard to the presenting problem? Are both of the two perspectives (guidelines regarding effective practice, including interventive choices, should be empirically proven when possible *or* complexity of life situations argues against practice guidelines) presented ethically correct? In an attempt to convince potential clients to enter treatment, a social worker may claim or promise that she can help the client (perhaps even obtain a cure) when she only hopes that she can do so. Is this ethical? What do you think?

Preparation and Readiness for Private Practice

Professional life in social agencies is influenced by rules, limitations on interventive modes that can be used, relatively low salaries, and—in general—the constraints of employment in complex organizations. In addition, many graduate social workers carry debt burdens from their educations. In a market economy, the establishment of private practices can be seductive since they potentially can provide the practitioner greater autonomy, freedom to select clients, and greater choice of treatment interventions.

Ethical social workers will assess their qualifications and readiness to establish private practices. Part of this assessment is objective. One either has a professional license or other credentials or not. Other criteria are more subjective, such as one's motivations and sense of discipline, skill levels, and the ability to deal with one's own difficulties and limitations. For example, private practice requires arrangements be made for office space, insurance, referrals, record keeping, management of crises, and supervision and consultation (Matorin, Rosenberg, Levitt, & Rosenblum, 1987); the social worker must assess her ability to successfully make these arrangements. What other resources need to be available to ensure ethical practice within a private practice setting; for example, do experienced social workers need to be available to provide supervision or consultation?

Ethical standards (NASW *Code*, 1999, 1.04a, b) require that a social worker "provide services and represent themselves as competent within the boundaries of their education . . . or other relevant professional experience." How does one know prior to establishing a private practice that one is sufficiently prepared to engage in such an entrepreneurial effort? The "standard of care" and professional actions of social workers are judged against what a majority of practitioners in the profession would do with a particular type of client in a particular type of situation. As an ethical issue, how does one know with reasonable assurance what other private practitioners are doing with particular cases?

Noncompetition: An Unexplored Ethical Dilemma

The use of restrictive covenants or noncompetition agreements has a long history in the professions. In these situations, prior to employment, employees agree that they will not establish a private practice and take agency clients away from the agency. There are no systematic data about these practices, and the extent to which they exist in mental health services is unclear. Nevertheless, given the current economic context, it is likely such covenants exist and raise ethical dilemmas.

When an employee leaves the employing organization and cannot establish a private practice with former agency clients, the disposition of the client caseload is not self-determined by the client but by the terms of a noncompetition agreement. This protection against "insider raiding" ensures client retention in the event that a social worker leaves to set up her own practice. However, both the employer and the employee may be making unethical decisions that lose sight of the client's right to self-determination (e.g., whether the client would like to continue receiving services from the employee who is leaving).

Employers have a legitimate interest in attempting to protect their organizations from competition. The employee who leaves for private practice is likely to have benefited from her employment in the organization and takes with her confidential information and skills acquired as a result of the employment. The employee departing to start a private practice may feel that it is in the clients' best interest to continue to be seen by her, while the agency may feel that the clients' best interests are served by their continued involvement with the agency; however, who is really best qualified to decide which option serves the clients' best interest?

According to Wyatt, Daniels, and White (2000), there is no consensus about the legality of these types of restrictions. It is reasonable to assume social workers are not immune to these types of employment agreements. One ethical dilemma connected with such agreements is the degree to which clients are making informed choices. It is highly unlikely that social workers and employers inform clients of arrangements such as these at the beginning of services.

Do you think such covenants are ethical? The *Code of Ethics* (NASW *Code*, 1999, 3.09a) states "social workers generally should adhere to commitments made to employers and employing organizations." Where can you find guidance in the *Code* for agreeing to the restriction or not? What does "generally adhere" mean? If you decide the agreement the agency asks you to sign is unethical, what actions should you take? Are the issues the same for a social worker who is leaving an agency to go work for another, possibly better, agency?

EXERCISES

1. Some social workers have argued against the use of diagnosis, but most believe that diagnosis is an essential and necessary step in the treatment process. Have every student in the class select a partner. In each group of two, have one student role-play the pro diagnosis position and the other, the antidiagnosis position. Try to convince each other of the ethical problems that the other's position causes.

2. Consider the case of Barry (Exemplar 11.3). What ethical aspects does this case present? How would you resolve them? Use the ethical decision screens to answer these questions.

3. Did Ms. Aberdeen, the social worker of Ms. Martin (Exemplar 11.4), conduct herself in an ethical way? What other options could she have employed?

4. Consider the ethical questions raised in the Misrepresentation section of this chapter. Instead of simply saying that such behavior is unethical, note arguments that may be offered by a social worker who does present herself in one of these ways. Then answer these arguments.

SUGGESTIONS FOR ADDITIONAL READINGS

Kutchins and Kirk (1995, 1997) critically examine the utility, scientific evidence, and ethical and other problems related to the use of the DSM-IV-TR. A reasoned condemnation of client dumping by private practice practitioners can be found in an editorial in the *Journal of Independent Social Work,* written by the editor and one of the leading academic experts on private practice (Barker, 1988a). Myers and Thyer (1997) advocate that the NASW *Code* include a standard that requires empirically proven interventions as the first intervention choice by practitioners. Howard and Jenson (1999) argue that formal guidelines for practice should be created and that the use of those guidelines be included as a provision in the *Code.*

12 CHAPTER | **Changing World/Changing Problems**

In this chapter, we cover a medley of topics. We will examine ethical issues and dilemmas in areas that are relatively new for social workers or are rapidly evolving, such as family and domestic violence, including elder abuse; managed care and mental health; technology in information systems and direct practice; genetics; and end-of-life decisions, as well as dilemmas related to evidence-based practice and research in practice settings.

DOMESTIC VIOLENCE

Domestic violence is also known as partner abuse, spousal assault, or spouse abuse. We use the term to refer to violence between adults who are intimates, regardless of their marital status, living arrangements, or sexual orientations. Domestic violence comes in several forms: physical, sexual, psychological, economic, social isolation, stalking, and coercive control (Austin & Dankwort, 1999). Females are more often the targets of violence. There are estimates that nonfatal assaults occur in one of every six American homes, with 2 million females severely injured annually. Almost 9% of homicides in the United States are spousal homicides (Lystad, Rice, & Kaplan, 1996).

Over two-thirds of clients in family therapy clinics engaged in some form of physical violence against their partners within the year prior to the initiation of therapy. One study by the American Association of Marriage and Family Therapy members found that 60% did not consider family violence to be a significant clinical problem in their practice. Another study in a family therapy clinic found that more than half of all cases involving physical violence are not detected during routine interviews prior to the start of treatment (Aldarondo & Straus, 1994).

Physical violence hinders therapy and harms the quality of family life and welfare of clients, yet one needs time to develop a trusting relationship before domestic violence may be revealed. Even if someone denies the occurrence of domestic violence early in the client-social worker relationship, it may be necessary to be aware of possible signs of domestic violence and to be willing to bring the issue up again later in the relationship. What should a social worker do who is working with a client she suspects is in a violent relationship when the client denies this and the professional contract has been time-limited? After all, the clients determine what they will state. Should the social worker use valuable time to come back to this issue again? How can the social worker balance what she knows about reluctance to probe for domestic violence early in the helping relationship with an ethical responsibility to respect the client's right to self-determination?

Studies on the effectiveness of couple therapy for intimate partner violence confirm that therapy results in temporary decreases in violence, but generally, therapy does not result in stopping domestic violence in the long term (Jory, Anderson, & Greer, 1997). Many agencies are understaffed. Others have long waiting lists. All give priority to serving those currently in treatment. Remember this when you consider the ethical implications for not providing frequent follow-up services to present and past clients who have been involved in domestic violence. How would you respond in Exemplar 12.1?

❖ 12.1 A Leaving and Returning

Maria Christo arrived at the Women's Shelter a week ago; she had a black eye, a broken arm, and several other bruises. This is the fourth time in two years that Mrs. Christo has stayed in the shelter after leaving her husband. Each of the previous three times Mrs. Christo returned home after her husband begged her to return and promised to get help. Mr. Christo has completed a batterer treatment program, but the treatment has not been successful, as demonstrated by Mrs. Christo's return to the shelter. Mrs. Christo just came to you to tell you that she is returning home to her husband again. She says a woman's place is with her husband, for better or worse. You don't agree with her and you believe that there is a strong possibility of continued violence if Mrs. Christo returns to her husband.

What is your ethical responsibility in this situation? How can you balance your desire to protect Mrs. Christo with her right to self-determination? What would you do if the Christos have two young children at home who have witnessed the domestic violence? Would your choice differ if there are no children involved? Would it make a difference if you don't agree with her view of a "woman's place"?

HIV AND FAMILY ISSUES

The *Tarasoff* principle referred to in Chapter 5 requires social workers to inform those who are the targets of potential violence. This guideline, however, can lead to an ethical quandary in the case of clients who are HIV positive. Many persons who are HIV positive became so through transmission by intravenous drug use and sexual contact with persons infected with the virus. From a public health and social work perspective, the general assumption is that it makes sense for the patient to notify her sexual partners of her HIV positive status in order to protect uninfected partners from future infection and to inform those persons who have already been exposed so they may be tested and—if positive—seek appropriate medical care. The ethical issue for a social worker is what to do if the client who is infected with HIV positive refuses to notify his or her partner. Under what circumstances should a social worker inform health authorities, medical persons, or the partner who is not being told the facts? Is this an overruling of the self-determination of the client or the protection of health and life?

Many women are at risk of harm from their partners if the partners are informed of their HIV positive status. They can be injured. Is the ethical action to promote the public health strategy by informing those involved and promoting condom use? Furthermore, which is more ethical: to attempt to get the female to warn her partner, which risks her being abused or not to warn her partner, which risks his illness (North & Rothenberg, 1993)? Issues around HIV transmission, confidentiality, and the duty to warn will be discussed in further detail in Chapter 13. In this chapter, we will focus on HIV as it relates to family issues, such as domestic violence, pregnancy, and parenting.

In addition to the risks of domestic violence when a partner is notified of HIV status, there are other ethical issues around pregnancy and parenting. Research suggests that "when antiretroviral therapies are administered prophylactically to the woman during pregnancy, labor, and delivery and administered to the infant in the postpartum period and further exposure is avoided by bottle-feeding, the risk of MTCT [mother-to-child transmission] may be reduced from approximately 25% to between 2% and 8%" (Wolf et al., 2001). Given the potential risks of refusing prophylactic treatment and/or breast feeding, how should a social worker respond to a woman who knows she is HIV positive but wants to breast feed her child? How should a social worker balance the mother's right to autonomy and making her own decisions for herself and her child with the child's needs?

Table 12.1 provides the case recommendations for seeking a court order in this situation that Wolf et al. (2001) provide for pediatricians. Do these recommendations seem reasonable for social workers? Are these recommendations consistent with the NASW *Code of Ethics* (1999) and the ethical principles screen provided in Chapter 4?

Exemplar 12.2 raises several issues related to HIV status, child bearing, and domestic violence:

Table 12.1 | Case Recommendations for Seeking a Court Order

Action	Case
Ethically mandatory to seek a court order	Parent is incapable of making an informed decision because of (1) severe psychiatric illness; (2) effects of substance abuse; or (3) false belief on fact essential to medical decision.
Ethically permissible to seek a court order	Human immunodeficiency virus-infected woman's clinical situation is such that her refusal of antiretroviral prophylaxis and her decision to breast feed poses significant risk of transmission.
Ethically impermissible to seek a court order	Human immunodeficiency virus-infected woman is taking steps to reduce the risk of transmission to her infant but is unable to adhere to all recommendations because of strong social or cultural reasons.

From Wolf, et al., When Parents Reject Interventions to Reduce Postnatal Human Immundeficiency Virus Transmission, *Arch Pediatr Adolesc.*, 2001; 155:927–933. Copyright 2001, American Medical Association. Used with permission.

❖ 12.2 Should Mrs. Adams Have a Child?

Kiera Adams is HIV positive; she has been compliant with the antiretroviral therapy prescribed by her physician and has been symptom free so far. Mrs. Adams has been married for approximately two years and has not told her husband of her HIV status. Neither of them wanted children when they got married, however, recently Mr. Adams has been putting pressure on Mrs. Adams to have children. Mrs. Adams describes her husband as a good man who sometimes has trouble controlling his temper. Mrs. Adams has come to you for assistance in deciding whether to have a child.

Mrs. Adams' situation raises several issues: (1) Should her husband be notified of her HIV positive status? (this will be discussed more in Chapter 13) (2) Mrs. Adams' description of her husband as sometimes having trouble controlling his temper suggests that domestic violence may be an issue. Should you ask about that even though it was not the purpose of Mrs. Adams's visit? If you do ask and find that she is in a domestically violent relationship, or one that is likely to become violent if she does not agree to her husband's wishes, which issue takes precedence—dealing with the domestic violence, notifying Mr. Adams that his wife is HIV positive, or addressing the issue that Mrs. Adams came to you about? (3) Given the potential risk of HIV transmission from mother to children during pregnancy, labor, delivery, or breast feeding, how would you help Mrs. Adams decide about having a child? Do you have any responsibility to explore related issues with Mrs. Adams, such as whether she would breast feed if she had a child? If Mrs. Adams reports that her husband strongly believes that bottle feeding is not appropriate, is it possible to balance all the demands of this situation? (4) At what point do the as-yet-unconceived child's needs and interests enter into consideration?

Powderly (2001) raises some other issues in working with women who are HIV positive and are parents. First, a woman with HIV needs to consider having an advance directive so that her wishes will be met in the event that she is unable to make decisions for herself. Second, it is also important to develop permanency plans for her children in case she becomes unable to care for them. Powderly presents a case study of a woman who made arrangements for her partner to care for her children if she died; the partner was also HIV positive and was a drug dealer who was shot to death six weeks after the children's mother died. This case illustrates the need to not only have a permanency plan, but also to have alternative or backup plans. At what point should a social worker bring these issues up with a client who has HIV? Are these appropriate issues to bring up when a woman is considering becoming pregnant as was Mrs. Adams in Exemplar 12.2?

ELDER ABUSE

General issues of aging will be discussed in Chapter 13; in this chapter, we will briefly discuss some of the ethical issues that can arise in situations where older people are victims of abuse. According to the National Elder Abuse Incidence Study (National Center on Elder Abuse, 1998, cited in Bergeron & Gray, 2003), approximately 450,000 people age 60 and over experienced abuse or neglect in 1996, and fewer than 20% of these cases were reported to elder protection agencies even though every state has some form of elder abuse reporting law. Bergeron and Gray (2003) discuss the ethical issues that can arise for social workers who facilitate caregiver support groups and make the following recommendations:

1. Know the elder abuse reporting law—"because elder abuse laws are not criminal laws, some social services benefits are available to the victim . . . at no charge . . . if a report is filed" (p. 102). This can benefit both the victim and the caregiver.
2. Develop rapport with elder abuse protection practitioners—because many of the potential ethical dilemmas that arise in caregiver support groups have no definitive answers, developing rapport with elder abuse professionals in advance can help the facilitator be prepared to address issues as they arise.
3. Develop clear expectations of confidentiality—group members need to be informed of the limits of confidentiality in relation to elder abuse reporting requirements.
4. Monitor group members' self-disclosures—facilitators need to "monitor the group process so that information is not being shared prematurely and

to ensure that members have sufficient knowledge about the outcome of their disclosures" (p. 103).

5. Prepare support group members for the report—group members should be informed of the policies for working with members who reveal abusive behaviors.
6. Cultivate peer supervision and mentoring among facilitators.
7. Contribute to the research in this area.

These recommendations provide some guidance for social workers who facilitate caregiver support groups. If one of the purposes of the caregiver support group is to allow members to vent frustrations and concerns, is there a possibility that the "normalization of feelings may send subtle messages to members that certain levels of consistent abusive actions, such as yelling, isolating the elderly person, or not obtaining adequate in-home services, are acceptable" (Bergeron & Gray, 2003, pp. 103–104). In earlier chapters, we raised the "who is the client" issue; who is the client for these recommendations? Does the elderly abused person who is not physically present ever become the group facilitator's client? Is the facilitator's only responsibility to make the report to an elder abuse protection agency?

MANAGED CARE AND MENTAL HEALTH

Since the early 1980s, health care costs have escalated beyond the rate of inflation. As a result, there has been an increasing demand to control expenditures and to use managed health and mental health care systems as cost savers wherever possible (U.S. Census Bureau, 2001). Managed care systems attempt to contain costs by limiting the types of services that are reimbursed; for example, home or school visits or ancillary interviews with family members or significant other persons are generally not reimbursable. Only mental health services (therapy with DSM-IV-TR diagnoses) are reimbursed, thus limiting procedures that may be absolutely necessary in particular situations (Brill, 2001).

Managed care is one major strategy developed in an attempt to control health and mental health costs by monitoring access to and the type of health care patients receive from health care practitioners or health maintenance organizations (HMOs). Costs are reduced by placing controls on health practitioners and by fostering competition among HMOs. Managed care plans attempt to reduce these costs through controlling the type of health practitioners used, limiting access to service, and prescribing the type and length of service provided.

Practitioners from several disciplines have objected to the ways in which cost-conscious managed care plans are limiting patient service. Some have even argued that managed care is unethical since the professional autonomy of practitioners is threatened by the controls exerted by the managed care organization. (Strom-Gottfried, 1998b). There is concern that practitioners are selected not for their excellence but because they are willing to accept lower fees and more controls over their practice. Those selected by the managed care organization agree to these limitations, it is argued, in exchange for an assurance of a high volume of patients and guaranteed payments. Those not selected suffer the loss of income. Further, there is concern that the various controls instituted will result in poorer-quality service and reduce the ability of practitioners to provide what they consider to be high-quality professional service. Social workers are forced to choose between giving priority to the needs of the client, the interests of the insurer and/or society, and their own financial interests. On the other hand, it must be remembered that clients may not receive any services unless health care organizations remain viable.

Managed care not only has an impact on professional persons in private solo or group practice but also on social agencies as they become ever more dependent on third-party payments. Carpenter and Platt (1997) found that managed care produced a greater sense of strain between personal and professional values among social workers in agency settings than it did social workers in private practice. The impact of managed care creates a number of ethical dilemmas for social work practitioners, whether in private or agency-based practice. Among the ethical dilemmas arising from managed care are those concerning confidentiality and informed consent (see Chapter 5 for a discussion of these two issues), duty to assist and access, honesty, participation in treatment decisions, quality of care, and professional autonomy. Furthermore, the mission of social work and the mission of managed care organizations are often in conflict, and social workers have to be alert to the potential conflicts in their roles. Social workers are committed to service, and managed care organizations, although committed to service, have a mission of remaining financially viable and profitable.

The *Code of Ethics* has several standards that are of special relevance in these situations. (1) "Social workers should use clear and understandable language to inform clients of the purpose of the services, risks related to the services, limits to services because of the requirements of a third-party payer, relevant costs, reasonable alternatives, clients' right to refuse or withdraw consent, and the time frame covered by the consent." (NASW, 1999, I.03a). (2) "Social workers should not disclose confidential information to third-party payers unless clients have authorized such disclosure" (1.07h). (3) "Social workers should take reasonable steps to avoid abandoning clients who are still in need of services" (1.16b).

Other standards may also be relevant to managed care settings. Consider, for example, the issue of informed consent (1.03). Clients may have limited financial resources that force them to choose their health plan on the basis of cost. As a result, in certain situations, they are not free-agents and may not understand the possible rationing of services that may occur when managed care organizations use cost-saving devices. Similarly, there may be limits on refusals by clients to participate in the managed care organization's recommended treatment that minimizes their sense of voluntariness. Managed care programs may place the social worker in situations in which their compliance with standard 4.04 (NASW *Code*, 1999) may become questionable. For example, in order to provide a "reimbursable service" for a client, the practitioner may have to consider fudging the diagnosis in some way, as was discussed in Chapter 11.

There are many other ethical dilemmas practitioners can encounter in regard to managed care situations. Difficult issues arise when the cost containment goals of managed care place limits on the length of treatment, deny care, or insist on certain treatments. When a client's situation is not improved or the problem is unresolved, managed care may deny further reimbursed treatment. Nonetheless, the client may require a continuation of services. This problem becomes accentuated for a practitioner when two similarly situated clients both need professional social work service but have different benefit packages. On what basis does this social worker decide how to distribute services when both have equal needs. Should the client with the more generous benefit package receive more service?

Certain ethical dilemmas arise from the requirement to continue treatment if it is needed (NASW, 1999, 1.16b) or terminate treatment once it is no longer needed (NASW, 1.16a). What should the practitioner do if the client who needs continued treatment has reached the maximum on his annual or lifetime benefits but is unable to pay? A practitioner can state at the beginning of treatment that the family agency policy limits the number of sessions. What if during treatment the client resolved several of the problems that had brought him into treatment but another problem had emerged, and the social worker's supervisor denied permission for additional sessions? What is the ethical thing to do?

Many social workers have been pressured by managed care organizations to provide group therapy for their clients in place of individual treatment because group service is time and cost efficient. The insurance companies stress that outpatient services in time-limited groups have been found to be very effective. For example, persons with panic disorder who received cognitive-behavioral group therapy in addition to medication "had lower posttest anxiety scores than those who received medication alone" (Mitchell, 1999, p. 188). What is the ethical responsibility of a social worker inexperienced with groups? Should she offer group service (even while learning how to do this)? Must she tell clients that they must look for help elsewhere?

Practitioners in private practice may also be tempted to agree to emphasize group treatment because this can result in greater income—even when professional judgment counterindicates this mode of treatment. Here, the social worker faces another ethical dilemma: how to juggle the demands of her own professional judgments, those of the insurance company, and her desire for economic security. This dilemma is not limited to workers in private practice; it also occurs in agency practice, as shown in Exemplar 12.3.

❖ 12.3 What the Pine Tree Insurance Company Wants

Dr. Felicia Montevideo, director of social work clinical services for Family and Children's Services of Pleasant City, was surprised when she received a letter from the Pine Tree Insurance Company (Managed Care Division) and later a phone call, both of which subtly suggested that more of the agency's treatment services be offered in time-limited groups. When she raised the issue with the agency's administrative executive committee, some argued in favor of complying because the money received from the insurance company made up a substantial part of the agency's income. Others were concerned that such a change in operating procedures would upset the staff. Others wanted to know what would be most helpful to clients? Still others argued that compliance would mean yielding their professional judgment to the Pine Tree Insurance Company.

Among the options suggested by committee members are the following: (1) to ignore the suggestion because it had not been explicitly stated; (2) to comply as soon as possible with the suggestion; (3) to refuse to comply and to begin to advocate with Pine Tree Insurance for the current mix of service modalities; (4) to examine and review research on the relative effectiveness of various treatment methods; and (5) to meet with Pine Tree representatives to explore ways to slowly phase in more group treatment. What are the ethical implications of each option?

Davis (1997) discusses the need to ensure the availability of culturally competent standards of care and diagnostic and treatment services to underserved groups. In addition, managed care organizations need to provide accessible services "located within reasonable geographic distance to Black neighborhoods" (Davis, 1997, p. 636). What should the social worker do in Exemplar 12.4?

❖ 12.4 Where Are the Services?

Ms. Anita Dee is a social worker in a state psychiatric hospital that primarily serves low-income people of color. The Medicaid recipients are served through a managed care system that is privately operated. Generally, administrators and supervisors in this public hospital seek harmonious relationships with the managed care organization located in another state. Ms. Dee recently realized that when chronically ill psychiatric patients are discharged, the managed care company refers them to outpatient sites that are seldom near where they reside; transportation to the treatment sites is not provided. Consequently, the discharged persons are not receiving the help they need. Ms. Dee believes the managed care company is discriminating against poor and minority persons, but her supervisor says her job is to help prepare persons to leave the hospital and anything after that is not her concern. What should she do?

It is clear from the *Code of Ethics* that a practitioner should advocate for her client to receive appropriate services. The issue of advocacy raises several questions. How does one balance advocacy for one client versus the services that other clients need? Advocacy for one client can be time consuming and deprive others of services they need. How far should one appeal? How much unpaid time should be devoted to such efforts? Should one appeal when there is little chance for success? Furthermore, one can advocate once too many times and risk being removed from the managed care panel (Wineburgh, 1998).

TECHNOLOGY: INFORMATION SYSTEMS AND DIRECT PRACTICE

Social work, like many other professions, has been affected by computers and other modern technologies. Many persons, including social workers, believe that things, unlike people, are value-free. However, since technology exists within a human context, it reflects and shapes human choices. Human choices always involve value choices and ethical priorities.

At first, social workers were concerned that the introduction of information technologies into social agencies and social work practice would result in more critical ethical dilemmas because these technologies were thought to be insensitive to variations in human needs and individual differential values and cultures. Additional problems were expected in the areas of confidentiality and of protecting the ownership of personal data (Fodor, 1999). It was believed that it would be more difficult to protect information from inappropriate prying and from inappropriate control. These fears have remained of a concern, perhaps even intensified over time as invasions of privacy have increased.

As coordinating agencies, grant-funding agencies, third-party payers, and others seek to obtain detailed data that can be obtained easily from computerized data banks, improved methods for guaranteeing the confidentiality of records will be needed (Davidson & Davidson, 1996). When multiple agencies become linked in networks in order to promote collaborative case management, new problems arise. Is client permission needed for one agency/worker to share or receive the information held by another agency about a common client? To what extent can agencies successfully limit the client data they have computerized, and how can clients actually be sufficiently informed so as to be able to limit the information transferred to another agency? Another question is whether clients or patients understand the realities of the information networks to which agencies and their personal records are tied. To whom do these data belong? How can clients be assured privacy? (Relevant sections of the *Code of Ethics* (1999) are discussed in Chapter 5.) These problems are not entirely new and they also occurred in the precomputer era. However, the ease and quickness of information transfer make these ethical issues ever more critical in social work practice. Earlier in Chapter 5, the Health Insurance Portability and Accountability Act (HIPAA) was introduced. This legislation was enacted to protect the privacy of patients and of electronic communications about them. As the act is implemented, its success at ensuring such protections will be determined (Department of Health and Human Services, 2002).

Employees in social agencies can work at computer monitors whose screens face a hallway path and are exposed to view by anyone who passes by. Furthermore, if an agency's computer system can be accessed externally, it is potentially open to hackers, even when security systems are in place. Hackers are experts and have been able to penetrate the Defense Department and other computer systems. If interested, they would have little difficulty entering a social agency security system.

Ethical dilemmas can also arise in regard to requirements by funding and other supervisory external groups to provide data they know are available. These requests can raise ethical questions regarding confidentiality of data, how data will be used, as well as the informed consent of those whose personal information is being forwarded.

Concerns about computer security are not limited to interorganizational electronic communications. Caputo (1991) set forth an ethical framework for information systems that asserts the primacy of clients as citizens. The ethical framework fulfills the following functions:

1. It provides a way to inform clients about the existence of a computerized client-information system.
2. It enables clients to give informed consent in regard to the uses of information about themselves.
3. It offers an opportunity for individuals to inspect, correct, or add information about themselves, allowing them to expunge all or parts of their records, except where such records are legally required.
4. It develops an information-needs matrix to guide unit allocation decisions on the basis of critical success factors.
5. It holds professionals to a professional practice that is mindful of ethical standards, including respect for clients' autonomy, their right to information and privacy, the need to weigh the efficacy of demands for efficiency against the principle of human dignity, and adherence to confidentiality regarding the use of routinely collected information about clients.

Other ethical issues arise out of still newer developments. Among these are data bases that can be used for screening and assessment; the selection of practice and service recommendations; expert systems for evaluating various risks, such as foster care, parole, and suicide; and interactive treatment games and various forms of therapy. Among the ethical dilemmas that have developed as a result of these developments are questions of beneficence (autonomy versus paternalism), equity of access to scarce resources (ensuring equality of opportunity), and the promotion of the common good (ensuring that the maximum number of individuals benefit from the introduction of information technology). The assumption of many advanced software and expert systems (computerized decision making) is that there is always one "right" decision that should be followed. As a result, problems concerning client autonomy and worker flexibility have become more critical. How is it possible for the worker simultaneously to defend the autonomy of the client, meet the expectations of the agency, and avoid paternalism and control of clients?

The introduction of information systems into social agencies with very tight budgets means that scarce resources must be deployed to pay for the new technology and for staff with specific expertise even while other agency programs and client supports will be reduced or eliminated. Work patterns and organizational structure will change, and some resources will not be available for some kinds of client services.

Consider the common dilemma that confronts the social worker in Exemplar 12.5.

❖ 12.5 Computerized Information System or Services?

Miri Neidig, a social worker, is a member of the board of directors of a Neighborhood Service Center that provides counseling and other services, including services for low-income minority teens at a local shopping mall. This service has recently been instituted and is highly valued by community members concerned about sexually transmitted diseases and by teenagers because of the privacy afforded by the location and the likeable staff. The agency recently purchased several computers and some members of the board are pressuring the executive director to computerize its operation. They believe it is essential for agencies to become technologically up-to-date. According to the United Way, the current funding situation has become precarious and expenses must be reduced. The board will meet tonight to review the agency budget.

The board and Ms. Neidig are faced with the question of what services to reduce or cut. Some argue that it is more important to upgrade the technology in the agency, and others argue there are too few services provided now. There are waiting lists for almost all services. The board, including Ms. Neidig, is faced with difficult choices. For the future, improved use of computers by the agency will be a positive step. If they vote in favor of further computerization, other services will be diminished. A vote for computerization will deny the community services that are desperately needed. What recommendation would you make to Ms. Neidig about her vote? How would you choose?

TECHNOLOGY IN DIRECT PRACTICE

Called by a variety of names, online therapy is a developing method of delivering services via typed text communication, without being able to observe the client, provided by for-profit companies and individual therapists. For-profit organizations employ social workers to provide these services. They argued that it is a "low-risk means of making extra money from the comfort of home with no office expense" (O'Neill, 2001a). The employing corporation provides a virtual office, Web page, assesses suicide risk, does practice management, provides billing services, and pays for services rendered. Some of the benefits of online therapy are accessibility for rural area and home-bound clients, anonymity for those reluctant to see a therapist, availability 24 hours a day for seven days a week, low cost, and screening and follow-up care. Although there are claims that social workers who provide these services do so at low risk, there are ethical issues involved. Aside from the management services provided, a social worker has no way of seeing the person directly and so misses all non-verbal clues, is dependent on distant and perhaps unknown persons regarding the suicide assessment, and has to trust the business in regard to everything they claim they will do. Where in the *Code* would you find support suggesting that providing services in this way is ethical or unethical?

In addition to newly developing online therapy, even newer Web cameras can alter the way Internet therapy is provided. Clients can go to their computers, key in a password, and begin talking to their therapists with full-screen video and audio. In its infancy, Web camera therapy efforts need improvement and greater availability, both of which are dependent on technical engineering matters in order to grow as a method of providing therapy (O'Neill, 2001b).

Internet-based therapy is not without its critics. The Clinical Social Work Federation raised serious ethical and practice issues regarding its use. Among the areas of concern were the following: (1) Confidentiality is impossible to ensure when information is transmitted over the Internet; (2) The existence of a real-time record of the client-therapist interactions can provide a useful document for attorneys to subpoena; (3) There is no assurance that presenting information is accurate and no empirical evidence of the efficacy of online therapy; (4) There is a high potential for doing harm to clients through breach of confidentiality, misdiagnosis because of limited or incorrect information, and jurisdictional problems such as practicing in a state in which you are unlicensed. The California Board of Psychology as early as 2000 announced that psychologists who provide internet psychological services must be licensed in California (NASW News, September 2000). Therapists may also risk lawsuits (Carlson, 2002). O'Neill (2002) found that some social workers thought it a mistake and unethical for social workers to offer online therapy prior to the establishment of practice standards and before the liability issues have been clarified. Other social workers were critical of the criticisms and claimed that online therapists are equally as well prepared as those who provide off-line therapy, relative anonymity can increase willingness of clients to participate in the therapy, and both client and therapist can be freed from preconceived notions about each other (O'Neill, 2002).

It is likely that regardless of the undecided practical and ethical issues, Internet services will continue to expand. In 2001, Medicare expanded its coverage of telehealth services for Medicare beneficiaries to include certain individual psychotherapy services. Eligible clinical social workers can receive reimbursement for specified services. However, the services are reimbursable only if clients receive the services at "originating sites" such as physician and practitioner offices, hospitals, and rural health-care clinics. In general, these sites must be in rural areas designated as health professional shortage areas or counties that are not part of a metropolitan statistical area (a city with more than 50,000 people) (Ballie, 2001).

A number of broad issues in need of development have been identified by Goutham Menon: (1) The *Code of Ethics* should be revised to reflect technological innovations; (2) NASW practice standards need to consider Internet counseling; (3) empirical research is needed to examine the efficacy of online practice; continuing education requirements should be defined for online counselors; (4) limits need to be placed on cross state/national borders counseling (NASW, 2001).

Although as this is being written the social work profession has not developed systematic guidelines, we are including guidelines prepared for the National Board for Certified Counselors for the reader's consideration. Among the suggested guidelines are ensure client confidentiality through encryption methods; check on liability issues; inform the client how long session data will be saved; check on client and counselor identities through codes; verify identities of adults when consent is needed for minors; establish a local on-call counselor or crisis resources; screen out problems not appropriate for Internet counseling; explain and have contingency plans if technical problems occur; explain how to cope with potential misunderstandings that arise due to lack of visual cues; and discuss with the counselor what to do if the counselor is off-line or when there are delays in sending and receiving messages (Fukuyama, 2001).

The increasing use of electronic mail makes available unsought information that may confront a practitioner with critical ethical dilemmas. Note Exemplar 12.6.

❖ 12.6 E-Mail from Europe and Suicidal Thoughts

A university student used an electronic mail discussion group to inquire about a drug that could be used for a painless suicide. A professor in Europe who read this request communicated his concern to the sender's university, which forwarded this message to the university's counseling department. The counselor assigned to this case obtained more information before deciding what to do. She contacted the director of the Computer Center, who broke into the student's account where additional messages on suicide were discovered. At this point, the counselor decided to contact the student's parents. (This situation was described on a Social Work electronic discussion list and is used with permission of Steve Marson of Pembroke University. The counselor was not a social worker.)

Exemplar 12.6 has been presented because it reflects the rapidly expanding use of electronic mail and because it raises some issues that social workers must consider. One issue facing the counselor is whether to act on the basis of third-party information from someone unknown to her. Because the situation was potentially life threatening, this counselor decided to take the information conveyed by the third party seriously, but she also wanted to obtain verification of the facts, if possible. Here, the worker decided that intervention was justified. More generally, questions can be raised regarding the circumstances under which a social worker should seek access to a confidential electronic file. Is there any issue short of life-threatening situations that might support such an action? Under what circumstances does the Computer Center or a social agency have a right to examine someone's personal computer account? What should the counselor have done if the Computer Center (or agency) stated such an invasion was illegal or against the rules? Although the counselor felt justified in asking the Computer Center for verification because of the potential life-threatening nature of the situation, was it ethical for her to enter the student's computer account without obtaining his permission?

Because the student is at the university and the counselor is a university employee, she has some responsibility for his welfare, especially after she gained information about what was in his file. What should she have done if the student's account did not include life-threatening materials?

We do not know the counselor's reasons for contacting the student's parents rather than the student himself. Is telling the parents about their son's behavior an improper invasion of the student's right to privacy and confidentiality? What should the counselor do if, instead of contacting the student's parents, she spoke to the student, and he simply stated that he has an intellectual interest in painless suicide as a chemical problem? Which standards in the *Code of Ethics* provide guidance in this type of situation?

GENETICS

Genetic Screening

Researchers at a large number of academic centers, genome institutes, and private organizations are rapidly decoding the human blueprint. As a result, genetic knowledge is growing rapidly. As more medical technologies and scientific information become available, it becomes easier to identify genetic disorders such as cystic fibrosis, hemophilia, muscular dystrophy, sickle-cell anemia, and certain cancers, including breast and ovarian cancers.

Ethical dilemmas regarding genetic counseling that confront social workers are not limited to those employed in hospital and medical settings but can occur in other settings as well. The newly available information can be life-saving and life-enhancing, but situations can arise which are quite complex. Ethical issues can arise in areas related to who is the client, honesty and dishonesty, informed consent and coercion, confidentiality, to whom loyalty is owed, competing interests, and other issues.

The results of genetic testing are based on probability, and those involved with testing and genetic counseling express concerns that people will take irrevocable actions or make decisions based on hope or fear and not facts. Freedman (1998) studied those seeking genetic screening through participant observation of counseling sessions and in-depth interviews of women who sought susceptibility testing. The vast majority of those who requested such testing were white, middle class, educated, and not deprived economically. Dilemmas of a socioeconomic character also arose. Those who were middle class or wealthy could benefit more because they had the economic means to take advantage of medical and other care that could arise from the new knowledge. Others might have risked more when they learned test results. Poor persons might be at greater risk where money matters played a part in decision making.

Some ethical issues regarding susceptibility testing relate to confidentiality and privacy. Can the information learned be kept confidential and private? What rights do family members or significant others have to the information learned through the testing? To what use will employers and insurance companies put the information? What are the potential future liabilities for social workers?

Consider the following situations in Exemplar 12.7.

❖ 12.7 Genetic Disorders and Adoption—Who Should Be Informed?

Samantha Gross, 18 years old, was adopted about 14 years ago. She has been diagnosed with muscular dystrophy, a genetic disorder. Samantha lives in a state where the identities of the birth couple legally may not be revealed. Is it the ethical responsibility of her social worker, Emily Needham, to find her biological parents and inform them of this occurrence regardless of how much time and effort it will take? After all, this is a very serious illness and shouldn't the parents be warned so the family knows?

Conversely, a serious genetic disorder is diagnosed in Mrs. Essie Swift, the biological mother who gave up her daughter (Samantha Gross) 14 years ago. If Mrs. Swift is served by a social worker and that worker learns of the diagnosis and also knows of Samantha's adoption, must that social worker track down the adoptee and inform her? What are the ethical and legal implications for doing so? For not doing so?

A number of ethical issues are raised by the examples. Who is the client in each case? What rights and privacy belong to clients? Is everyone involved entitled to confidentiality? Do others involved have a right to know developments that can affect their lives and the lives of their family members? Who owns genetic information?

Reproductive Technology

Medically assisted conceptions involving donor insemination are growing more common. Typically, the identification of the donor is forbidden. This situation is similar to adoption in that the donor—and the biological parent—may have identifiable latent inherited diseases. For example, the sperm donor's genetic background is unknown. When the child born from the insemination process becomes an adult and has children of their own, there is the risk of illnesses occurring either later in his own life or in the life of the child.

Is it ethical to keep the identification of the donor secret? In addition to needed genetic information that may be unobtainable, the agency and social workers protect the anonymity of the donor through secrecy. These actions are incongruent with the demands for honesty and trust established by the *Code* and are contrary to the *Code*'s insistence that people's well being be protected and they be given equitable treatment. On the other hand, there is no attempt to protect the child's basic right to his genetic inheritance. This is dishonesty that protects the family image of a mother and a father with their child and keeps the donor lurking ambiguously in the background (Landau, 1998a, b). Is participation in situations where the donor is kept secret and important genetic information is kept from the family and child ethically correct?

An ethical dilemma occurs when relatives want access to genetic information that may be of importance to their health or to the future of their children. What ethical issues does the request by Roberta Jackson pose in Exemplar 12.8?

❖ 12.8 The Dilemma of Huntington's Disease

Roberta Jackson is eager to have a baby and has just asked you as her social worker not to tell her husband or family members that she has a genetic marker that identifies her as a carrier of Huntington's disease, a disease for which there is no cure but which will not show up until 20 to 30 years from now when she hopes a cure will have been discovered. This is an inherited condition that potentially affects all family members and inflicts premature senility on those affected. She is afraid that her husband will not be willing to have a child if he knows about her genetic condition. When the welfare of other people is at risk, does their right to such information take precedence over your client's right to privacy?

Confidentiality is only one of the several ethical issues present in this situation. There are others. What is the best interest of the as-yet-unborn child? Who is the person, or are the persons entitled to make such decisions? What are the religious implications for all concerned (if any)? Who speaks for the fetus? What are the statistical relationships between a genetic marker and the actual occurrence of the genetic defect, and what bearing do they have on making a decision? Does Ms. Jackson's husband have a right to know and make *his* decision on the basis of complete information? What is society's best interest in this situation?

The social worker in Exemplar 12.8 has to consider several ethical issues, including client self-determination and protection of human life, confidentiality and privacy and who has a right to information, honesty, and priorities of values. A social worker involved with susceptibility testing also will face such dilemmas. In some susceptibility test facilities, the staff—including social workers—concerned that employers and insurance companies will misuse the information gained through the testing, create "shadow charts." These charts contain correct information (record of counseling, family history, clinical exams, and the test results of genetic tests) but are kept separate from official charts. Is this a correct ethical choice when the social workers cannot assure their case records will be confidential and secure?

END-OF-LIFE DECISIONS

In 1993, the NASW Delegate Assembly approved a policy statement on "Client Self-Determination in End-of-Life Decisions." The policy statement offers guidance to social workers. The NASW's position was based on the principle that client self-determination should apply to all aspects of life and death. The policy statement contains the following ideas:

- The social work profession strives to enhance the quality of life; to encourage the exploration of life options; and to advocate for access to options, including providing all information to make appropriate choices.
- Social workers have an important role in helping individuals identify the end-of-life options available to them.
- Competent individuals should have the opportunity to make their own choices but only after being informed of all options and consequences. Choices should be made without coercion.
- Social workers should not promote any particular means to end one's life but should be open to full discussion of the issues and care options.
- Social workers should be free to participate or not participate in assisted-suicide matters or other discussions concerning end-of-life decisions depending on their own beliefs, attitudes, and value systems. If a social worker is unable to help with decisions about assisted suicide or other end-of-life choices, he or she has a professional obligation to refer patients and their families to competent professionals who are available to address end-of-life issues.
- It is inappropriate for social workers to deliver, supply, or personally participate in the commission of an act of assisted suicide when acting in their professional role.
- If legally permissible, it is not inappropriate for a social worker to be present during an assisted suicide if the client requests the social worker's presence.
- The involvement of social workers in assisted-suicide cases should not depend on race or ethnicity, religion, age, gender, economic factors, sexual orientation, or disability.

Essentially, end-of-life decisions focus on three different stages of ethical concern: palliative care, death by choice or otherwise, and grief among survivors. Social workers have a long history of care with persons in the process of dying and with dealing with grief following deaths. The end-of-life policy promulgated by the NASW is a relatively new development in social work which is met by social workers and others with differing sets of values. Little is known about these phenomena. Some social workers believe that promulgation by the NASW of guidelines regarding social workers' potential roles in physician-assisted suicide in effect suggest it is ethical to do so. Others oppose providing assistance in ending-of-life situations (Manetta & Wells, 2001). In some states, to assist in a suicide is against the law.

Though the NASW's policy statement is based on the principle of self-determination, many doubt whether meaningful self-determination and voluntary consent prevail in situations in which a person wishes to harm himself or commit suicide because "only abysmal ignorance or deep emotional trauma can lead persons to extreme measures like these" (Gewirth, 1978, p. 264). Others also take issue with the autonomy (self-determination) argument by suggesting that active physician-assisted suicide is more than a matter of self-determination. From this point of view, it has been suggested by Callahan (1994) that it is a mutual decision by two people, one of whom is to be killed and the other to do the killing (cited in Csikai, 1999). In certain situations, medical treatment for palliative care or harsh treatments such as chemotherapy reach a limit beyond which there is no ultimate benefit to the patients and there is no enhancement of quality of life. Some persons feel that quality of life is ethically irrelevant, and the ethical issue is to take or not take a life.

The policy statement raises many questions, among which are the following: Whose quality of life is supported by assisted suicide? Whose life is harmed? What is competence in such a situation? How does one judge competency? Is coercion entirely absent when people are considering suicide? What should one do if the option chosen creates issues for other family members, significant others, friends, or other professionals? What should one do if there are conflicts among those involved—some wanting to maintain life at all costs, others supporting the person's decision? What does it mean to be present but not participate? Is this just another form of approval of the act?

The definition of terminal illness is not always clear. Sometimes even the best of medical practitioners makes a mistake, and persons judged to be terminally ill live beyond the projected time. Can "comfort care" and the control of pain offset the desire to end one's life?

Since 1997, the State of Oregon's Death with Dignity Act has been implemented and more than 100 persons have used the law to bring an end to a terminal illness with a physician's assistance. Four states considered similar legislation but none has passed as of March 2003. Most states prohibit physician-assisted suicide. Supreme Court rulings on physician-assisted suicide for terminally ill persons left the door open for individual states to define their own statutes in this area and suggested the Court could revisit the issue.

Two basic ethical issues have to be weighed: one concerns the society; the second concerns the social work profession itself. In regard to society, there are those concerned about the "slippery slope" effect of condoning assisted suicide. In at least one nation where assisted suicide has been permitted, the definition of who is eligible has grown looser and outside the specific guidelines over time (Citizen Link, 2003). As far as social work is concerned, will social workers' participation in assisted-suicide situations result in their being less trusted by those groups that reject assisted suicide? Assisted suicide requires assistance being provided only for those who are undeniably competent to make such requests and for whom there are no alternative ways of relieving their suffering through palliative care. One observer suggests that there are two essential ethical requirements of professionals: to seek to deliver the kinds of services they profess to provide and to be trustworthy. To be trusted as a profession, social work must be viewed as honest, fair, and avoiding acting unjustly (Jackson, 2000). It is against these ethical standards that assisted-suicide participation needs to be weighed.

ACCOUNTABILITY, EFFECTIVENESS, AND ETHICAL DILEMMAS: EVIDENCE-BASED PRACTICE AND RESEARCH

Both public and private organizations and third-party payers increasingly are pressuring social workers and human service organizations for evidence that they are accountable and their services are beneficial to those they are serving. This trend is reflected in the *Code of Ethics* where several standards are relevant to discussions of evidence-based practice and the use of research findings: "Social workers should critically examine and keep current with emerging knowledge relevant to social work . . . [and] should routinely review the professional literature" (NASW *Code,* 1999, 4.01b). In addition, "social workers should base practice on recognized knowledge, including empirically based knowledge" (NASW *Code,* 1999, 4.01c). Furthermore, social workers are also encouraged to "critically examine and keep current with emerging knowledge . . . and [to] fully use evaluation and research evidence in their professional practice" (NASW *Code,* 1999, 5.02c). Many social workers, especially students, are not convinced that research is relevant to what they do; but more and more demands are made on social workers that they be accountable for their methods and the outcomes of their services. These demands can create ethical dilemmas for social workers.

Recently, there has been a great deal of discussion about evidence-based practice and how it should be used in social work (see Gambrill, 2003; Howard, McMillen, & Pollio, 2003). Research knowledge, clinical expertise, and client values are all integrated in evidence-based practice, which involves five steps:

1. Converting information needs related to practice decisions into answerable questions
2. Tracking down . . . the best evidence with which to answer them
3. Critically appraising that evidence . . .
4. Applying the results of this appraisal to practice and policy decisions. This involves deciding whether evidence found (if any) applies to the decision at hand (e.g., Is a client similar to those studied?) and considering client values and preferences in making decisions as well as other applicability concerns.
5. Evaluating our effectiveness and efficacy in carrying out steps and seeking ways to improve them in the future (Sackett et al., 2000, pp. 3–4, cited in Gambrill, 2003, p. 7)

Many social workers feel unprepared or unable to perform these five steps and/or they may feel that they are already overburdened and do not have the time to perform them. A social worker may even wonder if evidence-based practice is really ethically necessary. The *Code* (1999, 4.01) suggests that clients have a right to expect that social workers will be competent in their area of practice; can a social worker remain competent if she does not stay up-to-date with current developments in the field? Consider Exemplar 12.9:

❖ 12.9 Mrs. Johnson Wants Immediate Relief

Sheryl Adams is a social worker in a solo private practice; one of her clients, Mrs. Johnson, was referred to her after Mrs. Johnson's physician, who often makes referrals to her, made a diagnosis of depression. Mrs. Johnson's physician wanted to prescribe an antidepressant, but Mrs. Johnson, who is breast feeding her three month old son, refused to take the medication prescribed. She is afraid that the medicine will harm the baby, but she refuses to stop breast feeding or to take the prescribed medication because she previously had been prescribed medications for depression which made her life miserable with headaches, dry mouth, and sweating. Because of Mrs. Johnson's refusal to take the anti-depressants, her physician referred her to Ms. Adams for counseling. He expected Ms. Adams to convince Mrs. Johnson to take her medication. The physician expressed great concern about the infant's health. Ms. Adams has little experience treating depression, but there are no other licensed social workers in the area. At the first session, Mrs. Johnson stated that she is very concerned that due to the depression she is not adequately caring for her son and that she needs immediate relief so she can be a better mother but she cannot manage to cope with the medications.

What are the ethical dilemmas facing Ms. Adams? Who is her client—the infant, Mrs. Johnson, the physician, her practice? How can she decide who takes priority? What additional information is needed so that Mrs. Johnson can give informed consent for the treatment? Are there nonmedication treatments for depression? Is this situation a repeat of Mrs. Johnson's earlier depressive episode or situational postpartum depression? How much time will it take to find and review the relevant research literature? What harm can be done in the interim? Should Mrs. Johnson be told about the available treatment options, the risks and benefits of each, and the likely efficacy of each, including the fact that Ms. Adams is not experienced in delivering some of these treatment options? What should she do if she cannot learn the most effective new treatments easily or Mrs. Johnson when informed of the situation refuses to participate? Review the *Code of Ethics* (1999) for relevant standards.

Evidence-based practice involves five steps. Let us consider how Ms. Adams could apply those five steps to this situation. First, Ms. Adams could develop "answerable questions," such as, what non–medication-based treatments are available for depression? Also, given that Mrs. Johnson has a three-month-old son, what distinguishes major depression from postpartum depression, which is the most appropriate diagnosis for her, and are the treatment options different? Once Ms. Adams has developed answerable questions, she can move to the second step, "tracking down the best evidence." How should Ms. Adams proceed? Assuming that she is a busy professional, does she have time to find and review all the relevant research literature? There are a growing number of Internet-based resources available that provide summaries and critiques of the research literature in a number of areas. What if Mrs. Johnson has heard about a treatment for depression called transcranial magnetic stimulation (given the ease with which information can be obtained from the Internet, it is possible for clients to find information on treatments that the social worker is not familiar with) and has asked Ms. Adams to convince the insurance company to pay for this treatment? Should Ms. Adams do so? How could she decide if this is an appropriate referral? Ms. Adams could check with a library or look for Internet-based resources, such as the Cochrane collaboration, which provides systematic reviews on a number of health-related topics, including depression (see Martin et al. [2002] in the Cochrane Library at www.cochraneconsumer.com for a review of transcranial magnetic stimulation). More such sites will probably be developed in the near future, and readers are encouraged to explore the Internet for similar resources.

Once Ms. Adams has found the relevant research evidence, she needs to move to step three, "critically appraising that evidence." Some social workers find research intimidating and/or have difficulty evaluating research methodology—how should they proceed with this step? Is it ethical to uncritically accept the conclusions of study authors without examining the adequacy of the research methodology used? Is this step easier if one has reliable and trustworthy sources of information? In step four, the results of steps one through three are applied, including considerations of whether what has been found is relevant to the client's issue and how these findings relate to the client's values. What should Ms. Adams do if after all of this she finds that the most effective treatment is one she does not know how to provide or is unacceptable to Mrs. Johnson? Finally, in step five, the effectiveness and efficacy of steps one through four are evaluated. For most social workers, this process may be quite time-consuming, especially the first few times it is used. Does this cause any ethical dilemmas?

RESEARCH AND EVALUATION IN PRACTICE SETTINGS

In addition to keeping up-to-date with current research findings, social workers are encouraged to "promote and facilitate evaluation and research to contribute to the development of knowledge" (NASW *Code,* 1999, 5.02b). Many funding sources now require that agencies provide outcome data in order to continue receiving funding. While this requirement is not inconsistent with the *Code of Ethics* or evidence-based practice, it may create a number of ethical dilemmas for social workers. Consider the following situation in Exemplar 12.10:

❖ 12.10 Fundalot Foundation Wants Evidence

The Sidestreet Agency provides services to runaway adolescents; for the past three years, over 80% of their funding has been provided by the Fundalot Foundation. The board of directors of the Fundalot Foundation recently voted to change the criteria for continued funding; specifically, they now want all programs to provide evidence of their efficacy. They have not been specific about what type of evidence will be acceptable, but they have decided to let each agency determine what types of data should be collected and reported. Funding will be discontinued if programs have inadequate data collection and reporting, or findings that do not support the program's efficacy.

Kathleen Hall is the social worker for the Sidestreet Agency; for the past three years, she has written the funding proposal for the Fundalot Foundation. Given the new requirements, Ms. Hall has asked to meet with the other members of the staff to discuss how they will address them. During the meeting, a number of issues are raised: (1) Should the agency respond or not respond to these requirements? (2) Is informed consent required to collect this sort of outcome data? What if clients refuse to give consent? Will they be dropped from the treatment program? (3) If the agency's clients are children and adolescents, at what age can they give informed consent, and how can it be obtained for those clients who are too young or not yet competent enough to give consent? Is the consent of their parents required? (4) What if the findings are not good enough? (5) If "we know it works," why isn't that enough proof for the foundation? (6) Who or what takes ethical priority here: the agency that needs funding, the clients being served, the staff who want to retain their jobs, or honesty that requires accurate recording?

How should a social worker respond to these issues?

If an agency decides to evaluate its services, the collection of outcome data raises a number of additional ethical dilemmas. The NASW *Code of Ethics* (1999) has a number of standards for evaluation and research (see 5.02 a–p), including an injunction against dual relationships (5.02 o). "Despite this injunction, however, the current priority given to establishing the efficacy of clinical programs through research is now demanding that clinicians include research in the scope of their practice. . . . The dual role of clinician and researcher, although advantageous, poses risks to the self-determination of clients who are potential study participants" (Antle & Regehr, 2003, p. 140). Is the clinician-researcher dual role avoidable for a social worker in an agency that requires the collection of outcome data? If this dual role is unavoidable, how can the social worker protect the client's rights, including self-determination, while meeting the needs of the agency to establish its efficacy? What should a social worker do who works for an agency that will not provide services without the client's agreement to provide outcome data? Finally, let us consider the case of an agency that has collected the outcome data required by its funding agency, but the results are not positive (e.g., there is no evidence that the agency's services are effective). What would you do in this situation?

EXERCISES

1. In a group, discuss how technologies present ethical dilemmas for your agencies and for social workers. Identify how these ethical dilemmas could be avoided and/or dealt with ethically. How are HIPAA requirements being addressed?
2. You are on a committee to consider the fate of a severely disabled infant whose survival is questionable. Identify standards in the *Code of Ethics* that help you to weigh the welfare of the parents versus the welfare of the child.
3. You are serving on the committee in Exemplar 12.3, "What the Pine Tree Insurance Company Wants." Which of the options suggested by committee members would you choose? What standards in the *Code of Ethics* support your choice?
4. If you were confronted as a social worker with the issue of assisted suicide, can you identify your personal values about such actions? What would be your position? What justification would you provide for your decision?
5. A claim has been made that the mission of social work is the attainment of social justice, and that mental health services are outside the social worker's realm (Wakefield, 1988). Are the only goods associated with social justice economic and social goods? Is providing help for internal psychological states that are impediments to attaining economic and social goods connected to the ethical commitment to social justice? Is the search for meaning and self-respect through social worker services contributory to social justice (Dean, 1998)? Would it be unethical for social workers to desist from delivering mental health services?
6. Have a class discussion or debate about whether evidence-based practice is ethically necessary?

SUGGESTIONS FOR ADDITIONAL READINGS

Hughes (1993a, b) presents a guiding ethical paradigm for use in child welfare settings in relation to catastrophically ill newborns. Social Work Speaks (NASW, 1994) includes "Client Self-Determination in End-of-Life Decisions," the NASW policy statement on this issue. Callahan (1994) presents arguments in opposition to the NASW policy position on end-of-life decisions. Lo, Dornbrand, Wolf, and Groman (2002) discuss the legal and ethical issues of withdrawing life support from patients who are incompetent, but not terminally ill. Maher and Ford (2002) discuss the legal and ethical issues in the case of cojoined twins who were separated against the wishes of the parents. Issues concerning privacy, confidentiality and security of communications, and informed consent in telehealth are examined in "Telehealth: Implications for Social Work Practice" by McCarty and Clancy (2002).

Social Work with Selected Client Groups

In this chapter, we discuss ethical dilemmas arising out of work with selected client groups. The topics covered in this chapter are as diverse as the client populations discussed. Although these dilemmas are presented in the context of specific groups, including the elderly and the ill, many of these problems are also relevant to other groups.

A PLURALITY OF IDENTITIES AND CLIENT GROUPS

American society is growing more and more diverse, leading to an increasing number of group identities in the United States. Such identities serve as political and social forces, as a means of personal expression, as well as a way of achieving meaning in people's lives. One result of this increasing diversity is that social workers deal with a growing number of people who come from a variety of cultures that differ from mainstream American society and whose lives are affected by their own cultures and those of other persons and groups.

Among general American society and among social workers, there is an affirmation of diversity. Enunciated in the *Code* (Ethical Principles) is the expectation that "social workers treat each person in a caring and respectful fashion, mindful of individual differences and cultural and ethnic diversity." The *Code's* standard on cultural competence and social diversity (NASW *Code*, 1999, 1.05) requires that ethical social workers understand culture and its function in human behavior, and have a knowledge base of and be sensitive to their clients' cultures. Furthermore, social workers are expected "to obtain education about and seek to understand the nature of social diversity and oppression with respect to race, ethnicity, national origin, color, sex, sexual orientation, age, marital status, political belief, religion, and mental or physical disability."

People may belong to several groups and have multiple identities. Even when a person is strongly identified with a single culture, his identity can be based on additional characteristics such as national origin, gender, social class, sexual orientation, disability, and age. In the process of learning much about many different groups, there are dangers of stereotyping persons by a primary group identity. However, cultures are varied and complex, and social workers need to create methods to avoid false generalizations or overgeneralization about groups (Walker & Staton, 2000). A White woman, for example, can be born and raised in Africa, be poor, a Baptist, 80 years old, and a lesbian.

Illustrative of this point, Fellin (2000) proposed a way of assessing cultures of identification and participation, which emphasizes the multiple groups and degrees of group membership and participation an individual may have. Clients belong to various racial and ethnic groups and subgroups, religions, social classes, sexual orientations, and may have disabilities of various types. When dealing with these differing persons and families, a social worker has to determine the degree of identification each person has with the groups they belong to, the level of their psychological sense of membership, and their level of participation in the groups.

Thus, a person can hold membership in various groups, identify themselves psychologically more or less with various groupings, and participate socially to varying degrees in each of the groups. We have introduced this conceptual scheme because it enables social workers to more correctly/ethically understand and assess the clients and families whom they serve from a multicultural and complex perspective. To think a person possesses only one identity is to engage in stereotyping because each person belongs to many groups and the strength of his identities may shift over time. To understand each person as an individual requires being sensitive to and informed about a client's series of identities.

Misdiagnosis and Treatment

Because there are often major cultural differences *within* different cultural groups, it is difficult to offer generalizations that apply to a community as a whole. For example, the Filipino community is a diverse population itself. Individuals and their families differ in respect to when they arrived in the United States, socioeconomic background, educational level, language, factors surrounding their immigration, dialect, geographic orientation, social class, and level of acculturation. There is diversity among groups and within groups (Agbayani-Siewert, 1994).

Understanding of a particular person and culture can be informed and accurate, but discrimination exists at many levels, including at the practitioner level. Diagnoses appear to be connected to race, class, cultural background, or gender of clients. African Americans and Hispanics are more likely to be diagnosed with affective or personality disorders. Whites are more likely to be diagnosed with organic disorders. African American children are diagnosed as hyperactive more than White children who are in turn diagnosed as hyperactive more often than are Asian American children (Solomon, 1992).

At least two theories are suggested to explain these discrepancies. Misdiagnosis is a result of different cultural expressions of symptoms or by clinician bias. These kinds of misdiagnoses based on misunderstanding or on bias are both unethical. Would these misdiagnoses be considered ethical if they were arrived at inadvertently and be a product of poor professional practice? Is the practitioner's intention to misdiagnose necessary before a person can be held guilty of an ethical violation? A social worker can encounter ethical dilemmas related to confidentiality and respecting a client's culture. For example, a young Asian American woman might be extremely shy about truthtelling and disclosure. In her culture, many important decisions may be made by the elders and not by the young client. On the other hand, social workers are trained to encourage disclosure and honesty in their clients. For a social worker to report bad news to such a client (e.g., that they need to make a report for child abuse or suggest HIV testing) could be interpreted as contributing to the illness, depriving the client of hope, and even casting a curse on the client and her family, in addition to bringing shame to the client and her family. Is it ethical to explore for more information when the client is culturally protective of family and personal secrets? What should one do if the client does not want you to report abuse since that would shame her family and ruin their life in their community?

❖ 13.1 How Much to Tell Mrs. Cho?

Mrs. Cho, an Asian American and recent immigrant in her early 50s, was referred to the Western Neighborhood Counseling Center by a non-Asian lady friend whom she admired and who had been helped at the Center. Mrs. Cho explained to Haley Traylor, her social worker, that she started having stomachaches accompanied by becoming quite anxious following her husband's being laid off. A visit to a physician found no physical problems. As treatment proceeded, things went quite well for a time, and Mrs. Cho began to feel better and more in control of her life. It was at that point that Mrs. Cho told Ms. Traylor that although she is feeling better, a woman at her church told her she should not be using the Western Neighborhood Counseling Center but should use Asian methods and Asian persons to deal with her problems. She announced that she appreciates the help she has been given but thinks her friend is correct, and she intends going to a "healer" who emphasizes meditation and green tea. This decision surprised Ms. Traylor because she had heard that the particular "healer" Mrs. Cho is going to visit is not helpful and that several persons had seen him and had their physical problems worsen after his treatment. What is the ethical choice for

Ms. Traylor? Should she tell Mrs. Cho what she knows about other persons' experiences with the neighborhood "healer"? Would that lead to an informed choice? Should she remain silent about her knowledge and accept without question Mrs. Cho's decision?

There are "culture-bound" syndromes that practitioners may encounter in their practices. For example, social workers in certain locations may be confronted with client symptoms, such as *ataque de nervios* (out of consciousness state resulting from evil spirits); *amok* (outbursts of violent and aggressive behavior); and *dhat* (extreme anxiety associated with a sense of weakness and exhaustion) (Glossary, 2003). These unfamiliar syndromes when confronted raise several ethical issues: (1) Does a practitioner have sufficient training to recognize and deal with them? (2) What should one do when managed care will not reimburse unless a practitioner assigns a DSM diagnosis, or what should one do when managed care refuses to reimburse treatment for the symptoms you have identified? (3) Can a social worker raised in American culture accept these as valid symptoms since these are not part of her own cultural experience? (4) Finally, how much multicultural training is required for a practitioner to practice ethically with diverse populations?

FAMILY AND MARITAL THERAPY

Family and marital therapy in social work focus on context, relationship, shared and unshared perceptions of reality, and the meaning persons give to their situations. Many—but not all—of the marital and family therapy theoretical approaches are influenced by systems theory and define the boundaries of people and their contexts as open, assuming that people and their relationships (family members with each other and families with their environments) are shaped constantly by their physical, social, and cultural environments (Hartman, 1995).

A number of ethical dilemmas are encountered in marital and family therapy situations. In some cases, the ethical dilemmas of marital and family therapists are like those of individual therapists, but in other situations, there are unique differences. Numerous complex ethical dilemmas have to be dealt with by marital and family therapists, such as defining who is the client, the family or the individual; handling family secrets such as the sexual or other problems of parents or extramarital affairs; honesty and dishonesty; diagnostic labeling which may later be used as part of litigation regarding child custody or other matters; and boundary dilemmas, including sexual boundaries (Goldenberg & Goldenberg, 2000).

As in individual therapy, marital and family therapists can encounter boundary dilemmas. Negretti and Wieling (2001) studied the use of electronic communication technologies in clinical work. Therapist availability is therapeutically important because it encourages involvement, confirms the client and their relationship, and contributes to problem resolution. Therapists must be available to clients and provide them with methods for contacting them in emergencies or for needed support. Each therapist, however, must define how vulnerable or responsible she is willing to be with clients and at what cost. Consider the following dilemmas. Family members seen privately in a therapist's office can locate a therapist's e-mail address through the Internet and extend the relationship beyond office visits to e-mail or other electronic devices. Since one cannot see the family member, how is one to assess the needy family member's situation when you are pursued repeatedly by him?

THE ILL

Changes in health care that result from new technologies, new disease entities, and reorganization of the health care system cause social workers to face difficult ethical choices. The following situations in Exemplar 13.2 illustrate some of the difficult ethical choices that confront health care social workers employed in these services.

❖ 13.2 To Treat or Not to Treat—At What Costs?

Jorge Gaudi, an HIV-positive person, has contracted a strain of TB that is virulent and drug resistant. He is extremely infectious. If he is successfully treated, he will no longer be able to infect others, and his life will be extended. Successful treatment depends on his consistent compliance with the treatment regimen, but he does not comply with his treatment regimen while in the hospital and wanders the hallways where he "bothers" staff and others. He has had to be restrained. He is homeless, lacks family support, and is drug addicted. Any possible cure depends on his complying with a difficult regimen, which is unlikely in his current life pattern.

    The patient's inability to comply with the demands of treatment creates a number of ethical dilemmas for the health team. When the team meets they discuss his situation, including what should be done following discharge so the social worker can begin preparations. Among the options are to (1) arrange a special comprehensive discharge plan that will require coordination among many agencies and persons and motivate Mr. Gaudi through special incentives for compliance—that is, provide housing, drug treatment, and psychiatric treatment *while others wait for* such resources; (2) provide monetary incentives, and pay him to comply; (3) involuntarily confine him and/or let him live in the community but put him on directly observed therapy, having him mandatorily observed while taking his medications; (4) discharge him and leave him to make his own decisions; and (5) provide a specialized foster home placement.

He is drug addicted, homeless, and will never regain full health. Is it ethical to single out poor and minority persons for confinement and mandatory programs? Is it fair to deprive other hospital patients of resources they need in order to help Mr. Gaudi? Which is the higher priority? If you were the social work member of the hospital team considering what to do, what would you suggest? Why?

Neonatology

Technological advances in neonatology have made it possible to sustain the lives of many newborn infants who in the past would not have survived. Survival for some, however, will mean chronic disabilities, perhaps lifelong institutionalization; keeping some extremely low-birthweight infants alive raises questions about the immediate and future quality of life of the child, the parents, and other family members.

There are three ethical issues that are generally involved in these situations: the welfare of the parents versus the welfare of the child; the freedom of choice of the parents versus the rights of the child; and whether societal funds should be used to maintain a marginal life instead of allocating these funds to increasing the quality of life for other children who in time will become productive members of society. Embedded in these issues is one background issue illustrated by Exemplar 13.3: Under what circumstances should extraordinary actions be taken to enable the birth of a live fetus or to sustain a newborn child with multiple life-threatening problems?

❖ 13.3 One Baby and Two Parents Who Want Guidance

Dr. Jane Newhouse just informed Mr. and Mrs. Lanier that their newborn son has kidney failure, gastrointestinal obstructions, brain damage, and recurrent seizures. A bowel operation, dialysis, and a kidney transplant will be needed. Dr. Newhouse was extremely pessimistic about the immediate survival possibilities and even more certain that if the infant lives, he will face survival crisis after survival crisis. The ultimate prognosis will be a child who will require institutionalization very early in life. After Dr. Newhouse discussed the options, Mr. and Mrs. Lanier, who must authorize any surgery, ask to meet with you, their social worker, because they trust you.

Mr. and Mrs. Lanier ask you to confirm that their infant is hopelessly ill, and they tell you that they do not have funds to save the life of the infant by taking extraordinary measures, nor funds to support the infant at home if he leaves the hospital. They are confused, anxious, and unsure what they should do.

How should you respond when the Laniers ask your advice? (1) Should you tell them that, for many health conditions, it is very difficult to predict with any certainty what will occur in the future but that Dr. Newhouse was very clear about the prognosis? You can encourage them to stop treatment. (2) Should you tell them that miracles do happen and encourage them to continue the infant's treatment? (3) Should you tell them that you can listen and help them think the problem through but that you cannot give them guidance about what they should decide? (4) Should you encourage them to speak again to Dr. Newhouse and get her opinion? Where in the *Code* will you find guidance so you can make the correct decision? In the ethical principles screen (Chapter 4), the highest value is the principle of the protection of life. Does this mean any life, even the life of a severely disabled person?

Child Illnesses, Disability, and Child Welfare

Following the "Baby Doe" case, Congress passed the Child Abuse Amendments of 1985 and assigned public child welfare agencies the responsibility of policing decision making concerning catastrophically ill neonates. Public child welfare agencies became responsible for assuring that decisions regarding medical treatment that would either end or sustain life would be in the newborn's interest and would not be neglectful or abusive.

Thousands of disabled children are born each year with life-threatening medical complications. State and county departments of social services have moved to protect children from abuse and neglect, guided by the child's best interests. One result is that child welfare agencies sometimes find themselves responsible for making such life-and-death decisions when the Department of Social Services has legal guardianship over the child for the following reasons: (1) the mother is dying or has already died; (2) the mother is incompetent; or (3) the child has been abandoned or otherwise has become the ward of the agency. When social workers are faced with making recommendations in such cases, where in the *Code of Ethics* will they find guidance?

Hughes (1993a, b) concluded that in our pluralistic society there is no consensus that can provide guiding principles for child welfare workers and agencies. Nevertheless, he suggested a "guiding ethical paradigm" that can serve child welfare agencies faced with these critical and difficult decisions. This guiding ethical paradigm consists of two principles for those with responsibility for treatment and case management for catastrophically ill newborns: (1) The quality-of-life principle can be described as the need to assess and consider the future quality of a person's life as an important variable in deciding whether to intervene to prolong life; this principle suggests that some lives are worse than death; and (2) The principle of social transcendence expresses the traditional principle of the sanctity of human life, no matter how damaged that person may be. This principle requires that decisions not be based upon the potential relative social utility of a person's life. It requires that treatment not be withheld on the basis of an assessment of a child's future potential to contribute to society or upon the priorities of social utility. Hughes believes that quality of life and social transcendence are consistent with the intent of the historical child welfare principle of best interests of the child. Suppose you are the child welfare social worker assigned to the Lanier infant (Exemplar 13.3). Apply these principles to the situation. Do they help you in making a decision? Would they do so in another and different case situation?

Do the two principles form a sufficient base for decision making? What limitations can you identify for each of these principles separately and for the two in combination? Do you see any conflicts with the NASW *Code of Ethics* or your state child maltreatment laws? Does the ethical principles screen suggest a different course of action?

Exemplar 13.4 also raises questions about the role of the social worker and involves several ethical dilemmas.

❖ 13.4 Our Daughter or Our Lives?

Irma Bream, a social worker at Heartland Children's Hospital, is meeting with Albert and Sorelle Clayton about the forthcoming discharge of their disabled 18-year-old daughter, Alice. The options upon discharge are a nursing home that accepts very young persons; a specialized foster care placement; or home care. However, no community services are available to support home care. Therefore, the latter option would require that her parents commit 24 hours per day to care for their daughter without hope of respite time or any other help. As the parents see it, their only real choice is whether to give up their lives for the care of Alice or to give up Alice to foster care or the nursing home. Despite long discussion and after several meetings with their social worker, Albert and Sorelle can't come to a decision. Now they ask Ms. Bream what she thinks is the right thing to do. Can you identify the ethical dilemmas facing the social worker in this situation?

Where in the NASW *Code of Ethics* would this social worker find guidance?

CLIENTS WITH HIV AND AIDS

The HIV (human immunodeficiency virus) infection has now spread to every nation in the world and has infected millions of people worldwide. In the United States, AIDS (acquired immunodeficiency syndrome) seems to be holding, but in South America, sub-Sahara Africa, and Asia, the disease is fast reaching epidemic proportions. In Africa, it is becoming endemic and hard to eradicate. The United Nations in a long-term forecast claims 65 million persons will die worldwide by 2020, more than triple the number who died in the first 20 years of the epidemic (Altman, 2002). Over 1.1 million people in the United States have been infected with HIV (Sharma et al., 2003). National population-based estimates in the United States have been unavailable since 1995 when the Survey of Childbearing Women was discontinued. As a result, only estimates can be made of HIV infection in the general population. Trend data are available from several groups: men who have sex with men, injection drug users, and other selected population groups. The prevalence of HIV infection has been found to be low among youth, military applicants, and among first-time blood donors. The prevalence differs by race/ethnicity. The HIV epidemic has slowed from a period of rapid growth (approximately 150,000 new infections per year) during the mid-1980s to a more stable 40,000 infections annually since the mid-1990s (Department of Health and Human Services, 2001).

The progression of the disease varies widely among individuals who may be in certain cases symptomless for more than 10 years. AIDS, the most advanced stage of HIV infection, refers to all HIV-infected people who have blood containing particular antigens. The death rate has been reduced for those who respond favorably to new combinations of drug treatments. However, many people are unable to follow through on the very demanding drug regimen because of their own limitations, because of the costs of drugs, or because they have HIV infections that are resistant to the drug combinations (Altman, 1999). More effective medical treatments have prolonged the lives of many people living with HIV/AIDS. All social workers, even those who are practicing with populations (or in areas of the country) that have so far had a low incidence of human immunodeficiency virus (HIV/AIDS) may sooner or later serve clients who have AIDS or who test HIV-positive. When this happens, they will face many new ethical problems. Ethical dilemmas may be encountered related to survival and lengthy chronic care balanced against increasingly applying resources to prevention and behavioral change efforts aimed at reducing high-risk behaviors. Other such ethical dilemmas may relate to mandatory screening of newborns, mothers who do not want their children on protease inhibitors (anitiviral medications), follow-up of mothers who gave birth to infected children, confidentiality and adolescents, and illegal drug use by those on medications.

Several drugs have been created to fight HIV infection. These drugs fight the infection and associated infections and cancers. One result is a more extended life for many victims. Medical treatments aim at controlling the progress of the disease and providing palliative care intended to relieve suffering and improve the quality of life. Life-prolonging care is available, but at the same time, current therapies do not benefit all patients. Regimens of "successful" treatment can lead to prolonged suffering from the adverse effects of medications.

Some patients die of HIV infection and its complications either because they do not have access to such therapies or despite the available treatments. Suffering includes multiple symptoms, pharmaceuticals, and losses; personal experiences with illness and death related to HIV disease; social stigma and isolation; the unpredictable course of the disease; and changing treatment approaches (Oppenheim & Hay et al., 2002).

AIDS is not an "ordinary" disease. People who have AIDS or who test HIV positive cannot be discussed in quite the same way as people who suffer other kinds of diseases. AIDS is a life-threatening disease; and people with HIV/AIDS have to come to terms with their own potential mortality, frequently at an early age. Although there are other diseases that are also life-threatening at early ages, there is a very high degree of stigma associated with AIDS, more stigma than is true for almost any other illness. This is because AIDS was first discovered among groups that are traditionally labeled as deviants—gay people, drug users, and prostitutes. Because of this stigma, many people with AIDS do not want others to know that they have the disease. They often go to considerable lengths to conceal the illness, even from those who are closest to them. They need support to ask for the help that they desperately need.

Social workers' concern for persons with AIDS is not new, but goes back to the very beginning of the public recognition of this epidemic. When social workers from 16 countries and 30 states met at the First International Conference on Social Work and AIDS in 1989, they resolved that:

> social workers and social work agencies are ethically obligated to provide appropriate services to all people affected by HIV/AIDS. These agencies and social workers are further obligated to ensure that direct care providers, supervisors and administrators have necessary training, education and support to maintain high standards of service provided with full protection of civil liberties and without discrimination or fear of working with people affected by HIV/AIDS . . .

Adopting policy statements is only a beginning, but it is an important beginning. Much work needs to be done to improve the effectiveness of interventions with this population. Social work with such clients requires a great deal of knowledge and expertise; this places a special responsibility on social workers to gain training and direction for work with HIV/AIDS-infected clients.

People who are infected by HIV/AIDS require a great many services, including medical, legal, employment, housing, and social services. Social workers are particularly well equipped to meet several of the special needs of this population, including the following:

1. Mental health, housing, entitlements, education, case management services
2. Advocacy to protect these clients against discrimination and to ensure that they will receive all the services they need
3. AIDS education for the general public, for the families of infected persons, and for those with HIV/AIDS themselves
4. Bereavement counseling for the families and loved ones of those who have died from AIDS

Biases about AIDS

Some social workers want to avoid working with HIV/AIDS-infected persons because they are worried that they might "catch" the disease. Is it unethical to avoid serving such clients when this fear is unfounded? Medical sources agree that HIV/AIDS is not spread by casual contact. Social workers can be certain that they are not at risk of HIV infection when serving clients who have AIDS. Yet these fears, false as they are, exist and must be overcome if social workers are to provide service to people with HIV/AIDS.

The AIDS epidemic has become widespread. Many persons have become infected, including spouses and significant others of infected persons, recipients of infected blood, newborn babies of infected parents, persons who shared needles, and others. Some of these persons may share the general public's biases about AIDS, and the stigma associated with AIDS may keep them from asking for the help they need when they know they are HIV positive. Social workers must find ways to open communication channels with all of these people, both those who are diagnosed as HIV positive and those who have developed AIDS.

Confidentiality and the Rights of Partners

A study by Abramson (1990) suggests that the issue of secrecy is a major ethical problem for social workers who have people with AIDS or people who are HIV positive on their caseload. The ethical dilemma facing these social workers arises out of the obligation or duty to warn a third party that he or she is endangered by unprotected sex (this will require breaking confidence). Often HIV-positive clients fear rejection, abandonment, and/or loneliness if their partners find out that they are infected. Exemplar 13.5 illustrates one aspect of this dilemma.

❖ 13.5 Gary Has Unsafe Sex

You staff a support group for HIV-positive adults. During one of the group meetings, Gary Damian relates that he continues to engage in unprotected sexual relations with his wife. When challenged by a group member, he admitted that he was not being fair to his wife but that he was afraid she would leave him if she found out that he was HIV positive.

What is your responsibility? If you cannot help Gary talk to his wife and/or convince him that he should change his behavior, should you break confidentiality? Does the *Tarasoff* ruling require you to notify his wife of the danger she faces? Whether a social worker is required by law to warn a third party when there is a threat of HIV infection differs from state to state. Among the legal arguments bearing on this question is the proposition that harm from a gunshot is virtually certain, but there is somewhat less certainty with regard to harm from unprotected sex with an HIV-infected partner. Not every person who has sex with an infected partner will become infected. Legal arguments aside, from an ethical point of view, the risk faced by the partner of an HIV-infected person may be sufficiently great to require breaking confidentiality and warning the potential victim (Girardi, Keese, Traver, & Cooksey, 1988; Melton, 1988).

In the language of our ethical principles screen (EPS), this ethical dilemma can be resolved by determining whether or not Ethical Principle 1 (preserving life) is involved. If the danger to the partner's life is direct and immediate (as most social workers think it is), this principle takes precedence over Ethical Principle 6 (privacy and confidentiality). The medical profession has dealt with this ethical dilemma in a similar way. The Council on Ethical and Judicial Affairs of the American Medical Association (AMA) suggests that if a physician fails to persuade the HIV-infected person to inform a third party, the physician should inform public health officials. Only if public health officials refused or were unwilling to take on the responsibility of warning does the physician have an obligation to act directly. The notion that physicians should have the right to breach confidentiality in order to warn the unsuspecting persons was endorsed by the Presidential Commission on the HIV Epidemic. The commission held that the decision about whether to breach confidentiality remained with the physician and was not imposed as a matter of law. Instead of a duty to warn, there was a "privilege to disclose" (Bayer, 1998).

Other Ethical Problems

There are many other ethical dilemmas and problems that social workers face when working with HIV-positive clients. "Rationing" medical care presents one set of ethical problems that require a social worker's advocacy services. Childless adults living with HIV infection typically only qualify for Medicaid coverage once they become eligible for SSI. Becoming eligible for SSI depends on becoming disabled. Those persons with asymptomatic HIV infection are not eligible for Medicaid until the condition has become fully developed AIDS. As a result, childless adults who are HIV positive are ineligible for Medicaid except in several states with Medicaid waivers to extend benefits to nondisabled persons living with HIV. These states conduct demonstration projects to evaluate the cost effectiveness of expanding services to this group in order to slow the progress of the disease and prevent opportunistic infections (Human Rights Campaign, 2003). Does a social worker have an ethical obligation to advocate for such services? How does one decide which deserves priority use of your time? Advocacy efforts? Service to your ever-expanding caseload? Advocacy for universal health care? For the homeless? For children without health care? Yourself and your time and energy?

Exemplar 13.6 concerning condoms for teens presents such issues at several levels. Both exemplars may require advocacy efforts by social workers.

❖ 13.6 School Policy, Condoms, and Parental Permission

You are a social worker in a high school, assigned to the school's health team. HIV and AIDS are threatening teenagers, many of whom ignore "safe sex" practices. The school system recently adopted a policy that condoms can be distributed only to students whose parent(s) have given written permission. Because of this rule, the team members can no longer provide condoms, even when students who are known to be sexually active request them. This morning such a sexually active student asked you for condoms. How do you respond? Later in the day, there will be a team meeting at which the new condom policy will be discussed. What can the team do about it?

This social worker is faced with the ethical dilemma of choosing between agency policy and protection of life in this specific instance. What about other sexually active students? At another level, what are the ethical dilemmas that face the team as they consider the school system's policy? Does the *Code of Ethics* provide direction for this social worker and for the team?

What does the *Code* suggest is the ethical thing to do in the following situations?

- An undocumented and illegal immigrant comes to your agency seeking care and treatment? Should you report the person to the Immigration and Naturalization Service? Refer him to a hospital?
- What if an adolescent informs you he is HIV positive and asks that you not inform his parents? Who is your client? To whom do you owe loyalty? The adolescent? His parents? Society?
- What should you do if a patient with AIDS who is on "medication cocktails" tells you he is also using illegal drugs and claims that you owe him confidentiality? What does the *Code* suggest you do? Do the principles in Chapter 4 help you decide what you should do as a social worker?

THE AGING

The "graying" of America continues to increase at a moderate rate as the elderly population increases numerically but remains stable as a percentage of the population (Hetzel & Smith, 2003). In the not too distant future, this growth will become rapid. In 1900, only one in every 25 Americans was over 65. By 2000, one in eight persons was in this age group. According to Census Bureau projections, the elderly population is expected to double to 80 million persons by 2050 (U.S. Census Bureau, 2003).

As the size of the aging population increases in the coming decades, communities must prepare for an increase in the size of the disabled population. It must be remembered, however, that socioeconomic status influences the pattern of disabilities. The patterns of morbidity and the incidence of disease reported among middle-aged people (45 to 64) in the two lower socioeconomic levels are not reported for the higher socioeconomic levels until the age group of 75 and above (Smyer, 1993).

As the number of aging persons increases and the number of such persons with cognitive and/or physical disabilities grows, one can anticipate an increase in the number of ethical dilemmas. Many of these dilemmas will focus on complex decision making in regard to autonomy, informed consent, self-determination (Dickson, 1997), and rationing of limited resources.

Informed consent is an ethical issue when working with people of any age, as discussed in Chapter 5, but it becomes critical when working with the aged. Informed consent implies a rational process. The person has a right to understand the situation, the choices, and the projected results of the decision to be made. In the case of aging persons who are clearly incompetent, courts may appoint a guardian. There are, however, many aged persons who have a limited capacity for understanding and decision making, who are legally competent and have a right to make their own decisions. Should the social worker do what she thinks is best for such clients? After all, they are aged, and there are real limits to the possibility of independent decision making and functioning. Since such persons may have limited understanding and the social workers have limited time, is it fair to use more of available time to help them understand more completely the implications of their decisions? What is the necessary degree of informed consent required in such a situation?

Proctor et al. (1993) found when they studied ethical dilemmas in hospital social work that most involved conflicts between client self-determination and client best interest; dilemmas were more likely when a patient's mental status was impaired and decision making was problematic. They found that these dilemmas related to delayed discharge, in-hospital mortality, and less than adequate post discharge care. A large proportion of these conflicts were connected to decisions about discharge destinations—that is, going home or going to a nursing home. When there were disputes among various parties, four out of five disputes were over the discharge plan or medical care. There were conflicts between families and medical teams or specific physicians; patients and staff members; social workers and medical staff persons; patients and everyone else; or among family members. Ethical dilemmas were found to be more likely when patients were physically dependent and mentally confused.

Both the person with serious health problems and family caretakers risk a great deal when ill persons receive health care at home rather than moving to assisted living, nursing centers, or other health care facilities. Conflicts often arise between the autonomy of the client and the helping activities of caretakers and social workers. During their time at home, an erosion of abilities often ensues, either as a result of the progress of the disease, because of aging, or both. Difficulties arise when physical deterioration occurs at a faster rate than mental deterioration. In these cases, clients become more dependent physically but remain alert intellectually. Under what circumstances should a social worker act on her own when it appears that her client receiving home health care is not impaired cognitively and has been exploited or neglected? Is such intervention by the social worker ethical if she does not involve the client in making choices for himself?

Moving from home care to long-term care residences is a traumatic life transition. Reinardy and Kane (1999) in a retrospective study of 260 older adult foster care residents and 179 cognitively intact nursing home residents in Oregon reported on the nature and circumstances surrounding their decision to move to a foster care or nursing home, including among other variables their perception of the decision-making process and who influenced it. High proportions of residents in both types of residences perceived that they had been manipulated into the move or that the move had been inevitable with little opportunity for choice. In this study, many of those persons who moved to an adult foster care home saw themselves as in control and choosing an alternative to nursing care. Foster care residents more frequently moved from their homes to foster homes, perhaps seeking homelike atmospheres, privacy, and more flexible routines. However, the nursing home residents tended to relocate from acute care to the long-term residence. Movement from an acute care facility to the long-term residence was associated with less control over the decision to move. Persons in both types of residences see family members as major influences on the move that tended to reduce rather than support a sense of control.

Hospital discharge planning and other transitions raise ethical dilemmas. Is it possible always to respect the autonomy and decision making of the older person and not discourage the involvement of family members (Reinardy & Kane, 1999)? Conflicts may arise from other factors. Aside from mental impairment and mental confusion, the societal definition of aging may produce ethical problems. Social workers must remain sensitive to situations in which the aging person may hold different values, choose different lifestyles, and have different expectations than those customary in the younger-generation social workers. When such conflicts exist, this does not make the older person "incompetent," but the social worker is faced with a value clash with ethical implications.

One of the fastest growing segments of health care is home health care. One hundred and eighteen social workers employed by both proprietary and nonprofit agencies participated in the first study of social workers' professional functions and ethical concerns in home health care. Patient autonomy and self-determination were found to be major ethical issues (Egan, 1999).

Knowledge about the potential effects of one choice or another also can play a part in ethical decision making. A study of depression and mortality among nursing home residents showed a significant difference in the mortality rates of residents with depressive disorder and those without (Wicclair, 1993). Given this information, the choice facing Rosalind Lippe and her social worker, Teresa Richards, is difficult.

❖ 13.7 Depression, Day Treatment, or the Nursing Home

Rosalind Lippe, 70 years of age, has been depressed for some time, Teresa Richards has been visiting her at home and helping her in a number of ways, but Ms. Lippe's depression has only slightly lifted, even with medication. A psychiatrist has recommended a day treatment program, but Ms. Lippe cannot afford payment for this service. However, Ms. Richards knows that treatment would be available for Ms. Lippe if she were to enter a local nursing home. Medicaid will pay the nursing home because of Ms. Lippe's low income.

Nursing home placement tends to be irreversible, yet in this case, placement may be the best option. Ms. Lippe is a younger aged person, but she is in difficulty. Right now, a bed is available in the nursing home, something that does not occur often. A decision will have to be made very quickly; if a mistake is made, it will probably not be possible to correct it. Many ethical issues need to be considered. How can Ms. Richards ensure informed consent by Ms. Lippe? Very few people want to enter a nursing home. Torn among her need for help, her ambivalence, and her depression, how can Ms. Lippe make a fully voluntary decision? Given what is known about mortality rates among nursing home residents, what factors must Ms. Richards balance? On the one hand, Ms. Lippe needs help for her depression; on the other hand, there will be a loss of freedom and possible health risks if Ms. Lippe enters the nursing home. In what ways can Ms. Richards resolve these ethical dilemmas?

SOCIAL WORK WITH GROUPS

Social workers are involved with groups in many different kinds of settings. No matter what type of setting they practice in, they will encounter many of the ethical dilemmas met with in other direct service roles. One ethical issue social workers who work with groups have to deal with occurs when they have to choose between group members as illustrated in Exemplar 13.8.

❖ 13.8 Charlie's Special

When Charlie, a ten-year-old emotionally disturbed youngster, joined the group, Emo Wilkommen, the social worker, took an immediate liking to him. Charlie's mother died some years ago, and his father is imprisoned. In order to ease Charlie's way into the therapy group, Emo set firm limits on two rambunctious group members and set up several opportunities for Charlie to shine. Group members claimed that the worker is favoring Charlie.

To what extent is Charlie entitled to unequal treatment in the group in order to make up for past deprivations and difficulties? Should Emo be entirely honest with the group members? What approach would do the most good and the least harm? Is it ever ethical for a social worker to be manipulative with a group?

In some situations, social workers serve as coleaders of therapy groups. In Exemplar 13.9, a social worker is faced with an ethical dilemma resulting from the group coleadership model.

❖ 13.9 Concern for Group? Self? Colleague?

Andrea Miller and Pat Stoner are social workers who colead a therapy and support group for psychiatric patients. They have worked together on many groups during the past few years. Recently, tensions have escalated between them because Ms. Stoner has shown up late for sessions, contradicts Ms. Miller during group sessions in front of the patients, disagrees on how to run the group, and has occasionally left the group early. One result has been that group members pay attention to the split instead of their own problems, and Ms. Miller has heard two group members commenting outside the sessions about the tensions they observed. Ms. Miller attempted to solve the problem outside the group setting, but the tension and the behavior have continued. As a long-term colleague of Ms. Stoner, Ms. Miller is not sure what she should do. Obviously, Ms. Stoner has some personal problems, but it is unclear whether they will pass by quickly or continue.

What is the ethical choice? Discussion has not worked. Ms. Miller can ignore the behavior. She can ask to be relieved of the assignment. If asked why, she can choose not to tell or say she is tired of the assignment, she can tell their supervisor and put the problem "on the table." Ms. Miller is torn between loyalty to group members, to herself, and to her colleague. Is there any guidance about these issues in the *Code of Ethics*? From an ethical point of view, how would you handle this situation?

Social workers often work with task groups in the community. Some of the ethical dilemmas that arise concern confidentiality, self-determination of the group and individual members, inclusion or exclusion of members, and conflicts of interest (Congress & Lynn, 1997). What is the ethically correct choice in the following dilemmas?

You are a social worker employed by a city housing authority, and you are working with a group of mothers to improve a playground for their children. One resident brings a friend with her to the meeting. During the meeting, you discover the friend is living with the group member's family in the same apartment. This is unknown to both the housing authority and your employer, and it is against the law. What should you do?

You are a social worker assigned to work with a community group concerned about trash pickup, speeding traffic that endangers neighborhood children, and public transportation accessibility. Your values and those of the group have been congruent regarding every concern so far. At this evening's meeting, a highly influential group member introduced the news that the state mental health department intends to establish a community residence in the neighborhood. When she took the leadership on this issue, the entire group agreed to make their opposition to the proposed residence their highest priority. You know there is a great need for such residences. If, however, you oppose their actions, you are concerned that it will undermine your effectiveness with all the other issues. How will you balance your values with those of the group? To whom do you owe loyalty? The group? Yourself? The neighborhood? Those who need such residences? Society in general?

MACROPRACTICE

Some professional social workers hold stereotyped views of their colleagues who engage in macropractice. They believe that practitioners who engage in agency-wide change efforts, social planning, neighborhood and community organization and development, social action, and social policy efforts are operating in a highly politicized arena. They think that this practice area is grounded on techniques and methods based on pragmatism rather than on ethical considerations. This perception is fostered not only by the nature of the settings in which macropractitioners practice but also by the language they use, especially such terms as *tactics, strategies, conflict,* and *advocacy.* Indeed, references to ethics are only rarely found in macropractice textbooks (exceptions include Netting, Kettner, & McMurtry, 1998, and Tropman, Erlich, & Rothman, 2001).

Nevertheless, macrosocial workers do encounter many difficult ethical dilemmas in their daily practice. The NASW *Code of Ethics* applies to all NASW members, including those in macropractice. The *Code of Ethics* states that "Social workers' primary responsibility is to promote the well-being of clients" (NASW, 1999, 1.01) and "Social workers should promote the general welfare of society, from local to global levels. . . ." (NASW, 1999, 6.01). Further, "the social worker should engage in social and political action that seeks to ensure that all people have access to the resources, employment, services, and opportunities they require to meet their basic human needs and to develop fully" (NASW, 1999, 6.04a).

When the social worker is attempting to comply with all of these standards, many dilemmas are encountered. These dilemmas include determining who is the client to whom primary responsibility is owed and selecting the persons who have access to resources when not every needy person can be supplied because these resources are in short supply. Another type of dilemma occurs when there are several similarly disadvantaged groups. How does the worker choose the one group that will receive her priority attention?

In the following social planning situation, the social worker has to choose between many different groups. The choices to be made clearly deal with promoting the "general welfare of society." In this instance, who is society? Which group deserves priority consideration?

❖ 13.10 Establishing a Cancer Treatment Unit

You are the director of social work in a large urban community hospital located in a low-income area serving people from various economic levels. You have been assigned to staff the planning committee charged with creating a plan for the future of the hospital. You grew up in the community and have family and long-standing friends who reside there. You also have relationships with many community human service administrators and staff members.

As the planning process proceeds, it becomes clear that most committee members favor the creation of a specialized cancer treatment unit, which will gain status and recognition for the hospital and also attract patients from throughout the state. Such a recommendation, however, will make it impossible to recommend improvements for emergency and ambulatory care that are desperately needed by the neighborhood. A recommendation for a cancer treatment unit will change the nature of the available health care, who will get the jobs, use of community space, kinds of housing that will be available, and so forth.

It becomes clear to you that the local community will gain very little and lose much if a cancer treatment unit is installed. You are torn between loyalties to the hospital, to the community in general, to the social and human service agencies in the community, and to the community's population, including your friends and relatives who need a different type of service.

As a member of the planning group, you are faced with the dilemma of choosing between groups to determine who will benefit from the distribution of resources. What criteria will help you choose between the cancer patients who do not necessarily come from the immediate community and the health needs of your family, friends, and neighbors? Choosing between two groups, both of which have real health needs, is a typical ethical dilemma faced by social workers who are social planners. Whose good is primary? As a social worker, you owe first priority to the potential recipients of health services, but which of the groups has a higher priority? In addition, is the hospital's long-term viability a consideration that should affect the ethical decision-making process?

A review of the ethical principles screen (EPS) in Chapter 4 can be helpful as one thinks about the dilemma confronting this social planner. We would suggest that a consideration of Ethical Principles 1 and 2 is most compelling in the present case.

Principle 1—Protection of life. All medical services ultimately deal with the protection of life. Cancer patients are at a great risk and inevitably face life-threatening situations that require early treatment—the earlier the better. On the other hand, the emergencies typically treated in a hospital ER range from routine treatments to life-threatening situations that require immediate treatment, for the latter, any delay may be a death sentence. Principle 1 does not provide unambiguous guidance, but it can be used to buttress either choice.

Principle 2—Equality and inequality. Cancer is today a very high-profile disease. A cancer treatment unit will be established in at least one hospital in the state, no matter what the board of Neighborhood Hospital decides. For the neighborhood residents, however, the Neighborhood Hospital is the only chance for receiving timely emergency services; transportation to the next nearest hospital would add 10 to 15 minutes' travel time—too much time when every minute counts. Under this principle, neighborhood persons have the ethical right to expect preferred consideration. The social worker, therefore, can support a recommendation in favor of improving emergency services.

Social workers are expected to be open and honest. Among the standards in the *Code of Ethics* is the expectation that "social workers should not participate in, condone, or be associated with dishonesty, fraud, or deception" (NASW Code, 1999, 4.04). At every step in their education and later in agency practice, social workers are encouraged not to engage in secretive, hidden, or disguised actions or to be manipulative. Much attention has been paid in the literature to efforts to change social agencies, always with the justification that one's efforts are designed to improve services for clients or to attain some general good. In some cases, concealed and unacknowledged action may be thought necessary to gain a greater good for a community or for clients. In these cases, social workers have to weigh the ethical balance between a greater good and hidden actions.

What is the best way for the worker to respond in the situation presented in Exemplar 13.11?

❖ 13.11 How to Fight the Half-Truths of the Real Estate Lobby

Ed Corey is a community organizer, employed by a social agency to develop new housing in a neighborhood. Ed staffs a community coalition that is vigorously working on the new housing. The early activities of the coalition were very successful, but powerful real estate interests who wanted to block the development of the new housing began to spread rumors about Ed's personal history and life. They also used deceptive and distorted facts in advertisements to destroy the coalition's efforts and to undercut Ed's potential influence.

Ed, for his part, knows about the "shady" dealings of some members of the real estate group. He senses there will be no new housing unless aggressive action is taken, but he is unsure what he should do to combat the half-truths and lies of the opponents of the new housing. How should Ed use the information he has? Should he be open and rebut the charges of the opponents? Should he retaliate and fight "fire with fire" behind the scenes? Should he use the facts he possesses with strategically located opinion molders to undermine the influence of the real estate group?

SOCIETAL ISSUES

Standard 6.01 of the *Code* states "social workers should promote the general welfare of society . . . their communities, and their environments." Before leaving this section, we want to point out an example of ethical responsibility of social workers at a societal level. African American, Latino, and certain Asian minority populations suffer morbidity and mortality disproportionately in the United States (Hogue & Hargraves, 2000). From birth to death, African Americans are at greater risk for debilitating social, psychological, and physical conditions that negatively affect the quality of their individual and family lives, including "premature" deaths (Jackson & Sellers, 2001). Similarly, Latinos are most likely to be the most uninsured of all racial and ethnic groups, less likely to use health care services for preventive care, and those with existing health and mental health conditions are less likely to use health services than Whites (Carter-Pokras & Zambrana, 2001). Are such matters the ethical concern only of social workers who are practicing macromethods? If not, what does this suggest are the ethical roles of direct service and clinical social workers in regard to these situations?

Whatever the difficulties and dilemmas for social workers in macropractice, the *Code of Ethics*—for all social workers—explicitly requires engagement by social workers in social and political action "to prevent and eliminate domination of, exploitation of, and discrimination against any person, group, or class on the basis of race, ethnicity, national origin, color, sex, sexual orientation, age, marital status, political belief, religion, or mental or physical disability" (6.04d).

EXERCISES

1. If you are confronted by the ethical dilemma that faces the director of social work in Exemplar 13.10, "Establishing a Cancer Treatment Unit," what do you think your decision would be? What arguments support your decision? What arguments exist contrary to your point of view?

2. What are the ways in which aging persons attempt to make health decisions in advance of medical operations? What dilemmas occur that affect social workers when such arrangements either have not been made or are unclear in some important way?

3. Can you identify ways in which ageism appears in American society and in social work practice? How do these relate to the social work *Code of Ethics*? What can a social worker do to minimize ageism?

4. The legislature of your state has been alarmed by a sudden sharp increase in the incidence of HIV-positive findings among several populations. A bill has been introduced calling for mandatory HIV screening of all persons applying for a marriage license. The problem is a real one; the solution suggested may or may not be effective, but it does raise a number of ethical issues. Your local NASW chapter has asked you to discuss these questions at the next membership meeting.

5. You are a social worker for a hospital support group of young adults recovering from serious illnesses. The group has been told they can make decisions "within agency policy" in a democratic fashion. When the group is informed that a new member will be joining, one member recognizes the person, says she is disruptive, and the group joins in and says the new member cannot join. What should you do? Support the group or the new member?

SUGGESTIONS FOR ADDITIONAL READINGS

Hughes (1993a, b) reviews the life-and-death decisions facing child welfare workers when dealing with severely disabled children. Ward and Drotman (1998) systematically examine the demographics of HIV and AIDS. Yu and O'Neal (1992) analyze the issue of confidentiality that faces social workers who work with clients with AIDS. Dolgoff and Skolnik (1996) report on the findings of an empirical study of decision making by social workers with groups. Dickson (1997) reviews the complex relationships between law, ethics, social work, and self-determination among the aging. Egan (1999) reports on social workers' ethical concerns in an expanding field, home health care. Torczyner (1991) examines ethical issues in social action. Freeman and McDonnell (2001) provide very detailed case examples from medical settings, some of which present the basic case information, ask the reader to make a decision, and then provide follow-up information allowing the reader to see potential consequences of some decisions. Walker and Staton (2000) caution about the dangers of stereotyping in "Multiculturalism in Social Work Ethics."

14 CHAPTER | Whose Responsibility Are Professional Ethics?

Ethical decision making is often presented in a way suggesting that the social worker who must make a decision is completely alone and cut off from every support system that might give her guidance. Many have questioned this view. Philosopher W. D. Walsh wrote, "morality is first and foremost a social institution, performing a social role, and only secondarily, if at all, a field for individual self-expression" (Frankena, 1980, p. 33).

While every social worker is, of course, responsible for her ethical decisions, it must be recognized that she is a participant in a number of networks and social systems that support—or should support—her ethical decision making. One of the purposes of the *Code* is to help social workers "identify relevant considerations when professional obligations conflict or ethical uncertainties arise" (NASW *Code*, 1999, Purpose of the NASW *Code of Ethics*). Decision making, however, always occurs within a social setting that influences, rewards, or guides certain behaviors and limits, sanctions, or disapproves others. The social agency employing the social worker is one such setting, the service delivery team or office is another, and the professional association is a third. Any discussion of steps designed to facilitate and strengthen ethical decision making is incomplete if it fails to take these systems into consideration. Professional ethical actions are not only a result of individual choices. Organizations also must play a part in supporting correct ethical decision making by social workers.

Granted there will never be a time when clear guidelines will be available for every ethical decision that a social worker must make, yet various societal and institutional mechanisms have been developed to provide guidance and support. Here we want to discuss a number of mechanisms that have been found particularly helpful by some social workers.

Agency Risk Audits

Audits for many reasons are conducted in human service agencies—financial, safety, quality control, and utilization review. Agencies can conduct an audit of professional knowledge of social work ethics. The audit can include two major foci: (1) social workers' knowledge of identified ethics-related risks (complaints and lawsuits filed against social workers, ethics committees' experiences, and law suits and court cases) in their field of service and practice settings; and (2) current agency procedures and procedures for handling ethical issues, dilemmas, and decisions.

Among the ethical risks are client rights, confidentiality and privacy, informed consent, service delivery, boundary issues and conflicts of interest, documentation, defamation of character, client records, supervision, staff development and training, consultation, client referrals, fraud, termination of services and client abandonment, practitioner impairment, and evaluation and research. Agencies that periodically engage in social work ethics audits have the opportunity to strengthen their own ethical performance, but they also provide support and preparation for practitioners and supervisors, thus sharing as an organization the burden of ethical decision making by staff members (Reamer, 2001).

Peer Review and Committees on the Ethics of Social Work Practice

Peer review permits a social worker to test her ethical decision making against that of her colleagues, either informally in groups that practitioners create for mutual aid or formally in agencies. In the past, social workers have used informal groupings to review their professional practice decisions. Such groupings can also be useful for reviewing ethical decisions. Peer review groups are particularly important for social workers in private practice because they are more isolated than workers in agency-based practice and because they have less opportunity for interaction with peers. Controls and accountability of private practice social workers depend almost entirely upon the sensitivity and knowledge of the individual practitioner. Peer pressures, which are so immediate in agency practice, are much less evident in private practice. Because of these considerations, social workers in private practice may want to organize peer review systems that are specifically geared to review their ethical decision making. In this way, they can be more certain that their decisions will be of the highest quality.

Each agency should establish a Committee on the Ethics of Social Work Practice, analogous to Committees on the Rights of Human Subjects that exist in every academic research organization. Practitioners who have an ethical question may consult with the committee about a problem. Such a committee is a forum where social workers can think through difficult ethical questions occurring in everyday practice. Most important, this committee can be the locus for the routine monitoring of ethical practice within the agency.

The NASW also provides consultation on ethical issues by appointment and displays monthly on its Web site ethical dilemmas submitted by members. The dilemmas are examined in relation to the *Code.*

Accountability Systems

Professional social workers for the foreseeable future, whether they work in agencies or in private practice, will practice in an environment in which they will be held accountable for their professional activities. Courts, third-party payers, governmental regulators, and empowered clients and patients as citizens play roles in regard to accountability in our increasingly litigious society. Social agencies are accountable for what they do. Social agencies that want to implement this responsibility in a positive way must develop and operate accountability systems. These systems are characterized by the following features: information systems and monitoring; methods for sampling activities and decisions; clear indicators of the desired quality of performance; clear indicators or criteria of the desired quantity; and feedback systems that permit an early alert to problem situations.

Accountability systems relate primarily to practice performance, but there is no reason why such systems could not incorporate additional indicators that focus on the ethical aspects of practice. Just as agencies evaluate the effectiveness and efficiency of the services they deliver and the social work practices of their social work employees, agencies can also track and evaluate systematically the ethical decision making of social work practitioners.

In-Service Training and Consultation

Most agencies make a heavy investment in providing in-service training, continuing education opportunities, and consultation for their staff. Though the focus is often on more effective practice and more efficient administration, these sessions should also include a focus on the ethical implications of practice in order to strengthen the ethical level of practice.

Agency Appeals Procedures and Ombudsmen

Many agencies have appeals procedures, but clients are often not aware of them. "Forgetting" to inform clients about them may simplify the life of the practitioners and administrators, but this does not make for a high level of ethical practice. The use of appeals procedures does more than correct mistakes made by social workers. One of their most valuable functions is to sensitize social workers to the ethical aspects of practice. An ombudsman or another type of appeals procedure should be readily available to clients, who should be able to use these procedures without any risk of stigma. Ethical social workers will welcome such strategies. Administrative review procedures also have a place in the support system, but they do not take the place of appeals procedures freely available to clients.

Clients' Bill of Rights

Many hospitals and other service organizations distribute a bill of rights to new clients and patients. These brief statements inform people of the type of information they are entitled to know about their situation. They are also told they can expect to be treated with dignity and respect, they will participate in decision making about their situation, they will be informed about available options, and they have a right to speak to an ombudsman or other person if they are dissatisfied with their treatment.

Social workers should consider the use of a clear and informative statement to inform new clients about what they can expect from the professional personnel they will encounter, the mechanisms for raising questions or seeking clarification where needed, and the procedures for registering grievances. While social workers can and should inform their clients about these things, transmitting such information verbally is *not* a "Bill of Rights." This must be in writing and can be issued only by the *Agency*, not by the individual social worker. The situation is different for those in private practice who can and should issue such a written document to every new client. The document should include statements about what the client can and cannot expect to happen in the professional service.

Essential to all techniques that agencies employ to establish ethical norms and enhance ethical conduct (e.g., staff education and training, accountability systems, etc.) is the establishment of an ethical climate in the agency that is visible, deemed important, and understood by all participants. The establishment of such a climate involves the use of the executive leadership influence and the participation of staff members and other parties at every level of the system to ensure high ethical standards throughout the work and life of the agency (Grundstein-Amado, 1999).

Professional Associations

Professional associations, such as NASW, can play a key role in strengthening ethical practice. The promulgation and periodic revision of the *Code* needs to be strengthened through the inclusion of case references and interpretive guidelines because the standards of practice and the limits of ethical behavior are difficult to define. Jayaratne et al. (1997) found in a study of Michigan NASW members that there is much confusion and disagreement as to what constitutes appropriate ethical practice. This disturbing finding suggests that the NASW and other professional associations of social workers must develop additional strategies if they want to encourage the strengthening of ethical decision making within the profession. The following are some of the ways to do so:

1. Continue to revise and refine the *Code of Ethics*. It may be helpful to add case precedents.
2. Encourage the formation of formal and informal groups to study and review critical ethical decisions arising from actual practice experiences.
3. Develop a data bank of precedents with ethical implications. Knowledge about ethical decisions is valuable, but identifying and learning about

those actions found to be unethical can also have positive consequences, including being instructive and prewarning members of the profession.

4. Continue to schedule activities that focus on the ethical aspects of practice, both at professional conferences and as part of continuing education programs.

5. In addition to discussion of monthly dilemmas on NASW's Web site, publish an "Ethics Reporter" or a regular ethics column in *Social Work* or in the *NASW News* in order to make social workers more familiar with their *Code of Ethics*.

6. Further develop NASW's ethics hotline so that practitioners, supervisors, and administrators can obtain advice on ethical issues that arise in their practice. Modern communication technologies, such as fax and electronic mail, can provide instant communication over long distances. At the same time, these technologies give the consultant sufficient time to reflect on the question or to consult with others.

7. The NASW should publish an annual report, as does the American Psychological Association, regarding the number and types of ethical complaints investigated and the disposition of those cases.

8. State licensing boards can also play a part in reporting on their activities and in other ways educating practitioners, supervisors, and administrators in their respective states.

It is desirable that the professional organization and its local chapters, as well as individual social agencies, begin to collect data on ethical decision making. Such a data bank should not be limited to "success stories" but should also include errors, unanswerable questions, and embarrassing situations. Collection of this type of data will be helpful to practitioners as well as to students. This information will explicate the ethical quandaries experienced by social workers, the preferred solutions, and the results achieved. Such a data base will also be helpful in the creation of case materials, which are so necessary for the systematic development of new social work knowledge. Just as lawyers can draw on case law for guidance in making the difficult decisions, so social workers should be able to receive guidance from the suggested data bank.

NASW Professional Complaint Procedures

Requests for professional review (RPRs) may be submitted by any individual, group, or organization. The complainant need not be a member of the NASW. A member who wishes to have his or her own conduct reviewed may self-refer. The individual against whom the RPR is filed must have been a member of the NASW at the time of the alleged violation. A chapter member may serve as a Surrogate Complainant when a member appears to have violated the NASW *Code of Ethics* and this information is in the public domain, that is, a matter of public record. With the approval of the National Committee on Inquiry, a person other than the individual with direct knowledge of the situation may serve as a Representative Complainant if the affected person is incapacitated, unavailable, or a minor child. Alleged violations of personnel standards by an employer or agency may also be filed, including allegations the employer or agency imposed limitations on, or penalties for, professional action on behalf of clients (NASW, 2001).

One effort to streamline procedures concerns resolution at the chapter level of disputes involving professional ethics and agency personnel standards. A first step since 1998 allows chapters to determine whether a dispute meets the criteria for acceptance into the adjudication process before designating it as a complaint. This step helps to protect social workers against harm from unfounded complaints.

In this final chapter, we have presented ideas that may help social workers in their search for more effective ethical practice. The values of the social work profession form the background for ethical decision making. In turn, ethical decision making is the cornerstone for ethical practice.

Ethical decision making begins with familiarity with the *Code of Ethics* and the clarification of one's own values. Knowledge of what one really believes is an inescapable basic step for social workers seeking to strengthen their ethical practice. Beyond this, it becomes important for social workers to clarify the values of society and of the various groups with which they work. Clarification of these values permits social workers to become more sensitive to and more aware of the values of others and of possible conflicts between different value systems.

Individual practitioners sometimes feel that they are alone when facing ethical dilemmas, but there are others who can share these ethical problems. Formal peer review, agency consultations, and the professional association must share the burden of thinking through these dilemmas. Some persons have suggested that ethics do not exist outside of community. To base ethical decisions strictly on one's individual conscience can lead a person into very difficult situations and into playing God. All ethics are integral to community. There are many reasons for a professional social worker to "connect" with the professional community. Fellow professionals can provide opportunities to think through ethical questions and dilemmas, to discuss one's ethical concerns with other social work professionals, and to gain colleague support.

EXERCISES

1. Identify your strengths and limitations in regard to ethical decision making when you are engaged in social work practice. How can you better prepare yourself for being an ethical social worker?
2. Identify in your field instruction placement, your agency of employment, or other social agency what you consider to be the limitations of the ethical decision-making patterns used. If you could improve one thing about ethical decision making in this organization, what would you choose to alter and how could you go about trying to improve the situation?

3. Review the *NASW Procedures for Professional Review* (2001) to become familiar with the filing of a complaint with the professional association.

SUGGESTIONS FOR ADDITIONAL READINGS

Csikai and Sales (1998) report on the explosive growth of hospital ethics committees and the roles and expectations of social workers as related to them. Jayaratne et al. (1997), in "Social work professional standards: An exploratory study," found that practitioners and those who judge practitioner behavior are making decisions with relatively little guidance from the profession. Strom-Gottfried (2003) helps practitioners and others to increase their understanding of adjudication as she reviews the origins, targets, and outcomes of ethics complaints.

Additional Exemplars

The exemplars in this appendix have been chosen to illustrate ethical practice problems occurring in the real world of social workers. For each exemplar, identify the ethical dilemmas and the relevant sections of the NASW *Code.*

❖ A.1 Discriminatory Practices and an Agency Employee

Several social agencies in your city, including the one for which you work, engage in discriminatory practices against minority group children. There is now a court case about this matter, lawyers for the plaintiff have asked you to testify about specific instances of such discriminatory practices. You oppose these practices and repeatedly have spoken against them at staff meetings, but you hesitate to testify in court because (1) you are afraid that you may be fired if you testify against your agency, (2) you are not sure whether the confidential relationship you have with your clients permits you to reveal this information, and (3) you are not certain whether it is ethical for you to use agency records for this purpose.

❖ A.2 Olympus Products or Michael Crawford?

Angela Ross is a social worker in the Mephisto EAP program. Michael Crawford has been referred to her by a supervisor in the Olympus Products mailroom for taking longer than usual lunches, coming in late, and often asking to leave early. By the time she met with him, she

245

learned from files that he had a drug problem and completed a 30-day rehabilitation program. His work performance has been satisfactory until this recent behavior. When referred earlier for the rehab program, he had been warned that the business would not continue his employment if he relapsed again. Mr. Crawford started off by telling Ms. Ross that he has been using drugs once again. He begged her not to tell the "bosses" since he has a wife and children; and if he loses this job, it will be very difficult for him to find another. Did she have a responsibility earlier to clarify with Mr. Crawford how information he gave would be shared with his employer? What should Ms. Ross do? Should she report a different problem? Who takes priority for correct action—Mr. Crawford? Ms. Ross? The EAP program? The supervisor? Mr. Crawford's family? Olympus Products?

❖ A.3 Continued Funding and Unqualified Staff

Les Granger is the executive director of Southwest Newtown, a community development agency organizing in a poor neighborhood. He received a phone call from Kenneth Harrick, a very influential legislator, who called to ask Mr. Granger to hire his daughter Gretchen for a job in his agency. Gretchen is very impressed by the work they are doing, as is Mr. Harrick, who is pleased he could be helpful in maintaining the agency's state funding. When Mr. Granger meets with Gretchen, it becomes very clear that she simply is unprepared for the job, lacks skills, and even has attitudes that will undermine the work of the other staff members. Mr. Granger was uncomfortable following the phone call sensing that Mr. Harrick expected his daughter would be hired. Although Mr. Harrick did not say so in just those words, Mr. Granger was convinced that if she is not hired there would be negative consequences. Granger believes he faces a choice: either the agency funding will be cut or eliminated or he can hire a person who will not be able to do the job and will require much assistance and time. What is the ethically correct choice—protect the agency funding so good work can continue or possibly undermine services with lower quality staff?

❖ A.4 Cheating Medicaid

Melissa Walker told Mrs. Strong, her supervisor, that her client Mrs. Anderson has Medicaid family coverage, including young children. She also informed her that she is cheating and had been encouraged to do so by an earlier social worker when she applied. She tells you that if she does not have Medicaid the family will be ruined financially; they are just beginning to see "light at the end of the tunnel," and she could never afford the medical care she and her children are receiving. The eligibility rules are clear; all taxpayers are providing funds for the Medicaid program. Mrs. Anderson and her family need the medical services provided. Because of a shortage of Medicaid funds, however, others even more needy may not receive services if a large number of ineligible persons use the services provided. What is Melissa Walker's obligation to the taxpayers? What is her responsibility to enable a family to make a comeback? What is the right thing to do?

❖ A.5 The Ethics of Team Practice

Timothy Land is a social worker in a day treatment program for deinstitutionalized persons. Professionally, Mr. Land is respected by other members of the team and is viewed as a social worker of great promise who will move ahead quickly in his career.

Clients in the program are assigned to treatment groups on the basis of the decision of the psychiatrist and the social worker. There is no written contract as to what is expected of either patients or of staff. Clients are never involved in decisions about group assignment or tasks. If a client does not fulfill the assigned tasks, he or she is typically labeled "disruptive" or "decompensating." These comments are written on the clients' charts.

Land questions the ethical aspects of these procedures. He feels strongly that social work ethics require client participation in all phases of the decision-making process. Land is not certain to whom he owes primary loyalty and responsibility. Is it to the team? To the clients? Or to his career?

❖ A.6 Can a Former Co-Worker Be a Client?

Kate Pecknold, the intake worker in the Midstream Counseling Center, refers a new client to you. She is seeking help because of anxiety about many changes taking place in her life at the same time. Her last name — Granger — is familiar but her first name is unknown to you. When she appears for the appointment, you realize Hayley Granger was formerly a co-worker in another agency a few years ago. She tells you that she realizes you have this former work relationship, but she admires you very much and feels that because she knows some of the other workers, it is likely that you are the only staff member she would trust. What should you do?

❖ A.7 A Friendly Neighbor in Need

Your middle-aged neighbor, Sally Roth, has been having problems with her teenage son, Kirk. You are employed as a social worker at the Prime Senior Center, your family lives two doors away from her house, and your children have gone to school and played together. She tells you she is having a very difficult time with her son, is unable to pay for counseling, and does not want to use her husband's health insurance coverage because it can cause him trouble at work. You like Sally and her family and value her friendship, and you would like to be helpful to her.

What should you do when she asks that you see her privately to help her "solve" these problems. What ethical problems do you see in this situation?

❖ A.8 A Social Worker Strikes It Rich

An elderly man, Mr. Silvano, has been your client for several years. He feels you have been a wonderful "friend," and he is telling you that he wants to leave you a sizeable sum in his will. The agency has strict rules against accepting gifts from clients, but you won't receive the money until after he dies. The money would certainly be helpful, after all, you have expenses also. What should you do? Tell Mr. Silvano you're sorry, but you can't accept being placed in his will? Keep quiet and wait to see what happens?

❖ A.9 Your Colleague or Your Client?

As required by her agency, a social worker has developed a resource file that identifies resources needed to do her job—hospital beds, Medicare contacts, inexpensive housing, and other needed services. Other workers in her unit have not prepared themselves to identify systematically helpful contact persons and resources at various social agencies. One of these social workers has just approached you and asks for help finding a room for rent so she can complete the discharge arrangements for Mr. Sisyphus, but you know you will need to have that potential room for your own client, Mr. McDonald. The situation is complicated by the fact that if Mr. Sisyphus is not discharged today, he will have overstayed the time limit in this facility, and his worker will be reprimanded, which could affect his evaluations and pay. To whom do you have responsibilities? To protect your resource file and a potential bed for your client, Mr. McDonald? Help Mr. Sisyphus get a room? Help your colleague avoid being reprimanded?

❖ A.10 Responding to Concerned Family Members

Mrs. Ruggiero is a social worker in a psychiatric facility. All information about voluntary patients is to be kept confidential unless there is a signed consent form. Officially, when a relative calls to inquire whether the person is hospitalized there, staff members are not supposed to acknowledge his or her presence. Sometimes an especially tearful parent or sibling calls stating that the patient is expecting to move in and live with them, and they need to know if the patient is there or on the "street." Mrs. Ruggiero usually is very sympathetic to their requests. Even when a consent form is missing, she will find ways around the issue. Sometimes she learns information that can be very helpful regarding the treatment provided for the patient. It is possible the patient has distorted his history, and the family member can fill you in on the history and verify and clarify facts, including identifying medication being used. She might say, "I am not allowed to give you information, but I will listen to whatever you want to tell me. What you are describing to me sounds very familiar, and we do have persons here who have problems similar to those you are describing. Yes, there is a pay phone here, visiting hours are early evening, and the hospital is located on Elm Street." Is it ever correct to act against agency policy? What types of situations might suggest avoiding the hospital's policy? Who takes priority in this situation? The patient? After all, you can learn information that could prove helpful. The hospital by obeying the rule? The parent or sibling?

❖ A.11 Taking on a Private Client

Christine Ross is the only MSW social worker in a remote mountain community where she staffs the county welfare office. Her friend, Kay Jordan, the principal of the county high school, has told her about a very disturbed student in her school. This student has lately engaged in some very bizarre behavior, and Kay has no doubt that he needs professional help. Since the nearest mental health clinic is 130 miles away, Kay asked Christine to provide therapy for this student.

The student is not eligible for service from the county welfare department (which in any case does not provide therapy). Therefore, Kay asked Christine to take him on as a private client. Christine has never before provided therapy for this kind of very disturbed person, but she is willing to try. Is it ethical for her to do so when there is no possibility of obtaining supervision?

❖ A.12 A Dual-Role Bargain

Priscilla is a senior in high school who is being seen at the Blackburn Youth Counseling Service. She was referred by a school guidance counselor after she told the counselor she uses drugs recreationally with classmates. Her school attendance lately has been erratic, and her grades have been dropping each semester. Since beginning her treatment with Joyce Breckenridge, she often threatened to discontinue treatment. Last week, she bargained with Ms. Breckenridge. Priscilla would stay in treatment and not do drugs if Ms. Breckenridge would attend her graduation. The agency policy is to never meet with clients in person other than at the agency or not to attend clients' family or other celebrations. Ms. Breckenridge believed that Priscilla would never graduate unless she—as her social worker—did something special. Ms. Breckenridge said that if Priscilla stays in treatment, she will attend the graduation. What would be your choice, bargain with Priscilla and agree to her request? Comply with agency policy? Is this a dual-role situation? What should Ms. Breckenridge do?

❖ A.13 Threats from Your Client

You have been treating Jason Conger, a severely disturbed person, for several months. In recent weeks, he has become increasingly aggressive toward you, claiming (wrongly) that you are planning to harm him. Today, he told you that if you do not stop persecuting him, he will get even with you by harming your child.

You are very concerned since you know that Jason has been involved in the past in physically abusing children. Should you report this threat to the police? Should you arrange for a commitment to a mental hospital? Should you withdraw from this case? What should you do? What are the ethical dilemmas you must resolve before you can make a decision?

❖ A.14 An Interracial Marriage

Chris, age 28, has many problems. Until now, he has coped with them, but now he has a problem that is too big for him to handle alone. Chris has fallen in love with Amy and wants to marry her. The problem is that both of their families are vehemently opposed to this interracial marriage—Chris is a White Anglo, while Amy is a Vietnamese American.

The social worker to whom he has turned for help sees nothing wrong with an interracial marriage. She herself is White and has a Native American daughter-in-law. Should the worker share this information with Chris and help him deal with the prejudices of his and Amy's family? Is it ethical for the worker to talk about her own values?

What if this worker felt that interracial marriages made for many difficulties in our society and in this community in particular? Should she share with Chris the problems that her son and daughter-in-law have encountered? Is this ethical?

❖ A.15 Getting Help for Clyde Lukke

Clyde Lukke voluntarily entered Sunnyside Psychiatric Hospital on Wednesday afternoon. He complained of severe depression and was afraid that he might commit suicide. The admitting psychiatrist diagnosed his case as *depression, recurrent.* The usual treatment at Sunnyside for this diagnostic category is two to three weeks hospitalization, followed by long-term intensive individual therapy and medication.

Five days after admission, Angela Mennikke, the floor social worker, was notified by the business office to prepare the patient for discharge. Ms. Mennikke was surprised since discharge orders are usually discussed by the floor staff before they are entered. Rarely is discharge an administrative decision. Upon inquiry she learned that Mr. Lukke's HMO benefits are limited to one week of psychiatric hospitalization. She also learned that this HMO, like many similar organizations, reimburses only for time-limited group therapy, not for individual therapy.

Should the social worker prepare a routine discharge and let the HMO staff worry about how to help Lukke? Should she take an advocate stance to ensure that Lukke will get the treatment he needs? What is expected in this situation from a professional social worker who wants to engage in ethical practice?

❖ A.16 Who's to Know?

A local psychologist has just completed a battery of intelligence tests for a teenager with mental retardation served by your agency. You have learned that this boy's test results are just above the score required to continue services for him and his family. Your supervisor, concerned about what will happen if services are cut off, asked you to suggest to the psychologist that she report a slightly lower score, thus ensuring that the agency could continue to provide services to this client.

❖ A.17 A New Friend and Peer Consultation

Last night, social worker Mark Sussna met Valery Aylon at a party at a friend's apartment. In the course of the evening, they discovered that they shared many interests. It was almost a case of "love at first sight." Mark made a date to meet Valery the following evening.

Today, one of Mark's colleagues discussed a complicated case with him. Mark soon realized that the client being discussed was his new friend, Valery Aylon. What should he do? Should he tell his colleague to consult with someone else? Should he keep silent so that he can find out more about Valery, information which will help him determine whether they are really suitable? Should he terminate his friendship with Valery? (Note: Peer consultation is the accepted practice in this agency, so *confidentiality* is not an issue.)

❖ A.18 One Job or Two?

Joseph Leggio is a 25-year-old man with mental retardation. He has no living relatives and is able to live in protected environments in the community. Alice Patella, a social worker, recently placed him at a board and care home run by Mrs. Collins, a person with whom Alice has had a long relationship. Mrs. Collins has been supportive of the clients placed in her home, something that is found infrequently. Alice just discovered that Mrs. Collins—who needs the money—has not been supervising the clients placed in her home. Instead, she has hired a discharged psychiatric patient to monitor the residents while she works part-time in a local store. Alice knows that Mrs. Collins needs the income and her assistant, the discharged patient, needs both the extra money and the sense of accomplishment from performing the job. What would you suggest Alice do?

❖ A.19 Who Makes Social Work Decisions?

In the Whitehurst Children's Agency, the social work staff is supervised by Gloria Tabaka, a licensed social worker, who is an excellent teacher and supervisor. When Ms. Tabaka has to be away from the agency, whether for a few hours or a day, the only person she trusts sufficiently to act for her is the office manager, Monica Monteleone, who is not a professional social worker nor is she trained in any human service. When Ms. Tabaka is not present and cannot be reached, the staff must go to Ms. Monteleone for decisions about the clients. Admittedly, Ms. Monteleone does know a great deal about many things, but the social work staff is not sure whether social work decisions should be made by a person who has not been certified. Today, while Ms. Tabaka is away, you have to make a decision about an emergency child welfare situation that needs your supervisor's approval. Ms. Monteleone disagrees with your recommendation and suggests an option which you feel is not professionally defensible. What should you do?

❖ A.20 Obey the Law or Help?

Daphne Ranesco, a social work student, will graduate next week. Today, one of her clients, Harry Plimkin, called distraught saying he has become violent with his wife and that he wants help. He tells her he has much respect for her since she has been very helpful to him, especially in controlling his temper. He wants to see her privately for a few sessions because he does not trust anyone else at the agency to help him in this emergency. State regulations do not allow social workers to practice privately until they have had two years of postgraduation professional experience under supervision. Does an emergency such as this one justify breaking the law? Is the prevention of violence more important than abiding by the law? What are Daphne's options? What ethical considerations must be considered for each option?

❖ A.21 No Other Way to Gather Resources

You are employed by a rural County Department of Education, which has no funds available to help Tom Bishop, your homebound young client or his family to purchase a cheap computer and modem which would enable him to communicate with many learning facilities and with other teenagers. Tom is desperate for activity but cannot travel out of his house because of his physical disabilities, which resulted from a diving accident. You have already asked your colleagues if they know how you might gather these resources, but no one had any helpful suggestions. Tom and his parents have now given you permission to advertise his needs on the electronic network. In your e-mail message you identified your client by gender, age, and a general description of his physical problems, but you did not use his name nor indicate the specific nature of his disabilities. Is this a responsible and ethical use of information? Can your client be recognized in a relatively small and sparsely populated area? What are the ethical issues involved when you use an electronic network to gain needed resources for your client?

❖ A.22 A Reporter After Death

A year ago when you were employed by St. Paul's Family Center, you served as social worker of Nicholas Karros, who had been experiencing problems on his job that affected him and his family. About eight months ago, Nicholas was killed in an altercation at a local bar. Roberta Frei, a reporter for the local newspaper, approached you yesterday to ask for information about Nicholas because she heard he had been abusive to his wife and children. Ms. Frei wanted this information as part of her preparation for an article on local domestic violence. What should you do? Does the *Code of Ethics* protect dead persons? What ethical issues are involved here?

❖ A.23 How to Be Fair?

Your community is in the midst of an annual enrollment period for qualified aging persons to obtain tax-supported inexpensive transportation. Not every applicant will be accepted because only limited funds are available. As you help older persons fill out applications, you know some persons are needy but not providing all the income information in order to qualify. Should you confront them? Should you inform the authorities? Should you advocate for more dollars to support services?

❖ A.24 Insider Trading?

Recently, Mr. Wellington, a friend and neighbor, approached you in the supermarket. You were pleased to see him. Some years ago, he helped your parents several times when they were late on mortgage payments by loaning them money free of charge. He tells you that his nine-year-old child has been "acting up" and driving his wife crazy. They went for an initial interview at the local mental health clinic where you serve as the executive director and learned that it would be approximately one month before their son could be seen on a regular basis. Could you do anything to move up the appointment? What should you do?

❖ A.25 A House in a New Development

You are employed in a social agency and have developed a very positive relationship with a client, Chip, a very successful real estate agent who is appreciative of the help you have been able to provide for him. You and your wife are interested in buying a house in a new development where construction has been unable to keep up with the demand for new homes. However, you have less of a down payment than is needed, and you also are not high on the waiting list to get into this desirable area.

When you asked Chip about these two problems, he responded by telling you that he would be glad to move you up on the waiting list and would arrange for a loan for the difference in the down payment. Is there a difference between being moved up on the list and accepting the loan which you will repay? What are your choices?

❖ A.26 Christopher, Stella, or Clients?

Garnet Hinckley, a social worker in private practice, is exceptionally conscientious and an excellent practitioner, but she works too many hours and too many days because her family needs money for expensive medical care for her son, Christopher. At the same time, she is driven to provide service to her clients who have difficulty paying fees. She feels she is not paying enough attention to other family members. Her daughter, Stella, has often complained that she misses her and would like her to be home when she arrives home from school in the afternoon. However, if she is home when Stella wants her to be, she will lose part of her clientele and further reduce her income. To whom does Ms. Hinckley owe priority loyalty?

❖ A.27 But I Don't Like Him

Joe Sirocco appeared for an initial interview with Marti Holmgren, social worker in the Mt. Everest Counseling Center. He explains what is bothering him. As he talks, Ms. Holmgren feels more and more negative toward him. Eventually, she tells him she can't accept him as a client, although she will help him find another therapist. Mr. Sirocco asks why he is not being accepted. Ms. Holmgren responds that her caseload is too full at this time. Was she justified in giving this answer? Should she have told Joe Sirocco the real reason for her decision?

❖ A.28 Must There Be No Relationship?

Arthur Baker has been a client of Anton Forsyte for about six months. Mr. Baker feels that Mr. Forsyte has been very helpful to him, and in fact, the relationship has been very friendly. Mr. Forsyte admires Mr. Baker and enjoys his sense of humor, courage, and problem-solving ability. They also share many common interests, including music and art. The time has come, however, for terminating the relationship because all Mr. Baker's problems at home and work seem to have worked out well. Mr. Forsyte would like to continue the friendship but wonders at what point he can do so in terms of the *Code*'s prohibitions against dual-role relationships. When does the client role end? When can they be friends? Is there a time limit?

❖ A.29 It All Depends on the *Code* and How Social Work Is Defined

Dr. Curtis Worley is a licensed social worker in private practice with extensive credentials, professional training, and a thriving private practice. At one point, he became interested in Eastern philosophies and mysticism, meditation, uses of herbs, and other alternative treatment methods. As he became more educated in these methods, he gradually began to introduce them into his practice. Some patients felt his work was appropriate and helpful; some even were "worshipful" of his personality and skill. Others believed these new approaches were not helpful and discontinued treatment. One of these latter persons complained to the State Licensing Board that Dr. Worley is unethical and no longer practicing social work. To date, there are no reports of personal harm being done to patients. You are a member of the board and are being asked whether you believe his behavior is ethical.

❖ A.30 To Report or Not to Report a Crime

Lindsey Robertson has been seeing Tom Bland at the Big Bend Psychiatric Outpatient Center. She was told early in her treatment of Mr. Bland that he had been tried and found not guilty of embezzlement. Later, he told her that he actually had committed the crime 10 years ago. Ms. Robertson decided not to report these facts to anyone because she thought no one could be retried for felony crimes when he had been found innocent at trial but was later found to have committed the crime. Is her assumption correct? Does it make a difference that the worker-client relationship is occurring in a mental health setting?

❖ A.31 The Whole Truth . . . ?

A social worker is trying to find an adoptive family for a child. A potential adoptive family has been found. The birth mother was a heroin addict, was malnourished, and the child was born in distress but has now recovered. If you tell the entire story, you believe the family will not adopt the child. You believe that if you don't tell the whole story, they will adopt the child. How much should you tell? Is not telling "all the truth" ethical?

❖ A.32 You're Needed in Bayville

A social worker was attacked and killed last week at a community outreach program serving mentally ill persons in Bayville. You found this especially unnerving. Even before the death, you worried because you heard that from time to time guns were fired in the neighborhood, although no one had been injured. The agency is a subunit of a citywide system of services for this group of people. Your supervisor talks with you and explains that your skills and experience are needed at the outreach site because the death left relatively inexperienced social workers employed there. You don't want to go. What should you do?

❖ A.33 The Foundation Has Its Own Priorities

Southside Advocacy Center has a long history of service to the people of the southern part of the city. In fact, the agency is beloved by many persons. The center receives large grants from the Anon Foundation that enable the agency to exist. The foundation, because of its own agenda, asks the agency to move its operation to the southeast, another poor community. It is impossible for the center to serve both neighborhoods, and there has been a clear indication the foundation has developed a special concern—for whatever reason—about the southeast section. They regret having to make the demand but insist they must do so. Both neighborhoods need and deserve help. The southeast section, perhaps, may need help more because the support extended there over the years has been limited. To whom does the agency owe loyalty? Its continued existence? To the south community? To the southeast community?

❖ A.34 Regina Has Cancer and Her Parents Can't Agree

Regina Benson is a three year old with terminal cancer who needs palliative care until her expected death. The hospital wants the child to go home to die among her family members. When Susan Blank, social worker, discusses the situation with Patty and Carl Benson, Regina's parents, Mrs. Benson wants Regina to come home for her last months, but Mr. Benson is adamantly opposed. He feels the situation will be destructive to their other children. They simply cannot agree. When Susan Blank checks with the hospital administrator, he says the insurance company will pay, and the hospital would keep the child until her death. What are Ms. Blank's ethical options in view of the father's adamant position? What is best for the child? For the family? For the insurance company?

Glossary

autonomy self-determination, self-rule, being able to make free choices.

autonomous ethics ethical systems in which humans determine the moral rules.

client bill of rights a statement distributed to all clients/patients informing them that the information they are entitled to know about their situation, treatment expectations, and participation in decision making; that they will be informed about available options; and that they have a right to speak to an ombudsman or other person if dissatisfied with treatment.

code of ethics a collection of aspirations, regulations, and guidelines that represent the values of a group or profession to which it applies; a compilation of ethical standards.

competence the ability to give informed consent to some or all decisions, clients/patients are located along a range of capabilities, extending from completely competent to those who are somewhat competent to those who are not at all competent.

competing loyalties two or more loyalties that cannot be honored at the same time.

competing values two or more values that cannot be honored at the same time.

confidentiality a rule of duty requiring one entrusted with private or secret matters to refrain from divulging them; a contract not to reveal information about an individual except with his or her consent.

conflicting obligations two or more obligations that cannot be fulfilled at the same time.

deontology a philosophy of ethics holding that ethical rules for the right course of action are self-evident, can be formulated, and should hold under all circumstances.

direct liability supervisors may be charged with ethical breaches or negligence when harm is caused by the supervisor's acts of omission or commission.

dual-role relationship situation in which professionals fill more than one role at a time and should avoid conflicts of interest that interfere with the exercise of professional discretion and impartial judgment, especially to protect clients' interests and not to take unfair advantage of them.

duty to warn an obligation to use reasonable care to protect intended victims, also referred to as the *Tarasoff* principle.

effectiveness criterion the degree to which a desired outcome is achieved.

efficiency criterion relative cost of achieving a stated objective.

ethical absolutism any ethical theory that claims there are ethical rules that hold regardless of society, culture, or religion; correct standards applicable to everyone everywhere.

ethical decision making the process of analyzing and assessing the ethical dimensions of practice in order to develop ethically appropriate professional behavior.

ethical dilemmas choice by the social worker between two or more relevant but contradictory ethical directives; when every alternative results in an undesirable outcome for one or more persons.

ethical problem identifying the right thing to do in a given practice situation.

ethical priorities screen (EPS) a guide for rank-ordering ethical principles and priorities.

ethical relativism the belief that there is no absolute or universal moral standard and what is right or wrong is relative to an individual, group, or culture.

ethical rules screen (ERS) used as a step in ethical decision making by consulting the *Code of Ethics* for guidance.

ethics branch of philosophy that deals with the rightness or wrongness of human actions.

general ethics the obligations that are owed by one person to another.

group values values held by subgroups within a society.

heteronomous ethics ethical systems that derive moral rules from nonhuman sources.

informed consent the knowledgeable and voluntary agreement by a client/patient to undergo an intervention that is in accord with the patients's values and preferences.

least harm principle when harm will come to someone in the situation, it is the choice of the option that results in the least harm, the least permanent harm, or the most easily reversible harm.

malpractice professional negligence or misconduct; failure to exercise a degree of care that a similar professional of ordinary prudence would demonstrate under the same circumstances.

morality a concern with personally held ethical beliefs, theories of obligation, and the social elements that reinforce ethical decisions.

paternalism the act of overriding the autonomous decisions of a person or making decisions for the person with the intention of benefiting that person.

personal (individual) values the values held by one person but not necessarily by others.

prima facie **correct** apparently correct upon first viewing.

privacy a zone of individual autonomy in which people ought to be free to behave as they wish; the constitutional right protecting individuals from unwarranted governmental interference in intimate personal relations or activities.

privileged communication a legal concept protecting against forced disclosure in legal proceedings that would break a promise of privacy—based on ethical principles of confidentiality and privacy.

professional code of ethics a compilation of values, ethical principles, and ethical standards of a particular profession.

professional ethics codification of the special obligations that arise out of a person's voluntary choice to become a professional, such as a social worker.

professional social work ethics those ethical standards promulgated by the social work profession through its *Code of Ethics* and other publications.

professional values those values proclaimed by a professional group.

religious ethics ethics based upon a religion and its beliefs.

self-determination a person's right to make his or her own decisions.

situational ethics the position that all ethical decisions must be made in the light of individual circumstances and not according to moral rules or universal laws.

societal values values recognized by major portions of the entire social system or, at least, by the leading members or spokespersons *of* that system.

teleology philosophy of ethics that justifies ethical decisions on the basis of the context in which they are made or on the basis of the consequences they create.

unethical behavior violations of the profession's principles established by the profession's *Code of Ethics*.

utilitarianism a philosophy of ethics that defines right action as that which results in the greatest happiness for the greatest number of people.

value dilemmas two or more values that cannot be reconciled and simultaneously enacted.

values preferences that serve as guides or criteria for selecting good or desirable behaviors.

vicarious liability a supervisor is responsible for a supervisee's conduct during the course of employment, or field instruction, including ethical lapses.

voluntariness acting on the basis of meaningful and free consent obtained without coercion.

Selected Internet Sources of Information About Values and Ethics

http://www.casw-acts.ca   See Library, Publications, *Code of Ethics*.

http://www.feministtherapyinstitute.org   Feminist Code of Ethics, 1999.

http://www.unc.edu/professional/NABSW.html   National Association of Black Social Workers Code of Ethics.

http://www.naswdc.org/code.html   NASW Code of Ethics, 1999.

http://www.naswnyc.org/ethics.html   Ethics and professional liability. Material on a variety of topics related to the *Code*.

http://www.globalethics.org   Institute for Global Ethics.

http://www.ethics.ubc.ca   Centre for Applied Ethics, University of British Columbia.

http://www.nyu.edu/socialwork/wwwrsw/   World Wide Web Resources for Social Workers codes of ethics, ethics on the Web, ethics updates, journals and newsletters, professional associations, social work values and ethics.

http://www.cswf.org   *Code of Ethics* (1997), Clinical Social Work Federation.

http://www.ifsw.org/Publications/4.4.pub.html   International Federation of Social Workers *Code of Ethics*, Ethical Committee.

http://www.nbcc.org/depts/ethicsmain.htm   National Board for Certified Counselors Standards for the Ethical Practice of Web Counseling.

Bibliography

This bibliography lists the books and articles cited in this book, as well as additional literature on ethical problems in professional practice that may be of interest to the reader.

Abramson, M. (1984). Collective responsibility in interdisciplinary collaboration: An ethical perspective for social workers. *Social Work in Health Care, 10* (1), 35–43.

Abramson, M. (1985). The autonomy-paternalism dilemma in social work practice. *Social Casework, 66,* 387–393.

Abramson, M. (1989). Autonomy vs. paternalistic beneficence: Practice strategies. *Social Casework, 70,* 101–105.

Abramson, M. (1990). Keeping secrets: Social workers and AIDS. *Social Work, 35,* 169–173

Abramson, M. (1996). Toward a more holistic understanding of ethics in social work. *Social Work in Health Care, 23* (2), 1–14.

Adler, S.S. (1989). Truth telling to the terminal ill. *Social Work, 34,* 158–160.

Advocate Web. (2002). Helping overcome professional exploitation. Sexual exploitation litigation issues. http://www.advocateweb.org Search helping overcome professional exploitation. Brochure 2000f.cdr

Agbayani-Siewert, P. (1994). Filipino American culture and family: Guidelines for practitioners. *Families in Society, 75,* 429–438.

Aguilera, E. (2003, February 10). Cuba's low HIV rate belies the stigma, ignorance many face. *Denver Post.* http://www.denverpost.com/stories/O, March 11, 2003.

Albert, R. (1986). *Law and social work practice.* New York: Springer Publishing.

Aldarondo, E., & Straus, M.A. (1994). Screening for physical violence in couple therapy: Methodological, practical, and ethical considerations. *Family Process, 33,* 425–439.

Algana, F.J., et al. (1979). Evaluating reaction to interpersonal touch in a counseling interview. *Journal of Counseling Psychology, 26,* 465–472.

Almason, A. L. (1997). Personal liability implications of the duty to warn are hard pills to swallow: From *Tarasoff* to *Hutchinson v. Patel* and beyond. *Journal of Contemporary Health, Law and Policy, 13,* 471–496.

Altman, L. K. (1999, August 31). Focusing on prevention in fight against AIDS. *New York Times,* p. F5.

Altman, L. K. (2002, July 3). U.N. forecasts big increase in AIDS death toll. *New York Times,* pp. A1, A6.

American College of Physicians ACP Observer. (1997). Patients often forget physician's diagnosis. *News Briefs,* www.acponline.org/journals/news/feb97/brief297.htm.

American Medical Association (1997). *Code of ethics.* http://www.ama-assn.org.

American Psychiatric Association. (2000). *Diagnostic and statistical manual of mental disorders* (4th ed.). Washington, DC: Author.

Anderson, S., & Mandell, D. (1989). The use of self-disclosure by professional social workers. *Social Casework, 70,* 259–267.

Andrews, A. B., & Patterson, E. G. (1995). Searching for solutions to alcohol and other drug abuse during pregnancy: Ethics, values, and constitutional principles. *Social Work, 40,* 55–64.

Antle, B. J., & Regehr, C. (2003). Beyond individual rights and freedoms: Metaethics in social work research. *Social Work, 40,* 135–144.

Arendt, H. (1963). *Eichmann in Jerusalem: A report on the banality of evil.* New York: Viking Press.

Ashton, V. (1999). Worker judgements of seriousness about and reporting of suspected child maltreatment. *Child Abuse and Neglect, 23* (6), 539–548.

Ashton, V. (2001). The relationship between attitudes toward corporal punishment and the perception and reporting of child abuse. *Child Abuse and Neglect, 25* (3), 389–400.

Austin, J. B., & Dankwort, J. (1999). Standards for batterer programs. *Journal of Interpersonal Violence, 14,* 152–168.

Baier, K. (1958). *The moral point of view: A rational basis of ethics.* New York: Random House.

Ballie, R. (2001). Medicare will now cover some telehealth psychotherapy services. *Monitor on Psychology, 32* (10). http://www.apa.org/monitor/nov01/telehealth.html.

Barker, R. L. (1988a). "Client dumping": Some ethical considerations. *Journal of Independent Social Work, 2,* 1–5.

Barker, R. L. (1988b). Just whose code of ethics should the independent practitioner follow? *Journal of Independent Social Work, 2* (4), 1–5.

Barker, R. L. (1992). *Social work in private practice* (2nd ed.). Washington, DC: NASW Press.

Barksdale, C. (1989). Child abuse reporting: A clinical dilemma. *Smith College Studies in Social Work, 59,* 170–182.

Barnett-Queens, T. (1999). Sexual relationships with educators: A national survey of masters-level practitioners. *The Clinical Supervisor, 18* (1), 151–172.

Basham, K. K., Donner, S., Killough, R. M., & Rozas, L. W. (1997). Becoming an anti-racist institution. *Smith College Studies in Social Work, 67,* 564–585.

Bates, C. M., & Brodsky, A. M. (1989). *Sex in the therapy hour: A case of professional incest.* New York: Guilford.

Bauman, Z. (1996). Morality in the age of contingency (pp. 49–58). In P. Heclas, S. Lash, & P. Morris (Eds.), *Detraditionalization: Critical reflections on authority and identity.* Cambridge, MA: Blackwell Publishers.

Bayer, R. (1998). AIDS and the ethics of prevention, research, and care. In G. Wormser (Ed.), *AIDS and other manifestations of HIV infection* (3rd ed., pp. 799–807). Philadelphia: Lippincott-Raven Publishers.

Bayles, M. D. (1981). *Professional ethics.* Belmont, CA: Wadsworth Publishing.

Beck, J. C. (1998). Legal and ethical duties of the clinician treating a patient who is liable to be impulsively violent. *Behavioral Sciences and the Law, 16,* 375–389.

Beder, J. (1998). The home visit, revisited. *Families in Society, 79,* 514–522.

Beit-Hallahmi, B. (1975). Encountering orthodox religions in psychotherapy. *Psychotherapy, 12,* 357–359.

Bergeron, L. R., & Gray. B. (2003). Ethical dilemmas of reporting suspected elder abuse. *Social Work, 48,* 96–105.

Berkman, C. S., Turner, S. G., Cooper, M., et al. (2000). Sexual contact with clients: Assessment of social workers' attitudes and educational preparation. *Social Work, 45* (3), 223–235.

Berman-Rossi, T., & Rossi, P. (1990). Confidentiality and informed consent in school social work. *Social Work in Education, 12,* 195–207.

Berliner, A. K. (1989). Misconduct in social work practice. *Social Work, 34,* 69–72.

Bern, D. J. (1970). *Beliefs, attitudes and human affairs.* Pacific Grove, CA: Brooks/Cole Publishing.

Bernsen, A., Tabachnik, B. G., & Pope, K. S. (1994). National survey of social workers' sexual attraction to their clients: Results, implications, and comparison to psychologists. *Ethics & Behavior, 4* (4), 369–388.

Bernstein, S. (1960). Self-determination: "King or citizen in the realm of values." *Social Work, 5,* 3–8.

Bernstein, S. B. (1993). What happened to self-determination? *Social Work with Groups, 16* (1/2), 3–14.

Bernstein, S. R. (1990). Contracted services: Issues for the nonprofit agency manager. In *Towards the 21st century: Challenges for the voluntary sector.* Proceedings of the 1990 Conference of the Association of Voluntary Action Scholars. London, England.

Besharov, D. J., & Besharov, S. H. (1987). Teaching about liability. *Social Work, 32,* 517–522.

Besharov, D. J., & Laumann, L. A. (1996). Child abuse reporting. *Society, 33* (4), 40–46.

Beyerstein, D. (1993). The functions and limitations of professional Codes of Ethics. In *Applied ethics.* (pp. 416–425). Eds. Winkler, E. R. & Coombs, J. R. Cambridge, MA: Blackwell.

Black, D. (1972). The boundaries of legal sociology. *Yale Law Journal, 81,* 1086–1101.

Bloom, M. (1975). The paradox of helping: Introduction to the philosophy of scientific helping. New York: John Wiley & Sons.

Bogodanoff, M., & Elbaum, P. L. (1978). Touching: A legacy from the encounter movement to social work practice. *Social Work in Health Care, 4,* 209–219.

Bonosky, N. (1995). Boundary violations in social work supervision: Clinical, educational, and legal implications. *The Clinical Supervisor, 13* (2), 79–95.

Borenzweig, H. (1983). Touching in clinical social work. *Social Casework, 64,* 238–242.

Borys, D. S., & Pope, K. S. (1989). Dual relationships between therapist and client: A national study of psychologists, psychiatrists, and social workers. *Professional Psychology: Research and Practice, 20,* 283–293.

Bowers v. Hardwick, 106 S. Ct. 2841 (1986).

Brabeck, M. M., & Ting, K. (2000). Feminist ethics: Lenses for examining ethical psychological practice. In M. M. Grabeck (Ed.), *Practicing feminist ethics in psychology.* Washington, DC: American Psychological Association.

Brager, G. A. (1968). Advocacy and political behavior. *Social Work, 13* (2), 5–15.

Brandeis, L. D., & Warren, S. D. (1890). The right to privacy. *Harvard Law Review.* IV (5), December 15.

Brill, C. K. (2001). Looking at the social work profession through the eye of the NASW Code of Ethics. *Research on Social Work Practice, 11* (2), 223–234.

Broadie, S. (1991). *Ethics with Aristotle.* New York: Oxford University Press.

Brown, H. J. (1970). Social work values in a developing country. *Social Work, 15* (1), 107–112.

Bullis, R. K., & Harrigan, M. P. (1992). Religious denominational policies on sexuality. *Families in Society: The Journal of Contemporary Human Services, 73,* 304–312.

Butz, R. A. (1985). Reporting child abuse and confidentiality in counseling. *Social Casework, 66,* 83–90.

Cain, L. P. (1979). Social worker's role in teen-age abortion. *Social Work, 24*, 52–56.

Callahan, D. (1987, October/November). Terminating treatment: Age as a standard. *Hastings Center Reporter*, 21–25.

Callahan, J. (1988). *Ethical issues in professional life.* New York: Oxford University Press.

Callahan, J. (1994). The ethics of assisted suicide. *Health and Social Work, 19*, 237–244.

Canda, E. R. (1988). Spirituality, religious diversity, and social work practice. *Social Casework, 69*, 238–247.

Caputo, R. K. (1991). Managing information systems: An ethical framework and information needs matrix. *Administration in Social Work, 15* (4), 53–64.

Carlson, S. (2002, November 15). Virtual counseling. *The Chronicle of Higher Education,* pp. A35–36.

Carlton, W. (1978). *In our professional opinion: The primacy of clinical judgment over moral choice.* Notre Dame, IN: University of Notre Dame Press.

Carpenter, M. C., & Platt, S. (1997). Professional identity for clinical social workers: Impact of changes in health care delivery systems. *Clinical Social Work Journal, 25*, 337–351.

Carter-Pokras, O., & Zambrana, R. E. (2001). Latin Health Status. In M. Aguirre-Molina, C. W. Molina, R. E. Zambrana (Eds.), *Health Issues in the Latino Community,* (pp. 23–54). San Francisco: Jossey-Bass.

Cervera, N. J. (1993). Decision making for pregnant adolescents: Applying reasoned action theory to research and treatment. *Families in Society: The Journal of Contemporary Human Services, 74*, 355–365.

Chow, J. (1999). Multiservice centers in Chinese American immigrant communities: Practice principles and challenges. *Social Work, 44*, 70–80.

Christensen, K. E. (1986). Ethics of information technology. G. R. Geiss & N. Viswanathan (Eds.), *The human edge* (pp. 72–91). Binghamton, NY: Haworth Press.

Citizen Link (2003). Dutch (Holland/Netherlands) euthanasia: The Dutch disaster. www.family.org/cforum/research/papers/a0001021.html, January 8, 2003.

Clemens, E. L. (1995). Multiple perceptions of discharge planning in one urban hospital. *Health and Social Work, 20*, 254–261.

Cohen, R. (1980). The (revised) NASW Code of Ethics. *NASW News, 26* (April), 19.

Coleman, E., & Schaefer, S. (1986). Boundaries of sex and intimacy between client and counselor. *Journal of Counseling and Development, 64*, 341–344.

Congress, E. P. (1992). Ethical decision making of social work supervisors. *Clinical Supervisor, 10*, 157–169.

Congress, E. P., & Lynn, M. (1997). Group work practice in the community: Navigating the slippery slope of ethical dilemmas. *Social Work with Groups, 20* (3), 61–74.

Conrad, A. P. (1988). Ethical considerations in the psychosocial process. *Social Casework, 69*, 603–610.

Conte, C. K., Fisher, D. S., & Roffman, R. A. (1996). Training and supporting the telephone intake worker for an AIDS prevention counseling study. *Social Work, 41*, 314–319.

Conte, H. R., Plutchik, R., Picard, S., & Karasu, T. B. (1989). Ethics in the practice of psychotherapy. *American Journal of Psychotherapy, 43*, 32–42.

Corey, G., Corey, M. S., & Callanan, P. (1998). *Issues and Ethics in the Helping Professions* (5th ed.). Boston: Brooks/Cole Publishing Co.

Coughlin, B. J. (1966). Interrelationship of governmental and voluntary welfare services. In *The Social Welfare Forum 1966.* New York: Columbia University Press.

Council on Social Work Education (2001). *Educational Policy and Accreditation Standards.* Alexandria, VA: Author.

Courtney, M. E., Barth, R. P., Berrick, J. D., Brooks, E., Needell, B., & Park, L. (1996). Race and child welfare services: Past research and future directions. *Child Welfare, LXXV*, 99–137.

Csikai, E. L. (1999a). Euthanasia and assisted suicide: Issues for social work practice. *Journal of Gerontological Social Work, 31* (3/4), 49–63.

Csikai, E. L. (1999b). The role of values and experience in determining social workers' attitudes toward euthanasia and assisted suicide. *Social Work in Health Care, 30* (1), 75–95.

Csikai, E. L., & Sales, E. (1998). The emerging social work role on hospital ethics committees: A comparison of social worker and chair perspectives. *Social Work, 43* (3), 233–242.

Curtis, P. A., & Lutkus, A. M. (1985). Client confidentiality in police social work settings. *Social Work, 30,* 355–360.

Cwikel, J. G., & Cnaan, R. A. (1991). Ethical dilemmas in applying secondwave information technology to social work practice. *Social Work, 36* (2), 114–120.

Cyrns, A. G. (1977). Social work education and student ideology: A multivariate study of professional socialization. *Journal of Education for Social Work, 13* (1), 44–51.

Daro, D. (1988). *Confronting child abuse: Research/or effective program design.* New York: Free Press.

Davidson, J. R., & Davidson, T. (1996). Confidentiality and managed care: Ethical and legal concerns. *Health and Social Work, 21,* 208–215.

Davis, K. (1997). Managed care, mental illness and African Americans: A prospective analysis of managed care policy in the United States. *Smith College Studies in Social Work, 67,* 623–641.

Dean, H. (1998). The primacy of the ethical aim in clinical social work: Its relationship to social justice and mental health. *Smith College Studies in Social Work, 69,* 9–24.

Dean, R. G., & Rhodes, M. L. (1992). Ethical-clinical tensions in clinical practice. *Social Work, 37,* 128–132.

Delaronde, S., King, G., Bendel, R., & Reece, R. (2000). Opinions among mandated reporters toward child maltreatment reporting policies. *Child Abuse and Neglect, 24* (7), 901–910.

Dent, S. (2000). Illiteracy: 'Hidden Disability' creates health care confusion. *FP Report, 6* (1), http://www.aafp.org/fpr/20000100/illiteracy.html, October 16, 2002.

Department of Health & Human Services, Centers for Disease Control and Prevention (2001). *HIV Prevalence Trends in Selected Populations in the United States: Results from National Serosurveillance, 1993–1997.*

Department of Health and Human Services (2002). Modifications to the Standards for Privacy of Individually identifiable Health Information—Final Rule. http://www.hhs.gov/news/press/2002pres/20020809.html, November 25, 2002.

DeSmidt, G., & Gorey, K. M. (1997). Unpublished social work research: Systematic replication of a recent meta-analysis of published intervention effectiveness research. *Social Work Research, 21,* 58–62.

Deutscher, I., Pestello, F. P., & Pestello, H. F. G. (1993). *Sentiments and Acts.* New York: Aldine de Gruyter.

DeYoung, M. (1988). The good touch/bad touch dilemma. *Child Welfare, 67,* 60–68.

Dickson, D. T. (1997). Law, ethics and social work with the elderly: Self-determination. *Journal of Law and Social Work, 7* (2), 105–125.

Diggs, B. J. (1970). Rules and utilitarianism. In K. Pahel & M. Schiller (Eds.), *Readings in contemporary ethical theory* (pp. 260–82). Engle-wood Cliffs, NJ: Prentice-Hall.

Dobrin, A. (1989). Ethical judgments of male and female social workers. *Social Work, 34,* 451–455.

Dolgoff, R. (2002). An exploration in social policy and ethics: Ethical judgment before or after the fact? *Social Work Forum, Wurzweiler School of Social Work, 35* (Winter/Spring, 2001–2002), 67–86.

Dolgoff, R., & Skolnik, L. (1992). Ethical decision making: The NASW Code of ethics and group work practice: Beginning explorations. *Social Work with Groups, 15* (4), 99–112.

Dolgoff, R., & Skolnik, L. (1996). Ethical decision making in social work with groups: An empirical study. *Social Work with Groups, 19* (2), 49–65.

Dryden, W., & Ellis, A. (1988). Rational-emotive therapy. In *Handbook of Cognitive-Behavioral Therapies.* New York: The Guilford Press, 214–272.

Dumont, M. P. (1996). Privatization and mental health in Massachusetts. *Smith College Studies in Social Work, 66,* 293–303.

Dworkin, G. (1985). Behavioral control and design. *Social Research, 52,* 543–554.

Edward, J. (1999). Is managed mental health treatment psychotherapy? *Clinical Social Work Journal, 27,* 87–102.

Egan, M. (1999). The social worker in the emerging field of home care: Professional activities and ethical concerns. *Health & Social Work, 24* (1), 43–55.

Egley, L. C. (1992). Defining the *Tarasoff* Duty. *Journal of Psychiatry and Law, 19,* 93–133.

Ellis, A. (1973). *Humanistic psychotherapy: The rational-emotive approach.* New York: McGraw-Hill.

Ewalt, P. L., & Mokuau, N. (1995). Self-determination from a Pacific perspective. *Social Work, 40,* 168–175.

Ewing, C. P. (2002). *Tarasoff* update: psychotherapy threats alone provide no basis for criminal prosecution. *Monitor on Psychology, 33* (2), 1–3. http://www.apa.org/monitor/feb02/jn.html, July 17, 2002.

Federal Psychotherapist-Patient Privilege (*Jaffee v. Redmond,* 518 U.S. 1): History, Documents, and Opinions, http://psa-uny.org/jr/, September 5, 2002.

Feldman, K. A., & Newcomb, T. M. (1994). *The impact of college on students.* New Brunswick, NJ: Transaction Publishers.

Fellin, P. (2000). Revisiting multiculturalism in social work. *Journal of Social Work Education, 36* (2), 261–278.

Felthous, A. R., & Kachigian, C. (2001). The Fin de Millenaire Duty to Warn or Protect. *Journal of Forensic Science, 46* (5), 1103–1112.

Festinger, L. (1957). *A Theory of cognitive dissonance.* New York: Harper & Row.

Finkelhor, D. (1990). Is child abuse over-reported? *Public Welfare, 48,* 22–29.

Finkelhor, D. (1998). Improving research, policy, and practice to understand child sexual abuse. *Journal of the American Medical Association, 280,* 1864–1865.

Finn, J. (1990). Security, privacy, and confidentiality in agency microcomputer use. *Families in Society: The Journal of Contemporary Human Services* (May), 283–290.

Fisher, D. (1987). Problems for social work in a strike situation: Professional, ethical, and value considerations. *Social Work, 32,* 252–254.

Fishkin, J. S. (1982). *The limits of obligation.* New Haven, CT: Yale University Press.

Flaherty, J. (2002, August 14). Girls link their use of family planning clinics to keeping parents in the dark. *New York Times,* A14.

Fleck-Henderson, A. (1991). Moral reasoning in social work practice. *Social Service Review* (June), 185–202.

Fletcher, J. F. (1966). *Situation ethics, the new morality.* Philadelphia: Westminster Press.

Flexner, A. (1915). Is social work a profession? *Proceedings of National Conference of Charities and Corrections* (pp. 576–590). Chicago: Hindman.

Fodor, J. L. (1999, February). Computer ethics in higher education. *Syllabus,* 12–15.

Frank, J. (1991). *Persuasion and healing* (Rev. ed.). New York: Schocken Books.

Frankena, W. K. (1973). *Ethics* (2nd ed.). Englewood Cliffs, NJ: Prentice-Hall.

Frankena, W. K. (1980). *Thinking about morality.* Ann Arbor: University of Michigan Press.

Franki, V. (1968). *The doctor and the soul.* New York: Alfred A. Knopf.

Frankl, V. (1968). *The doctor and the soul.* New York: Alfred A. Knopf.

Frans, D. J., & Moran, J. R. (1993). Social work education's impact on students' humanistic values and personal empowerment. *Arete, 18* (1), 1–11.

Freedberg, S. (1989). Self-determination: Historical perspectives and effects on current practice. *Social Work, 34,* 33–38.

Freedman, -T. G. (1998). Genetic susceptibility testing: Ethical and social quanderies. *Health & Social Work, 23,* 214–222.

Freeman, J. M., & McDonnell, K. (2001). *Tough decisions: Cases in medical ethics* (2nd ed.). New York: Oxford University Press.

Freud, S. (1999). The social construction of normality. *Families in Society, 80* (4), 333–339.

Fukuyama, M. A. (2001). Counseling in colleges and universities. In D. C. Locke, E. L. Herr, & J. E. Myers (Eds.), *The handbook of counseling* (pp. 319–341). Thousand Oaks, CA: Sage Publications.

Galambos, C. M. (1997). Resolving ethical conflicts in providing case management services to the elderly. *Journal of Gerontological Social Work, 27* (4), 57–67.

Galambos, C. M. (1999). Resolving ethical conflicts in a managed health care environment. *Health & Social Work, 24* (3), 191–197.

Galinsky, M. J., Schopler, J. H., & Abell, M. D. (1997). Connecting group members through telephone and computer groups. *Health & Social Work, 22,* 181–188.

Gambrill, E., & Pruger, R. (Eds.) (1997). *Controversial issues in social work ethics, values, and obligations.* Boston: Allyn and Bacon.

Gambrill, E. D. (2003). From the editor: "Evidence-based practice" Sea change or the emperor's new clothes? *Journal of Social Work Education, 39,* 3–23.

Garb, H. N. (1994). Cognitive heuristics and biases in personality assessment. In L. Heath (Ed.), *Applications of heuristics and biases to social issues* (pp. 73–90). New York: Plenum Press.

Gerhart, U. C., & Brooks, A. D. (1985). Social workers and malpractice: Law, attitudes, and knowledge. *Social Casework, 66,* 411–416.

Gewirth, A. (1978). *Reason and morality.* Chicago: University of Chicago Press.

Gibelman, M., & Schervish, P. H. (1997). *Who we are: A second look.* Washington, DC: NASW.

Gillis, J. S. (1974). Social influence therapy: The therapist as manipulator. *Psychology Today, 8* (7), 90–95.

Girardi, J. A., Keese, R. M., Traver, L. B., & Cooksey, D. R. (1988). Psychotherapist responsibility for notifying individuals at risk for exposure to HIV (AIDS). *Journal of Sex Research, 25,* 1–27.

Givelber, D., Bowers, W., & Blitch, C. (1984). *Tarasoff:* Myth and reliability. *Wisconsin Law Review, 2,* 443–497.

Glaser, R. D., & Thorpe, J. S. (1986). Unethical Intimacy: A survey of sexual contact and advances between psychology educators and female graduate students. *American Psychologist, 41* (1), 43–51.

Glasser, P. H. (1984). Being honest with ourselves: What happens when our values conflict with our clients? *Practice Digest, 6* (4), 6–10.

Glassman, Carol. (1992). Feminist dilemmas in practice. *Affilia, 7,* 160–166.

Glossary of Culture-Bound Syndromes. http://weber.ucsd.edu/~thall/cbs_glos.html, March 17, 2003.

Gochros, H. L. (1988). Risks of abstinence: Sexual decision making in the AIDS era. *Social Work, 33,* 254–256.

Goffman, E. (1959). *The presentation of self in everyday life.* Garden City, NY: Doubleday.

Goldenberg, I., & Goldenberg, H. (2000). *Family therapy: An overview* (5th ed.). Belmont, CA: Brooks/Cole.

Goldstein, E. G. (1997). To tell or not to tell: The disclosure of events in the therapist's life to the patient. *Clinical Social Work Journal, 25,* 41–58.

Goldstein, H. (1973). *Social work: A unitary approach.* Columbia: University of South Carolina Press.

Goldstein, H. (1987). The neglected moral link in social work practice. *Social Work, 32,* 181–186.

Goldstein, H. (1998). Education for ethical dilemmas in social work practice. *Families in Society: The Journal of Contemporary Human Services, 79,* 241–253.

Golton, M. (1971). Private practice in social work. In R. Morris (Ed.), *The encyclopedia of social work.* New York: National Association of Social Workers.

Goodban, N. (1985). The psychological impact of being on welfare. *Social Service Review, 59,* 403–422.

Goode, E. (2001, August 27). Disparities seen in mental care for minorities. *New York Times,* pp. 1, 12.

Gorey, K. M., Thyer, B. A., & Pawluck, D. E. (1998). Differential effectiveness of prevalent social work practice models: A meta-analysis. *Social Work, 43,* 269–278.

Gottleib, M. C., & Cooper, C. C. (1993). Some ethical issues for systems-oriented therapists in hospital settings. *Family Relations, 42* (2), 140–144.

Greenhouse, L. (1998, December 2). High court curbs claim on privacy in a house. *New York Times,* All.

Greenhouse, L. (1999a, April 11). Check out your driver. *New York Times, Week in Review,* p. 2.

Greenhouse, L. (1999b, April 6). Supreme court roundup; police searching car may include passenger's things. *New York Times,* A19.

Greenwood, E. (1957). Attributes of a profession. *Social Work, 2* (3), 45–55.

Grisso, T., & Appelbaum, P. S. (1998). *Assessing competence to consent to treatment: A guide for physicians and other health professionals.* New York: Oxford University Press.

Group for the Advancement of Psychiatry (1994). *Forced into treatment: The role of coercion in clinical practice.* Report No. 137. Washington, DC: American Psychiatric Press.

Grundstein-Amado, R. (1999). Bilateral transformational leadership: An approach for fostering ethical conduct in public service organizations, *Administration & Society, 31* (2), 247–260.

Guttmann, D. (1996). *Logotherapy for the helping professional: Meaningful social work.* New York: Springer Publishing Co.

Haley, J. (1976). *Problem-solving therapy.* New York: Harper & Row.

Halmos, P. (1965). *Faith of the counselor.* London: Constable.

Handler, J. E., & Hollingsworth, E. J. (1971). *The deserving poor.* Chicago: Markham.

Haney, C., Banks, C., & Zimbardo, P. G. (1973). Interpersonal dynamics in a simulated prison. *International Journal of Criminology and Penology, 1,* 69–97.

Harris, G. C. (1999). The dangerous patient exception to the psychotherapist-patient privilege: The *Tarasoff* duty and the *Jaffee* footnote, *Washington Law Review, 74,* 33–68.

Hartman, A. (1995). Family Therapy. In R. L. Edward (Ed.), *Encyclopedia of Social Work* (19th ed., Vol. 2). Washington, D.C.: National Association of Social Workers, 983–991.

Hasenfeld, Y., & Weaver, D. (1996). Enforcement, compliance, and disputes in welfare-to-work programs. *Social Service Review, 70* (2), 235–256.

Hayes, D. D., & Varley, B. K. (1965). The impact of social work education on students' values. *Social Work, 10* (4), 40–46.

Healy, T. C. (1998). The complexity of everyday *ethics* in home health care: An analysis of social workers' decisions regarding frail elders' autonomy. *Social Work in Health Care, 27* (4), 19–37.

Hetzel, L., & Smith, A. (2001). The 65 years and over population: 2000. *Census 2000 Brief.* Washington, D.C. U.S. Census Bureau. www.census.gov/prod/2001pubs/C2kbr01-10.pdf, October 9, 2003.

Hiratsuka, J. (1994). When it's a helper who needs help. *NASW News* (June), 3.

Hodge, D. R. (2002). Does social work oppress Evangelical Christians? A "new class" analysis of society and social work. *Social Work, 47* (4), 401–414.

Hogue, C. J. R., & Hargraves, M. A. (2000). The commonwealth fund minority health survey of 1994: An overview. In C. J. R. Hogue, M. A. Hargraves, & K. S. Collins (Eds.), *Minority Health in America.* Baltimore: Johns Hopkins University Press, 1–18.

Hokenstad, M. C. (1987). Preparation for practice: The ethical dimension. *Social Work Education Reporter, 25,* 1–4.

Holmes, S. A. (1998, December 6). Right to abortion quietly advances in state courts. *New York Times,* Section 1, p. 1.

Holroyd, J., & Brodsky, A. (1977). Psychologists' attitudes and practices regarding erotic and nonerotic physical contact with patients. *American Psychologist, 32,* 843–849.

Horner, W. C., & Whitbeck, L. B. (1991). Personal versus professional values in social work: A methodological note. *Journal of Social Service Research, 14* (1/2), 21–43.

Houston-Vega, M. K., Nuehring, E. M., & Daguio, E. R. (1997). *Prudent practice.* Washington, DC: NASW Press.

Howard, M. O., & Jenson, J. M. (1999). Clinical practice guidelines: Should social work develop them? *Research on Social Work Practice, 9,* 283–301.

Howard, M. O., McMillen, C. J., & Pollio, D. E. (2003). Teaching evidence-based practice: Toward a new paradigm for social work education. *Research on Social Work Practice, 13,* 234–259.

Howe, E. (1980). Public professions and the private model of professionalism. *Social Work, 25,* 179–191.

Hughes, E. C. (1965). Professions. In K. S. Lynn (Ed.), *The professions in America.* Boston: Beacon Press.

Hughes, R. C. (1993a). Child welfare services for the catastrophically ill newborn: Part I—A confusion of responsibility. *Child Welfare, 72,* 32–40.

Hughes, R. C. (1993b). Child welfare services for the catastrophically ill newborn: Part II—A guiding ethical paradigm. *Child Welfare, 72,* 423–437.

Human Rights Campaign (2003). Medicaid Expansion. www.hrc.org/issues/hiv_aids/background/medicaid.asp, 1/27/2003.

Illich, I. (1977). *Disabling Professions.* Salem, NH: M. Boyars.

Imbert, R. C. (2002). Personal letter (December 18). NASW Insurance Trust and the American Professional Agency.

Imre, R. E. (1989). Moral theory for social work. *Social Thought, 15* (1), 18–27.

Iserson, K. V. (1986). An approach to ethical problems in emergency medicine. In K. V. Iserson et al. (Eds.), *Ethics in emergency medicine* (pp. 35–41). Baltimore: Williams & Wilkins.

Ivanoff, A., Biythe, B. J., & Tripodi, T. (1994). *Involuntary clients in social work practice: A research-based approach.* New York: Aldine de Gruyter.

Jackson, J. (2000). Duties and conscience in professional practices. In Q. de Stexhe and J. Verstraeten (Eds.), *Matter of Breath: Foundations for Professional Ethics* (pp. 239–258). Leuven, Belgium: Peeters.

Jackson, J. S., & Sellers, S. L. (2001). Health and the elderly. In R. L. Braithwaite & S. E. Taylor (Eds.), *Health Issues in the Black Community* (pp. 81–96). San Francisco: Jossey-Bass Publishers.

Jayaratne, S., Croxton, T., & Mattison, D. (1997). Social work professional standards: An exploratory study. *Social Work, 42,* 187–199.

Jones, W. T., Sontag, F., Beckner, M. O., & Fogelin, R. J. (1977). *Approaches to ethics.* New York: McGraw-Hill.

Jory, B., Anderson, D., & Greer, C. (1997). Intimate justice: Confronting issues of accountability, respect, and freedom in treatment for abuse and violence. *Journal of Marital and Family Therapy,* 399–419.

Joseph, M. V. (1983). The ethics of organization. *Administration in Social Work, 7,* 47–57.

Joseph, M. V. (1985). A model for ethical decision-making in clinical practice. In C. B. Germain (Ed.), *Advances in clinical social work practice* (pp. 207–217). Silver Spring, MD: NASW.

Judah, E. H. (1979). Values: The uncertain component of social work. *Journal of Education for Social Work, 15* (2), 79–86.

Kagle, J. D., & Gielbelhausen, P. N. (1994). Dual relationships and professional boundaries. *Social Work, 39,* 213–220.

Kalichman, S. C. (1999). *Mandated reporting of suspected child abuse: Ethics, law, and policy.* Washington, DC: American Psychological Association.

Karis, J. M., & Wandrei, K. E. (1992). PIE: A new language for social work. *Social Work, 37* (1), 80–85.

Kaslow, F. (1998). Ethical problems in mental health practice. *Journal of Family Psychotherapy*, 9 (2), 41–54.

Keith-Lucas, A. (1977). Ethics in social work. *Encyclopedia of social work* (pp. 350–355). Washington, DC: National Association of Social Workers.

Kirk, S.A., & Kutchins, H. (1988). Deliberate misdiagnosis in mental health practice. *Social Service Review*, 62, 225–237.

Kiselica, M.S., & Ramsey, M.L. (2001). Multicultural counselor education. In D.C. Locke, J.E. Myers, & E.L. Herr (Eds.), *The handbook of counseling* (pp. 433–451). Thousand Oaks, CA: Sage Publications.

Kitchner, K.S. (1984). Intuition, critical evaluation and ethical principles: The foundation of ethical decisions in counseling psychology. *Counseling Psychology*, 12, 43–55.

Kluckhohn, C. (1951). Values and value-orientations in the theory of action: An exploration in definition and clarification. In T. Parsons & E.A. Shils (Eds.), *Toward a general theory of action* (pp. 388–433). Cambridge, MA: Harvard University Press.

Kohlberg, L. (1984). *The psychology of moral development*. New York: Harper & Row.

Kopels, S., & Kagle, J.D. (1993). Do social workers have a duty to warn? *Social Service Review*, 67, 101–126.

Kugelman, Wendy (1992). Social work ethics in the practice arena: A qualitative study. *Social Work in Health Care*, 17 (4), 59–80.

Kuhse, H., & Singer, P. (1985). Ethics and the handicapped newborn infant. *Social Research*, 52, 505–542.

Kupperman, J.J. (1999). *Value . . . and what follows*. New York: Oxford University Press.

Kurzman, P.A. (1995). Professional liability and malpractice (pp. 1921–1927). *Encyclopedia of social work* (19th ed.). Washington, DC: NASW Press.

Kurzweil, Z. (1980). Why heteronomous ethics? In M. Kranzberg (Ed.), *Ethics in an age of pervasive technology* (pp. 68–71). Boulder, CO: Westview Press.

Kutchins, H. (1991). The fiduciary relationship: The legal basis for social workers' responsibilities to clients. *Social Work*, 36, 106–113.

Kutchins, H., & Kirk, S.A. (1987). DSM-III and social work malpractice. *Social Work*, 32, 205–211.

Kutchins, H., & Kirk, S.A. (1988). The business of diagnosis: DSM-III and clinical social work. *Social Work*, 33, 215–220.

Kutchins, H., & Kirk, S.A. (1995). Review of diagnostic and statistical manual of mental disorders (4th ed.). *Social Work*, 40, 286–287.

Kutchins, H., & Kirk, S.A. (1997). *Making us crazy*. New York: The Free Press.

Laing, R.D. (1967). *Politics of experience*. New York: Pantheon Books.

Landau, R. (1996). Preparing for sudden death or organ donation: An ethical dilemma in social work. *International Social Work*, 39, 431–441.

Landau, R. (1998a). Secrecy, anonymity, and deception in donor insemination: A genetic, psychosocial, and ethical critique. *Social Work in Health Care*, 28 (1), 75–89.

Landau, R. (1998b). The management of genetic origins: Secrecy and openness in donor assisted conception in Israel and elsewhere. *Human Reproduction*, 13 (11), 3268–3273.

Lee, M.Y., & Gaucher, R. (2000). Group treatment for dually diagnosed adolescents: An empowerment-based approach. *Social Work with Groups*, 23 (2), 55–78.

Lens, V. (2000). Protecting the confidentiality of the therapeutic relationship: *Jaffee v. Redmond*. *Social Work*, 45 (3), 273–276.

Levy, C. (1976a). Personal versus professional values: The practitioner's dilemma. *Clinical Social Work Journal*, 4, 110–120.

Levy, C. (1976b). The value base of social work. *Journal of Education in Social Work*, 9, 34–42.

Lewis, H. (1984). Ethical assessment. *Social Casework*, 65, 203–211.

Lewis, H. (1989). Ethics and the private non-profit human service organization. *Administration in Social Work*, 13 (2), 1–14.

Lewis, K. N., & Walsh, W. B. (1980). Effects of value-communication style and similarity of values on counselor evaluation. *Journal of Counseling Psychology, 27,* 305–314.

Lidz, C. W., Mulvey, E. P., & Gardner, W. (1993). The accuracy of predictions of violence to others. *Journal of American Medical Association, 269* (8), February 24, 1007–1011.

Lipsyte, R. (2002, November 17). Johnson and Augusta Mask Bigger issues, *New York Times, SportsSunday,* p. 5.

Lo, B., Dornbrand, L., Wolf, L. E., & Groman, M. (2002). The Wendland case—Withdrawing life support from incompetent patients who are not terminally ill. *The New England Journal of Medicine, 346,* 1489–1493.

Loewenberg, F. M. (1987). Another look at unethical professional conduct. *Journal of Applied Social Sciences, 11,* 220–229.

Loewenberg, F. M. (1988). *Religion and social work practice in contemporary American society.* New York: Columbia University Press.

Loewenberg, F. M. (1992). Notes on ethical dilemmas in wartime: Experiences of Israeli social workers during Operation Desert Shield. *International Social Work, 35* (4), 429–439.

Lott, B., & Bullock, H. E. (2001). Who are the poor? *Journal of Social Issues, 57* (2), 189–206.

Lum, D. (2000). Social work practice and people of color (4th ed.). Belmont, CA: Brooks/Cole.

Lyden, J. (1998). Christian ethics, Protestant. In R. Chadwick (Ed.), *Encyclopedia of applied ethics* (pp. 457–469). Boston: Academic Press.

Lystad, M., Rice, M., & Kaplan, S. J. (1996). Family violence. In S. J. Kaplan (Ed.), *Domestic violence* (pp. 139–180). Washington, DC: American Psychiatric Press.

MacIver, R. (1922). The social significance of professional ethics. *Annals, 101,* 5–11.

MacMurray, J. (1961). *Persons in relation.* Atlantic Highlands, NJ: Humanities Press.

Maesen, W. A. (1991). Fraud in mental health practice: A risk management perspective. *Administration and Policy in Mental Health, 18,* 431–432.

Maher, V. F., & Ford, J. (2002). The heartbreak of parens patriae. *Jona's Healthcare, Law, Ethics, and Regulation, 4,* 18–22.

Manetta, A. A., & Wells, J. G. (2001). Ethical issues in the social worker's role in physician-assisted suicide. *Health and Social Work, 26* (3), 160–166.

Manning, R. C. (1992). *Speaking from the heart: A feminist perspective on ethics.* Lanham, MD: Rowman & Littlefield Publishers.

Manning, S. S., & Gaul, C. E. (1997). The ethics of informed consent: A critical variable in the self-determination of health and mental health clients. *Social Work in Health Care, 25* (3), 103–117.

Manstead, A. S. R. (1996). Attitudes and behavior. In G. R. Semin & K. Fiedler (Eds.), *Applied social psychology.* Thousand Oaks, CA: Sage Publications.

Marcuse, P. (1976). Professional ethics and beyond: Values in planning. *Journal of the American Institute of Planners, 42,* 264–274.

Maritain, J. (1934). *Introduction to philosophy.* London: Sheed & Ward.

Marson, S. (1993). Social work discussion list (SOCWORK@UMAB.BIT-NET). October 18, 1993.

Martin, J. L. R., Barbanoj, M. J., Schlaepfer, T. E., Perez, V., Kulisevsky, J., & Gironell, A. (2002). Transcranial magnetic stimulation for treating depression (Cochrane Review). In *The Cochrane Library, 2.* Oxford: Update Software.

Maslow, A. H. (1962). *The farther reaches of human nature.* New York: Penguin Books.

Maslow, A. H. (1969). Toward a humanistic biology. *American Psychologist, 24,* 724–735.

Mason, R. O. (1994). Morality and models. In W. A. Wallace (Ed.), *Ethics in modeling* (pp. 183–194). Tarrytown, NY: Pergamon.

Matorin, S., Rosenberg, B., Levitt, M., & Rosenbaum, S. (1987). Private practice in social work: readiness and opportunity. *Social Casework, 68* (1), 31–37.

Mattison, D., Jayaratne, S., & Croxton (2002). Client or former client? Implications of ex-client definition on social work practice. *Social Work, 47* (1), 55–64.

McCann, C. W. (1977). The codes of ethics of the NASW: An inquiry into its problems and perspectives. In B. E. Olvett (Ed.), *Values in Social Work Education* (pp. 10–19). Salt Lake City: University of Utah Graduate School of Social Work.

McCarty, D., & Clancy, C. (2002). Telehealth: Implications for social work practice. *Social Work, 47* (2), 153–161.

McGowan, B. G. (1995). Values and ethics. In C. H. Meyer & M. A. Mattaini (Eds.), *The foundations of social work practice* (pp. 28–41). Washington, DC: NASW Press.

McMahon, A., & Allen-Meares, P. (1992). Is social work racist? A content analysis of recent literature. *Social Work, 37*, 533–539.

Melton, G. B. (1988). Ethical and legal issues in ATOS-related practice. *American Psychologist, 43*, 941–947.

Meyer, C. H. (1985). Different voices: Comparable worth. *Social Work, 30*, 99.

Meyers, C. J. (1997). Expanding *Tarasoff*: Protecting patients and the public by keeping subsequent caregivers informed. *The Journal of Psychiatry & Law*, Fall, 365–375.

Mickelson, J. S. (1995). Advocacy. In R. L. Edwards (Ed.), *Encyclopedia of social work*. Vol. 1 (19th ed., pp. 95–100). Washington, DC: National Association of Social Workers.

Miller, D. J., & Thelen, M. H. (1986). Knowledge and beliefs about confidentiality in psychotherapy. *Professional Psychology: Research and Practice, 17*, 15–19.

Miller, H. (1968). Value dilemmas in social casework. *Social Casework, 13*, 27–33.

Millstein, K. (2000). Confidentiality in direct social work practice: Inevitable challenges and ethical dilemmas. *Families in Society, 81* (3), 270–282.

Mitchell, C. G. (1999). Treating anxiety in a managed-care setting: A controlled comparison of medication alone versus medication plus cognitive-behavioral group therapy. *Research on Social Work Practice, 9*, 188–200.

Moran, J. R. (1989). Social work education and students humanistic attitudes. *Journal of Education for Social Work, 25* (1), 13–19.

Moreno, J. D., Caplan, A. L., & Wolpe, P. R. (1998). Informed Consent. *Encyclopedia of Applied Ethics*. Vol. 2. New York: Academic Press, 687–697.

Moser, C. (1980). Letter. *NASW News, 25* (9), 6.

Murdach, A. D. (1996). Beneficence re-examined: Protective intervention in mental health. *Social Work, 41*, 26–32.

Murphy, M. J., DeBernardo, C., & Shoemaker, E. (1998). Impact of managed care on independent practice and professional ethics: A survey of independent practitioners. *Professional psychology: Research and Practice, 29*, 43–51.

Myers, L. L., & Thyer, B. A.- (1997). Should social work clients have the right to effective treatment? *Social Work, 42*, 288–298.

NASW Ad Hoc Committee on Advocacy. (1969). The social worker advocate: Champion of social victims. *Social Work, 14* (2), 16–23.

National Association of Social Workers. (1987). *AIDS: A social work response*. Washington, DC: National Association of Social Workers.

National Association of Social Workers. (1990a). People in the news. *NASW News, 35* (5), 17.

National Association of Social Workers. (1990b). *Standards for Social Work Personnel Practices*. Washington, DC: National Association of Social Workers.

National Association of Social Workers. (1993). A study of trends in adjudication of complaints concerning violations of NASW's code of ethics—overview of results.

National Association of Social Workers. (1994). Client self-determination in end-of-life decisions. In *Social work speaks* (pp. 58–61). Washington, DC: Author.

National Association of Social Workers. (1995a). Lawsuits: No more immunity. *NASW News, 40* (1), 7.

National Association of Social Workers. (1995b). A study cites most reported ethics breaches. *NASW News, 40* (4), 4.

National Association of Social Workers. (1999a). Assembly lowers BSW's dues, alters ethics code, eyes itself. *NASW News, 44* (9) (October), 1,10.

National Association of Social Workers. (1999b). *Code of ethics.* Washington, DC: Author.

National Association of Social Workers. (2000). Agency restricts internet counseling. *NASW News, 45* (8), 12.

National Association of Social Workers. (2001a). Caution urged before web counseling. *NASW News, 46* (January), 5.

National Association of Social Workers. (2001b). *NASW Procedures for Professional Review.* Washington, DC: Author.

National Association of Social Workers. (2002). HIPAA Alert! http://www.socialworkers.org/practice/hipaa/default.asp, October 1, 2002.

National Research Council. (1993). *Child abuse and neglect.* Washington, DC: National Academy Press, Author.

Negretti, M. A., & Weiling, E. (2001). The use of communication technology in private practice: Ethical implications and boundary dilemmas in therapy. *Contemporary Family Therapy, 23* (3), 275–293.

Netting, F. E. (1987). Ethical issues in volunteer management and accountability. *Social Work, 32,* 250–252.

Netting, F. E., Kettner, P. M., & McMurtry, S. L. (1998). *Social work macro practice* (2nd ed.). White Plains, NY: Longman Publishing Group.

Newhill, C. E. (1992). Assessing danger to others in clinical social work practice. *Social Service Review, 66* (1), 64–84.

North, R. L., & Rothenberg, K. (1993). Partner notification and the threat of domestic violence against women with HIV infection. *New England Journal of Medicine, 329,* 1194–1196.

Nurcombe, B., & Partlett, D. F. (1994). *Child mental health and the law.* New York: The Free Press.

Nyberg, D. (1996). Deception and moral decency. In R. A. French, T. E. Vehling, Jr., & H. K. Wettstein (Eds.), *Midwest studies in philosophy, vol. XX, moral concepts.* Notre Dame, IN: University of Notre Dame Press.

Odell, M., & Stewart, S. P. (1993). Ethical issues associated with client values conversion and therapist value agendas in family therapy. *Family Relations, 42* (2), 128–133.

O'Neill, J. V. (2001a). Online therapy on verge of major launch. *NASW News, 46* (1), 5.

O'Neill, J. V. (2001b). Webcams may transform online therapy. *NASW News, 46* (7), 4.

O'Neill, J. V. (2002). Internet-based therapy draws criticism. *NASW News, 47* (4), 12.

Oppenheim, S., Hay, J. B., et al. (2002). Palliative Care in Human Immunodeficiency Virus: Acquired Immunodeficiency Syndrome, In A. M. Berger, R. K. Portenoy, & D. E. Weissman (Eds.), *Principles and Practice of Palliative Care and Supportive Oncology* (pp. 1071–1085) New York: Lippincott Williams and Wilkins.

Oregon Health Services Commission. (2003). http://www.ohppr.state.or.us/index.htm, March 11, 2003.

Orovwuje, P. R. (2001). The business model and social work: A conundrum for social work practice. *Social Work in Health Care, 34* (1/2), 59–70.

Padilla, Y. C. (1997). Immigrant policy: Issues for social work practice. *Social Work, 42,* 595–606.

Parrott, C. (1999). Towards an integration of science, art and morality: The role of values in psychology. *Counseling Psychology Quarterly, 12* (1), 5–24.

Peckover, S. (2002). Supporting and policing mothers: An analysis of the disciplinary practices of health visiting. *Journal of Advanced Nursing, 38,* 369–377.

Pellegrino, E. D. (1991). Trust and distrust in professional ethics. In E. D. Pellegrino, R. M. Veatch, & J. P. Langan (Eds.), *Ethics, trust, and the professions* (pp. 69–85). Washington, DC: Georgetown University Press.

Pemberton, J. D. (1965). Is there a moral right to violate the law? *Social Welfare Forum, 1965* (pp. 183–196). New York: Columbia University Press.

Perlman, H. H. (1965). Self-determination: Reality or illusion? *Social Service Review, 39,* 410–422.

Perry, C., & Kuruk, J. W. (1993). Psychotherapists' sexual relationships with their patients. *Annals of Health Law, 2,* 35–54.

Pike, C. K. (1996). Development and initial validation of the social work values inventory. *Research in Social Work Practice, 6,* 337–352.

Planned Parenthood of Southeastern Pa. v. Casey, 505 U.S. 833 (1992).

Pope, K. S., & Bouthoutsos, J. C. (1986). *Sexual intimacy between therapist and patient.* New York: Praeger Publishers.

Pope, K. S., & Feldman-Summers, S. (1992). National survey of psychologists' sexual and physical abuse history and their evaluation of training and competence in these areas. *Professional Psychology: Research and Practice, 23* (1), 353–361.

Pope, K. S., Levenson, H., & Schover, L. R. (1979). *American Psychologist, 34* (8) (August), 682–689.

Pope, K. S., Tabachnick, B. G., & Keith-Spiegel, P. (1987). Ethics of practice: The beliefs and behaviors of psychologists and therapists. *American Psychologist, 42,* 993–1006.

Pope, K. S., & Vasquez, M. J. T. (1998). *Ethics in Psychotherapy and Counseling* (2nd Ed.). San Francisco: Jossey-Bass.

Powderly, K. (2001). Ethical and legal issues in perinatal HIV. *Clinical Obstetrics and Gynecology, 44,* 300–311.

Powell, W. E. (1994). The relationship between feelings of alienation and burnout in social work. *Families in Society, 75,* 229–235.

Proctor, E. K., Morrow-Howell, N., & Lett, C. L. (1993). Classification and correlates of ethical dilemmas in hospital social work. *Social Work, 38,* 166–177.

Pumphrey, M. W. (1959). The teaching of values and ethics in social work education. New York: CSWE.

Rabkin, J. G., & Struening, E. L. (1976). *Ethnicity, social class and mental illness.* New York: Institute on Pluralism & Group Identity.

Raines, J. C. (1996). Self-disclosure in clinical social work. *Clinical Social Work Journal, 24,* 357–375.

Rawls, J. (1971). *A theory of justice.* Cambridge, MA: Harvard University Press.

Reamer, F. G. (1983). Ethical dilemmas in social work practice. *Social Work, 28,* 31–35.

Reamer, F. G. (1993). *The philosophical foundations of social work.* New York: Columbia University Press.

Reamer, F. G. (1995). Malpractice claims against social workers: First facts. *Social Work, 40,* 595–601.

Reamer, F. G. (1998). The evolution of social work ethics. *Social Work, 43,* 488–500.

Reamer, F. G. (1999). *Social work values and ethics* (2nd Ed.). New York: Columbia University Press.

Reamer, F. G. (2001). *The social work ethics audit: A risk management tool.* Washington, DC: NASW Press.

Regehr, C., & Antle, B. (1997). Coercive influences: Informed consent in court-mandated social work. *Social Work, 42,* 300–306.

Reid, W. J. (1997a). Long-term trends in clinical social work. *Social Service Review, 71* (2), 200–213.

Reid, W. J. (1997b). Research on task-centered practice. *Social Work Research, 21,* 132–137.

Reinardy, J., & Kane, R. A. (1999). Choosing an adult foster home or a nursing home: Residents' perceptions about decision making and control. *Social Work, 44* (6), 571–585.

Reiser, S. J., Burstajn, H. J., Applebaum, P. S., & Gutheil, T. G. (1987). *Divided staffs, divided selves: A case approach to mental health ethics.* Cambridge, England: Cambridge University Press.

Rice, D. S. (1994). Professional values and moral development: The social work student. Unpublished Dissertation. University of South Carolina.

Roberts, C. S. (1989). Conflicting professional values in social work and medicine. *Health and Social Work, 14*, 211–218.

Roberts, L. W., Battaglia, J., & Epstein, R. S. (1999). Frontier ethics: Mental health care needs and ethical dilemmas in rural communities. *Psychiatric Services, 50*, 497–503.

Robertson, J. A. (1985). The geography of competency. *Social Research, 52*, 555–579.

Rogers, C. R. (1951). *Client-centered therapy.* Boston: Houghton Mifflin.

Rogers, C. R. (1977). *Carl Rogers on personal power.* New York: Delacorte.

Rooney, R. H. (1992). *Strategies for work with involuntary clients.* New York: Columbia University Press.

Rosa, L., Rosa, E., Samer, L., & Barrett, S. (1998). A close look at therapeutic touch. *Journal of the American Medical Association, 279*, 1005–1010.

Ross, J. W. (1992). Editorial: Are social work ethics compromised? *Health and Social Work, 17*, 163–164.

Rothman, J. (1989). Client self-determination: Untangling the knot. *Social Service Review, 63*, 598–612.

Rothman, J., Smith, W., Nakashima, J., Paterson, M. A., & Mustin, J. (1996). Client self-determination and professional intervention: Striking a balance. *Social Work, 41*, 396–405.

Rothstein, E. (2002, July 13). Moral relativity is a hot topic? True. Absolutely. *New York Times*, A 13, A 15.

Roy v. Hartogs. 366 N. YS. 2d297 (1975).

Royce, D., Dhooper, S. S., & Rompf, E. L. (1999). *Field instruction: A guide for social work students* (3rd ed.). New York: Longman.

Rubin, A., Cardenas, J., Warren, K., Pike, C. K., & Wambach, K. (1998). Outdated practitioner views about family culpability and severe mental disorders. *Social Work, 43* (5), 412–422.

Rust v. Sullivan, 500 U.S. Supreme Court, 173 (1991).

Ryder, R., & Hepworth, J. (1990). AAMFT ethical code: "dual relationships," *Journal of Marital and Family Therapy, 16* (2), 127–132.

Saenz v. Roe, U.S. Supreme Court, 1518, 1999.

Sammons, C. C. (1978). Ethical issues in genetic intervention. *Social Work, 23*, 237–242.

Sasson, S. (2000). Beneficence versus respect for autonomy: An ethical dilemma in social work practice. *Journal of Gerontological Social Work, 33* (1), 5–16.

Schamess, G. (1996). Who profits and who benefits from managed mental health care? *Smith College Studies in Social Work, 60*, 209–220.

Schild, S., & Black, R. B. (1984). *Social work and genetic counseling: A guide to practice.* Binghamton, NY: Haworth Press.

Schlossberger, E., & Hecker, L. (1996). HIV and family therapists' duty to warn: A legal and ethical analysis. *Journal of Marital and Family Therapy, 22*, 27–40.

Schoener, G. R. (1995). Assessment of professionals who have engaged in boundary violations. *Psychiatric Annals, 25* (2), 95–99.

Schopler, J. H., Abell, M. D., & Galinsky, M. J. (1998). Technology-based groups: A review and conceptual framework for practice. *Social Work, 43*, 254–267.

Sedlak, A. J., & Broadhurst, D. D. (1996). *Third national incidence study of child abuse and neglect: Final report.* Washington, DC: U.S. Department of Health and Human Services.

Selznick, P. (1961). Sociology and natural law. *Natural Law Forum, 6*, 84–108.

Advocate Web. Helping Overcome Professional Exploitation. (2002). Sexual exploitation litigation issues. http://www.advocateweb.org/hope/litigation.asp, July 18, 2002.

Sharma, S., & Patenaude, A. (2003). HIV-AIDS. *Medicine: Instant Access to the Minds of Medicine.* www.emedicine.com/aaem/topic252.htm, January 24, 2003.

Sharwell, G. R. (1974). Can values be taught? *Journal of Education for Social Work, 10*, 99–105.

Shaw, G. B. (1932). *The doctor's dilemma.* London, England: Constable.

Shea, S. C. (1999). *The Practical Art of Suicide Assessment.* New York: John Wiley Sons, Inc.

Shillington, A. M., Dotson, W. L., & Faulkner, A. O. (1994). Should only African-American community organizers work in African-American neighborhoods? In M. J. Austin & J. I. Lowe (Eds.), *Controversial issues in communities and organizations*. Boston: Allyn & Bacon, 128–111.

Shirk, E. (1965). *The ethical dimension*. New York Appleton-Century-Crofts.

Simon, R. I., & Gutheil, T. G. (1997). Ethical and clinical risk management principles in recovered memory cases: Maintaining therapist neutrality. In P. S. Appelbaum, L. A. Uyehara, & M. R. Elin (Eds.), *Trauma and memory* (pp. 477–495). New York: Oxford University Press.

Siporin, M. (1982). Moral philosophy in social work today. *Social Service Review, 56*, 516–538.

Siporin, M. (1983). Morality and immorality in working with clients. *Social Thought, 9* (Fall), 10–28.

Siporin, M. (1985a). Current social work perspectives for clinical practice. *Clinical Social Work Journal, 13*, 198–217.

Siporin, M. (1985b). Deviance, morality and social work therapy. *Social Thought, 11* (4), 11–24.

Siporin, M., & Glasser, P. (1986). Family functioning, morality and therapy. In P. Glasser & D. Watkins (Eds.), *Religion and social work*. Newbury Park, CA: Sage Publications.

Sloan, L., Edmond, T., Rubin, A., & Doughty, M. (1998). Social workers' knowledge of an experience with sexual exploitation by psychotherapists. *Social Work, 43*, 43–53.

Smyer, M. A. (1993). Aging and decision-making capacity. In M. A Smyer (Ed.), *Mental health and aging: Progress and prospects*. New York: Springer Publishing.

Social Work (1991) 36 (2), 106–144. This issue contains a series of articles on the theme "Ethics and Professional Relationships."

Soderfeldt, M., Soderfeldt, B., & Warg, L. E. (1995). Burnout in social work. *Social Work, 40*, 638–646.

Sokolowski, R. (1991). The fiduciary relationship and the nature of professions. In E. D. Pellegrino, R. M. Veatch, & J. P. Langan (Eds.), *Ethics, trust, and the professions* (pp. 23–39). Washington, DC: Georgetown University Press.

Solomon, A. (1992). Clinical diagnosis among diverse populations: A multicultural perspective. *Families in Society, 73* (6), 371–377.

Soyer, D. (1963). The right to fail. *Social Work, 8* (3) (July), 72–78.

Specht, H., & Courtney, M. E. (1994). *Unfaithful angels: How social work has abandoned its mission*. New York: Free Press.

Spero, M. H. (1990). Identification between the religious patient and therapist in social work and psychoanalytic psychotherapy. *Journal of Social Work and Policy in Israel, 3*, 83–98.

Steinberg, K. L., Levine, M., & Doueck, H. (1997). Effects of legally mandated child-abuse reports on the therapeutic relationship: A survey of psychotherapists. *American Journal of Orthopsychiatry, 67*, 112–122.

Stevens, J. W. (1998). A question of values in social work practice: Working with the strengths of black adolescent females. *Families in Society, 79*, 288–296.

Stoesen, L. (2002). Recovering social workers offer support. *NASW News*, http://www.socialworkers.org/pubs/news/2002/07/recovering.asp?back=yes.

Strean, H. S. (1997). Comment on James C. Raines, "Self-Disclosure in Clinical Social Work." *Clinical Social Work Journal, 25*, 365–366.

Strom, K. (1992). Reimbursement demands and treatment decisions: A growing dilemma for social workers. *Social Work, 37*, 398–403. *Social Work, 45* (3), 251–261.

Strom, K. (1994). Social workers in private practice: An update. *Clinical Social Work Journal, 22*, 73–89.

Strom-Gottfried, K. (1998a). Informed consent meets managed care. *Health and Social Work, 23*, 25–33.

Strom-Gottfried, K. (1998b). Is "ethical managed care" an oxymoron? *Families in Society: The Journal of Contemporary Human Services, 79*, 297–307.

Strom-Gottfried, K. (1999). When colleague accuses colleague: Adjudicating personnel matters through the filing of ethics complaints. *Administration in Social Work, 23* (2), 1–16.

Strom-Gottfried, K. (2000). Ensuring ethical practice: An examination of NASW Code violations, 1986–97. *Social Work, 45* (3), 251–261.

Strom-Gottfried, K. (2003). Understanding adjudication: Origins, targets, and outcomes of ethics complaints. *Social Work, 48* (1), 85–94.

Strug, D. L., Grube, B. A., & Beckerman, N. (2002). Challenges and changing roles in HIV—AIDS social work: implications for training and education. *Social Work in Health Care, 35* (4), 1–19.

Sunley, R. (1997). Advocacy in the new world of managed care. *Families in Society, 78,* 84–94.

Sutherland, P.K. (2002). Sexual abuse by therapists, physicians, attorneys, and other professionals. *The Worldwide Legal Information Association,* http://www.lia.org, July 17, 2002.

Szasz, T. S. (1994). *Cruel compassion: Psychiatric control of society's unwanted.* New York: Wiley.

Tarasoff v. Regents of the University of California. S. Ct. of CA (1976).

Taylor, L., & Adelman, H. S. (1989). Reframing the confidentiality dilemma to work in children's best interest. *Professional Psychology: Research and Practice, 20,* 79–83.

Taylor-Brown, S., & Garcia, A. (1995). Social workers and HIV-affected families: Is the profession prepared? *Social Work, 40,* 14–15.

Timms, N. (1983). *Social work values: An enquiry.* London, England: Routledge & Kegan Paul.

Tong, R. (1998). Feminist ethics. In *Encyclopedia of applied ethics,* vol. 2 (pp. 261–268). New York: Academic Press.

Torczyner, J. (1991). Discretion, judgment, and informed consent: Ethical and practice issues in social action. *Social Work, 36,* 122–128.

Toren, N. (1972). *Social Work: The Case of a Semi-Profession.* Beverly Hills, CA: Sage Publications.

Tower, Kristine D. (1994). Consumer-centered social work practice: Restoring client self-determination. *Social Work, 39* (2), 191–196.

Towle, C. (1987). *Common human needs.* Silver Spring, MD: National Association of Social Workers.

Trolander, J. A. (1997). Fighting racism and sexism: The CSWE. *Social Service Review, 71,* 110–134.

Tropman, J. E., Erlich, J. L., & Rothman, J. (2001). *Tactics and techniques of community intervention* (4th ed.). Itasca, IL: F. E. Peacock Publishers.

Tully, C. T., Craig, T., & Nugent, G. (1994). Should only gay and lesbian community organizers operate in gay and lesbian communities? In M. J. Austin, & J. I. Lowe (Eds.), *Controversial Issues in Communities and Organizations* (pp. 86–96). Boston: Allyn & Bacon.

Turner, F. J. (2002). *Diagnosis in social work: New imperatives.* New York: Haworth Social Work Practice Press.

Ulrich, B., & Beck-Gemsheim, E. (1996). Individualization and "precarious freedoms." In P. Heclas, S. Lash, & P. Morris (Eds.), *Detraditionalization: Critical reflections on authority and identity* (pp. 23–48). Cambridge, MA: Blackwell Publishers.

U.S. Census Bureau. (2001). National health expenditures by type: 1990 to 1999, *Statistical Abstract of the United States: 2001* (121st Ed.). Washington, DC.

U.S. Census Bureau. (2003). Hobbs, F. B. (2003) The elderly population. January 30, 2003. http://www.census.gov/population/www/pop-profile/elderpop.html.

U.S. Census Bureau, Hetzel, L., & Smith, A. (2003) U.S. Census Bureau. *The 65 Years and Over Population: 2000,* http://www.census.gov/prod/2001pubs, January 30, 2003.

VandeCreek, L., Knapp, S., & Herzog, C. (1988). Privileged communications for social workers. *Social Casework, 69,* 28–34.

Van Hoose, W. H., & Kottler, J. A. (1985). *Ethical and legal issues in counseling and psychotherapy* (2nd ed.). San Francisco: Jossey-Bass.

Varley, B. K. (1963). Socialization in social work education. *Social Work, 8* (4), 102–105.

Varley, B. K. (1968). Social work values: Changes in value commitment of students from admission to MSW graduation. *Journal of Education for Social Work, 4,* 67–76.

Verschelden, C. (1993). Social work values and pacifism: Opposition to war as a professional responsibility. *Social Work, 38,* 765–769.

Vigilante, J. L. (1974). Between values and science: "Education for the profession during a moral crisis or is proof truth?" *Journal of Education for Social Work, 10,* 107–115.

Vigilante, J. L. (1983). Professional values. In A. Rosenblatt, & D. Waldfogel (Eds.), *Handbook of clinical social work* (pp. 58–69). San Francisco: Jossey-Bass.

Wagner, L., Davis, S., & Handelsman, M. M. (1998). In search of the abominable consent form: The impact of readability and personalization. *Journal of Clinical Psychology, 54,* 115–120.

Wakefield, J. (1988). Psychotherapy, distributive justice and social work (Parts 1 and 2). *Social Service Review, 62,* 187–209, 353–381.

Walcott, D. M., Cerundolo, P., & Beck, J. C. (2001). Current analysis of the *Tarasoff* duty: An evolution towards the limitation of the duty to protect. *Behavioral Sciences and the Law, 19,* 325–343.

Walden, T., Wolock, L., & Demone, H. W., Jr. (1990). Ethical decision making in human services: A comparative study. *Families in Society, 71,* 67–75.

Walker, R., & Staton, M. (2000). Multiculturalism in social work ethics. *Journal of Social Work Education, 36* (3), 449–462.

Walrond-Skinner, S., & Watson, D. (1987). *Ethical issues in family therapy.* London, England: Routledge & Kegan Paul.

Ward, J. W., & Drotman, D. P. (1998). Epidemiology of HIV and AIDS. In G. P. Wormser (Ed.), *AIDS and other manifestations of HIV infection* (3rd ed., pp. 1–17). Philadelphia: Lippincott-Raven.

Weick, A. (1999). Guilty Knowledge. *Families in Society, 80* (4), 327–332.

Weinstein, B., Levine, M., Kogan, N., et al. (2000). Mental health professionals' experiences reporting suspected child abuse and maltreatment. *Child Abuse & Neglect, 24* (10), 1317–1328.

Wheeler, D. L. (1993). Physician-anthropologist examines what ails America's medical system: Instead of treating patients, Melvin Konner probes health care in general. *Chronicle of Higher Education,* June 2, A6–A7.

Wicclair, M. R. (1993). *Ethics & the elderly.* New York: Oxford University Press.

Wigmore, J. (1961). *Evidence in trials at common law* (Rev. ed.). Boston: Little, Brown.

Williams, R. M., Jr. (1967). Individual and group values. *Annals, 371,* 20–37.

Willis, C. (1987). Legal and ethical issues of touch in dance/movement therapy. *American Journal of Dance Therapy, 10,* 41–53.

Wilson, C. A., Alexander, J. R., & Turner, C. W. (1996). Family therapy process and outcome research: Relationship to treatment ethics. *Ethics & Behavior, 6,* 345–352.

Wineburgh, M. (1998). Ethics, managed care, and outpatient psychotherapy. *Clinical Social Work Journal, 26,* 433–443.

Witkins, S. L. (1998). The right to effective treatment and the effective treatment of rights: Rhetorical empiricism and the politics of research. *Social Work, 43,* 75–80.

Wodarski, J. S., Pippin, J. A., & Daniels, M. (1988). The effects of graduate social work education on personality, values and interpersonal skills. *Journal of Social Work Education, 24,* 266–277.

Wolf, L. E., Lo, B., Beckerman, K. P., Dorenbaum, A., Kilpatrick, S. J., & Weintraub, P. S. (2001). When parents reject interventions to reduce postnatal human immunodeficiency virus transmission. *Archives of Pediatrics & Adolescent Medicine, 155,* 927–933.

Wolfson, E. R. (1999). The fee in social work: Ethical dilemmas for practitioners. *Social Work, 44* (3), 269–273.

Woody, J. D. (1990). Clinical strategies to promote compliance. *American Journal of Family Therapy, 18,* 285–294.

Wyatt, T., Daniels, M. H., & White, L. J. (2000). Noncompetition agreements and the counseling profession: An unrecognized reality for private practitioners. *Journal of Counseling & Development, 78* (1), 14–20.

Yu, M., & O'Neal, B. (1992). Issues of confidentiality when working with persons with AIDS. *Clinical Social Work Journal, 20,* 421–430.

Yurkow, J. (1991). Abuse and neglect of the frail elderly. *Pride Institute Journal of Long Term Home Health Care, 10* (1), 36–39.

Zur, O., & Lazarus, A. A. (2002). Six arguments against dual relationships and their rebuttals. In A. A. Lazarus, & O. Zur (Eds.), *Dual Relationships and Psychotherapy.* New York, NY: Spring Publishing Co., 3–24.

Zygmond, M. J., & Boorhem, H. (1989). Ethical decision-making in family therapy. *Family Process, 28,* 269–280.

Index